The Cambridge Companion to Metal Music

Since its beginnings more than fifty years ago, metal music has grown in popularity worldwide, not only as a musical culture but increasingly as a recognised field of study. This Cambridge Companion reflects the maturing field of 'metal music studies' by introducing the music and its cultures, as well as recent research perspectives from disciplines ranging from musicology and music technology to religious studies, Classics, and Scandinavian and African studies. Topics covered include technology and practice, identity and culture, modern metal genres, and global metal, with reference to performers including Black Sabbath, Metallica, and Amon Amarth. Designed for students and their teachers, contributions explore the various musical styles and cultures of metal, providing an informative introduction for those new to the field and an up-to-date resource for readers familiar with the academic metal literature.

JAN-PETER HERBST is Reader in Music Production at the University of Huddersfield, UK, where he is Director of the Research Centre for Music, Culture and Identity (CMCI). His primary research area is popular music culture, in particular rock/metal music and the electric guitar.

Cambridge Companions to Music

Topics

The Cambridge Companion to Ballet
Edited by Marion Kant

The Cambridge Companion to Blues and Gospel Music
Edited by Allan Moore

The Cambridge Companion to Caribbean Music
Edited by Nanette De Jong

The Cambridge Companion to Choral Music
Edited by André de Quadros

The Cambridge Companion to the Concerto
Edited by Simon P. Keefe

The Cambridge Companion to Conducting
Edited by José Antonio Bowen

The Cambridge Companion to the Drum Kit
Edited by Matt Brennan, Joseph Michael Pignato and Daniel Akira Stadnicki

The Cambridge Companion to Eighteenth-Century Opera
Edited by Anthony R. DelDonna and Pierpaolo Polzonetti

The Cambridge Companion to Electronic Music
Edited by Nick Collins and Julio D'Escriván

The Cambridge Companion to the 'Eroica' Symphony
Edited by Nancy November

The Cambridge Companion to Film Music
Edited by Mervyn Cooke and Fiona Ford

The Cambridge Companion to French Music
Edited by Simon Trezise

The Cambridge Companion to Grand Opera
Edited by David Charlton

The Cambridge Companion to Hip-Hop
Edited by Justin A. Williams

The Cambridge Companion to Jazz
Edited by Mervyn Cooke and David Horn

The Cambridge Companion to Jewish Music
Edited by Joshua S. Walden

The Cambridge Companion to K-Pop
Edited by Suk-Young Kim

The Cambridge Companion to Krautrock
Edited by Uwe Schütte

The Cambridge Companion to the Lied
Edited by James Parsons

The Cambridge Companion to Medieval Music
Edited by Mark Everist

Composers

Instruments

The Cambridge Companion to Metal Music

Edited by

JAN-PETER HERBST
University of Huddersfield

Shaftesbury Road, Cambridge CB2 8EA, United Kingdom

One Liberty Plaza, 20th Floor, New York, NY 10006, USA

477 Williamstown Road, Port Melbourne, VIC 3207, Australia

314–321, 3rd Floor, Plot 3, Splendor Forum, Jasola District Centre,
New Delhi – 110025, India

103 Penang Road, #05–06/07, Visioncrest Commercial, Singapore 238467

Cambridge University Press is part of Cambridge University Press & Assessment,
a department of the University of Cambridge.

We share the University's mission to contribute to society through the pursuit of
education, learning and research at the highest international levels of excellence.

www.cambridge.org
Information on this title: www.cambridge.org/9781108845861

DOI: 10.1017/9781108991162

First published 2023

A catalogue record for this publication is available from the British Library.

A Cataloging-in-Publication data record for this book is available from the Library of Congress

ISBN 978-1-108-84586-1 Hardback
ISBN 978-1-108-99398-2 Paperback

Contents

Figures

Tables

Notes on Contributors

Edward Banchs is an independent researcher and freelance writer based in Pittsburgh, Pennsylvania. His writings about the metal subculture in the African continent have primarily focused on how metal has interacted with its locality and how metal fans have risen to confront the challenges that they have faced. His writings have appeared in publications such as *Metal Hammer*, *The Guardian* and *Afropop*.

Tom Cardwell is an artist and researcher based in London, UK. His PhD thesis (2017) employed painting practice and ethnography to examine the customised jackets made by heavy metal fans. His research interests include contemporary and historic painting, subcultural symbolism and expressions of personal narrative and identity in popular image traditions. Cardwell's book *Heavy Metal Armour* (Intellect, 2022) brings together his battle jacket paintings and academic research to offer an interdisciplinary study of jacket making in metal subcultures. In 2022, Cardwell was awarded the Postdoctoral Fellowship in the Arts at the Helsinki Collegium for Advanced Studies. He is Senior Lecturer in Painting at Camberwell, University of the Arts London.

Hale Fulya Çelikel has been working at Sabancı University for over a decade and teaches courses on classical music history, opera and twentieth-century music history, encompassing popular music. Simultaneously, she has a popular music career as a metal keyboardist, singer and synthesiser artist, having worked in the audio sector as a product manager for SynthMaster since 2018.

Owen Coggins is a Leverhulme Early Career Fellow in Social and Political Sciences at Brunel University London, investigating ambiguity, ideology and marginal religion in black metal music cultures. His book *Mysticism, Ritual and Religion in Drone Metal* (Bloomsbury Academic 2018) won the 2019 IASPM Book Prize, and writing on noise, extreme music and religion have appeared in publications such as *Metal Music Studies*, *Popular Music* and *Riffs*. Coggins is also working on a co-authored book about the folk instruments in global metal music, and runs drone record label Oaken Palace as a registered charity raising money for environmental causes.

ANDREW L. COPE is a freelance musicologist, educator and performer of rock and metal music. A protégé of the late Professor Sheila Whiteley, and PhD graduate of the University of Salford UK, Cope is best known as the author of *Black Sabbath and the Rise of Heavy Metal Music* (Ashgate 2010) and the award-winning *Status Quo: Mighty Innovators of Rock* (Routledge 2019). Cope has also taken part in a range of film, radio and podcast interviews to offer his erudite insight into the world of rock and metal music.

ROSS HAGEN is Associate Professor of Music Studies at Utah Valley University in Orem, UT, USA. Hagen's research interests include underground music scenes, black metal music, medievalism and avant-garde music. He has published articles and reviews in a number of academic journals, edited volumes and encyclopaedias and is a regular presenter at international conferences. Recent publications include co-editing *Medievalism and Metal Music Studies: Throwing Down the Gauntlet* (2019), chapters in *The Oxford Handbook of Music and Medievalism* (2020) and *Researching Subcultures, Myth, and Memory* (2020) and a book on Darkthrone's 1992 album *A Blaze in the Northern Sky* for Bloomsbury's 33.3 book series (2020). In addition to his academic work, Hagen has long been active as a performer and composer, specialising in black metal and other extreme and/or marginal music styles.

PIERRE HECKER is Senior Researcher and Lecturer at the Centre for Near and Middle Eastern Studies at Philipps-University of Marburg, Germany. He holds a PhD from Leipzig University and is the author of the book *Turkish Metal: Music, Meaning, and Morality in a Muslim Society* (Ashgate, 2012). Recent publications include 'Islam: The Meaning of Style' (*Sociology of Islam*, 2018), 'Satan, Sex and an Islamist Zombie Apocalypse' (UCL Press, 2022) and 'Tired of Religion: Atheism and Nonbelief in "New Turkey"' (2022). He heads the research group 'Atheism and the Politics of Culture in Contemporary Turkey' funded by Stiftung Mercator and co-edited the volume *The Politics of Culture in Contemporary Turkey* (Edinburgh University Press, 2022).

IMKE VON HELDEN holds a PhD in Scandinavian Studies and has written about cultural identity, history and mythology in Norwegian metal music. She is the manager of an academic institution at the University of Koblenz, Germany, and a vocalist of the all-female metal project Chaos Rising.

JAN-PETER HERBST is Reader in Music Production at the University of Huddersfield (UK) where he is Director of the Research Centre for Music, Culture and Identity (CMCI). His primary research area is popular music culture, in particular rock music and the electric guitar, on which he has published widely. Currently, he is undertaking two funded research projects on metal: one that explores how heaviness is created and controlled in metal music production, and one investigating extreme metal vocals. Herbst's editorial roles include *IASPM Journal* and *Metal Music Studies*.

ROSEMARY LUCY HILL is Senior Lecturer in Media and Popular Culture at University of Huddersfield, where she is the Director of the Popular Music Studies Research Group. She is the author of *Gender, Metal and the Media: Women Fans and the Gendered Experience of Music* (Palgrave) and has published widely on issues around gender, popular music and digital spaces. She co-created the *Five Step Guide to Writing a Safer Spaces Policy* (www.saferspaces.org.uk) for music venues to improve safety at live music events. She is also the co-editor of Intellect's *Advances in Metal Music Studies* book series. She is currently investigating sexual violence in the music industry.

CATHERINE HOAD is Senior Lecturer in Te Rewa o Puanga/School of Music and Creative Media Production, at Te Kunenga Ki Pūrehuroa/Massey University, Aotearoa/New Zealand, and Chair of the Australia-New Zealand branch of the International Association for the Study of Popular Music. Her research explores constructions of identity and belonging in heavy metal and hardcore scenes, practices and communities.

LEWIS F. KENNEDY is a musicologist and Curriculum Manager (Popular Music) at Leeds Conservatoire. In 2018, he completed a PhD in Music at the University of Hull writing a thesis on functions of genre in metal and hardcore music, conceptualising genre as an active, emerging and determining force in the production and consumption of contemporary popular music. Having been involved in metal studies for several years, he is the current Treasurer and Membership Officer of the International Society for Metal Music Studies. He has co-edited the 'Metal & Musicology' special issue of *Metal Music Studies* (2019). Recent publications include book chapters on New Wave of American Heavy Metal and notions of heritage(-making) in metal/hardcore historiography, a study of the interplay between aidoru and metal themes in the lyrics of Babymetal, and an ethnography of the Hull metal/hardcore scene.

MARK MARRINGTON is currently Associate Professor in Music Production at York St John University, having previously held teaching positions at Leeds College of Music and the University of Leeds (School of Electronic and Electrical Engineering). His research interests include metal music composition and production, music technology and creativity, the contemporary classical guitar and twentieth-century British classical music. Marrington has published chapters with Cambridge University Press, Bloomsbury Academic, Routledge and Future Technology Press, and has contributed articles to journals *Metal Music Studies*, *British Music*, *Soundboard*, the *Musical Times* and the *Journal on the Art of Record Production*. His recently published monograph, *Recording the Classical Guitar* (2021), won the 2022 ARSC Award for Excellence in Historical Recorded Sound Research (Classical Music).

MARK MYNETT, as well as Senior Lecturer in Music Technology and Production at the University of Huddersfield (UK), is a live music engineer, and record producer, engineer, mix and mastering engineer with his own studio – Mynetaur Productions. He has had an extensive career as professional musician with six worldwide commercial album releases with his band Kill II This, along the way working with renowned producers Colin Richardson and Andy Sneap and several years of high-profile touring in Europe.

DANIEL NEVÁREZ ARAÚJO is Assistant Professor in the Department of English at the University of Puerto Rico – Río Piedras. He has published work in a wide array of topics, including Disability Studies, AIDS/HIV literature and film, comedy, documentary film, immigration, identity, and heavy metal music in publications such as *The Journal of Fandom Studies*, *The Massachusetts Review*, *Trespassing Journal*, *Sargasso*, and *Metal Music Studies*. He has co-edited the books *Heavy Metal in Argentina: In Black We Are Seen* (2020), *Heavy Metal in Latin America: Perspectives from the Distorted South* (2021), and *Defiant Sounds: Heavy Metal Music in the Global South* (2022).

PETER PICHLER is Postdoctoral Researcher at the University of Graz, where he leads the research project 'Breaking the law?! Norm-Related Sonic Knowledge in Heavy Metal Culture. Graz and Styria since 1980'. His fields of expertise are European Union cultural history, metal music studies and historical theory. His latest book is *Metal Music, Sonic Knowledge, and the Cultural Ear in Europe since 1970: A Historiographic Exploration* (2020).

PAULA ROWE is a social work scholar at the University of South Australia. Her research focus is on community building and belonging, and the political activation of marginalised groups and individuals, most often through a critical youth studies lens. Rowe is a member of the Editorial Advisory Board for *Metal Music Studies*. She has occupied numerous roles in the metal music industry over three decades, and her current metal research is investigating the youth uptake of decolonial metal.

ERIC SMIALEK researches musical meaning through music analysis and reception studies. His most recent article, on Taylor Swift and LGBTQ allyship, appears in *Contemporary Music Review*. A frequent contributor to edited collections, Smialek has forthcoming publications in *Heavy Metal Music and Dis/Ability*; *Music and Genre: New Directions*; *The Routledge Handbook of Metal Music Composition*; and *The Routledge Handbook of Progressive Rock, Metal, and the Literary Imagination*. He serves on the editorial advisory board for the journal *Metal Music Studies* and is an assistant editor for *IASPM Journal*. Smialek is currently Senior Research Fellow at the University of Huddersfield to research musical expression, technique and cultural meaning in extreme metal vocals.

KARL SPRACKLEN is Professor of Sociology of Leisure and Culture at Leeds Beckett University. He has written extensively about belonging and exclusion in leisure spaces, leisure theory and subcultures of music. He was one of the founding editors of *Metal Music Studies* and is the Editor-in-Chief of the *International Journal of the Sociology of Leisure*.

DANIEL SUER studied music education and English at the University of Siegen and musicology at the University of Music and Dance Cologne. Currently, he is a research assistant and PhD student at the University of Siegen (Germany) within a DFG-funded project on the relation between music and dance in metal. His research interests focus on music–movement–corporeality, metal studies, qualitative research methods and x-disciplinarity in popular music studies.

JEREMY SWIST is Lecturer in the Department of Classical Studies at Brandeis University in his home state of Massachusetts. He holds a PhD in Classics from the University of Iowa. He has published on rhetoric, historiography, philosophy and medicine under the Roman Empire, with a special interest in the emperor Julian the Apostate. His publications in metal studies include "Satan's Empire: Ancient Rome's anti-Christian appeal in extreme metal" in *Metal Music Studies* (2019) and "Headbanging to Byzantium: The Reception of the Byzantine Empire in

Heavy Metal Music" in *What Byzantinism Is This Is Istanbul?* (ed. E. Alışık, 2021). He has devoted multiple invited lectures and public pieces to addressing appropriations of Greco-Roman antiquity, especially Sparta, by far-right metal bands. In 2022, he and Charlotte Naylor Davis co-organised the first *Heavy Metal & Global Premodernity* conference.

NIALL THOMAS is Senior Lecturer in music production at the University of Winchester (United Kingdom). His research explores the phenomenology of record production in a number of contexts, most recently in metal music. Thomas is also interested in the use of music technology for inclusive practice in higher education.

SAM VALLEN is the lead guitarist and musical director of Australian progressive metal band Caligula's Horse, as well as a producer, songwriter and music academic. He holds a doctorate in music from the Queensland Conservatorium.

NELSON VARAS-DÍAZ is Professor of Social-community Psychology at Florida International University. His work related to metal music addresses issues of community formation, linkages between culture and music and metal music as a decolonial strategy in Latin America. He co-edited the books *Heavy Metal Music and the Communal Experience* (2016), *Heavy Metal in Argentina: In Black We Are Seen* (2020) and *Heavy Metal in Latin America: Perspectives from the Distorted South* (2021). He authored the book *Decolonial Metal Music in Latin America* (2021) published by Intellect. He has produced and directed the award-winning documentaries *Songs of Injustice: Heavy Metal Music in Latin America* and *Acts of Resistance: Heavy Metal Music in Latin America*. He is one of the editors of the *Metal Music Studies* journal.

JEREMY WALLACH is Professor in the Department of Popular Culture in the School of Cultural and Critical Studies at Bowling Green State University. A cultural anthropologist specializing in popular music and globalisation, he has written or co-written more than thirty research articles; co-edited, with Esther Clinton, a special issue of *Asian Music* (2013); and authored the monograph *Modern Noise, Fluid Genres: Popular Music in Indonesia, 1997–2001* (Univ. of Wisconsin, 2008; Indonesian Ed., Komunitas Bambu, 2017). In 2011, he co-edited, with Harris M. Berger and Paul D. Greene, the collection *Metal Rules the Globe: Heavy Metal Music around the World* (Duke University Press). Wallach has given research presentations in Austria, Canada, Finland, France, Germany, Indonesia, Italy, Mexico, the Netherlands, the Philippines, Puerto Rico and throughout the United States.

DUNCAN WILLIAMS is Lecturer in Acoustics and Audio Engineering at the University of Salford, Manchester, UK, where he is also Course Leader of the Sound Engineering and Production BSc(Hons) degrees. His recent published work includes library music for EMI Production Music, SonyATV, DeWolfe and KPM MusicHouse, with several major television credits. Contemporary music performances include concerts at the Royal College of Music, London (2015), International Computer Music Conference (2014), installations at Los Angeles' UCLA Art|Sci Gallery (2014), the Peninsula Arts Contemporary Music Festival in Devon (2013–14), New Scientist Live (2022), British Science Festival (2018), Berlin Science Festival (2018), South by Southwest (2019), Silbersalz (2019), the Science and Media Museum (2021) and the Museum of Science and Industry (2021).

JAN-PETER HERBST

Numerous bands and their fans see themselves as having revolutionised rock music in the late 1960s and the early 1970s and given birth to a harder style that was to become known as heavy metal. British bands Black Sabbath, Deep Purple, Led Zeppelin and The Kinks are considered pioneers within the two countries of metal's origin; their counterparts in the US were Steppenwolf, Iron Butterfly and Blue Cheer. Although it is safe to say that these bands were among those that gave the initial spark for a musical genre that has taken hold around the globe in the more than fifty years of its existence, this introduction is not meant to debate the origins of metal.

Today, metal music is a genre popular with fans worldwide, facilitated by a vast industry with specialised professions, such as journalists, artist and repertoire managers, record producers, concert promoters and stage crews. In the premier league of internationally-selling pop artists are some of the most prominent metal acts, including Metallica, Def Leppard, Guns'n'Roses, Linkin Park, Van Halen and Kiss, with over a hundred million records sold each. *Metallica* (1991), known as Metallica's 'Black Album', officially spent five hundred weeks on the Billboard 200, and their latest record, *Hardwired ... To Self-Destruct* (2016), climbed to number two on the Billboard Charts. Judas Priest's current (nineteenth) record is their highest-charting album, and Ozzy Osbourne's classic *Blizzard of Ozz* (1980) was recently awarded five-time platinum in the US. But metal music is not only flourishing in the mainstream. By the time of writing, the *Encyclopaedia Metallum* lists 156,453 metal bands around the globe, and *The Spirit of Metal* identifies 28,726 record labels dedicated to the genre – numbers expected to continue growing fast. Metal festivals like Rock in Rio, Exit, Hellfest, Graspop Metal Meeting, Rock am Ring, Download or Wacken attract hundreds of thousands of visitors every year. At the same time, countless smaller festivals for specific subgenres and subcultures take place throughout the world. A recent trend is heavy metal cruises like '70,000 Tons of Metal' hosting about one hundred bands and several thousand fans.

Considering its beginning as a rebellious subculture that never ceased to pride itself on its transgressiveness,[1] it is perhaps surprising that metal has become part of popular culture. Evidence of a growing mainstream acceptance comes from heritage places like museums dedicated to metal. One such example is Birmingham-based *Home of Metal*[2] in the English West Midlands region, a government-sponsored network holding exhibitions and events. Given the enormous influence of forerunners Black Sabbath, Birmingham and the Black Country as the genre's supposed birthplace is the network's main focus. Developments that followed in Black Sabbath's wake in other parts of the world are also covered. The latest exhibition of Home of Metal was in 2019 at Birmingham Museum and Art Gallery, celebrating the fiftieth anniversary of the recording of Black Sabbath's seminal self-titled album, which many see as the origin of the metal genre.[3] A similar initiative is the *Rock and Metal Museum*,[4] whose RAM Gallery, curated by Bloodstock festival founder Paul Gregory, exhibits metal artwork by various artists. These two initiatives are examples of 'self-authorised heritage'[5] within the metal scene, supported and thus 'legitimised' by councils and local funders. Yet another prominent example supports the impression that metal has become a 'legitimate' part of popular culture deemed valuable. The *GRAMMY Museum* – an affiliate of the prestigious GRAMMY Music Awards – hosted a year-long exhibition from 2012 to 2013 on the theme of 'Golden Gods: The History of Heavy Metal',[6] showcasing the genre's origins, subgenres, bands and controversies, alongside interactive scream booths, tutorials on metal drum and double bass, and a metal guitar riff station. Should such an appearance in mainstream popular music not be proof enough of metal's cultural impact, then two more museums show that countries have begun to embrace metal music as part of their national heritage. The Finnish Music Hall of Fame in *Helsinki's National Museum* opened the special exhibition 'Metal Export' in July 2020 with artefacts from the legendary Nosturi Club, live videos of Insomnium, Moonsorrow and Amorphis, and instruments of Apocalyptica and Children of Bodom.[7] The second museum is the *Rockheim Museum* in Trondheim, which pays tribute to the cultural influence of Norwegian black metal through a dedicated 'black metal room' containing exhibits such as posters, vinyl, artwork, videos and instruments like the Pearl drum kit played by Mayhem, Satyricon, Burzum, Darkthrone, Enslaved, Emperor and Arcturus.[8]

Much like museums and exhibitions, there is also a wealth of metal documentaries, from early examples like Metallica's *Some Kind of Monster* (2004) and Sam Dunn's *Metal: A Headbanger's Journey* (2005) and *Global Metal* (2008) to a plethora of films about individual bands and metal subgenres, many of which are nowadays being streamed on mainstream platforms such as Amazon Prime and Netflix.

Moreover, metal has found its way into vocational and higher education institutions. The *Metal Factory*[9] in Eindhoven, Holland, opened in 2013 as the world's first school for metal, teaching vocalists, drummers, bassists, guitarists and keyboardists how to build a career in the music industry. Among the former beneficiaries of government-funded popular music performance programmes are Floor Jansen (Nightwish), Ruud Jolie (Within Temptation), Stef Broks (Textures) and Johan van Stratum (Stream of Passion). The fact that these musicians became instructors at the Metal Factory indicates the success of the programme and national sponsoring schemes.[10] Other institutions follow a more theoretical approach. The University of Helsinki and the Massachusetts Institute of Technology (MIT) offer dedicated metal music modules, two examples of the many existing. Institutions around the globe have begun to integrate metal into the curricula of their general popular music courses and modules.

Long before metal music became a subject taught in the academy, it had been researched. Pioneering book-length works in the 1990s stem from Deena Weinstein,[11] Robert Walser,[12] Donna Gaines[13] and Harris M. Berger.[14] Journalistic literature also embraced metal early on, featuring specific subgenres, bands and record labels on a large scale.[15] However, it was not until the late 2000s that a series of symposia and conferences – most notably the 2008 *Heavy Fundamentalisms: Music, Metal and Politics* conference in Salzburg, Austria – set the start for metal music studies to develop into a distinct field of study with its own learned society, the International Society for Metal Music Studies, and dedicated journal, *Metal Music Studies*. Since then, metal music studies have proliferated and diversified, encompassing many research traditions from the arts and humanities to the sciences. Hence academia and society have increasingly recognised metal music as a valid field of research.[16] Metal-related publications appear in general popular music journals and edited volumes, and research on metal is also found in publications of popular music's various parent disciplines. But perhaps one of the most evident indicators of the growth of metal music as a distinct field of study is the rapid increase in the number of collected editions and monographs over the last five years, along with an equally growing number of dissertations.

As the academic field grows, books and dissertations are becoming more thematically focused. This *Cambridge Companion to Metal Music* sets itself apart from this trend of specialisation by providing a broader scope and an overview of metal music studies. It strikes a balance between introductions to key themes and state-of-the-art discussions of emerging issues and musical phenomena. Given this perspective, this volume is intended as a textbook for new generations of scholars, from undergraduate and postgraduate students to early career researchers. The chapters have been written by a diverse group of contributors, ensuring a well-balanced mix of emerging to experienced scholars from varied disciplines: musicology, music technology, media and communication studies, leisure studies, youth studies, religious studies, classical studies, history, sociology, art and design to Scandinavian and African studies. This range of approaches and methodologies reflects the discipline of metal music studies. The volume is divided into six parts spanning all-time classic and nascent themes in metal scholarship.

Part I, *Metal, Technology and Practice*, acknowledges the relevance of music technology and offers valuable insights into the perspectives of metal music creation for those involved, i.e., artists and recording professionals. Part II, *Metal and History*, contains selected case studies and examples of the common practice of appropriating historical themes and mythologies in metal for a purpose in the present. Part III, *Metal and Identity*, covers some of the mainstream themes in metal scholarship, such as gender, class and race. Part IV, *Metal Activities*, focuses on a less researched area with topics relevant to the practising metalhead, including leisure activities such as concerts, festivals and dancing/moshing. Part V, *Modern Metal Genres*, explores more contemporary topics, that is, lesser researched metal subgenres such as technical death metal, metalcore and djent, and how established and influential subgenres such as black metal are developing today. In the final Part VI, *Global Metal*, the focus shifts away from the historically early (and dominant) metal scenes in Central Europe, North America and selected Asian countries to acknowledge metal music cultures worldwide, as is popular within current metal scholarship. Like any compendium, this volume cannot be comprehensive. However, it is a starting point for broader discussions, provides an informative introduction for metal music scholars new to the field and serves as a source for contemporary research for readers familiar with the academic metal literature.

This *Cambridge Companion* begins with an overview chapter on the history and stylistic developments of metal music. Andrew L. Cope outlines metal's sonic evolution and its continuous expansion over five decades. He also addresses more recent developments in metal, where contrasting musical idioms are increasingly used through the process of extensive and elaborate assimilation. These idioms serve as a foil for the prominence of established metal devices in new and unusual contexts. Cope argues that through a sequence of essential features and their relationship to key bands, tracks and albums, metal music developed in an accumulative process driven by a series of pioneering musicians who created and reiterated a specific combination of musical elements and performance practices to establish the metal sound.

Part I – *Metal, Technology and Practice* – provides a historical overview from a different perspective, focusing on record production and how technology has been utilised creatively to achieve ever-higher levels of heaviness in metal's ever-diversifying subgenres. Jan-Peter Herbst and Mark Mynett concentrate on the formative heavy metal in the 1970s, the thrash metal movement in the 1980s and the beginning of extreme metal in the early 1990s to trace how specific releases set standards and trends in metal music production, highlighting notable moments in the evolution of heaviness on metal records. They illustrate how the practice of live recording lost its importance and gave way to a hyper-real aesthetic beyond human performance capability through music production technologies. These shifts brought more extreme sounds through greater distortion and sonic weight, intended to achieve the ideologically desired heaviness as a key part or by-product of the genre's continued progress. The technological reflections are followed by Niall Thomas's chapter, which takes a closer look at the phenomenological perspective of record producers. Thomas argues that technological democratisation has transformed the experience of making metal records through creative flexibility and control, technologically and financially, an experience that would have been unattainable in the past. Drawing on the experiences of producers who shaped the recording careers of artists such as Black Sabbath and Judas Priest, Thomas connects the experiences of record production to musical, socio-cultural and technological development. Likewise phenomenological, but from the first-person perspective of a metal vocalist, Hale Fulya Celikel sheds light on how her professional career developed in the metal industry with a band performing and releasing original music. Reflecting on her role as singer of the Turkish progressive metal band Listana, Celikel addresses the following issues: high and low art, status and musical socialisation; metal-specific skill acquisition; songwriting practices; demo recordings and self-released albums; challenges in obtaining gig opportunities; discrimination as a female performer in a male-dominated environment. In the final chapter of Part I, Duncan Williams provides an overview of timbre in metal production from a psychoacoustic and computational musicology perspective, focusing on the use of acoustic feature extraction. Williams reflects on how the acoustic feature sets underlying performance and recording technology may inform production and analysis in the not-too-distant future. These considerations make him predict possible AI-driven approaches to machine listening, timbral metering and tone matching with great future potential for metal music practitioners.

Part II addresses *Metal and History*. Peter Pichler begins with his analysis of how contemporary extreme metal has found ways to incorporate the ancient cultures of Sumer and Mesopotamia into their music. Pichler examines how history is constructed in Mesopotamian metal, a discourse he sees as promoting a specific kind of historical politics that helps solve problems in the present, especially in the conflict-ridden region of the Middle East. Extending the scope to draw connections to two other discourses of history in metal – 'Oriental metal' and 'Viking metal' – Pichler argues that we can potentially learn from the past through metal music. Jeremy Swist takes us to ancient Greece to discuss another appropriation of classical tales, particularly the saga of Sparta and its representation in popular media. The Spartans' last stand at Thermopylae, the mythologised battle led by King Leonidas, has served as inspiration for metal bands worldwide since the 2006 film *300*. Swist argues that the battle resonates with political and nationalistic agendas and that Sparta's broad appeal harmonises with metal's ethos of hypermasculinity, the liberation of animal instincts and the disruption of systems of conformity and control, embodied by the battle in which the few stood defiant against the many. The section on metal and history concludes with Imke von Helden's examination of Viking metal, one of the most popular adaptations of history and imagined cultures in metal music. The chapter analyses different approaches by Viking metal bands to these lyrical themes and how they intersect with cultural aspects, authenticity, ideology and gender. Von Helden finds that Viking metal is one of the few subgenres of metal music defined less by its sonic characteristics than by its visual elements and lyrical contents, which revolve around the Viking Age, Old Norse mythology and the depiction of Nordic nature.

In the first chapter of Part III – *Metal and Identity* – Paula Rowe explores the nexus of metal identity formations and mental health, arguing that metal music and culture have the potential to promote mental health by creating a sense of belonging, empowerment, well-being and resilience. Examining the domains of psychosocial well-being through the lens of heavy metal identity formation, she reasons metal to have qualities that can protect mental health. Rowe concludes that internal identity dialogues can shield metal fans against some of modern life's most pervasive social and emotional threats. Rosemary Lucy Hill then investigates the gendered meanings of metal from the 1970s to the present, especially with a focus on the gendering of the genre, sexism and the continued male-dominance of musicians' roles, women's experiences of empowerment through metal, and metal as a vehicle for feminist rage. Hill argues that current thinking about metal and gender has been shaped, on the one hand, by gendered expectations of musical suitability mostly outside academia and, on the other, by angry reactions from metal fans, musicians and scholars. The section on metal identities ends with Catherine Hoad's thought-stimulating reflections on what it means for metal to be transgressive in the twenty-first century. She draws on notions of resistance, rebellion, transgression and outsiderness prevalent in the metal community, arguing that this spirit is challenged by metal's commercial success, geological diversification and generational shifts among fans, with 'resistance' taking on different trajectories as metal manifests itself in various political currents and contexts. Hoad explores how the politics of rebellion and resistance in metal play out in fragmented ways as metal fandoms around the world negotiate shifting ideological contexts and markets. In this context, she focuses on matters of performative transgression and commercial dissent, raising the provocative question of whether metal can still be rebellious in the twenty-first century or if it ever was.

Part IV focuses on *Metal Activities,* with Karl Spracklen introducing metal as a space for leisure and tourism. He discusses why metal is leisure for musicians and fans alike, exploring its meaning and purpose in modern society. Even though metal is part of the wider entertainment industry, best defined as commodified popular culture, Spracklen argues that metal still gives meaning to people's leisure lives by allowing musicians to make the music they love and fans to be moved by it. Spracklen points out that metal is less constrained than mainstream pop music and therefore provides a communicative leisure space where fans and musicians can find meaning, belonging and solidarity. He concludes that as long as metal does not become trendy and retains uncompromising riffs and unfashionable themes, it holds the potential as a form of leisure that resists conformity, commercialisation and control. Next, Daniel Suer gives an introductory overview of dance practices in metal and their social organisation. He examines the social organisation of mosh pits and discusses them as contested communities, as they offer communal experiences while perpetuating existent barriers to participation, especially in relation to gender identities. In addition, Suer outlines areas for further research, including dance practices in virtual spaces and the Global South, histories of metal dance and the relationship between music and movement in metal. Thomas Cardwell then explores the activity of battle jacket customisation. Battle jackets, he shows, are visible badges of identity in clothing that derive their individual significance through decorative patches, band insignia, studs and other embellishments. Cardwell traces the origins of such jackets in twentieth-century subcultures and the development of their making among fans since the 1970s. He argues that the jackets serve as documents of personal music history, with patches commemorating concert attendance and favourite bands. Based on a series of interviews, Cardwell notes that while each jacket is unique to its creator, most follow a set of tacitly agreed conventions and structures.

Part V – *Modern Metal Genres* – begins with Ross Hagen's reflections on the development of black metal, specifically how the emphasis on geographic location and local cultures has changed both in the bands' music and visual presentation and how they are practised today. Hagen looks at the Mountain West region in the United States, where the genre is being cultivated, recontextualising Norwegian black metal's musical and ideological tropes into forms that honour this new location while retaining key points of Norwegian black metal's worldview. The subsequent chapter by Lewis F. Kennedy examines the impact of subgenre qualifiers that modify a genre title. Using technical death metal as a case study, Kennedy analyses the prescriptive nature of creativity contained within a relatively precise definition of the modifier 'technical' that has developed through consistent use by artists, reliable recognition by audiences and continued reinforcement by critics. Kennedy concludes that subgenre qualifiers simultaneously describe and prescribe the specific focus of a particular subgenre, affecting composition, production, performance and reception. Owen Coggins is next to explore how the subgenre of drone metal evolved, incorporating influences from metal and classical avant-gardes that provided an overlap for otherwise relatively unconnected audiences. Coggins finds ambivalence in metal media; while sometimes drone metal's status is questioned, other times it is critically praised in more highbrow publications, particularly in avant-garde magazines like *The Wire*. Although a highly marginal subgenre, Coggins argues that drone metal significantly impacts how metal is perceived and understood, both within and outside metal culture, through its contested influences and deployment in legitimation strategies. Mark Marrington's chapter discusses djent as another controversial subgenre within the metal community. It examines the development of djent since the mid-2000s, taking into account the main musical, technological and environmental factors that have shaped the genre's identity. Marrington emphasises the important role of emerging digital technologies, both in the formation of the subgenre's musical and sonic characteristics and in its wider dissemination and expansion. Reflecting on djent's significance as a 'cyber-genre' within the domain of contemporary electronic music practice, Marrington concludes that djent aligns with recent trends that bring metal ever closer to the aesthetics of post-digital music practice. Part V on modern metal genres closes with Eric Smialek's analysis of metalcore. Smialek provides a reception history of metalcore, marked by disagreements over its definition and legitimacy, revolving around the idea of an 'abject genre' – a shorthand term for nu metal, screamo and a variety of '-core' subgenres that have been widely criticised by metal fans. After analysing commonalities metalcore shares with other abject genres, including mass popularity, stylistic alterations of traditional metal traits regarded by critics as simplified dilutions, and associations with marginalised categories of identity, Smialek outlines various historical accounts of the genre to conclude that a more complex consideration of chronological and conceptual boundaries is required than a single narrative allows.

The final part, Part VI on *Global Metal*, commences with Pierre Hecker's chapter on metal in the Middle East. Hecker deconstructs the semiotic baggage of the term 'Middle East' shaped by a history of Western imperialism. He critically examines the exoticisation of the Muslim metalhead, addressing the semantic disorder caused by the emergence of local metal scenes in different socio-political contexts and the associated moral panics over metal and Satanism. Hecker argues that prevailing Orientalist discourses have led to an exoticisation of the Middle Eastern and/or Muslim metalhead in academic and popular discourses, emphasising that there is still a perception that the dominance of Islam somehow precludes the existence of metal music and culture in the Middle East. The next chapter covers metal in Asia, where long-established scenes in Japan, Indonesia, Malaysia, Singapore and Nepal wield influence on the rapidly expanding scenes in India, China and mainland Southeast Asia, where heavy metal remains the preferred genre for only a small minority. Jeremy Wallach then explores the Asian metal universe as an increasingly interconnected field that has forged links with other regions. Wallach argues that by gradually attracting the enthusiastic attention of international audiences, Asian bands have achieved a shift in dominant representations of Asian musics, dismissed in the West as boringly derivative, inauthentic pop or featuring abstruse traditional styles inaccessible to non-Asian ears. Wallach concludes that Asian metal is neither and that its influence on the global music scene has only just begun. Edward Banchs gives an overview of African metal, focusing on sub-Saharan Africa. As Banchs suggests, the arrival of rock and heavy metal on the African continent was not uniform because the genres developed at different times in different countries and under different circumstances. He exemplifies how metal stories, regardless of the circumstances, tell of a genre that empowers performers and ardent fans alike, even if facing challenges such as authoritarianism, economic hardship and conservative cultural norms. Banchs concludes that metal expanded in Africa mainly for three reasons: many countries have an enthusiastic fanbase; the establishment of national scenes that produce bands, original recordings, record labels and media specialising in this particular industry; an ever-growing number of metal festivals. The subsequent chapter by Nelson Varas-Díaz and Daniel Nevárez Araújo takes a perhaps unusual approach. Instead of providing an overview of metal in Latin America, the authors examine the efforts of Latin American metal artists to address injustices of coloniality through their music's sounds, lyrics and aesthetics. With the question in mind, 'What has Latin American metal music ever done for us?', Varas-Díaz and Nevárez Araújo draw on the concept of the 'ethics of affront' to show how artists tell and simultaneously challenge the colonial history of their culture through sounds, images and words. The authors find the application of this concept to have implications for metal music as an academic field. They argue that metal music should be studied to comprehend how people in Latin America and the Global South use extreme forms of music, which sheds light on their context and allows for a deeper understanding of how social and political forces sustain practices of oppression. In the final chapter, Samuel Vallen introduces Australian metal music, pointing to the common theme of distance that inevitably comes with its geographical distance to metal scenes in Europe and the United States and the vast territorial (and cultural) space between Australia's largest population centres. He examines some of the distance-related negotiations Australian metal acts engage in to conceptualise their practice. Vallen argues that the negotiation of distance is a pervasive aspect of Australian metal that has far-reaching and tangible implications across the style's musical and paramusical developments. He concludes that one cannot write the history of Australian metal without considering this ongoing negotiation.

Notes

1. Keith Kahn-Harris, *Extreme Metal: Music and Culture on the Edge* (Berg, 2007).
2. Home of Metal (2022). https://homeofmetal.com (accessed 21 March 2022).
3. See, for example, Andrew L. Cope, *Black Sabbath and the Rise of Heavy Metal Music* (Routledge, 2010).
4. Rock and Metal Museum (2022). www.rockandmetalmuseum.com/about (accessed 21 March 2022).

5. Les Roberts and Sara Cohen, 'Unauthorising Popular Music Heritage: Outline of a Critical Framework', *International Journal of Heritage Studies* 20/3 (2014): 241–61.

6. GRAMMY Museum (2012). https://grammymuseum.org/event/golden-gods-the-history-of-heavy-metal (accessed 21 March 2022).

7. Klaudia Weber, 'FAME: Heavy Metal as Museum-Material?', *Stalker Magazine* (2020). https://stalker-magazine.rocks/en/2020/08/03/fame-heavy-metal-as-museum-material (accessed 21 March 2022).

8. 'To All Black Metal Fans: Legendary Drum Kit in the Rockheim Museum', *ThorNews* (2014). https://thornews.com/2014/12/21/to-all-black-metal-fans-legendary-drum-kit-in-the-rockheim-museum (accessed 21 March 2022).

9. Metal Factory (2022). www.metalfactory.education (accessed 21 March 2022).

10. See also Pauwke Berkers and Julian Schaap, 'From Thrash to Cash: Forging and Legitimizing Dutch Metal', in Lutgard Mutsaers and Gert Keunen (eds.), *Made in the Low Countries* (Routledge, 2017), pp. 61–71.

11. Deena Weinstein, *Heavy Metal: The Music and its Culture* (Lexington Books, 1991).

12. Robert Walser, *Running with the Devil: Power, Gender and Madness in Heavy Metal Music* (Wesleyan University Press, 1993).

13. Donna Gaines, *Teenage Wasteland: Suburbia's Dead End Kids* (University of Chicago Press, 1998).

14. Harris M. Berger, *Metal, Rock, and Jazz: Perception and the Phenomenology of Musical Experience* (University Press of New England, 1999).

15. A selected bibliography of academic texts and journalistic sources is provided at the end of the volume.

16. See Karl Spracklen and Niall Scott, 'Editorial', *Metal Music Studies* 1/1 (2014): 3–4; Jan-Peter Herbst and Karl Spracklen, 'Metal Music Studies at the Intersection of Theory and Practice', *Metal Music Studies* 7/3 (2021): 351–6.

Get Your Double Kicks on Route 666

The Sonic Evolution of Heavy Metal across Five Unholy Decades

ANDREW L. COPE

From its emergence in the early 1970s, heavy metal evolved into the collective of interrelated strands recognised as metal today. It is an extensive and ever-growing network that includes, amongst others, classic metal, thrash metal, black metal, death metal, melodic death metal, folk metal, symphonic metal, grindcore, metalcore, deathcore, nu metal, doom metal, progressive metal, industrial metal, gothic metal and djent. Whereas the nomenclature and boundaries are somewhat arbitrary, those strands are united by the common espousal of specific musical practices and performance techniques contributed by key bands and performers over the last five decades. It is a process that seems to fall naturally into three stages, which will be explored in this chapter: formation, expansion and fusion.

Formation

Many of the core features of metal to date first emerged in the early live performances and studio album tracks of Black Sabbath.[1] Hailing from Aston (Birmingham, UK) in the industrial heartlands of England, vocalist Ozzy Osbourne, guitarist Tony Iommi, bassist Geezer Butler and drummer Bill Ward took inspiration from the occult-centred writings of Dennis Wheatly and the Hammer horror film series, espoused the name Black Sabbath and created a lyrical and musical world that was in every way as dark, morbid and other-worldly as the cinematic and literary genres that inspired it. Lyrics not only engaged with the arcane world of gothic horror, paganism and fantasy but also displayed a growing interest in anti-war and anti-patriarchal rhetoric. It was an influential approach that inspired album art, dress codes, band names (Cradle of Filth, Deicide, The Haunted, System of a Down) and a wide range of lyrical interpretations[2] from Iron Maiden's macabre 'Hallowed be Thy Name' (1982) to Metallica's nightmarish 'Enter Sandman' (1991), Sepultura's polemic 'Refuse/Resist' (1993) and the Satanic atheism of Opeth's 'The Grand Conjuration' (2005). It was an approach best summed up by Osbourne when he said: 'For us the whole hippy thing was bullshit. The only flower you saw in Aston was on a gravestone. So we thought, let's scare the whole f**king planet with music.'[3]

Musically, Black Sabbath expressed that notion through a number of different compositional and performance-related strategies, all of which became central to the sound of heavy metal. Arguably, the most immediate of those were the band's aggressive performance techniques and extreme levels of amplifier volume.[4] Although a process initiated in the work of 1960s rock bands such as The Who and The Jimi Hendrix Experience,[5] Black Sabbath took it further by combining high-output distortion with a particularly brutal form of attack that seemed to mirror the architecturally decimated and industrial post-war environment from which they emerged.[6] Those muscular riffs were underpinned by Bill Ward's powerful and innovative drumming style, which paid scant regard to the established timekeeping and backbeat-focused[7] traditions of rock drumming and, instead, adopted an approach that often closely integrated with the shape of the compositions. For example, on the recordings 'Black Sabbath' and 'Iron Man' (both 1970), Ward's drumming emphatically traces the rhythmic contours of the guitar parts to intensify the visceral punch of those riffs. When Ward does incorporate backbeat-type features, it is much more to do with riff propulsion and symphony rather than timekeeping and dancing. That innovative approach redefined the role of the metal drummer, something more fully illustrated further on.

A guitar-specific metal characteristic to emerge at the same time was that of down-tuning, a tuning method where the standard pitch of a guitar is lowered in nominated increments of half steps or, more correctly, semitones. Down-tuning is not specific to metal, but when combined with brutal performance techniques and high-gain tones, it forms a context that *is* peculiar to metal. Tony Iommi first adopted that practice because of an unfortunate machine shop accident in which he lost the tips of his fretting hand middle and ring fingers. He did so initially to make playing more comfortable – slacker strings are more pliable and softer on the fingers. However, having seemingly discovered the inherent darkness of timbre that results from such low-pitched guitar strings, especially when combined with the loud, high-gain amplifier output and brutal performance style discussed earlier in this section, the band eagerly incorporated that practice into the fabric of their signature sound.

Although Black Sabbath's first two albums were recorded with the guitars tuned to standard pitch, all live performances during that time were in E flat standard, which is one semitone lower. From the release of their third album,

Master of Reality (1971), they not only committed to recording with the guitars down-tuned but also expanded the concept by dropping the pitch three semitones to C sharp standard for certain tracks, as in, for example, 'Children of the Grave' (1971), 'Under the Sun' (1972) and 'Symptom of the Universe' (1975). Although not all metal bands followed Black Sabbath's example by adopting, centralising and privileging down-tuning methods, most have, and that ubiquity is abundantly evident across the metal collective, a point more fully illustrated further on.

Synonymous with down-tuned heavy metal riffing is the power chord,[8] a key performative and compositional tool that, according to metal mythology, also originated as a direct corollary of Tony Iommi's accident. Unable to play barre chords in the conventional way following that life-changing incident, Iommi took to fretting just the two lowest notes of a regular barre chord using his unaffected index and little fingers, and the result was a simple two-note chord, five notes apart – a spacing known in musical terms as a perfect 5th.[9] He moved those two-note shapes up and down the fretboard to iterate the chord changes, and *et voila*, the power chord sequences of heavy metal were born. By composing riffs from sequences of 5ths, Iommi had invoked an age-old medieval device known as organum, something that went out of fashion many centuries ago but now repurposed as part of Black Sabbath's agenda to, as noted earlier in this section, 'scare the whole f**king planet with music' – unholy transgression indeed.

Equally important to the compositional processes of Black Sabbath, and of heavy metal thereafter, are monophonic phrases and motifs which work in tandem with power chords to provide the essential riff-centred core of metal's instrumental skeletal framework. It is an approach that highlights the conspicuous and notable absence of traditional chord progressions in metal, a remarkable phenomenon that emerged from Iommi's subversive approach to harmony, and one of the most striking features of the genre. Whereas it is recognised that metal bands make occasional or novel use of traditional harmonic movement, those instances, with the exception of fusions such as folk metal,[10] are aberrant within the wider context of their repertoires. Similarly, the eschewal, or down-playing, of pentatonic and blues stylisations in favour of modal syntax is equally striking. This, too, is a characteristic that originated in the early work of Black Sabbath, where the judicial privileging of specific medieval church modes[11] significantly contributed to articulations of the arcane and other-worldly aesthetics of their lyrical subjects. More specifically, they drew on the Aeolian, Dorian and Mixolydian modes to evoke gothic ambience and the rather eery-sounding Locrian mode to express fear, discomfort and discord.

For example, within the Locrian mode is found the tritone, a musical device known colloquially as *Diabolus in Musica* ('the devil in the music'). In 'Black Sabbath' (1970), the ominous 'figure in black' is made terrifying by the prominent reiteration of tritones. Those tritones are also multiplied across the texture of the music being heard in the guitar riffs, bass lines and tortured vocal parts of Osbourne. An equally distinctive feature of the Locrian mode is the very piquant flat 2nd,[12] a musical interval that dominates much of 'The Wizard' (1970) from the same album. In other places, flat 2nds are iterated in sequences to produce tense chromatic lines such as those found in 'War Pigs' (1970). From within the many creative configurations of those discordant musical devices emerged an unusual 'angular' style of writing that became the cornerstone, not only of Black Sabbath's own signature sound but of the whole, sonic edifice of metal itself, a ubiquity too monolithic to summarise here but represented by tracks as wide-ranging as Metallica's 'Enter Sandman' (1991), Pantera's 'Walk' (1992), Machine Head's 'Old' (1994), Drowning Pool's 'Bodies' (2001), Rammstein's 'Sonne' (2001), Lamb of God's 'Laid to Rest' (2004), DevilDriver's 'Hold Back the Day' (2005), Amon Amarth's 'Free Will Sacrifice' (2008), Slipknot's 'Psychosocial' (2008) and Judas Priest's 'Necromancer' (2018).

Expansion

As much as those tracks embody and perpetuate the compositional methods, brutal performance practices and lyrical themes initiated by Black Sabbath, clearly, there are a whole range of additional stylisations evident in those recordings that reveal a significant post-Sabbath expansion of metal coding. Such features include new performance practices such as vocal growling, guitar tremolo picking, drumming double kicks and blast beats, complex twin-guitar textures and significant advancements in sound technology. The inception of that process occurred during the latter half of the 1970s within the so-called New Wave of British Heavy Metal (NWOBHM).[13] It was a movement spearheaded by bands such as Iron Maiden, Judas Priest, Venom and Motörhead, who each built on select elements of Black Sabbath's unique coding to forge novel, metal-influenced identities. However, it was during the 1980s and 1990s that the techniques and lineaments noted earlier in this section synchronised with those earlier innovations to form the full range of metal coding recognised today.

One of the most notable developments of that formative period was an expansion of Bill Ward's integrated and orchestral approach to drumming, along with an elevation of the metal drummer to that of a highly specialised erudite technician. It was a process marked by the introduction, advancement and adoption of a range of new techniques, including double kick or double bass pedalling. This stylisation became the norm in many strands of the heavy metal collective and involves the use of two separate bass drum pedals to create fast and intricate mechanistic patterns that both propel the music and, often, synchronise with the guitar parts in a profuse assortment of configurations. Examples include Slayer's 'Raining Blood' (1986), Machine Head's 'Davidian' (1994), Strapping Young Lad's 'Love?' (2005), Grand Magus' 'Kingslayer' (2005), Ensiferum's 'In My Sword I Trust' (2012) and In Flames's 'Burn' (2019).

It was, in fact, Bill Ward who first indicated the future heavy metal context of double kicks in a brief passage of thundering double bass work, starting at 3:08, on 'Into the Void' (1971). Ward took his cue from the work of Louis Bellson, a drummer famed for his use of double kicks with the Duke Ellington band during the 1950s (for example, 'Skin Deep', 1952). Ian Paice of Deep Purple also pointed the way in 'Fireball' (1970), a recording that significantly influenced Judas Priest's 'Exciter' (1978) and Motörhead's 'Overkill' (1979), both of which were important landmarks in the evolution of metal drumming. Rob Hunter of Raven developed an even greater intensity of speed and drive on tracks such as 'Tyrant of the Airways' (1981); however, it was Dave Lombardo of Slayer whose catalytic development of that technique, for example, in Slayer's 'Haunting the Chapel' (1984), led more directly to the complex refinements and almost complete ubiquity found in metal today.

A second widespread development in metal drumming was the emergence of the blast beat, a single stick roll or rapid alternation of bass and snare drum – essentially, a fast backbeat or polka beat – synchronised with cymbals. The true blast beat seems to have first emerged in the mid-1980s with tracks such as 'Milk' (1985) by Stormtroopers of Death, but it was Motörhead who initiated the exponential acceleration of the backbeat tempo on recordings such as 'Ace of Spades' (1980). United Kingdom's hardcore punk innovators, Discharge, intensified that trend (for example, 'The Blood Runs Red', 1982), a process mirrored in the United States in the work of San Francisco's Dead Kennedys on their 1981 album *In God We Trust, Inc.* Those recordings were highly influential on bands such as Slayer and Metallica, key instigators of thrash metal. However, the most extreme form of blast beat is more readily associated with Napalm Death and the early grindcore movement,[14] where the superfast backbeat patterns of hardcore morphed into what was, essentially, a stylised arhythmic and non-metric blast of sonic violence. By the early 1990s, the blast beat, and its numerous variants, had evolved into a discrete and metronomically precise musical technique requiring astonishing levels of stamina and virtuosic skill, much like double kicks. More importantly, those stylisations became essential components in many strands of the metal collective, exemplified by such tracks as At the Gates' 'The Red in the Sky Is Ours' (1990), Cradle of Filth's 'Mother of Abominations' (2004), As I Lay Dying's 'Comfort Betrays' (2007) and Napalm Death's 'F**k the Factoid' (2020).

Whilst metal drummers were busily fashioning such distinctive new characteristics, their fellow guitarists were equally industrious in developing their own range of new stylisations. Such developments included the adaptation of a long-established folk guitar technique known as tremolo picking, a method involving rapid alternation of the plectrum to achieve a peculiar type of sustain. It was 1960s surf guitarists like Dick Dale who first remodelled that quaint folk technique within a rock context on tracks such as 'Misirlou' (1962). In metal, however, tremolo picking received a radical makeover, becoming a genre-specific technique used to both intensify aggression and mirror the double kick rhythms of the drummers. In this way, guitars and drum kit work in symphonic unison to accentuate the impact of the riffs. Examples include Slayer's 'War Ensemble' (1990), Cradle of Filth's 'Cthulu Dawn' (2000), As I Lay Dying's 'The Sound of Truth' (2007) and Amon Amarth's 'Live Without Regrets' (2011).

One further way in which guitarists contributed to the development of metal during this second stage of evolution was through the creative ontogeny of twin-guitar work. At the forefront of this initiative were Iron Maiden and Judas Priest who, building on the innovative 1970s work of Wishbone Ash and Thin Lizzy,[15] designed complex harmonic and contrapuntal[16] textures for twin guitars that merged effectively with their own unique take on the other-worldly/anti-war lyrical themes and modal syntax initiated by Black Sabbath.[17] Examples include Iron Maiden's 'Hallowed Be Thy Name' (1982) and 'The Trooper' (1983), along with Judas Priest's 'Tyrant' (1976) and 'Exciter' (1978). It was an approach that suited heavy metal's proclivity for complex design,[18] both in formal structure and in textural detail,[19] a trend widely embraced throughout the metal collective and illustrated by a wide range of examples, including Metallica's 'One' (1988), Megadeth's 'Hanger 18' (1990), In Flames' 'The Jester's Dance' (1996), Machine Head's 'Slanderous' (2006), Cradle of Filth's 'Nymphetamine Fix' (2004), Slipknot's 'Vendetta' (2008), Týr's 'Hold the Heathen Hammer High' (2009), Amon Amarth's 'First Kill' (2016) and Carcass' 'The Living Dead at the Manchester Morgue' (2020).

Guitarists' innovations were also driven by the desire to find ever-increasing extremes of down-tuning and distortion too. Whereas Black Sabbath had frequently down-tuned to C sharp standard, others, led by bands such as Carcass (for example, *Reek of Putrefaction*, 1988) and At the Gates (for example, *The Red in the Sky Is Ours*, 1992), took that principle further, lowering the pitch a huge five semitones to B standard. Since then, both C and B standard have become common across the metal collective. Additionally, many guitarists adopted 'dropped-tuning' – standard tuning (at standard pitch or any of the down-tuned equivalents), with the sixth string tuned one whole step lower. The string spacing between the sixth and fifth string in this method allows a power chord to be performed using a short barre with just one finger and, therefore, a faster and more efficient method of iterating that key metal device. Examples include Pantera's 'Walk' (1992) (dropped D) and Disturbed's 'Down with the Sickness' (2000) (dropped C). At the same time, guitarists eagerly pursued greater refinements of tone and power to drive those power chords, riffs and solos. Electronics developed accordingly with amplifiers and effects pedals emerging that could simulate highly saturated distortion, something amply illustrated in the previous examples.

One of the more radical developments of post-1970s metal was the emergence of new vocal techniques, particularly in the rabid screams and death growls that both originated on and are synonymous with the underground extreme metal scene. It was a process that began with Venom and Motörhead who, in a departure from the expected norm of tuneful intonation, engaged with a more raucous and monotone approach to vocalising in numbers such as Motörhead's 'Jailbait' (1980) and Venom's 'Black Metal' (1982). The vocals of Slayer and Death in the early 1980s intensified and broadened that approach pre-empting the wide range of rabid vocal stylisations that came to dominate much of the metal scene thereafter. That range encompasses all levels of pitch, from deep, guttural death growls through mid-range frenzied rasps to theatrical high-pitched screams.

Cradle of Filth vocalist Daniel Davey, aka Dani Filth, impressively covers the whole gamut of those stylisations, often within the confines of a single composition, something evidenced on 'Cruelty Brought Thee Orchids' (1998). Similarly, but in a less theatrical setting, Angela Gossow, in her time with Arch Enemy, not only helped establish the strong tradition of female growlers on the scene today but also developed a remarkably wide range of pitch in her brutal live and recorded performances. Others have chosen to specialise in one range or another. Johan Hegg (Amon Amarth), Mikael Åkerfeldt (Opeth) and Glen Benton (Deicide) favour low-pitched death growls, whilst vocalists such as Randy Blythe (Lamb of God), Corey Taylor (Slipknot and Stone Sour) and Rob Flynn (Machine Head) are noted for their mastery of ferocious mid-range snarls.

Of course, not all metal vocalists have embraced the idiomatic trend for the growled, snarled and screamed, preferring, instead, to engage with a more traditional and melodic approach, one that both perpetuates and enhances the vocal histrionics initiated by Rob Halford (Judas Priest) and Bruce Dickinson (Iron Maiden). Notable proponents of this approach are Joakim Brodèn (Sabaton), Janne Christoffersson (Grand Magus) and Heri Joensen (Týr). Also important in contributing to the same tradition are the many prominent female vocalists of the metal collective, a roster that includes Tarja Turunen (solo artist and ex-Nightwish), Floor Jansen (Nightwish and After Forever), Liv Kristine (Leaves' Eyes and various metal collaborations), Sarah Jane Ferridge, aka Sarah Jezebel Deva (Cradle of Filth collaborations), Cristina Scabbia (Lacuna Coil) and Doro Pesch (solo artist).

Fusion

By the early 1990s, then, the core coding of metal was established and, although the future trajectory would see ever-increasing levels of complexity and sophistication applied to those established codes (as in mathcore and djent, for example), metal, thereafter, would evolve by means of fusion or hybridisation. It was a process that occurred on two levels. Firstly, by the fusion of contrasting stylisations from within metal itself and, secondly, by the incorporation of elements taken from pop, folk, classical and other forms of music normally considered incongruous with metal.[20] In this way, bands were able to establish novel identities within the metal scene and explore new ways of evolving the metal genre. It is important to note that there was considerable overlap in the dual processes of expansion and fusion.

Given the bifurcation of vocal techniques that occurred during the second stage of metal's development, it was natural that metal musicians would seek to combine those highly contrasting techniques, something educed by Los Angeles band Fear Factory in their pioneering work in the early 1990s. Their vocalist, Burton C. Bell, developed a style that moved easily between juxtaposed sections of growled/screamed vocals and melodic singing, almost as if it were two different singers. It was an approach prefaced on their early recordings but more fully realised on their 1995 album *Demanufacture*. From the mid-1990s, notable outfits such as System of a Down and Slipknot grew that trend to become commonplace within the metalcore and melodic metalcore scene of the 2000s, a movement further developed and represented by such bands as Machine Head, Trivium and Bullet for My Valentine. Whilst those artists adopted the same episodic approach as Fear Factory, others have been more creative. For example, As I Lay Dying, on the track 'I Never Wanted' (2007), used three vocalists in a more integrated and contrapuntal way by combining growled/snarled vocals simultaneously with melodic singing and traditional two-part harmonies in an effective three-part ensemble that smoothly transitions between numerous textures and colours.

A more heterogeneous fusion of idioms occurs in the diverse world of nu metal, where elements of metal, hip-hop, industrial, funk and pop coalesce in a range of permutations and unique metal makeovers.[21] Korn were one of the earliest progenitors of that concept, but it was Limp Bizkit who, through their incorporation of funk grooves, hip-hop rapping and DJ scratching, helped shape the more commercial approach often associated with that style. The band's 1999 award-winning single 'Break Stuff', for example, gives the *Diabolus in Musica* guitar riff of the verse sections a funky makeover in its supporting role to Fred Durst's stylised rap technique – an incongruous, yet effective and unique contribution to the ever-expanding family of metal idioms. Linkin Park further exploited the commercial potential of that concept on their albums *Hybrid Theory* (2000) and *Meteora* (2003). Those recordings spawned a number of singles that blended elements of metal, pop, industrial and hip-hop into a unique metal-focused style with widespread global appeal. In 'Numb' (2003), for example, a creative counterpoint of rapping and strongly emotive vocal melodies weave through a rhythmic flow of highly contrasting dynamics and industrial keyboard sounds to deliver what may best be described as a metal-centric ballad. Even where Linkin Park focus more on the metal elements, as in their 2000 release 'One Step Closer', gentle melodic and rap vocal techniques temper the presence of rabid vocals, dropped-tuning, high-gain distortion, Black Sabbath-influenced angular syntax and prominent Locrian discords.

A common approach shared by nu metal bands such as Linkin Park and Limp Bizkit is a proclivity for the verse/chorus-style formatting found in much pop music, a tendency also evident, perhaps surprisingly, in the more guitar-centric circles of nu metal. For example, Drowning Pool's 2001 mosh pit favourite, 'Bodies', is not only verse/chorus/middle-8-led, but a strongly anthemic crowd-pleaser too. However, the prominence of metal syntax, timbres and vocal techniques eclipse any genuflections towards pop stylisations, an approach similarly encountered, for example, in Papa Roach's 'Last

Resort' (2000) and 'Between Angels and Insects' (2000), and also Five Finger Death Punch's 'Jekyll and Hyde' (2015) and 'Sham Pain' (2018).

For many metal musicians, romantic notions of bygone eras, traditional folklore and indigenous cultural practices have inspired a plethora of folk metal crossovers. This concept has been particularly strong in Western Europe and Scandinavia, where a proclivity for Celtic folk melody easily aligns with the modal syntax and medieval aesthetics already established in mainstream metal.[22] Within those numerous configurations, there are varying emphases placed on the folk elements. For example, in the so-called Viking metal of Nordic bands Amon Amarth and Ensiferum, lyrics and visual imagery are highly significant and hold parity with the modal-centric musical elements. Amon Amarth's 2016 hymnal anthem 'The Way of Vikings' praises the glorious might and bravery of the Viking warrior with noble and majestic folk melodies, archaic harmony, death growl vocals and other extreme metal characterisations. A similar approach marks Ensiferum's 2012 track 'In My Sword I Trust'. There, the rabid vocals and stirring synthesised choral lines give way to a rousing *esprit de corps* refrain, calling brothers to arms with triumphal melodic leaps. Finntroll celebrate their Finnish roots in a more playful way. Their 2004 track 'Fiskarens Fiende', for example, both parodies and subverts the Finnish folk dance known as 'humppa'. The song is underpinned by archetypal walking 'oompah' bass lines and (simulated) accordion parts of the humppa and overlaid with creepy-sounding Locrian motifs, rabid vocals, down-tuned, distorted guitars and double kicks to complete the quirky caricature.

Others have focused more on the incorporation of actual traditional instruments and performance techniques as a way of hybridising folk and metal. For example, Danish band Svartsot, building on the earlier work of England's Skyclad and Ireland's Cruachan, successfully combine metal stylisations such as death growl vocals, double kicks and distorted, down-tuned guitar riffs with traditional Celtic instruments such as the Irish whistle, Aeolian pipes and Bodhran. On Svartsot's 2007 track 'Gravollet', for example, the instrumental modal themes are shared equally between metal guitar and Irish whistle, and the spirit of a traditional ceilidh dance is clearly invoked by the skipping pseudo-bodhran rhythms of the opening and the polyrhythmic hemiola cadences of each section. Whilst fellow Scandinavian bands Turisas and Korpiklaani have followed a similar trajectory, the Scottish pirate metal band Alestorm have accommodated an even wider range of acoustic instruments in the creation of their rather quirky and subversive take on folk metal. Such instrumentation has not only included passages for fiddle, accordion and tin whistle but also for trombone, trumpet and vibraslap, a rich timbral pallet evidenced across their output, including their 2014 album *Sunset on the Golden Age*.

Although strongly Eurocentric, folk metal has developed globally too. For example, Israel's Orphaned Land blend metal coding with Middle Eastern syntax and dance rhythms along with the incorporation of idiomatic instrumental and vocal traditions, a styling abundantly evident on *All Is One* (2013). Taiwanese band Chthonic have significantly impacted the global metal scene with an innovative fusion of Orient folk and black metal. This is expressed through the telling of ancient and recent Taiwanese history along with the incorporation of East Asian instrumentation such as the Chinese erhu and Japanese koto. Those elements are well exemplified throughout the 2011 album *Takasago Army*.

Classical music has provided metal musicians with alluring opportunities for assimilation from the start; Black Sabbath's theatrical and structurally complex approach owes much to the world of Romantic-era music, and the layered tritones of 'Black Sabbath' (1970) itself were directly influenced by Gustav Holst's 'Mars' from *The Planets* (1914).[23] The theatrical and pseudo-operatic vocal style of Rob Halford of Judas Priest, for example, on *Stained Class* (1978), further strengthened metal's affiliation with classical music, an approach magnified in black metal where vocal histrionics combine with prominent orchestral and operatic keyboard sounds to significantly define the esoteric soundscapes of bands such as Cradle of Filth and Dimmu Borgir. However, it was in the work of Finland's Nightwish where the most overt interpretation of symphonic metal emerged on albums such as *Oceanborn* (1998) and *Wishmaster* (2000). The appointment of trained opera singer Tara Turunen and prominent use of synthesised orchestral parts on those albums emphatically signalled the band's intent to forge a classical/metal hybrid that was in every way as artistically grand in performance and composition as the symphonic muse that inspired it.

In a similar way, industrial references have been central to metal from the beginning, particularly in the mechanistic rhythms of the drum and guitar parts. Nevertheless, several artists have forged more discrete and genre-specific hybrids of industrial metal, including Fear Factory, Nine Inch Nails, Rob Zombie, Marilyn Manson and the German band Rammstein. In concert, Rammstein have staged a series of settings that play with themes of industrial desolation and deprivation redolent of the former German Democratic Republic from which they emerged.

The extensive use of pyrotechnics has been central to those productions and seen guitarists breathing fire, flaming mic stands, a firework-shooting crossbow, burning metallic angel wings and flames from stage pyro canons that fire with all the searing intensity of an industrial blast furnace.

Rammstein are also synonymous with the emergence of dance metal,[24] a crossover style that combines metal with electronic dance music idioms such as techno and ambient. That fusion is most readily recognised in their 1997 MTV hit 'Du Hast', where a techno-style 'four to the floor' bass drum beat is overlaid with gated loops, sustained, ambient keyboard chords, robotic, space-age synth tones and high-gain, drop-tuned heavy metal guitar riffing. An even greater interest in hybrid experimentations is evidenced within the remainder of Rammstein's extensive output, where a variety of unusual combinations may be found in addition to their industrial and dance metal offerings. For example, 'Te Quiero Puta!' (2005) combines brutal heavy metal riffing with pseudo-Tijuana brass, flamenco syntax and a quirky vocal contribution from Hispanic born Hollywood star Carmen Zapata. It is a spectacular and innovative fusion that generates intense discord by the simultaneous mix of Phrygian, Phrygian dominant[25] and Locrian elements whilst, at the same time, exuding playful and subversive humour.

The multi-hybrid style adopted by Rammstein foreshadows the most recent trends in metal, which take the concept of fusion to extreme levels, an approach spearheaded by Pittsburgh quintet Code Orange. Their 2020 album *Underneath* combines sound effects and samples with a huge range of metal stylisations and other related idioms. That pallet includes, amongst others, industrial, mathcore, thrash, grunge, electronica, ambient, metalcore, hardcore, djent, doom, sludge, black metal, death metal and progressive rock. It is an experimental and truly avant-garde approach that juxtaposes those highly contrasting stylisations in rapidly changing episodes to delineate a scrambled montage of sound that animates the subversive and often nightmarish content of their lyrics and videos.

As such, the work of Code Orange in 2020 reminds us that Black Sabbath's original agenda, back in 1970, to 'scare the whole f**king planet with music', is just as relevant today as it was fifty years ago. Furthermore, whereas metal has widely diversified during the course of its evolution, it is the core coding established by Black Sabbath and other early innovators that continues to both unify and identify the current diverse world of heavy metal music.

Notes

1. Andrew L. Cope, *Black Sabbath and the Rise of Heavy Metal Music* (Ashgate, 2010).
2. See also Deena Weinstein, *Heavy Metal: The Music and its Culture* (Da Capo Press, 2000), pp. 39–41.
3. Cope, *Black Sabbath*, p. 30.
4. See also Weinstein, *Heavy Metal*, p. 23.
5. Jim Marshall, *Jim Marshall: The Father of Loud* (Backbeat, 2004), pp. 52–61; Charles Shar Murray, *Jimi Hendrix and Post War Pop* (Faber, 2001), pp. 261–3.
6. Cope, *Black Sabbath*, pp. 26–30.
7. An alternating bass-snare pattern inherited from the dance bands of the 1940s.
8. Further illustrated in Robert Walser, *Running with the Devil: Power, Gender and Madness in Heavy Metal* (Wesleyan University Press, 1993), p. 43.
9. A transgressive and unconventional approach to chord playing because, according to classical theory, a basic chord should have three notes that combine the first, third and fifth degrees of a major or minor scale.
10. Where traditional harmonic movement is a vital part of the hybrid.
11. See also Walser, *Running with the Devil*, pp. 46–8.
12. Also prominent in the Phrygian mode, which became an important component of metal in subsequent decades.
13. Joel McIver, *Extreme Metal* (Omnibus Press, 2000), p. 13.
14. Albert Mudrian, *Choosing Death: The Improbable History of Death Metal & Grindcore* (Feral House, 2004), pp. 35–7.
15. Cope, *Black Sabbath*, p. 114; Mick Wall, *Run to the Hills: Iron Maiden, the Authorised Biography* (Sanctuary, 2004), pp. 27–30.
16. Not in the strict classical sense of counterpoint but, similarly, the simultaneous combination or weaving of two or more independent melodic stands.
17. Cope, *Black Sabbath*, pp. 117–20.
18. It is acknowledged that certain strands of metal represented the antithesis of that principle, a point made in the Fusion section of this chapter.
19. See also Walser, *Running with the Devil*, pp. 63–6.
20. Stuart Borthwick and Ron Moy, *Popular Music Genres* (Edinburgh University Press, 2004), pp. 139, 144.
21. Matthew Karpe, *Nu Metal Resurgence* (FastPrint, 2018).
22. Ruth Barratt-Peacock and Ross Hagen (eds.), *Medievalism and Metal Music Studies: Throwing Down the Gauntlet* (Emerald, 2019).
23. Confirmed by both Butler and Iommi in video interviews, including this one. www.classicalwcrb.org/post/gustav-holst-heavy-metal-pioneer (accessed 16 April 2021).
24. Also known as 'Tanzmetall' or 'Neue Deutsche Härte', a movement that developed in Germany and Austria during the early 1990s.
25. A stylisation synonymous with flamenco and Latin folk forms.

PART I

Metal, Technology and Practice

Personal Take I – Russ Russell

The Quest for Perfection

'All that matters is what comes out of the black boxes' – a saying that I've heard over and over since I first started working in studios, simply meaning whatever methods you employ, whatever technology you use, the final result is all that matters. Throughout history, every breakthrough in music technology has been met with the same reactions. Some hate it and view it as 'cheating', while others embrace it and utilise it to greater or lesser extent. Even things like the first microphones and early recording media like wax cylinders were seen as the devil's work and purists refused to accept them, claiming they stole the soul of the musicians.

Fast forward to today, and while technology has changed enormously, attitudes are still very similar. The big arguing points of today, particularly in the world of extreme heavy music, seem to be triggered drums and quantisation, both of which have been around for decades but have come under increasing scrutiny as they are used more and more in modern production. Everyone is different and has different tastes, which is the pure joy of music production, except that for me, for my own personal tastes, things have gotten to a point where everybody isn't different or unique anymore. There are, of course, many exceptions to this, with hundreds of fantastic producers, engineers and mixers making great records. But as an overall view of my field of music, there are ever-increasing armies of clones, thousands of them, all using the same methods, the same technology, copied rather than actually learned from the same 'rule books', and this is sadly having the effect of making many artists sound the same.

Technology is not being used to enhance the musicians' performance anymore but rather to replace it. It's totally fine to do that, of course, if that's your intention, but the thing I feel is missing most from a lot of bands now is the band, the humans, the subtle interactions between people all the way through the process of writing, rehearsing and recording a song. As I said, this is absolutely fine if that is the original intention of the artist and producer/engineer/mixer (often all the same person these days, but that's a whole other conversation). But from my own personal experience, when you keep a bit of that interaction, that push and pull, the interplay of great musicians, the band are often shocked but utterly thrilled to capture some of the energy, some of that magic that they feel when performing live and not have it all squeezed out of them in the quest for 'perfection'. So, from my perspective, I'd say use your technology in whatever way you want, whatever is right for the project, learn when to use it and when not to; just try to remember, musicians are humans too.

Russ Russell, metal music producer (Amorphis, At the Gates, Dimmu Borgir, Evile, Napalm Death, Samael, The Haunted)

3

Mapping the Origins of Heaviness between 1970 and 1995

A Historical Overview of Metal Music Production

JAN-PETER HERBST AND MARK MYNETT

In October 1969, Black Sabbath recorded their debut album in a single day-long session at London's Regent Sounds Studio. Especially when compared with the affordances of today's digital music production technology, the conditions were rudimentary: the studio had a four-track tape machine that allowed drums, bass and guitar to be tracked, then a separate guide vocal or second guitar, which were later merged to make space for vocals or additional guitar parts. Importantly though, these limitations did not, in any way, obscure the core ingredients for what was to become 'the sound of metal'. The heavily distorted guitars were recorded at excruciatingly loud levels and double-tracked to fill out both sides of the stereo field and create a wall of sound. The bass guitar was distorted – uncommon for the time – and primarily followed the guitar riffs to give them weight and heaviness. Whereas contemporary hard rock bands recorded multiple guitar parts to embellish melodies or play counterparts, Black Sabbath's arrangements and production approach aimed at maximising heaviness through sonic weight.

Though considered a fundamental quality of the music, it is unclear what exactly 'heaviness' is, not least because of its ambiguous, context-specific and subjective nature. According to Harris M. Berger, metal 'history is most often summed up by metalheads as a progressive quest for ever-heavier music. A rich and complex concept differentially interpreted across scenes, "heavy" refers to a variety of textural, structural, and affective aspects of musical sound and is crucial for any understanding of metal'.[1] There are indications that this quest for heaviness began with the birth of metal. Tony Iommi reflected in his autobiography that where Led Zeppelin relied on powering drums, Black Sabbath focused on a 'massive guitar and bass wall of sound', aiming to 'out-heavy Led Zeppelin'.[2] Francis Rossi, frontman of Status Quo, pointed out that in competition for heaviness in the early 1970s, no other band but Sabbath achieved such a thunderous and weighty sound.[3] Little has changed in the more than fifty years of metal music; bands still claim that their latest record is heavier than anything they have released before, seeing increased heaviness as a signifier of improvement and proof of not having sold out.

Heaviness seems to be a combination of compositional elements, performative features and sonic characteristics. Structural aspects, most of all perceived tempo and pitch, are essential contributing parts. Their realisation through performance is equally important, as only powerful playing and tight ensemble synchronisation create the individual and collective sounds perceived as heavy. In recorded form and on the live stage, technological mediation has increasingly helped metal artists in their enduring quest for greater heaviness. The decisive role of technology becomes apparent when comparing metal releases from different periods. While songs and performances have certainly changed, the quality and aesthetics of the produced sound have significantly altered metal's sonic signature.

This chapter gives a historical overview of the development of heaviness on metal records by tracing how specific releases set standards or trends in metal music production. It focuses on early heavy metal, the thrash metal movement in the 1980s and the beginning of extreme metal in the early 1990s, concluding with an outlook of contemporary and future production aesthetics.

Early Heavy Metal

The production possibilities for Black Sabbath's debut album were limited by both the recording technology of the time and engineers unfamiliar with the new, heavy aesthetic. But recording technology evolved rapidly and satisfied the consumers' growing hunger for heavier sounds. Most recording professionals had to learn how to harness ever-evolving production tools to effectively produce the increasingly more extreme forms of metal, which required different approaches than rock music. Partly due to the general willingness to engage with the relevant challenges and to explore, new metal-specific production approaches developed quickly.

Black Sabbath's second album, *Paranoid* (1970), was already produced with 24 tracks and more studio time, allowing greater freedom to craft the band's heaviness aesthetic. On their third album, *Master of Reality* (1971), the band emphasised sonic weight by tuning the guitars and bass down by three semitones for 'Into the Void', and in the process, laid the foundations for an often-default subsequent trend.

Other now-iconic metal bands also contributed to the advance of heaviness through pioneering performance and production styles on their influential releases in the 1970s and 1980s: British acts Judas Priest, Motörhead and Venom, to name a few. Although the distinction between hard rock and heavy metal was blurred in the 1970s, a specific metal aesthetic began to formulate. The grim and doomy atmosphere of Black Sabbath and the guitar/vocal virtuosity of Deep Purple and Judas Priest combined provided a performance template for many aspiring metal bands. Elsewhere Motörhead and Venom somewhat tore up or at least heavily revised this formula, and in the process, provided inspiration for thrash and extreme metal.

Bands, engineers and producers experimented with new forms of expression. A major step towards a heavier aesthetic was enabled by introducing two kick drums or double kick pedals on a single kick. Although jazz drummers and rockers like Cream, The Who and Rush had already experimented with this approach in the 1950s and 1960s, respectively, metal increasingly built its aesthetic around fast kick drum subdivisions. As exemplified on their second album, *Overkill* (1979), Motörhead drummer Phil Taylor was one of the earliest metal performers to fully exploit this technique. According to *Overkill*'s engineer Trevor Hallesy, ten of the 24 available tracks were used for drums, and the double kick was deemed important enough to be recorded with two microphones so that other essential instruments like the snare had to be captured with one microphone only.[4] The additional weight from the more prominent kick drum performance was particularly well-suited to the quest for greater heaviness. Evidence that the kick's role was rapidly growing is provided by engineer Tony Platt, who remembered the drum microphone setup for Motörhead's *Another Perfect Day* (1983). Pre-empting the modern practice of layering different kick drum microphones to control the high-end click, mid-frequency thump and sub-bass power, a valve microphone was blended with standard dynamic kick microphones to capture the sub-frequencies in a manner that reproduced the impact of moving air.[5]

Triggering, a technique allowing to add samples to the drum sound for more punch, was already available in the 1980s, before recording became digital. Studio reports on bands like Judas Priest and Motörhead nevertheless suggest that producers and bands avoided triggering drums and instead aimed to improve drum performance and recording quality. Whether ethical considerations prevented them from employing sampling technique is uncertain. According to producer Chris Tsangarides, and regardless of ethical considerations, numerous Judas Priest albums prior to *Painkiller* (1990) relied in part on programmed drums.[6] Such precise half-programmed drumming preceded the quantised drum sound that became common in the 2000s.

While the kick drum was generally gaining importance, one band experimented with the snare drum: Venom. For metal journalist Joel McIver, Venom drummer Tony Bray (Abaddon) invented thrash metal by doubling the speed of the snare, featured first in 'The Witching Hour' on Venom's debut *Welcome to Hell* (1981): 'It's that snare drum pattern which is the essence of thrash metal . . . Abaddon's drum part . . . was much faster than the usual rock and metal drum patterns, and now typifies the basis of all extreme metal.'[7] This release marked the beginning of a race for faster performances, soon to be exploited by thrash bands from the US (Metallica, Slayer, Exodus) and Europe (Kreator, Sodom, Destruction), and an increase in heaviness.

As for the bass, Judas Priest and Motörhead continued Black Sabbath's tradition of supporting the guitar, an aesthetic still prevalent in many modern metal productions. Lemmy Kilmister of Motörhead played his bass through guitar amplifiers with the treble turned up and the bass removed, much to the frustration of the band's engineers and producers. As Trevor Hallesy remembers: 'My bottom-end challenge came more from the bass drums than the bass really because Lemmy's playing is more of a guitar-playing style than a bass-playing style – you have to use the drums for bottom end. So if you listen to Motörhead, the bass drums are really pounding away there and the bass is almost another guitar part.'[8] Ryan Dorn similarly pointed out that even the guitars had more bottom-end than the bass.[9] This was not much different with Judas Priest. As Tom Allom remembered: 'I used to say they were the band with no bass player, as the bass kind of followed all of the parts of the guitar. It was the fatness of the guitar sound that I liked most about those Priest albums.'[10] The engineers and producers of both bands found creative ways of dealing with this problem. On Motörhead's *Another Perfect Day* (1983), Tony Platt split the bass signal to be recorded with different microphones through guitar and bass amplifiers to blend the instrument's low-end with the distorted sound of the guitar amplifier.[11] This technique has become standard in contemporary metal production. Judas Priest with producer Tsangarides employed a similar strategy on *Painkiller* (1990), but instead of mixing two amplifiers, they doubled the bass parts with a Moog synthesiser to receive the pick attack from the bass guitar and the low-end from the synthesiser.[12]

Guitars continued to be the backbone of metal in the 1970s and 1980s. Engineering practice hardly changed aside from the fact that higher track counts allowed two microphones, one for low-end and one for clarity and presence. Recording one guitar each for the left and right channels remained common. Some productions added ambience microphones (Judas Priest's *Painkiller*, 1990)[13] or short delay effects (Motörhead's *Another Perfect* Day, 1983)[14] to thicken the guitars.

Thrash Metal

Thrash metal's emergence and proliferation in the 1980s complemented the development of metal music's heaviness, with artists from the newly formed sub-genre not only competing for heaviness, as was the case in the 1970s, but now also for speed. Metallica's debut, *Kill 'Em All* (1983), marked a significant increase in speed, far surpassing the previous standards set by Motörhead. Tom Warrior of Celtic Frost noted that the new US-American thrash metal bands 'had a much more clinical approach to heaviness. Whereas the British bands had this publike aura around them, the Americans just sounded like heavy machines'.[15] Performances became faster and tighter and thus more effective, supported by new affordances in production technology. While the debuts of most thrash bands were raw, energetic and passionate, subsequent albums increasingly exploited overdubs recorded to a click track, alongside tape editing and punch-ins to craft clinically precise performances that were, from Metallica producer Flemming Rasmussen's perspective, almost 'computer-accurate'.[16] Partly due to metal artists now seeing their album's production aesthetics as an integral part of their art, metal music's overall production standards increased considerably.

In favour of a more direct and aggressive sound, an important departure from the earlier rock aesthetic was the decreased reliance on recorded or synthetic ambience. Eschewing reverb for an improved sense of clarity, Slayer's *Reign in Blood* (1986), as just one example, translated the band's aggressive style far better than their previous two albums.[17] Here it can be noted that, due to the fast performances (the album features ten songs delivered within 29 minutes), there was limited 'space' for ambience to exist and expire within, and the same can be said of slower low-frequency wave-lengths. According to metal journalist Ian Christe, it was the 'first time that Slayer's sharp speed ... was not dampened by muffled, dime-store production values'.[18] Metallica's transition to a dry and direct sound began with their second record, *Ride the Lightning* (1984), and culminated on their fourth album ... *And Justice for All* (1988). Although the latter album divided some fans due to its extremely dry and clinical sound, the record, and especially its dry drum aesthetic, was highly influential. Producer Rasmussen noted that no room microphones at all were used, and neither was reverb added in the mix.[19]

Drum samples were seldom employed in the major productions of the 1980s and early 1990s. They were not used on Metallica's first four albums nor on early records of other influential bands like Pantera,[20] at least according to claims of the respective engineers and producers.

Alongside the development of drum recording, editing and processing techniques, guitar engineering progressed significantly, itself becoming an art form. Thrash metal built an entire style around fast palm-muted guitar lines, resulting in a production requirement that adequately captured these fast and precise performances and translated them with the optimum balance between sonic weight and clarity. Rasmussen recalled the guitar tracking for 'One' on Metallica's ... *And Justice for All* (1988) one of the most 'produced' metal guitar sounds of the 1980s: 'The guys were in a layering mode, aiming for perfection ... By the end of the song there were six or eight rhythm guitars, played by James [Hetfield] on different amps with different sounds on top of each other. However, he was so tight that this just sounded like one big wall of guitars.'[21] In some respects, though, the guitars were not too different from earlier productions. They were still double-tracked, one left and one right, and they were in standard tuning; 1980s thrash bands seldom employed down-tuning. Rare examples of alternative tunings include Slayer's 'Hell Awaits' (1985) and Metallica's 'The Thing That Should Not Be' (1986), tuned down one and two semi-tones, respectively. Referencing the link between down-tuning and perceived heaviness concerning Metallica's 'The Thing That Should Not Be', metal journalist Joel McIver compared Metallica's *Master of Puppets* (1986) and Slayer's *Reign in Blood* (1986) as follows:

Sheer heaviness – the use of slow, downtuned, deliberately 'dark' and crunchy riffing – is an area which is difficult to quantify. Both [albums] are fearsomely heavy, but Puppets just takes it thanks to the numbingly weighty 'The Thing That Should Not Be'. The term 'heavy' in this context also refers to the crushing, intimidating or downright frightening atmosphere of the music ...[22]

It was not until their fifth album, *Metallica* (1991), that Metallica began consistently tuning down a semitone to increase heaviness through sonic weight.

Nevertheless, as in earlier metal productions, the bass guitar continued to stand in the shadow of the electric guitar, with the prime example being Metallica's ... *And Justice for All* (1988). The bass is all but inaudible on the album, and, as the band admitted themselves, this was linked to the passing of original bassist Cliff Burton.[23] The supporting role of the bass is nonetheless emblematic of metal productions, featuring a wall of guitars and dry, punchy drums at the expense of low-end thickness. Whether due to their grief or other factors, this popular record inspired subsequent bands to prioritise drums and guitars over the bass.

Metal productions in the 1980s were a playground for experimentation; bands devoted themselves to exploring the opposite extremes of meticulously produced and overly raw aesthetics. What stirred the metal community in 1991 was Metallica's self-titled record, also known as the 'Black Album'. Its slick, commercial and, to some, 'overproduced' aesthetic alienated many metal fans but nevertheless was highly influential.[24] Notwithstanding that the songs were less extreme – slower, simpler and more melodic – metal journalists have described *Metallica* as the 'album of heaviness'[25] that continued to 'push heavy metal further into new realms' while maintaining the genetic code of heaviness.[26] Under the new direction of Bob Rock, former Mötley Crüe and Bon Jovi producer, Metallica explored the limits of what was possible in production. With a view to achieving production perfection, the studio time for each Metallica album significantly increased from several weeks for *Ride the Lightning* (1984) to nine months for the 'Black Album' (1991).[27] The latter was the first album the band recorded live with additional overdubs, which did not keep the band from meticulously crafting and tweaking the sounds and performances.

The increased popularity of other music genres like hip hop in the early 1990s prompted rock and metal productions to strengthen their bottom-end to stay competitive and continue their quest for heaviness. Hired largely as a result of Mötley Crüe's drum sound on *Dr. Feelgood* (1989),[28] Bob Rock went to great lengths with Lars Ulrich's drum production on *Metallica* (1991). Almost contrary to the dryness featured on … *And Justice for All* (1988), a fully three-dimensional drum sound was sought, exemplified by the kick, snare and toms being amplified through an audio system in a large room and with the resulting ambience recorded and blended with the directly captured sound.[29] This approach resembles the modern way of producing metal with parallel dynamic range compression and controlled reverberation added to the drum mix. According to engineer Randy Straub, parallel compression is

something that Bob [Rock] and I started doing years ago, and that's now pretty standard … It is intended to make the drums and bass sound punchy, and larger than they really are. Part of mixing rock music is to get more excitement in a track than really is there, and compression seems to do that. Again, it makes it sound larger than life.[30]

As with previous Mötley Crüe productions, drum samples implemented via a digital delay unit enhanced the drum sound, with Rock revealing an intention to 'give as much weight to the drums as possible'.[31] For maximising the kick's bottom-end, a blanket tunnel with microphones enclosed within the tunnel was set up to capture the sub-sonic energy physically felt by the listener – a now-common technique in metal production.

Since 'weight' was the ultimate goal for the production, Rock convinced Metallica to tune down their guitars, an effect best heard in 'Sad but True'. Notably, the bass has improved audibility compared to previous Metallica records, contributing to the heavy impression of the 'Black Album'. Achieving a balance between powerful drums, solid bass and punchy guitars was a technical challenge, Rock admitted. The drums and bass needed heavy compression, but not the guitars. The solution was to compress the entire mix but bypass the guitars to maintain punch, directness and intelligibility.[32] In other respects, Rock continued the excessive engineering practice Metallica had adopted. Increasing the number of guitar tracks to three, with an additional one for the stereo centre, enhanced the density of the guitar wall. To fully realise this aesthetic, Rock employed

multiple amps, as well as using the differences in phasing, cabs, and heads that all combined to get one sound. Different volumes on different amps, for different frequencies and clarity. That's basically what I've always done to record guitars. Multiple amps and multiple mics, and finding that sound. It's basically a process of building the sound in the studio.[33]

As Rock explained, most rock productions aimed to capture the sound of a guitar played through an amplifier with one or two microphones to blend different tones and build a wall of sound.

The commercial aesthetic of *Metallica* (1991), with its catchy songs and slick production, was broadly criticised by fans. Bob Rock nonetheless inspired many metal producers of the 1990s and 2000s, showcasing the art form that metal music production has become; it spans technical sophistication and artistic craftsmanship, emblematising the high production quality expected in contemporary metal. Followers include producers Colin Richardson and Andy Sneap, who were instrumental in shaping the sound of extreme metal.

Extreme Metal

The transition from thrash and speed metal to other extreme subgenres, such as death metal, grindcore and black metal, was fluid. Death metal emerged in the mid to late-1980s and marked a significant increase in heaviness. Artists kept the fast pace of thrash metal but continued the formula of Venom and Slayer by featuring the double kick drum more prominently and making the 'blast beat' with fast snare hits a regular rhythmic element of their music. Guitars and bass were tuned down to add sonic weight, accompanied by grunting or growling vocal styles that emphasised depth in contrast to the sung vocal tenor of heavy metal or the screams and roars of thrash metal.

Death metal took a different course in the USA than in Europe. Both metal cultures had distinct production styles influenced by particular recording studios, engineers and producers who started to specialise in extreme metal. Several US studios became known for their focus on death metal production. The most well-known facility, Morrisound studio in Tampa, Florida, was centred around producer Scott Burns, attracting many bands from Florida and beyond. Musically, Morrisound is known for recording bands featuring technically demanding structures, including Death, Morbid Angel, Cannibal Corpse, Deicide, Obituary and Malevolent Creation.[34] Such highly technical performances are regularly described as 'brutal'. The lack of melodic elements, seemingly chaotic and unpredictable structures, fast double kick parts, sudden tempo changes and breaks, and rhythmically pronounced guitar riffs reinforce this impression.[35] Guitars in Floridan death metal tended not to be tuned as low as in other death metal, which can be explained by the technical nature of playing – very fast picking, especially tremolo-picking, can be challenging with increasingly lower tunings – as well as the challenges of tuning, plus definition and intelligibility that come with it. The precise performances translated well through Scott Burns' engineering style that placed clarity before sonic weight so that the production aesthetic can be described as 'clean' and 'clear', despite the focus on 'brutality'. Fitting examples of early Morrisound productions that defined the aesthetic include Death's *Scream Bloody Gore* (1987), Morbid Angel's *Altars of Madness* (1988), Obituary's *Slowly We Rot* (1989) and Cannibal Corpse's *Eaten Back to Life* (1990). The high production standard at Morrisound gave death metal a professional sound, which gained international attention, making the Tampa signature widely known and gathering many followers.[36]

Slightly later, European death metal was forming most famously in Sweden, specifically in Stockholm, with Tomas Skogsberg's Sunlight Studios as the centre of the scene and sound. The music emerging there was influenced by the punk-inspired German speed metal of bands like Kreator, Sodom and Destruction. With its sloppy, distorted, raw and less defined sound, Swedish death metal markedly differed from US death metal.[37] Entombed's album *Left Hand Path*, released in 1990, is generally considered to have defined the Stockholm sound.[38] The most characteristic element of the Stockholm signature is the guitar tone. By tuning their guitars down five semitones, Swedish bands popularised a tuning that was to become standard in extreme metal. More concerned with groove than technical complexity, the bands produced at Sunlight Studios favoured a highly distorted and muddy guitar tone over the tight sounds known from Morrisound productions, making 'rawness' and 'fat heaviness' emblematic of Swedish death metal.[39] The tone, reminiscent of a chainsaw,[40] was a combination of the 'buzzsaw' sound of the Boss HM-2 overdrive and the 'non-buzzsaw' sound of the Boss DS-1 pedal.[41] The HM-2 with all buttons turned to the maximum is recognised as the trademark of the Stockholm sound. It produced a mid-frequency-heavy sound, in stark contrast to the scooped, mid-lacking guitar sound on Morrisound productions, for a full, dense and heavy impression that influenced the coming metal in much the same way as the US competition. Other early releases produced at Sunlight Studios include Tiamat's *Sumerian Cry* (1990) and Carnage's *Dark Recollections* (1990). Subsequently, a new, melodic death metal sound began to form in Gothenburg, built around Fredrik Nordström's Studio Fredman. Although less extreme due to melodic elements, folk influences and a cleaner production style,[42] key releases such as At the Gates' *Slaughter of the Soul* (1995), Dark Tranquillity's *The Gallery* (1995) and In Flames' *The Jester Race* (1996) influenced many bands as well as engineers and producers by showing them how well a death metal production could work by balancing Tampa's precision with Stockholm's fatness.

In the evolution of heaviness, another phenomenon should not be missed: the grindcore sound of British bands like Napalm Death and Carcass. Napalm Death's first two releases, *Scum* (1987) and *From Enslavement to Obliteration* (1988), made their mark on the international death metal scene with their extremely fast songs and blast beats, inspiring other bands to play faster.[43] Carcass were founded by Napalm Death runaway Bill Steer, who can be credited with tuning the guitar five semitones lower to achieve a heavier tone, a practice that would soon spread and inspire Swedish death metal guitarists like those of the bands discussed before.[44] In an interview, Carcass guitarist Mike Hickey admitted that this tuning 'isn't the most practical tuning in the world, but it's probably the heaviest', while Steer stressed the 'crushing' sound, but as well its challenges:

it has a lot of shortcomings in terms of tone because it's a very unrealistic tuning; we've really had to struggle to make it work. Since we've been doing it so long we can just about pull it off, but to be brutally honest, I think D, or, at a push C# [the common tunings of US death metal bands at the time], are the best tunings.[45]

Carcass first delved into grindcore before releasing their most successful album, *Heartwork* (1993), which metal journalist Ian Christe described as 'the Metallica Black Album of death metal [. . . and] a meticulously constructed masterpiece'.[46] Like many releases of the British extreme metal label Earache, *Heartwork* was produced by one of the most influential extreme metal producers of the 1990s, Colin Richardson. Following Bob Rock's tradition, the production approach was similarly sophisticated to that of Metallica's 'Black Album'. Improving on established engineering approaches, *Heartwork* set the bar for production quality in extreme metal for years to come. The album's engineer, Keith Andrews, shared production trivia on various online message boards, giving rare insights into the production. For the drum sound, the production team experimented with the new affordances of digital technology, converting kick and snare hits to MIDI signals in the computer. Only the kick sound was eventually reinforced by an audio sample. Their experimentation still marked the beginning of an increasing preoccupation with drum enhancement, stressing its significance in metal production.

The album's guitar sound required considerable effort, as Steer wished for a bass-heavy yet defined tone. Inspired by the common kick drum engineering approach of blending low-end signal and high-end capture, the production team assembled two standard Marshall guitar cabinets into an oversized enclosure for the loudspeakers to increase the low-end content of the guitar signal. Later, oversized guitar cabinets from manufacturers like Mesa Boogie became popular in metal to provide a similarly deep sound. For the amplifier itself, the Peavey 5150 model was finally chosen after days of testing and combining different devices. Released shortly before the recording took place, the 5150 offered significant distortion capabilities and had a distinct character. An overdrive pedal was added to the signal chain to tighten up the oversized cabinet's flabby response. This was achieved by setting the pedal – often an Ibanez Tube Screamer, or similar – relatively flat from the perspective of gain, tone and level, which still allowed the three stages of high-pass-filtering contained in the pedal to have the desired effect. The combination of 5150 amplifier (or newer versions of this model) and overdrive pedal affords a heavy tone with high definition at extremely low tunings and, therefore, remains a common setup of extreme metal bands even today. Metallica's productions inspired the production team to blend the 5150 with several Marshall amplifiers for a denser texture; this technique has become an established approach in metal guitar engineering. Furthermore, instead of two guitars as typical of earlier metal, four guitar performances were recorded to enhance the wall of sound, establishing a new, enduring trend in many metal genres: quad-tracked guitars.

An alternative form of European extreme metal emerged in the late 1980s and early 1990s, most notably in Scandinavia, and became known as black metal. Ideological differences aside, black metal was clearly at odds with death metal, which professionalised production to pursue greater heaviness. Black metal artists felt that heaviness had reached its limits within the sonic confines of death metal, motivating them to go the opposite way by deliberately emphasising a lo-fi aesthetic, echoing the early releases of Venom and Bathory.[47] This sound, an alternative form of heaviness, became popular and has influenced bands to this day. Black metal's contributions to production and mainstream notions of heaviness were perhaps modest compared to those of the bands, producers and engineers described in this chapter. Notwithstanding that black metal merges and overlaps with other forms of extreme metal, it still exists in parallel with other contemporary metal that values high-quality production.

Conclusion

Metal music has changed a great deal in its more than fifty-year history. Technological advances and the professionalisation of production have accompanied and enabled the genre's ideological quest for ever-greater heaviness. Many of the techniques discussed have endured as standardised approaches in contemporary metal production. Production was incrementally brought to the fore, facilitating the music's core elements and qualities, in turn increasingly informing composition and performance. This development is reflected in many 'hyper-qualities', such as hyper-perfect performances and hyper-real sound staging. Digital audio workstations with ever more powerful editing and quantisation capabilities allowed productions to become faster, more technical and yet more precise. Hyper-compression made releases louder, partly contributing to the so-called 'loudness war'. Partly enabled by extended-range guitars with seven, eight or nine strings, advanced amplification technology and extreme audio processing tools and techniques, tunings were increasingly lowered, giving rise to entirely new metal subgenres like djent. The consequence of this development was that the commonplace practice in the 1980s – the live recording of basic tracks – practically vanished. Nowadays, drums are often recorded last and quantised to a grid or entirely replaced by programmed performances, and likewise, bass parts are sometimes programmed. Further complicated by decreasing budgets, the quest for greater heaviness demands performance precision and extremity beyond what is humanly possible.

Notes

1. Harris M. Berger, *Metal, Rock, and Jazz: Perception and the Phenomenology of Musical Experience* (University Press of New England, 1999), p. 58.
2. Tony Iommi, *Iron Man: My Journey through Heaven and Hell with Black Sabbath* (Simon & Schuster, 2012), p. 76.
3. Kory Grow, 'Heavy Metal, Year One: The Inside Story of Black Sabbath's Groundbreaking Debut', *Rolling Stone* (2020). www.rollingstone.com/music/music-features/black-sabbath-debut-album-heavy-metal-origin-interview-949070 (accessed 14 April 2021).
4. Jake Brown, *Motörhead in the Studio* (John Blake, 2010), p. 20.
5. *Ibid.*, pp. 78–9.
6. Jonathan Saxon, 'Chris Tsangarides: From Black Sabbath to Depeche Mode', *Tape Op: The Creative Recording Magazine* 70 (2009): 30–6.
7. Joel McIver, *Justice for All: The Truth about Metallica* (Omnibus, 2009), p. 52.
8. Brown, *Motörhead in the Studio*, p. 24.
9. *Ibid.*, pp. 148–9.
10. Jeb Wright, 'Producer Tom Allom: From Sabbath to Priest', *Classic Rock Revisited* (2013). www.classicrockrevisited.com/show_interview.php?id=978 (accessed 29 March 2021).
11. Brown, *Motörhead in the Studio*, pp. 75–6.
12. Saxon, 'Chris Tsangarides', p. 34.
13. Joe Matera, 'Tom Allom: "The Sounds on First Sabbath Albums Could Have Been Heavier"', *Ultimate Guitar* (2011). www.ultimate-guitar.com/news/interviews/tom_allom_the_sounds_on_first_sabbath_albums_could_have_been_heavier.html (accessed 14 April 2021).
14. Brown, *Motörhead in the Studio*, pp. 81–2.
15. Ian Christe, *Sound of the Beast: The Complete Headbanging History of Heavy Metal* (Harper, 2003), p. 90.
16. Richard Buskin, 'Metallica "One"', *Sound on Sound* (2011). www.soundonsound.com/people/metallica-one-classic-tracks (accessed 14 April 2021).
17. Jake Brown, *Rick Rubin: In the Studio* (ECW Press, 2009), p. 66.
18. Christe, *Sound of the Beast*, p. 150.
19. Buskin, 'Metallica "One"'.
20. Dan Epstein, 'How Vinnie Paul and Pantera Revolutionized the Art of Metal', *Rolling Stone* (2018). www.rollingstone.com/music/music-news/how-vinnie-paul-and-pantera-revolutionized-the-art-of-metal-666086 (accessed 14 April 2021).
21. Buskin, 'Metallica "One"'.
22. McIver, *Justice for All*, p. 149.
23. *Ibid.*, pp. 192–5.

24. Christe, *Sound of the Beast*, p. 217.
25. McIver, *Justice for All*, p. 208.
26. Christe, *Sound of the Beast*, p. 217.
27. McIver, *Justice for All*, p. 203.
28. Jake Brown, 'Bob Rock: Metallica, Mötley Crüe, & More', *Tape Op: The Creative Recording Magazine* 121 (2017): 60–4.
29. Sylvia Massy, *Recording Unhinged: Creative & Unconventional Music Recording Techniques* (Hal Leonard, 2016), p. 116.
30. Paul Tingen, 'Inside Track: Recording Evanescence's "What You Want"', *Sound on Sound* (2012). www.soundonsound.com/people/inside-track-recording-evanescences-what-you-want (accessed 14 April 2021).
31. Brown, 'Bob Rock', p. 60.
32. David Masciotra, *Metallica. 33 1/3* (Bloomsbury Academic, 2015), p. 52.
33. Brown, 'Bob Rock', p. 62.
34. Christe, *Sound of the Beast*, pp. 238–9.
35. Natalie J. Purcell, *Death Metal Music: The Passion and Politics of a Subculture* (McFarland, 2003), pp. 12–16.
36. *Ibid.*, p. 13.
37. Daniel Ekeroth, *Swedish Death Metal* (Bazillion Points Books, 2019), p. 18.
38. *Ibid.*, pp. 154–9; Purcell, *Death Metal Music*, p. 22.
39. Ekeroth, *Swedish Death Metal*, pp. 196, 214.
40. Purcell, *Death Metal Music*, p. 22.
41. Joe Matera, 'How Entombed and Sunlight Studios Gave Birth to Death-Metal Guitar Tone', *Guitar World* (2020). www.guitarworld.com/features/how-entombed-and-sunlight-studios-gave-birth-to-death-metal-guitar-tone (accessed 14 April 2021).
42. Benjamin Hillier, 'The Aesthetic-Sonic Shift of Melodic Death Metal', *Metal Music Studies* 4/1 (2018): 5–23.
43. Ekeroth, *Swedish Death Metal*, pp. 14–16; Purcell, *Death Metal Music*, p. 21.
44. Ekeroth, *Swedish Death Metal*, pp. 15, 119; Purcell, *Death Metal Music*, p. 22.
45. 'Death Lives', *Guitar World* (2004). www.goddamnbastard.org/carcass/interviews/gwinter.html (accessed 14 April 2021).
46. Christe, *Sound of the Beast*, p. 246.
47. Ian Reyes, 'Blacker than Death: Recollecting the "Black Turn" in Metal Aesthetics', *Journal of Popular Music Studies* 25 (2013): 240–57.

Technical Ecstasy

Phenomenological Perspectives of Metal Music Production

NIALL THOMAS

This chapter examines the lived experiences of UK-based record producers with notable credits in the metal genre:

- Romesh Dodangoda (Cardiff, UK): Bring Me the Horizon/Motörhead/Sylosis
- Mike Exeter (Birmingham, UK): Black Sabbath/Judas Priest/Cradle of Filth
- Tom Allom (London, UK): Black Sabbath/Judas Priest/Def Leppard
- Martyn Ford (Newport, UK): Skindred/Slipknot/Bullet for My Valentine
- Russ Russell (Northampton, UK): Dimmu Borgir/Napalm Death/SikTh
- Dave Chang (Reading, UK): Electric Wizard/Earthtone9/Orange Goblin
- Oz Craggs (Folkestone, UK): Feed The Rhino/Polar/Dead Harts

Interviews were conducted in 2014 to explore technology as a lens through which we can ask how knowledge is known rather than what is known. Importantly, the interviews prioritised asking participants how technology has influenced the experience of making recorded metal music.[1] The main impetus was to develop a deeper understanding of technological influence and the experience of using technology as part of their creative process. The intention was not to construct a production methodology for metal music but to use these lived experiences to explore the tensions caused by expectations and anticipations of the use of technology in the recording studio. The producers were asked to make sense of the music they work with and how it is defined by the objects (technology) that surround it, as well as their relationships with artists and recording studio occupants and the musical and metaphorical semantics of record production.

For these communities, production is understood to be an everyday activity.[2] This activity is situated within a life-world (recording studio) and enabled by a contextual influence (technology). Jonathan Smith et al. suggest that to be phenomenological, we must 'attend to the taken-for-granted experience of [an activity]'.[3] By asking record producers to consider the way in which they conduct their everyday activities, the small decisions that they may take for granted, or the techniques that they rarely think twice about, we can start building a more holistic view of the impact of technology on record production and the development of the sound of recorded metal.

The Recording Studio

The recording studio should be understood as a space in which music and unique technologies meet. It is a world that provides the opportunity to create systems and technologies from the activity that is contained within it. The space itself is unashamedly technological, transforming sound waves produced inside it, designed to create new artificial waveforms that could not be formed elsewhere.[4] Music technology has the potential to act neutrally and purely facilitate production, but it can also be seen to no longer be neutral through repeated use and developed practices, collating a number of social-cultural meanings. The recording studio is not passive in the act of making music; it is a world that encourages unique cultural (musical) phenomena.

In *Nature of Technology*,[5] W. Brian Arthur defines technology as singular, plural and collective. Singular technology 'originates as a new concept'[6] and internalises development. Plural technology develops its constituent parts and practices (installing new parts into a computer, for example) and becomes plural by building around phenomena. In a collective sense, technology 'encompasses the entire collection of devices and engineering practices available to a culture',[7] uses natural phenomena and develops through multiple technologies working together. Phenomena here are the acoustic variables (sounds) that music production technology exploits. The act of exploitation validates objects as technological, and the recording studio is a technological space because it affords creativity. The recording studio therefore demonstrates technological plurality: multiple groups of technologies and people that work together to capture acoustic energy and transform it into electrical energy, and back again. It affords the capture of a performance; it is a tool affording the documentation of cultural phenomena. It is a space for communities to interact with technological objects that tend to only exist in those spaces, influenced by socio-cultural applications of technology.

Over the last century, the primary act of performing music in the recording studio has changed dramatically in response to various technological and socio-cultural practices.[8] As these practices have evolved, production technology has become an integral part of all levels of music-making and is readily available to all musicians, professional or amateur. Personal computing affords musicians the ability to document their creativity away from recording studios outside of the temples of sound that have housed music production for the majority of the twentieth century.[9] Performers, songwriters and instrumentalists cross the threshold into music production with relative ease and understand how to recreate unique sonic aesthetics[10] whilst also employing the technology of studio production live on stage and in rehearsal rooms. Artists now expect more from recording studios and the people and technology that occupy them, forcing movement away from capturing whole performances to constructing them.

Because of these shifts, record producers have a very different role to play in the production of recorded music. They are not only facilitators of technical processes but creative overseers of unique projects that can encompass music-making over remote distances, time zones, multiple personnel and multiple socio-cultural influences. The relationship these producers have with the process has been dramatically changed by technology and has begun to normalise new approaches to making music in the studio environment. For example, contemporary recorded metal normalises performance-enhancing processes as a form of technological plurality rather than the singular documentation of performances.[11] It is the intersection of practice and the expectations of both technology and communities surrounding metal music that warrants a phenomenological analysis of metal music production.

Technological Ideologies

Significant literature surrounding the complex nature of contemporary metal recordings details how recordings are constructed from a technical perspective,[12] in-depth examinations of geographical and stylistic traits within productions,[13] and the analysis of discrete trends in the use of specific technology.[14] The producers who make up the sample of this chapter identified with all of the themes in the current literature but also a number of key descriptors that encapsulate the audible phenomena of metal music: impact; energy; precision; extremity. Historically, these audible phenomena are highly important to our understanding of the genre's technological narrative. Proto-metal artists drew inspiration from the sounds of the British blues scene in the 1960s and artists like Little Richard, Chuck Berry and The Kinks, incorporating cover versions into their live performances.[15] The ability to record isolated instruments on multitrack tape changed the way in which metal artists thought about the sonic qualities of the artists they drew inspiration from, including the subtleties and nuances (or indeed the lack of dynamic subtlety) in drum performances, the ability to drive valve guitar amplifiers into high levels of harmonic saturation, and the movement away from direct injection recording.[16] Metal's audible phenomena were created as performative interpretations collided with new technological possibilities.

These audible phenomena tend to be determined by a dominant commercial ideology[17] that has the potential to influence the choices made by record producers, who are expected to create the sound the artist (and often audience) envisions, as well as achieve audible intelligibility within the final production.[18] This ideology is expressed in a number of ways but often returns to the way technology can (or does) act deterministically during the production process.[19] Artists seem to embrace this determinism and accept it as a primary feature of the creative process. One of the interviewed professionals, Martyn Ford, suggested this is a unique problem with contemporary metal music as it exists in the recorded format: 'The most overlooked thing in metal or rock is the song . . . By having a great production, you can almost get away with existing as a band.' This is not just a technological issue. At the heart of what Ford claims is a suggestion that metal music is made in ways that disassociate the musicality of the work from the audible phenomena; if a record *sounds* good, it must *be* good. The prevalence of online resources[20] that are dedicated to metal production tips and guides, as well as the close links that metal musicians have with the contemporary studio environment, has changed the role of the producer in the minds of the artist and audience, and indeed the importance of production in the making of a record. Technology has allowed musicians to become producers in their own right, as they can now visualise more of the process of making records, changing the way in which they are consumed. If Ford is right in his assumption, then the same could be said for how audiences are now experiencing recordings. Are they listening to the song or the sound of the song? The other participants raised this same issue in slightly different ways, suggesting that technology has influenced the way metal records are made:

I'm not a massive fan of producers who aren't musicians, [record production] turns into technicalities with those kinds of people. (Exeter)

I think people are using the technology to make the genre better. As long as you ask the question along the way, am I using this because I have to or because I can? I think that's what people have forgotten about along the way. (Craggs)

I'm not saying you can't make good records on tape anymore ... but people's threshold of precision, not only in playing but in sound, people have got used to it now ... if you tried to do [contemporary metal] on tape, people would go what the f**k is that? (Russell)

You do need a lot of production to get things sounding like a modern metal record. (Chang)

The genre's sound has changed over time, no matter the similarities in musical or stylistic approaches, but it seems that the producers who are making it are at odds with the use of technology. The technological advances give the perception that using technology is critical in a genre-specific capacity and affords the explicit audible phenomena of recorded metal in the twenty-first century. The producers themselves seem to want to use it as little as possible, or at least in the least noticeable ways. However, they know that audiences and artists now expect certain things from recordings. Ford suggests that one of those things is precision, particularly in relation to timing and quantised performances[21]:

I am going to nail it to the grid if it's full-on metal. That's where the power comes from, when everything lands together. It is machine-like, but that's how modern metal sort of is now. In fact, a lot of the bands we are talking about ... wouldn't see the light of f**king day if that hadn't been done to it. (Ford)

The likening to machine only further implies the influence of technology on the audible and semantic phenomena surrounding metal production. The technological expectations that align with contemporary audible phenomena, namely: bass guitar distortion, brightness and heaviness of guitar timbres, and kick-drum sampling[22] start to support a view that production methods have become homogenised.[23] Oz Craggs draws on the idea that this homogeneity is explicitly linked to the idea of commercial ideologies:

The problem is I would love to sit here and say, 'I don't care about what other [records] sound like'. I wanna make things sound how I want it to sound, but it's not true. I think you always have to pay lip service to other stuff. (Craggs)

Heaviness becomes a conglomerate of these expectations and homogenous practices. As the outcome of these contemporary audible phenomena, it is linked intrinsically to the development of genre-specific production aesthetics that become more acute over time, and heaviness becomes a signifier of quality. As with Ford's assumption, if a record sounds heavier (i.e., it has more of the audible phenomena audiences expect), it is a *better* record. This is demonstrated in an early interview with Black Sabbath singer Ozzy Osbourne prior to the release of 1971's *Master of Reality*:

[*Master of Reality* is] the heaviest thing we've done. It's going to be heavier than before because that's what people want. I don't know if Led Zeppelin made a big mistake or not with their third album, but personally, I think a lot of people were disillusioned. . . . People want heavy music, the heavier, the better.[24]

This technological ideology demonstrates that recorded metal music embodies constant performative and sonic development through evermore overt show-cases of energy, extremity, impact, precision and speed. These performative qualities have been prompted by technology that affords the ability to deal with, and create, heaviness more efficiently.

Forging the Sound of Metal

To understand how these technologically informed ideologies are established, it is important to trace the history of the technological decisions being made and the resulting audible phenomena, which began arguably in 1969 at Regent Sounds Studio on Denmark Street in London, UK. Now the location of a guitar shop, the small basement recording studio was the site of a short recording session for a band that needed to record demos after attracting record label interest. That band returned later that year to record their first full-length album, which was released on 13 February 1970. The band was Black Sabbath, and the recording engineer was Tom Allom. Allom was interviewed to explore his role as recording engineer on the first three Black Sabbath records under producer Roger Bain and as producer for artists such as Judas Priest and Def Leppard. *Black Sabbath* (1970) was mostly recorded live over the course of a single day using Regent Sounds' limited technological setup:

The equipment was so simple by comparison to today. It was a simple 12 in 4 out console, one 4-track [tape] machine, a couple of 1/4" [tape] machines, an EMT plate [reverb]. I think one limiter compressor, that's all we had; no outboard EQ, no, there might have been one. We might have had a Pultec. The EQ on the board was really basic, and . . . we had a nice complement of mics, and it was a brilliant little studio. (Allom)

Whilst the simplicity of this type of setup is to be expected of the time, it emphasises that the genre's sonic foundations were not dissimilar to any other recording made in the late 1960s and early 1970s; there was nothing remarkable about the technology used. Artists would record live, together in one room with some acoustic separation. These sessions would have cap-tured multiple versions of full takes of songs, with the producer deciding which was the best performance. For Allom, using this technology was a test of his ability to work within its limitations.[25] He highlighted that 'the final mixes of the first Sabbath album . . . were mixing a fifth-generation 4-track'. It meant that additional parts would be layered on top of the selected performance, thus creating some of the first signs of the audible phenomena we recognise now, primarily double-tracked rhythm guitar parts.

This shift begins to make recording multiple passes part of the production methodology of metal music. It makes the process non-linear, and non-linear production practices are increasingly evident in the way contemporary producers work. Some of the participants highlighted that the heaviness that audiences now expect is created when employing these non-linear or fragmented production practices:

I think the expectation of the listener is one of clinical precision now. I think if you were to do a certain type of heavy band and not include the editing of tightness, maybe people would feel cheated, feel like it's not tight. The technology has made the performance element transcend. What was acceptable has now become unacceptable in some ways. (Craggs)

Craggs suggests that it just is not acceptable to make a record without intervention, whilst Ford suggests that because of the acceptance of non-linear production practices, some artists have adopted that into their writing and rehearsal approach: 'A lot of bands have never even played the song together. A lot of metal bands tend to do it that way these days'. This could be seen as removing a sense of creativity. For Allom, when working on some of the archetypal metal recordings, working in creative ways to fulfil artistic intention and swerving technical restrictions created new genre-specific audible phenomena: overdriven double-tracked guitar rhythms; the prominent bass guitar; drums that fill the extremes of the stereo space. Technological development that afforded new sounds and approaches embedded technology at the heart of metal music production. The earliest examples of recordings to exhibit these phenomena align with some of the earliest widespread availability of multitrack technology (four or eight tracks) in smaller recording studios.[26] Most interesting is that early metal artists were not using the technology in the more experimental ways that their contemporaries were outside of the genre.[27] There is little to suggest, by critically listening to early records by Black Sabbath or Coven, that the decisions made were meant to imitate the progressive sounds heard on records by The Beatles or Pink Floyd. Allom explained the practical impact of increased track count at Regent Sounds:

The boss [at Regent Sounds Studio, London] had just bought us a second 4-track [tape] machine. . . . We decided to record the drums in stereo, which wasn't done very often in those days. It was just a simple pair of overheads, one on the snare, and one on the kick. That was it. Then we did the basic tracks. It was bass and drums over two tracks and then guitar on track one and maybe a guide vocal on four. Then if you wanted to double the guitar, that would go on four, and you'd mix that lot to two tracks on the other machine and started over. (Allom)

Whilst limited compared with the affordances of contemporary recording technology, Allom was clearly excited by the possibilities the extra tape machine afforded.[28] Ford affirms the ways in which technological affordances present new opportunities for producers:

When eight tracks came out, they wouldn't say we aren't going to use eight tracks, that's cheating. Whatever is at your hands technology-wise, you are going to use it at some point to get a better result, or the best result you can. (Ford)

As an example of the space created and the resulting impact that each element of the mix has, 'Hand of Doom' from Black Sabbath's *Paranoid* (1970) features wide-panned, double-tracked overdriven rhythm guitar parts throughout. Not only does this create a dense and powerful guitar sound, but it allows the individual drum elements space to punctuate the mix (03:40–04:00). Without the ability to record individual elements of the instruments in detail, this sound would not have been created easily in the analogue domain. Allom's ability to control spatial imaging and overdub guitar riffs begins to set up a series of expectations that inform the construction – rather than the live capture – of contemporary metal recordings, putting 'the emphasis on carefully adding and shaping sounds is fundamental to the record's aesthetic quality'.[29] One of the drivers of recorded metal's unique production practices can also be its social consumption. It is driven by the live experience and the sound of a band in a venue, whether on stage or in the audience. Artists typically rehearse in practice rooms at loud volumes preparing for the sound they will have on stage, and recordings are often produced to sound 'mimetic of that form of large-scale space'.[30] The ability to orchestrate the position of the band in a recording with a sense of size and scale is key to creating the audible power of metal productions.

Fragmented Productions

These formative metal recordings not only allowed artists and producers to establish the audible phenomena of metal music, but they began to dictate some of the performative qualities that proliferate contemporary recordings. Allom further emphasises 'tightness' as a musical aesthetic that was key to the sounds achieved at Regent Sounds:

I didn't have any idea that that music was going to be so meaningful. When I think back at the time I did it, I remember being really impressed with how tight the band were. . . . It was almost a jazz band in a way, really amazing intricate patterns and everything. (Allom)

This points directly to the established production methodologies that have been developed for contemporary metal music. Performances that are virtuosic and create impact through precise musical synchronicity are integral to production of intelligible and impactful metal music.[31] These types of performances present one of the most challenging aspects of the genre's production and the element that contemporary technology often aims to create simple solutions for. These performances often rely on technology to be able to isolate minute detail and correct dynamic or temporal issues. The most isolated these edits or alterations become, the more fragmented and non-linear the production becomes. Fragmentation, particularly linked to multitrack technology, moves production further away from live performance and closer to total isolation and construction of individual instrumental parts that may have never even been played in the same acoustic space.[32] Typically, metal music exists decreasingly as a live phenomenon in the recording studio because of decreasing recording budgets and the increasing cost to maintain physical recording studios. The level of control now afforded by multitrack technology has promoted a movement away from using acoustic space to create the vast majority of contemporary metal recordings. Ford highlights this, drawing on his experience of playing with metal dub artist Skindred:

I remember being in studios, and everyone played together. [Nine times out of ten] even the vocals Benji [Webbe] did end up being the vocals we used, even if he was singing in the control room. We were all in separate booths. I miss that part; I do regret you can't do that [anymore]. You can do it, but it's going to cost. Setting up a whole band and capturing it as it is. In metal, you don't do that. (Ford)

Ford laments that the desire to make records this way has dissipated. He recognises that it will typically come down to cost and the availability of spaces that would accommodate this type of production style. There is much written about the changing finances of the music industry, and it would be safe to assume that bands in the genre are not going to be commanding the types of budgets that would afford them the use of studios to make records in these ways. There are, of course, exceptions, but on the whole, the experience of the producers interviewed is fairly modest when discussing budgetary influences on the scope of records they make:

The budgets just aren't there anymore to make the records and the way you'd ideally like to make them, and you have to adapt. Luckily, I've got [Longwave Studio, Cardiff], which when I've got a really tight budget allows me to adapt. The budgets have got smaller, but the expectations are still the same. [Record labels] want the same job done for less . . . You don't get as much time to work on a record now as you did a while ago. (Dodangoda)

Technology has been a real double-edged sword; through me being able to build small control rooms in artists' homes, I'm pretty sure I've contributed to the decline of studios. It's not really my fault, it's record company models and downloading and stuff like that . . . you've got that side, but you've also got the illegal side of that which tech has allowed. But on the plus side, you've got the ability to record an album day in, day out, in your own home, and I can mix in my home. (Exeter)

Interviewer: So that's a commercial issue then? You've mentioned the change in budgets quite a few times and record label models. Do you think that's forced a change in technology?

People have embraced the technology; you don't have to go into a big studio to make a record, and . . . the technology has enabled artists to get far better value for money, spend a bit longer doing an album, spend a bit more time in pre-production. (Exeter)

I am not one of these people that believes that having a DIY ethic is a good thing . . . I think there is an idea that [recordings] have to be done quicker and cheaper, and I think that's a sad state of affairs. (Craggs)

Mark Mynett's work on the production of contemporary metal music[33] supports the views expressed by the participants, recognising that record producers and engineers are often charged with creating an experience rather than capturing a performance that is the experience itself. It assumes that producers and artists alike are pre-empting the use of particular technological processes. The monumental shift away from recording performances of pieces of music has distinct advantages (e.g., performative inconsistencies are reduced, and records are made at significantly reduced cost) and disadvantages (e.g., homogenised production of dynamics and rigidity of mechanically edited performances).

Conclusion

The development of music technology has led to the dominant technological ideology that has been embraced by the participants, some more willingly than others, as part of the service they provide to artists. Tension between how technology is used and the perception of its use when producing metal music strengthens the case that contemporary music production has become increasingly fragmented and now constructs musical performances that adhere to idealistic representations. For metal music, these representations align with qualities such as extremity and precision, impact and energy. The dilemma that metal producers face is how they comply with the technologically influenced ideologies and how they assimilate them into their own practice. Recorded metal is now a separate entity from the live instance of the same music, as it is often influenced by a number of expectations and pressures. The interviewees highlighted how the uses of technology and a changing record industry have led to the establishment of accepted ideals for metal production, ideals that producers often feel obliged to provide.[34] Russ Russell surmised that technological development could only influence music to a finite point before it causes a problem:

Evolution is not always progression ... Some things accelerate you forward, and the same thing later down the line causes a massive pileup, and everything grinds to a halt for a while whilst everything sorts itself out. Then you carry on again. I think that's basically what's going on in music. The things that have helped have brought a whole new world of shit that has cluttered everything up; now, everyone is sorting it out again and forging ahead. (Russell)

The idea here is that perhaps technology has influenced the production of metal music to a pinnacle point, hence why homogenous production practices have been assimilated without resistance. This then presents an ethical dilemma that all producers face: how much do they let technology influence their approach and the recordings they make? It could be the case that music technology has advanced to a point that it removes the creative choices that informed many of the early, archetypal recordings made by the likes of Allom. It could also be that technology has restricted this creativity so that metal records cannot be made independently from the canon of contemporary metal productions. It seems appropriate to return to Arthur's *Nature of Technology*. Arthur suggests that bodies of technology 'give rise to the characteristic industries of an era'.[35] Metal music production has been defined by technological development, and the experience of the participants affirms that contemporary metal music production could indeed be described as a characteristic industry, an industry of accepted ideals afforded by creative technological exploration that has been assimilated into the practice of contemporary record producers. This has resulted in the prominence of technologically reinforced performance practices and an increasing dependency on technology to produce metal music.

Notes

1. Jonathan Smith, Paul Flowers and Michael Larkin, *Interpretative Phenomenological Analysis: Theory, Method and Research* (Sage, 2009).
2. The term 'production' is used throughout this chapter to encapsulate the multifaceted range of activities and roles that are part of making of a record, including (non-exclusive): recording engineer, mix engineer, producer, arranger and performer (as a non-band member).
3. Smith, Flowers and Larkin, *Interpretative Phenomenological Analysis*, p. 13.
4. Allan Williams, 'Divide and Conquer: Power, Role Formation, and Conflict in Recording Studio Architecture', *Journal on the Art of Record Production* 1 (2007). www.arpjournal.com/asarpwp/divide-and-conquer-power-role-formation-and-conflict-in-recording-studio-architecture (accessed 12 September 2021).
5. W. Brian Arthur, *The Nature of Technology: What it Is and How it Evolves* (Simon & Schuster, 2009).
6. *Ibid.*, p. 29.
7. *Ibid.*, p. 28.
8. Susan Schmidt Horning, *Chasing Sound: Technology, Culture, and the Art of Studio Recording from Edison to the LP* (Johns Hopkins University Press, 2013).
9. Paul Théberge, 'The End of the World as We Know it: The Changing Role of the Studio in the Age of the Internet', in Simon Frith and Simon Zagorski-Thomas (eds.), *The Art of Record Production: An Introductory Reader for a New Academic Field* (Ashgate, 2012), pp. 77–90.
10. Duncan Williams, 'Tracking Timbral Changes in Metal Productions from 1990 to 2013', *Metal Music Studies* 1/1 (2015): 39–68.
11. Niall Thomas and Andrew King, 'Production Perspectives of Heavy Metal Record Producers', *Popular Music* 38/3 (2019): 498–517.
12. Mark Mynett, *Metal Music Manual: Producing, Engineering, Mixing, and Mastering Contemporary Heavy Music* (Routledge, 2017).
13. Jan-Peter Herbst, 'Historical Development, Sound Aesthetics and Production Techniques of the Distorted Electric Guitar in Metal Music', *Metal Music Studies* 3/1 (2017): 23–46.

14. Jan-Peter Herbst, 'Old Sounds with New Technologies? Examining the Creative Potential of Guitar "Profiling" Technology and the Future of Metal Music from Producers' Perspectives', *Metal Music Studies* 5/1 (2019): 53–69.

15. Cory Grow, 'Black Sabbath on Sixties Origins: "We Were Rejected Again and Again"', *Rolling Stone* (2016). www.rollingstone.com/music/music-features /black-sabbath-on-sixties-origins-we-were-rejected-again-and-again-192645 (accessed 12 September 2021).

16. This was a technique commonly used until the mid-1960s, which required guitarists and bass players to plug directly into the mixing console rather than record their instrumentally acoustically or using an amplifier.

17. Theodore Gracyk, *Rhythm and Noise: An Aesthetics of Rock* (Duke University Press, 1996).

18. Mynett, *Metal Music Manual*.

19. Merritt R. Smith and Leo Marx (eds.), *Does Technology Drive History? The Dilemma of Technological Determinism* (MIT Press, 1994).

20. For example, Nail The Mix. www.nailthemix.com (accessed 12 September 2021).

21. Quantisation in music production is the process of editing audio transients (a kick drum being played, for example) onto a strict time-aligned grid inside of a digital audio workstation. This creates perfectly in-time performances and removes subtle nuances of timing in a metronomic fashion.

22. Williams, 'Tracking Timbral Changes'.

23. Niall Thomas, 'Innovation and Tradition in Metal Music Production', *Metal Music Studies* 7/3 (2021): 423–43.

24. Martin Popoff, *Black Sabbath: Doom Let Loose, an Illustrated History* (ECW Press, 2006), p. 55.

25. These limitations would not necessarily have been limitations at the time.

26. Black Sabbath's *Black Sabbath* (1970); Blue Cheer's *Vincebus Eruptum* (1968); Budgie's *Budgie* (1971); Coven's *Witchcraft Destroys Minds & Reaps Souls* (1969); Elf's *Elf* (1972); Spooky Tooth's *Spooky Two* (1969).

27. Greg Milner, *Perfecting Sound Forever* (Granta, 2017), p. 157.

28. In comparison to contemporary computer software digital audio workstations that afford limitless track count allowing engineers and producers to recorded unlimited inputs.

29. Jan-Peter Herbst and Mark Mynett, '(No?) Adventures in Recording Land: Engineering Conventions in Metal Music', *Rock Music Studies* 9/2 (2022): 137–156.

30. Simon Zagorski-Thomas, 'The Stadium in Your Bedroom: Functional Staging, Authenticity and the Audience-Led Aesthetic in Record Production', *Popular Music* 29/2 (2010): 255.

31. Mynett, *Metal Music Manual*.

32. Michael Chanan, *Repeated Takes: A Short History of Recording and its Effects on Music* (Verso, 1995).
33. Mynett, *Metal Music Manual*.
34. Thomas and King, 'Production Perspectives'.
35. Arthur, *The Nature of Technology*, p. 85.

5 | Not from the Mind But the Heart

The Metanarrative of Being in a Metal Band

HALE FULYA ÇELIKEL

A couple of decades ago, it would have been regarded as non-academic to pursue research, which involved not only being closely associated with a given field but also doing the activities within that field as a member of the studied community. The scholar was expected to be a respectful outsider and ensure that their presence did not alter the phenomenon they observed. It would not have been considered ethnography if the investigator acknowledged that their presence, decisions and personage were to be branded upon the outcome. The assumption was that the author should act like a camera and not assume the role of a film director. Their duty was to observe anything and everything in the form of thick description, audiovisual documentation or analysis, using one or a selection of the habitual tools of social sciences. In one of the core textbooks of ethnomusicology, Helen Myers admits that 'the act of anthropological observation is obtrusive, inevitably altering the behaviour of the observed'.[1]

Practice-led research, the method used in this chapter, proclaims to do almost the opposite. This method, at times, formulated with slightly different wordings, such as practice-based research, practice as research or artistic research, lends itself useful when researching any discipline that involves creativity or artistic expression. In her research, Lyle Skains puts forth that pursuing art as research does not only offer insights into art and the practice of art as it occurs, but can shed new and unexpected light on a range of topics, including cognition, discourse, psychology, history, culture and sociology.[2] In this sense, practice-led research is 'a targeted combination of autoethnomethodology, reflection applied to cognitive composition and creativity models, and post-textual media-specific analysis of the creative artefacts' akin to similar methods used for medicine and engineering'.[3] Accordingly, the creative process is both artistic and analytical: practice-led research is thus reminiscent of a hard-sciences researcher working in their laboratory. However, within humanities, perhaps due to the quest of presenting the research outcomes in a more 'scientific' sense and having as many shared attributes with hard sciences as possible, the use of practice-led research is relatively new.

This chapter is constructed around the mainly diachronic story of the Turkish metal band Listana. Metanarrative, used in the title, is a term developed by Jean Francois Lyotard to denote a grand narrative that seeks to connect separate events in a timeline to plausibly explain phenomena, such as social contexts and experiences.[4] A metanarrative must be grounded in the context of universal truth, similar to a causal chain, explaining and organising knowledge. In the context of the present chapter, metanarrative describes a 'self-directed form of ethnomethodology'[5] encompassing field notes, audio-visual material, formal and informal input of the involved parties and the musical products created to constitute the basis for analysing the creative process. The documentation is thus intertwined with the process itself, enabling a deep, subjective record of the entire procedure. Scholars who map out practice-led research as a method seem to agree upon not considering subjectivity as a problem. In this chapter, the intention is not to artificially elevate the band experience to the theory level by abstracting it or forcing generalisations. Instead, it gives a first-person account of a female-fronted metal band in Turkey.

Listana's Formative Period

Listana was founded in 2011 as a five-piece female-fronted metal band in Istanbul, Turkey, by amateur musicians who sought to develop their musical skills through exact covers. The initial aim was to perform known bands' music as close to the original as possible before turning to compose original songs. Despite being marginalised as a female-fronted band in the male-dominated metal music industry, Listana managed to survive the emerging phase, achieving the level of supporting international metal artists at domestic festivals and abroad in a relatively short time. Experiencing both setbacks and support, like many new metal bands, it became part of the vibrant Turkish metal scene Pierre Hecker describes.[6]

Initially, Listana performed the symphonic metal subgenre, common for female-fronted bands. Later, the band revised its playlist to form and occupy a niche of its own by turning to progressive metal, a technically demanding subgenre that is not very common or in demand in Turkey. Refraining from stereotypical themes of metal music, such as anger, violence, masculinity and promiscuousness, inevitably branded Listana also as an alternative metal band. Embracing being 'progressive', the band went on to create original music featuring daring harmonic effects, novel textures and odd time signatures. Despite drawbacks, such as frequent lineup changes, lack of experience in terms of producing and promoting original music, mediocre equipment and meagre stage experience, it was always possible to find gig opportunities and play to full venues.

Conflicts from Musical Socialisation

Having interviewed many metal performers with global careers, such as Zakk Wylde and Jordan Rudess, as well as some of the most prominent Turkish protagonists of the metal scene like Murat Ilkan during my research, I feel entitled to generalise that, unless they happened to grow up in a particularly musical environment (musicking parents, for example), most metal musicians pick up their instruments around the time they are in junior high school and start their musical career in their mid-teens. On the contrary, my exposure to metal music came at a later point in my life, when I was drawn to symphonic metal as a listener through its well-documented connection to classical music. I did not have any interest in performing metal until I received the offer to join Listana as a keyboardist and backing vocalist.

Unlike the other five members of Listana, I had no experience in amplified music at all, so I was much less skilled in the studio than my new colleagues. As a trained pianist and composer according to the Western Conservatory system, I never worked with musicians from diverse backgrounds. My musical experience consisted of classical music performances: solo piano, chamber music, accompaniment, acapella singing. Assuming that my new-found colleagues would have had at least some kind of musical education, I expected procedures I was familiar with through these settings. However, unexpectedly for me, adaptation and advancement became a difficult issue for everyone. Unfamiliar terms such as 'riff', 'groove' or 'guitar tone' seemed to belong to the genre we strove to perform, but I did not have any contextual grasp on them, my colleagues could not verbally define these to my satisfaction, and internet sources were in disagreement on their exact meaning. I was unable to communicate my knowledge, intentions or opinions through the musical jargon I was proficient with. Worst of all, I had limited skill and understanding of my new instrument: I had no notion at all of sound design or keyboard programming. Consequently, I was not able to use my entry-level Roland synthesiser to much effect, even though my keyboard technique was much more advanced than the parts I was required to play.

All in all, I found out that the expectations and performance standards of metal music differed from classical music. For instance, meticulousness and clarity were drowned in the noise during studio sessions at times, but colleagues did not seem to mind as long as the flow was not affected.

I worked closely with the band's semi-professional guitarist, who picked up the instrument at thirteen but never had any tutorage. Since both of us were required to play antiphonal, parallel or even unison solos, I constantly attempted to teach him music theory, notation and the 'correct' jargon, such as not calling lower strings 'upper' strings because they are vertically at a higher position. Yet, he did not show any significant interest, being content and successful with his mnemonatic and tactile musicianship; some issues of musical communication were thus forever left unresolved.

Reflections

When the problems described earlier affected my musical satisfaction, I felt it necessary to reflect on the reasons and began to analyse the experience. In Philip Bohlman's words: 'Thinking – or even rethinking – music . . . is at the base an attempt to claim and control music as one's own.'[7] Thinking along the lines, 'I have the longest and most comprehensive musical training, so I should have the authority on musical decisions' or 'it is my bandmates' shortcoming if they do not understand when I speak about third-degree modulations or thematic transformation', did not solve any problems. It was a revelation to discover that performing metal, thus learning another genre's performance practices, was a means to indulge in the pleasures of escapism for me. I was venturing into the realm of the musical 'Other',[8] behaving like many classically trained musicians, enjoying the popular music experience but without adopting it or declaring it an integral part of my musical identity out of unacknowledged subconscious contempt. Even though I was devoting ample time and resources to learning conventions and performance practices, I was still the superior, justified 'Self', who was presumably able to direct the musical experience in the manner I was taught during my studies. In short, I failed to understand 'one of the pillars of rock ideology: opposition to authority and discipline, and, by extension for musicians, opposition to a structured approach to the learning of music'.[9]

I needed to break with this attitude and accept that I had deficiencies and still things to learn in order to progress. For one, I discovered that I was completely insensitive to what popular musicians refer to as 'sound', and I only perceived the music through its quantitative parameters like pitch, rhythm or harmony. My approach was, in fact, very Adornian because I was seeking music's meaning and significance exclusively in its formal characteristics, notated or otherwise prescriptive, instead of the elusive and mysterious 'vibe' my bandmates sought. They seemed to respect my knowledge but did not evaluate the rehearsal techniques or aims I offered as useful or efficient: I was simply not metalhead enough for guiding a metal band, in their opinion. From their rebellious stance, the rigour and discipline of my classical training rendered me stiff.

As my experience grew, I came to understand that it is actually those elements between the notes that are making the music 'metal'. To a mind, which is programmed to use prescriptive Western notation to produce music, it is hard to accept the reversal of this idea. In the limited sense, notation gets to be used in metal music; it is an inadequate, descriptive tool. The idiomatic, instinctive 'licks' of the guitars, unwritten rules of composing bass and drums parts, timbral quality and treatment of scalar or modal material outside the conventional rules governing classical music are habitually captured by recordings. The composer and performer often being the same individual reinforces these characteristic properties to an extent few instrumentalists and composers of the Western musical canon, such as Chopin, ever achieve. Yet, again resulting from the seeming inadequacy and incompatibility of notation, if one is not skilled in treating a recording as a learning source, even an accurate transcription would not guarantee an authentic performance.

Becoming a Metal Musician

No study on metal music composition describes it as a standard procedure. Besides participant observation, I was able to gain some insight into how metal musicians and bands create music through interviews with professional metal musicians. It is unproven but potentially true that the stereotypical metal musician uses the ear more than the eye to create music. I eventually encountered a metal songwriter, who exclusively composes using Western staff notation and distributes this material among his band members, but new, original music arises from 'jamming' together for most bands. Michele Biasutti's work depicts a similar process, the compositional procedures of an Italian progressive rock band.[10] Biasutti analyses videotaped data to categorise his findings into five themes: context definition, experimenting, constructing, playing and evaluating. He uses an adaptation of the comparative ethnographic method to calculate how much time is spent on which respective compositional activity.

Returning to the microcosm of my own band, I can state that no Listana song was composed by the same band members in the same manner and employing the same procedure. Each song unfolded differently and took different amounts of time to write. Of the released numbers, the easiest to compose, 'Elveda' (2013), took only a few days, whereas some numbers, such as 'Persona non Grata' (2014), took a very long time, spanning a few months and undergoing drastic changes. As an active participant of the compositional sessions, I did not have the chance to employ similar data collection or analysis means as Biasutti did, who warns 'when actions are driven by the researcher, the participants are not free to express all possible behaviors'.[11] I have observed that it took Listana about a year to bring a piece from scratch to the recording phase, but this time requirement varies considerably between metal musicians and bands.

Once a band's endeavours reach the recording phase, its existence is confirmed. A 'demo recording' is an initial, usually technically flawed, sound or video recording that establishes the band's existence: the first outlet of a band to its potential audience. Without a demo, a venue would not let a band perform, as its musical inadequacy could cause them to lose their customers and even damage their inventory of sound or stage equipment. Therefore, as soon as a garage band decrees itself ready, its members attempt to record their output. Recording together in such a manner is called a 'rush' session and is seldom a flawless, immaculate affair. The recorded song could be a cover, especially if the band intended to perform at a venue or plan to attract a social media audience that would place them in the metal oeuvre due to their similarity to existing bands. Recording is a challenge for any band, be it in the relatively comfortable environment of a home studio or a fully equipped professional studio, where time and expertise must be paid for. Usually, less proficient musicians can only focus on their own instruments when jamming or gigging, without paying much attention to what the others are doing or how the ensemble sounds together; recording is therefore essential as a self-evaluation tool as well.

During Listana's existence, there have been innumerable recording sessions, some fruitful, others not. At the onset of the band, none of the members had enough proficiency with studio technologies or even minimum equipment to record at home, so even the earliest demo recordings had to be outsourced. From home studios with poor equipment to high-end studios where the hourly rent would be hundreds of liras, Listana explored many music production settings, gaining valuable insights. As the band members had day jobs, there were the financial means to hire professional studio staff and use proper equipment, but this did not ensure that a decent product emerged or that the resulting recording proved usable. Often, older recordings were discarded in favour of a newer recording that was meant to fix the flaws of the previous one. Another reason Listana's earlier recordings had to be discarded is that the band had to change vocalists four times in its initial two and a half years. If the replaced member had been an instrumentalist, the recording could have still been used with the permission of the former and current member, but there is no way to redeem or alter a finished recording with vocals short of re-recording. To avoid such issues in the future and to align the musical mastermind and the 'front' of the band, I was eventually 'promoted' by my fellow band members to be the band's lead singer as well as the keyboardist. For some time, to acquire live performances, we recruited a second keyboardist while I was using a keytar on the front stage.

For local metal artists, being on the stage of large-scale events is a rare occurrence. Metal artists, who must invest much time and capital to acquire their skills, equipment and networking, seldom make any money from gigging in Turkey. Metal clubs in Turkey usually have their selection of bands-in-residence that play covers of their regular customers' favourite music. These bands are formed by professional musicians, expected to play every week on their designated day, for a previously agreed fee per performance, split among band members, independent of the revenue of that particular day. Very few of these house bands have their own compositions or follow the same path as original bands that seek to establish themselves as metal artists on the domestic and international music market. Therefore, metal clubs that have live stages hardly ever hire new bands with an original discography. Since the supply is greater than the demand, most metal musicians must call their performances 'concerts with free entrance', where the expected outcome is exposure, beer and fun, rather than a professional opportunity for which they would receive some payment in money.

During the time it was actively performing, Listana was a conspicuous band because of the female lead and technically demanding music it sought to perform, which was rarely, if ever, attempted by cover bands. In the first half of the 2010s, the band gigged very often: besides a lively club scene, there were also open-air metal festivals in Turkey in that period. The average live club performance lasted around an hour, but there were also shorter appearances, such as at university festivals, which typically had a stage time of half an hour, including changeover and sound check. For a few months, the band even performed weekly in DoRock Taksim, the largest live metal club in Turkey, as a paid house band that performs a two-hour program – a very competitive gig. Listana even made it to the big stage to support international bands, such as Orphaned Land, Dark Tranquillity, Sonata Arctica and Theatres des Vampires, among others. A major achievement was to perform abroad in Ukraine in the summer of 2013, supporting Overkill,

Artillery and Dying Fetus. For an emerging band, an invitation to a festival meant that they would have to pay their travel and accommodation expenses themselves; such event organisations only have the budget to fully reimburse headliners and co-headliners. There is even a concept called 'buy-in', which means that a new band paying a certain sum might get a slot to perform at a festival or open for a more established band on tour. Major European festivals claim to shun this practice; I have witnessed the organisers of Hellfest state that a non-proficient band is not allowed on any of the festival's nine stages, and no sum of money can change that.

Performing Live

Most studies detailing the experience of live metal concerts are from the viewpoint of a spectator present among the audience or backstage. When considered from the performer's perspective onstage, there is next to no research available. I only encountered one other metal music scholar with a research design similar to my own: Jasmine Shadrack, who reports her experiences in black metal.[12] Acquiring the expertise to perform any music for an audience is a difficult task and more demanding with some music genres than others. For metal, the rules are clear: a performer must move and look representative enough on stage to communicate with and animate their audience. Inevitably, the focus is divided between performing well enough and interacting with the audience, verbally and nonverbally. Shadrack summarises: 'Make no mistake, if you are in a metal band, remaining static whilst you perform negates the performance itself. The physicality, endurance and focus required to ensure precise playing whilst head-banging for example, takes practice.'[13] No matter how much one practises on their own or with the band in the studio environment, genuine stage familiarity can only be acquired on stage in front of a real audience.

It was fortunate that I came to the front stage after being on the keyboards for two and a half years, which taught me how to connect with the audience to some extent. Learning to sing properly is no different from learning a new instrument, and it took me a long time to gain a semblance of confidence again. The audience walking in and out of the venue during performances, approaching to listen or going out for a smoke or chat, was not much of a concern for me before, but after I assumed the role of the vocalist, it often made me feel insecure. I kept asking myself if they were fleeing from my poor performance. The after-show adulations that I became used to in those first years of my metal musicianship were now replaced with some audience members avoiding eye contact with me or even ignoring me altogether, sometimes extending into anonymous derogatory comments on social media after shows. There would always be people charmed by my unusual voice, but I keep having detesters to this day.

A general procedure of a Listana concert was to arrive with equipment at the venue, sometimes several hours before the performance if we were the opening band, set up the rig, perform, disassemble our own gear and abandon the stage for a changeover. Although the stage mood resulted in extraordinary iconography in the form of photos and videos, there was not a single concert where everyone claimed to have been able to hear themselves and everyone else sufficiently and clearly, and where everything went smoothly. Performing meant all kinds of mishaps happening; very rarely everyone in the band would be satisfied with the outcome and leave the stage exhausted but satisfied.

Regardless of the genre they play, musicians have less time to devote to practise when they have day jobs. Lack of mental discipline, physical stamina or practice time compromises performing a distinctly virtuosic subgenre of metal through long playlists. During Listana performances, as with many other metal bands, we had instances of drummers rushing tempos that caused unclear passages or wrong entries in the case of instrumentalists. Irrespective of how much individual practice went into them, technically challenging parts sometimes became muddy with stage excitement.

When there are shortcomings among the internal factors that constitute the band's sound, 'outside' factors gain visibility beyond control, putting the outcome at risk. A band needs at least one person with an appropriately trained ear, who must be proficient in determining if the guitar and keyboard are properly compressed to not mask each other in the sonic spectrum, but this is often not the case, Listana being no exception. Without sufficient aural awareness, there is simply no guarantee that even the most advanced equipment would deliver the desired results. Let alone hiring a professionally trained live sound engineer, few venues take on the expense of dedicated staff operating the audio console for underground metal bands performing gigs. Therefore, the musical outcome is seldom the intended balance in terms of the mix.

Status and Gender Experiences

For Auguste Comte, music is the most social of all arts.[14] In the case of metal music, since it has a close and well-defined community, this statement rings even more true. Most metalheads I have made acquaintances with during my fieldwork decided to interact with me after learning about my band and performer status. My status as a researcher did not win them over, especially if they already had some dissatisfaction about their education or professional life. Some informants I attempted to interact with found it offensive that I was researching something like metal music, which is sacred to them, thus devaluing it. Fortunately, most of my informants made clear that I deserved their input since I was a metal musician as well as a researcher. In their eyes, my 'fakeness' and 'being a poser' was redeemed by the fact that I was performing metal.

As a musician and researcher, I disregarded the gender inequality in metal music as much as possible. There are two 'allowed' dress codes for a female metal figure: either to assume an utterly gender-neutral or even masculine dress code, or a hyperfeminine dress code.[15] According to the subgenre performed, variations of these two basic templates are possible. I was not comfortable with masculine or gender-neutral attire, nor did I wish to draw attention to my sexuality, so I always targeted a middle ground of femininity in my stage costumes. Neither Listana members nor other metal musicians we performed with treated me differently for being a woman: what mattered was music, not privileged chivalric treatment. The audience was another issue, though: there was no way to avoid the male gaze, which ranged from fervent admiration to outright misogyny. Although I refused to acknowledge it, I represented the 'Other' in some audience members' eyes: an anomaly, tolerated at best.

The initial two-year phase when I was solely the keyboardist, working hard on my live sets and performance skills, spared me from the negative end of this spectrum, but assuming the lead with a less-than-ready voice foregrounded my gender in the worst possible way. In Shadrack's words, I was bold enough to occupy a male space in an overtly male genre.[16] Considering that Listana performed progressive metal songs and most of these pieces are written for male voices, the initial reaction to my vocal performance was anything but favourable. We had performed some of those same numbers with our previous vocalists, but they were all more experienced singers than me, so the sexism they faced had a different nuance from what they told of their experiences. For me, the accusation was a gendered one: I was a poor vocalist who thought I could make up for my lack of talent by being an attractive woman and 'enthraling' my band members.

Interestingly, the strongest discouragement came from other women, who sometimes were not even musicians themselves or had projects in earlier stages than Listana. My interpretation is that the space for women is quite narrow in metal music performance, and competition is inevitable. From these female detesters' perspective, it is utterly unfair that I get to 'reign' on the stage, performing with more than adequate musicians and commanding *their* respect despite my obvious shortcomings. The men were another matter: for some, there is always the attraction, and the flaws in my performance thus serve as a pretext to approach me. For others, it is sacrilege that a woman, who happens to be an inexperienced singer, is offending their musical senses by daring to perform progressive metal numbers. Undeniably, I had much encouragement from within the band, partially stemming from the members' exasperation about the conflicts and problems we experienced with the four vocalists we tried. It is a cause of remorse for me that they had to endure the blows from the audience together with me; the process has been an eye-opener and led every band member to question musicianship and social pressure associated with metal.

Releasing an Album

The fertile environment and vibrancy of the Turkish metal scene meant that Listana could experience the thrill and driving motivation of an emerging band, similar to the accounts of comparable international bands. To consolidate this rising trend, an album was needed to be released: the presence of a solid recording of original music meant that Listana would be perceived as having enough identity and skill for large-scale events. However, such a band whose output was quite far from the Turkish mainstream had next to no chance of finding a local label willing to make a commitment in terms of promotion and digital distribution. Without the necessary know-how and connections to seek an international label, the decision was made to digitally release the Listana album *Unveiled* in 2013 as an indie band. Such an enterprise would have been immensely difficult without intermediaries just a decade ago, but online distribution companies such as CD Baby are now available to provide an artist's track with the UPC/EAN code, which is a validation for use on the internet. It is thus possible to legally release an act's output across the planet on a limited budget.

What is seldom mentioned in this bargain is that, without a proper marketing allowance, the visibility of any such release would be extremely limited. There is more than six centuries' worth in time of available music in streaming services worldwide. According to Daniel Sanchez, 99 per cent of all music streaming on Spotify and Apple Music comes from the top 10 per cent of songs. Less than 1 per cent of streams accounts for music other than what is popular, according to charts and sales graphics.[17] In essence, only those with the financial means to market a release by advertising on streaming platforms acquire visibility. Rather than implementing solutions for this discrepancy, music streaming platforms like Spotify and Apple Music admit to making money from advertising indie artists. Thus, listeners are put under the illusion of freely choosing what new music they would consume. The total production costs of Listana's 2013 release, with its recording, mixing, mastering, promotion photography, artwork design, music video production and digital publishing costs, were roughly 1,200 times higher than all the revenue from the released music.

Conclusion

In conclusion, the metal band experience enriched me both as a musician and a scholar: the most important revelation is that the procedure itself is sometimes even more important than the product. Listana had to remain dormant for some years now due to the pressures of academic career, family obligations and the declining economic situation in Turkey. However, if a project is close to one's heart, it can never be too far from the mind. I plan to resume both the work and the dream, armed with more skill and knowledge this time, of documenting the glocal and global metal music industry from within by doing practice-led research within the field.

Notes

1. Helen Myers (ed.), *Ethnomusicology: An Introduction* (Norton, 1992), p. 23.
2. R. Lyle Skains, 'Creative Practice as Research: Discourse on Methodology', *Media Practice and Education* 19/1 (2018): 82–97.
3. *Ibid.*, p. 85.
4. Jean-Francois Lyotard, *The Postmodern Condition: A Report on Knowledge* (Manchester University Press, 1984). After defining what a metanarrative is, Lyotard refutes himself by stating that postmodernism can neither be merely defined as a historical period nor a paradigm, it is an 'incredulity towards metanarratives' (p. 24). Metanarrative hereby represents the curation process of autoethnographic material and its significance in the researcher's identity.
5. Skains, 'Creative Practice as Research', p. 87.
6. Pierre Hecker, *Turkish Metal: Music, Meaning, and Morality in a Muslim Society* (Routledge, 2012).

7. Philip V. Bohlman, 'Ontologies of Music', in Nicholas Cook and Mark Everist (eds.), *Rethinking Music* (Oxford University Press, 1999), pp. 17–34.

8. The 'Self' and the 'Other' are used here in the academic binary context outlined by Hegel, Lacan, Sartre, Said and Derrida, among others.

9. Daniel Newsom, 'Rock's Quarrel with Tradition: Popular Music's Carnival Comes to the Classroom', *Popular Music and Society* 22/3 (1998): 10.

10. Michele Biasutti, 'Group Music Composing Strategies: A Case Study within a Rock Band', *British Journal of Music Education* 29/3 (2012): 343–57.

11. *Ibid.*, pp. 343–4.

12. Jasmine H. Shadrack, *Black Metal, Trauma, Subjectivity and Sound: Screaming the Abyss* (Intellect, 2020).

13. Jasmine H. Shadrack, 'Femme-Liminale: Corporeal Performativity in Death Metal', *University of Northampton* (2014). http://nectar.northampton.ac.uk/6795/1/Shadrack20146795.pdf (accessed 21 October 2021).

14. Auguste Comte, *A General View of Positivism* (Paris, 1848), p. 317.

15. See Sonia Vasan, 'The Price of Rebellion: Gender Boundaries in the Death Metal Scene', *Journal for Cultural Research* 15/3 (2011): 333–349.

16. Jasmine H. Shadrack, *Denigrata Cervorum: Interpretive Performance Autoethnography and Female Black Metal Performance*, doctoral dissertation (University of Northampton, 2017).

17. Daniel Sanchez, '99% of all Music Streaming Comes from Just 10% of Available Songs', *Digital Music News* (2018). www.digitalmusicnews.com/2018/02/14/spotify-apple-music-top-songs (accessed 21 October 2021).

Then, Now and What Next?

DUNCAN WILLIAMS

If you are a metal fan, the chances are that you will also play a musical instrument, or perhaps several instruments. However, for readers without any formal musical training, the word *timbre* might still not be familiar, although musicians are likely to have a well-developed sense of timbre without realising it. So, what is timbre, and why does it matter in metal music? When asked to describe a sound, a musician might use a combination of direct or metaphorical language: 'the bass is woolly', 'the kick drum needs more punch', 'the guitar is very harsh'.[1] This kind of descriptive vocabulary can present an obstacle for people who want to measure or manipulate sonic perceptual characteristics, such as musicians looking for a certain sound, producers responding to a client description, or engineers designing tools like equalisation or distortion algorithms. Essentially, the language of timbre is a way to communicate with others about the sound we hear. This extends beyond performance or recording and includes describing our experience of listening to music. For example, production critiques often fall instinctively under the purview of timbral analysis.

This chapter first introduces timbre from a formal point of view and reviews some specific metal-centred timbral studies from literature. Next, we look at the use of technology to meter timbral attributes. Finally, the chapter reflects on the ability to implement a machine learning system, a type of data-driven learning that falls under the umbrella of artificial intelligence, in music production tasks, which has borne fruit in automated mastering and mixing in recent years.[2] This chapter gives a brief overview of how these ideas work and how they might speculatively be implemented in the context of metal music and timbre, particularly with examples looking at convolution and tone matching.

Defining Timbre ('Then')

Listeners often struggle to describe their experience of music to others in a meaningful way. What do adjectives like 'warm', 'punchy' or 'heavy' really mean, and how can listeners, musicians and producers exploit this knowledge? To get a handle on timbre, we need to set a few definitions. The American Standards Association (ASA) defines timbre as 'that attribute of sensation, in terms of which a listener can judge that two sounds having the same loudness and pitch are dissimilar'.[3] This definition can be considered a difficult starting point, as it does not define what timbre *is* but rather what it is *not*. To illustrate this difficulty, we can consider unpitched or environmental sounds that would, according to the ASA definition, have no timbre. A more satisfactory definition is commonly given as 'the sensation on whereby a listener can judge that two sounds are dissimilar using other criteria than pitch, loudness or duration'.[4]

Tone colour and sound quality are terms that might be used synonymously with timbre. However, tone colour can imply that the spectral properties of the sound are solely responsible for its timbre, contradictory to research specifying the importance of temporal acoustic correlates with relation to the perception of timbre.[5] What this tells us is that timbre is a psycho-acoustic attribute. This means it is a perceptual parameter, something which is slightly different for each of us, but which has underlying acoustic contributing factors that can be quantified.

Fans of metal music are, in fact, particularly well trained for timbral analysis, as they will have a sense of what 'heavy' means and be familiar with at least three categories of instrumental timbral attributes: distorted guitar tones, screaming vocals, and polished closely microphoned and/or triggered drum sounds.

Metal Specific Timbral Attributes ('Now')

Let us consider our metal-specific timbral attributes in more detail. We might consider an ontological pyramid containing our descriptors, perhaps with 'heavy' at the top of the pyramid, as it pertains to individual instrumentation, the overall mix, lyrical content, and indeed the semantic whole of a performance. Below this, we might see our flavours of distortion, both for bass and guitar, perhaps then broken into smaller descriptors like 'bright', 'dirty' or 'chuggy'. Similarly, the second layer might feature other instruments, with a category for drums having sub-categories that include descriptors like 'punchy'. Perhaps the most unique and challenging of this second layer will be our category for vocals. There are very few genres of music with as much variety of timbre in their vocal delivery. To illustrate this, imagine a line of lyrics being delivered at the same pitch, loudness and spatial placement, but by different vocalists. Let us take Chris Barnes, the original vocalist of the death metal band Cannibal Corpse. The third layer of the pyramid might now include timbral descriptors like 'growly' or 'death grunt'. We might imagine a rather different vocal timbre if Barnes was replaced by, for example, Till Lindemann from the German industrial metal band Rammstein. Lindemann has a larger range than Barnes, and in German musicology, there is even a word for the type of spoken-word singing style he employs with Rammstein, *Sprechgesang*, literally spoken singing and not limited to the world of metal. For example, in the operatic idiom, it would be perfectly acceptable to mark a passage as *Sprechgesang* for singers. But in the metal world, we might fill our third layer of the timbral pyramid for Lindemann with descriptors like 'breathy' or 'raspy'. The vocal sound we hear in this case is a combination of several factors, including Lindemann's own performance, but also very much reliant on sound engineering and music production techniques. Closely microphoned vocals lend particular timbral properties, as does the use of dynamic range reduction, also known as compression. We also have, and often use colloquially, a generic timbral descriptor when considering metal vocals: 'clean'. In genres like metalcore, for example, vocalists might switch between a clean and a dirty style. These examples illustrate how psycho-acousticians borrow descriptors analogously from other domains, with 'clean' being semantically at the opposite end of a bipolar scale to 'dirty'.

'Heaviness' sits at the top of our pyramid of metal timbre. We all have an idea of what it means, and it pervades each of the lower levels of timbral attributes and their constituent descriptors. In the last fifteen years, we have started to see serious attempts by scholars and practitioners in qualifying and quantifying what we mean by this. We find across the literature qualities related to denser or distorted guitar timbres, perceived rhythmic difficulty,[6] and multiple combinations of perceptual and acoustic correlates.[7] The mechanism of distortion itself is quite well-known: additional harmonic overtones are added (perhaps with some inharmonic or noisy content) in particular ratios, which are akin to the physical sensation of distortion a listener might experience if their auditory mechanism was overloaded by a very loud sound in the real world. By rights, distortion should be a bad thing in sound engineering, and many technical training devices exist, which seek to teach the listener to identify and remove unwanted distortion. But in metal timbres, the key distinction is between wanted and unwanted distortion. Because of a technical focus by the sound engineering community on the latter, there are acoustic methods for describing distortion, both linear and non-linear types. As such, we can see that distortion is an acoustic parameter first and foremost, but it, in fact, has timbral descriptors that we might anchor to it, for example, 'clean' or 'dirty' as mentioned above, but also including 'crunch'. The difference between acoustic shape and type of distortion is of particular interest to metal, as the non-linear distortion found in overdriven tube amplifiers has a markedly different perceived response in listeners to linear distortion.[8] There are also studies suggesting that musicians and non-musicians have different responses to distorted timbres.[9]

By contrast to the favourable type of distortion, the drums in a metal performance are typically preferred to be 'clean', or other descriptors we might expect, such as 'punchy' or 'clicky'. There are always exceptions. Industrial metal, for example, has made creative use of distorted drums over the years. In modern metal drum sounds, we see a different lens passed over the timbre, then, that of realism and performance augmentation, whether it be through close microphone techniques or, more commonly, drum replacement and sample triggering strategies. For a detailed overview of the process of fine-tuning metal drums at the point of production, the interested reader might visit Mark Mynett's articles for *Sound on Sound* magazine,[10] which lift the curtain on these processes.

Applying Timbre in Performance and Production ('Next')

There are times when the lens of history allows us to see how timbre can be as fickle as fashion. In the mid-1990s, technology had sufficiently evolved to the point of being able to shape the production aesthetics of metal, giving rise to a new sub-genre: nu metal. Ross Robinson was arguably its most successful producer and had a distinctive sound characterised by a series of timbral attributes: detuned guitars or a 'ticky' bass sound. The first Korn record, *Korn* (1994), for all these trappings, is still a remarkably dynamic record, so much so that it features on recognised mastering engineer Bob Katz's shortlist for records deserving of praise in the face of the loudness war. Thus, we might consider a place somewhere in our timbral pyramid for the attribute set, which corresponds to specific sub-genres in metal. It has useful applications for listeners in terms of classifying their own choices of music and thus finding or recommending new music they might like. But beyond this, many examples are possible, taking advantage of recent advances in processing power and availability of digital signal processing, for example, digital convolution and the availability of machine learning techniques.

Proposing an AI Approach

One such example would be to propose tools that would allow us to harness what we know about metal-specific timbral features in our own music-making activities – whether as a performer, producer or simply a listener – using an artificial intelligence (AI) or machine learning approach. One example of a machine learning model would be a supervised learning algorithm. In our metal example, we could extract acoustic features from a dataset, for example, spectral centroid, which is correlated with *bright* guitar tones. We mark up the relative timbral descriptors for our example tones. The algorithm then seeks to discover how much of each acoustic feature there is in the *brightest* of tones and applies this as a weighting to each feature in the dataset. We now have a marked-up dataset of guitar tones with a series of weighted features contributing to specific timbral descriptors. Imagine now that instead of having traditional equalisation controls on your guitar amp (e.g., bass, middle, treble), you now have 'brightness', 'sharpness', 'heaviness' and other timbral descriptors of your choosing, trained on a dataset of metal tones that you enjoy.

Over a recorded audio mix, this tool might allow you to meter timbral qualities in your mix versus that of a reference mix that you, or a client, particularly enjoy. In fact, automatic mixing is one such example of which machine learning has already made great strides towards, and the LANDR platform uses exactly this technology in the world of music mastering.[11] Historically, an engineer or producer might spend many tedious hours automating a volume fader of a particular source – typically the lead vocal – to make sure that it sat correctly in the balance throughout a song. This can be a time-consuming process if done by hand, but it can be automated, freeing the engineer up for more creatively challenging, and ultimately enjoyable, work on the rest of the mix.

Beyond this, we might imagine future work combining machine learning for parameter control with the power of digital convolution going beyond tone matching and amplifier profiling and instead facilitating the creation of entirely new timbres. This process owes a lot to morphing,[12] in which a new timbre is created combining particular timbral attributes from two source sounds. It is, of course, impossible to predict what creative people will do with new tools once they become available. We can see historical examples of creative use of misused technology: the distortion created with electric guitar amplification was originally created by misuse of the amplification chain; equalisation that can now be used to carefully craft mixes, individual instrumental and vocal timbres was originally a tool to correct problems in the frequency response caused by telephony; sampling that in the metal world has given us consistent – perhaps overly consistent – kick drums, more or less gave rise to an entire genre in the shape of hip-hop music.

Feature-based Comparison as a Machine Learning Classifier

The following section provides a walk-through or 'thought exercise' as to how the ideas and techniques discussed earlier in this chapter might manifest in novel audio signal processing algorithms. It is important to emphasise that, at the time of writing, the idea illustrated here is somewhere between the realms of what we know now is possible and science fiction.

First, let us reiterate our goal: We imagine a technology that might apply acoustic measurement of specific features to describe the timbral attributes of a particular mix, perhaps in a sub-genre of metal, or with a desirable production characteristic – essentially, a well-mixed piece of music. Heaviness might be the goal, or clarity, or energy, or any number of timbral attributes that we enjoy in a song, album, artist or genre. We consider these as a hierarchical pyramid of idiom, with artists resting on a foundation of genre or sub-genre, and albums and songs on top of, or as divisions of, the artists' sound.

Why do we need this technology? To assist the artist in realising a sonic goal for an album or song in the context of the genre. There are, of course, sonic characteristics that we might ascribe to any of the layers of the pyramid described previously, but that are difficult for anyone outside of highly skilled production or engineering to really achieve. To put this in the simplest layman's terms: would it not be great if you could make your own recording sound exactly the way you want? This need not mean exactly like someone else's recording – although matching equalisation, loudness or distorted guitar tones is a common task for the working recording engineer – but rather a platform that allows a vocalisable production quality to be achieved by an artist. Those of us who have experimented with recording our own music will know the frustration of 'bad' recording or poor production quality more generally. Indeed, metal music more widely requires excellent production in comparison to many other genres, such as garage rock, which prizes a 'rough and ready' production style. Metal requires careful manipulation of the frequency spectrum, an understanding of harmonic distortion, triggering and phase in multi-microphone drum kit situations, and a host of other technical and aesthetic production decisions. In short, producing good-sounding metal is difficult.

Technology might now assist us, as many of the elements of production mentioned above are nowadays computer processes that operate on specific acoustic parameters. However, that would only be useful to our wider audience if such technology can first perceive the necessary processing differences. Thus, our goal is initially in metering, or *machine listening*. This gives us three questions:

(1) What does our machine hear (source)?
(2) What is its goal (target or training material)?
(3) What processing might then be required to bridge the gap (action)?

Here, we have stepped into science fiction, although just barely, as the world of machine learning is advancing so quickly that even at the time of writing, we see this paradigm in deep fake news items.

For the purposes of this chapter, let us illustrate this with a real-world example of the first stage – what does our machine hear – which is entirely possible already. Indeed, we could train a *classifier*, in machine learning terms, to deal with endless examples in the same manner, essentially creating the first stage of our machine listener: a *meter*. For this, we use audio stems of the main instruments of 'A Secret Kiss' from British doom metal band My Dying Bride's 2020 album *Macabre Cabaret*.[13] We are particularly interested in the elements that our production aid might help with: the relationship between the timbre of the guitars, the bass,[14] and the kick and remaining drum balance. We therefore analyse four stems: guitar, bass, kick drum and remaining drum mix.

Acoustic Feature Extraction

We extract the following features from each audio stem:

- *Spectral centroid*: A spectral 'centre of gravity' and commonly used psycho-acoustic parameter in music analysis (e.g., high-hats will have a higher spectral centroid than a kick drum), especially as a correlate for 'brightness'.
- *Spectral spread*: The 'instantaneous bandwidth' of a spectrum, used as a metric for tonality, where if a pair of tones converge, the spread decreases (e.g., we might expect a smaller spectral spread for harmonic distortion than inharmonic or partial distortion on a guitar tone).

- *Spectral skewness*: A degree of symmetry around the spectral centre, also known as 'spectral tilt' in speech analysis, indicating the relative strength of harmonic and fundamental content (e.g., useful in the analysis of the amount of distortion on both guitar and bass stems). A positive skew indicates the fundamental is more dominant than the upper harmonics or tones. In our case, power chords are the most relevant.
- *Spectral decrease*: The measure of the decrease in a magnitude spectrum. This parameter is not often seen in speech analysis but is common in musical instrument recognition (e.g., if we want to discriminate between an analysis of drums in a stereo mix and features that are guitar-driven, we might expect a minimal decrease in guitar spectrum, with a much more dynamic result in the spectra of the drums).
- *Spectral flux*: A simple metric of the amount of change in the spectrum over time (e.g., how consistent is the spectrum in the stems or the finished master we are listening to. This is especially interesting if we are considering emulating multiband compression parameters).
- *Spectral roll-off point*: Like the spectral decrease, a marker of the band-width of a signal over the total energy, helpful for instrument separation and also common in music genre classification.
- *Spectral crest*: A ratio of the peaks to the mean average (e.g., to reveal the amount of creative, production-informed compression).
- *mel spectrogram*: A pitch-related plot.
- *mel-frequency cepstral coefficient delta-delta*: A speech-derived cor-relate, which shows the rate of change in the spectrum of the spectrum (e.g., useful for reducing complex spectra to their most relevant components).

We might consider training our model on many more acoustic parameters, but the list above gives features that might be most useful in the analysis of metal production timbres.

It is beyond the scope of this chapter to provide each figure but let us examine some types of visualisations and consider a simple example from our sample material.

Figures 6.1–6.5 show a few of the types of visualisation we can produce to help our understanding of the numerical properties, which acoustic feature extraction produces. Sound engineers will likely be familiar with two of these types of presentation: (1) visualisation in the time domain, with time on the X-axis (as we see in common digital audio workstations when a waveform of a sound signal is presented); (2)

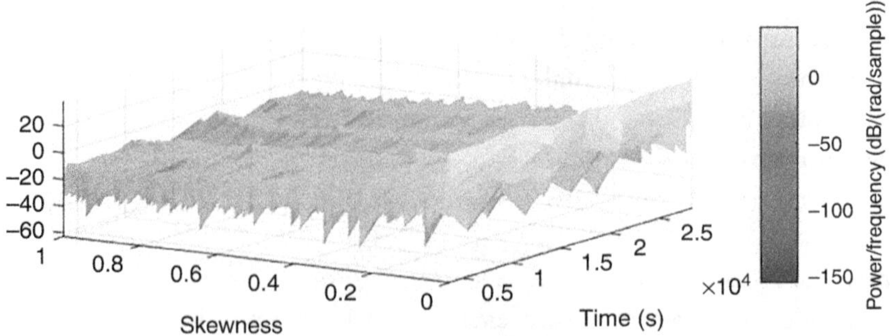

Figure 6.1 The spectral skew of the drum stems, rotated. It shows how the shape of the frequency content differs below the centroid in comparison to the mean. We can interpret this as being quite low-frequency-dominant, as might be expected from kick drums, but with a certain amount of time-varying, evenly distributed mid and high frequency content. Note the highs, in particular, remain very even and relatively smooth (© Duncan Williams)

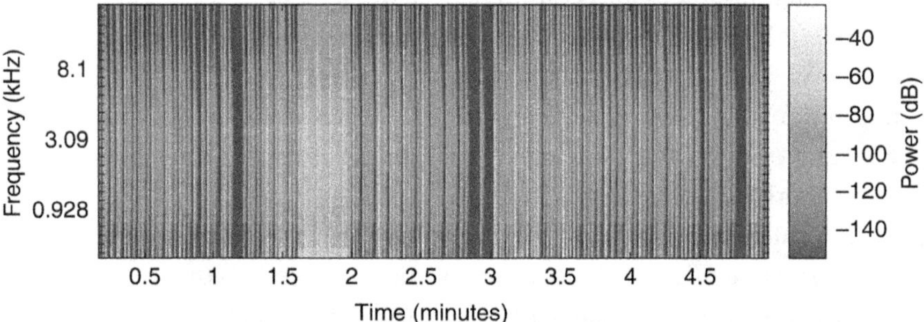

Figure 6.2 The mel-spectrogram of the kick drum. The interesting section at between 1.5 and 2 minutes is a section using a double pedal. Note that although there are marked amplitude differences, the frequency content of each instance of the kick (on the vertical axis) is markedly similar, suggesting multiband compression or triggering and a similar amount of reverb on each kick throughout the mix (© Duncan Williams)

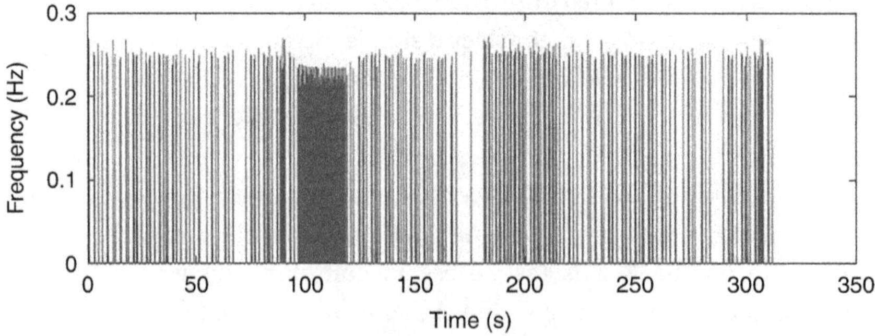

Figure 6.3 The spectral flux of the kick drum. Note there is limited spectral change, with a more marked drop in flux around the double pedal section (© Duncan Williams)

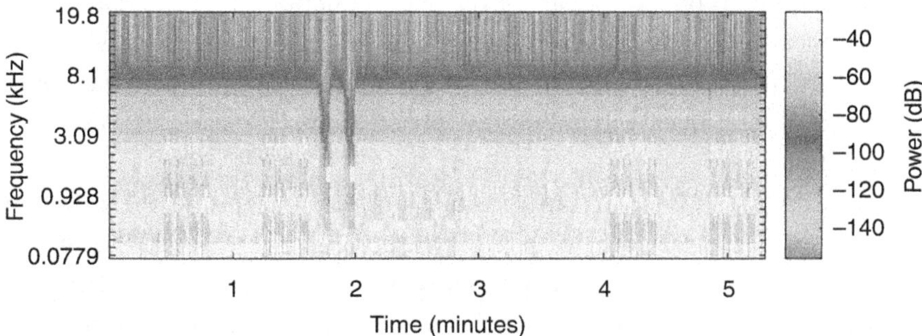

Figure 6.4 The mel-spectrogram of the guitar stem. Note a much fuller spectrum compared to the kick stem, with rich harmonics above the fundamental frequency up to a scooped region at approximately 3 kHz, with little to no content above the 'fizz' of 7 kHz (© Duncan Williams)

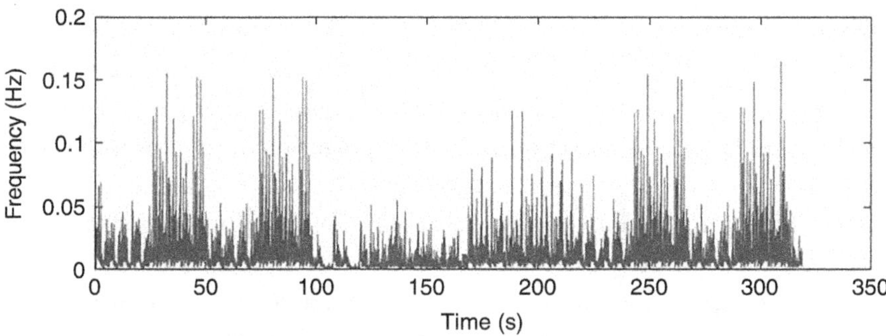

Figure 6.5 The spectral flux of the guitar stem compared to the relatively consistent spectral flux of the kick drum stems. This is a measure of change – how quickly the spectrum in each signal changes. Note the much greater variation in the guitar spectral flux, as opposed to the highly consistent measures from the drum stems (© Duncan Williams)

visualisation in the frequency domain, as in the mel-spectrograms, which show us amplitude (using the colour of the signal), time on the X-axis, and frequency on the Y-axis. As such a representation is 3D, we can rotate it as in the spectral skewness plot. In these figures, we can start to see immediate differences, as indeed we would hear them if we listened to the stems.

The next step of the AI learning process would be to *train* our machine listener to recognise these feature changes in order to provide novel metering or even suggest parameter adjustments based on a set of training material, for example, any set of stems the artist enjoyed and wanted to emulate. Note that we are not suggesting that sound engineers should be made redundant or that the art of record production might be reduced to a sequence of algorithms. New music will always require creativity and artistic interpretation. However, we might envision tools to take away some of the tedious learning curve in music production tasks and facilitate more creativity.

To spare the reader a complete overview of machine learning in the analysis of a training set, we will provide the shortest possible example here: let us say we want to emulate a guitar sound from a stem and therefore train a meter on the parameters listed above. First, we need to train our meter by linking the acoustic features in various ratios to a dependent output variable, the timbral descriptor. We then try a new input, which is classified according to the same features. The difference between source (our new input) and target (our training material) gives a suggestion for changes in a number and ratio of acoustic features. For example, to raise the spectral centroid, we might have a suggestion for some boost in the upper-frequency EQ of the guitar. Our fully-realised system could then analyse the perform-ance of this output in comparison to the input target (in machine learning terminology, this step is called *validation*), and adjust the suggestion accord-ing to 'how far out' it was (in machine learning terminology, this is the *error function*). We can see this type of classifier-optimisation problem in almost any example of machine learning. We end with a system that makes some recommendations in terms of audio production character, including EQ, dynamic range, harmonicity of distortion, amount of distortion, balance between harmonic distortion and fundamental frequency, spectral rate of change. All of those are measured from our acoustic analysis parameters. However, we are not bound by the suggestions. This is a jumping-off point, which might take the next generation of musicians in directions that are, at the time of writing, rather unimaginable, but no less exciting for it.

Conclusion

Psycho-acoustic research generally regards timbre as one of three perceptual attributes of sound along with loudness and pitch. This list of perceptual attributes can be expanded to include perceived duration, location and rever-berant environment. These are essentially a series of cues about the spatial properties of the sound source or, in the case of a mix, placement of a sound source in one, two or three dimensions: width, depth and height. The range of perceptual descriptors included in timbre studies is reflected in their acoustic correlates and the lack of a unidirectional scale suitable for timbre. Subsequent research has endeavoured to quantify these interrelationships in an effort to move towards a robust measure of timbre, usually through a combination of acoustic analysis and perceptual testing. The acoustic correlates of timbral descriptors determined by these approaches include harmonicity, which is particularly relevant for the distorted guitar, and various combinations of amplitude envelope and spectral or spectro-temporal variation.

Metal has its own specific timbral descriptors, which are a combination of performance and technology, all of which can fall under a pyramid with 'heavy' encompassing each subsequent timbral attribute. Vocal performance styles like growling and screaming are almost uniquely found in metal, and much like the distortion used in guitar or bass, and the triggering and layering used in drum production techniques, the technology can be used to enact large metal-specific timbral variation at the point of recording, mixing or live reproduction. Some work has been done by researchers looking at these metal-specific descriptors in the same vein as work by earlier psycho-acousticians, who looked at correlates for other timbral and perceptual descriptors like loudness and pitch. In this work, we see that timbral attributes can be either acoustical or descriptive, and some descriptive terms have been shown to overlap or agree in terms of their acoustic correlates. The nomenclature is mostly universal, although a large number of labels and descriptors have not been acoustically quantified as yet.

Work to reduce the range of descriptors, perhaps down to those which are acoustically independent, and a subsequent set of those with acoustic overlap, would be useful for our 'next' ideas. Similarly, attributes with acoustic overlap, or indeed attributes, which appear to have contradictory acoustic correlates, would also require the ratio between their acoustic correlates to be quantified (timbre metering, matching and designing). In the 'next' ideas, we can imagine a combination of these approaches with the now-readily available level of machine learning techniques to provide tools for musicians and producers that will help with timbre: to match existing timbres (streamlining the search for a good guitar tone or emulating favourite tones) and, perhaps most excitingly, to craft new timbres.

Notes

1. Colin G. Johnson and Alex Gounaropoulos, 'Timbre Interfaces Using Adjectives and Adverbs', *Proceedings of the 2006 Conference on New Interfaces for Musical Expression* (IRCAM, 2006), pp. 101–2.

2. Jonathan Sterne and Elena Razlogova, 'Machine Learning in Context, or Learning from LANDR: Artificial Intelligence and the Platformization of Music Mastering', *Social Media & Society* 5/2 (2019): 1–18.

3. 'American Standard Acoustical Terminology, Definition 12.9, Timbre', *ASA* (1960).

4. John M. Hajda, Roger A. Kendall, Edward C. Carterette and Michael L. Harshberger, 'Methodical Issues in Timbre Research', in Irene Deliège and Justin A. Sloboda (eds.), *Perception and Cognition of Music* (Psychology Press, 2004), pp. 237–87.

5. Paul Iverson and Carol L. Krumhansl, 'Isolating the Dynamic Attributes of Musical Timbres', *The Journal of the Acoustical Society of America* 94/5 (1993): 2595–603.

6. Calder Hannan, 'Difficulty as Heaviness: Links between Rhythmic Difficulty and Perceived Heaviness in the Music of Meshuggah and the Dillinger Escape Plan', *Metal Music Studies* 4/3 (2018): 433–58.

7. Vinoo Alluri and Petri Toiviainen, 'Exploring Perceptual and Acoustical Correlates of Polyphonic Timbre', *Music Perception* 27/3 (2010): 223–42.

8. William L. Martens and Atsushi Marui, 'Predicting Timbral Variation for Sharpness-Matched Guitar Tones Resulting from Distortion-Based Effects Processing', *Audio Engineering Society Convention* 118 (2005). www.aes.org /e-lib/browse.cfm?elib=13202 (accessed 11 September 2021).

9. Koji Tsumoto, Atsushi Marui and Toru Kamekawa, 'The Difference in Perceptual Attributes for the Distortion Timbre of the Electric Guitar between Guitar Players and Non-Guitar Players', *Audio Engineering Society Convention* 140 (2016). www.aes.org/e-lib/browse.cfm?elib=18244 (accessed 11 September 2021).

10. Mark Mynett, 'Extreme Metal: The SOS Guide to Recording & Producing Modern Metal', *Sound on Sound* 11 (2009): 120–33.

11. Sterne and Razlogova, 'Machine Learning'.

12. Edwin Tellman, Lippold Haken and Bryan Holloway, 'Timbre Morphing of Sounds with Unequal Numbers of Features', *Journal of the Audio Engineering Society* 43/9 (1995): 678–89.

13. These stems have been provided by the band's producer, Mark Mynett.

14. In metal productions, the bass often uses harmonic distortion and lives in a frequency domain closer to the guitar than in other genres.

PART II

Metal and History

Personal Take II – Brian Tatler

Got the Devil in Me

Was I evil? Am I evil? Will I be evil? The answer to all these questions is a succinct 'no', but what I was, am and always will be is a passionate writer and performer of heavy metal.

Heavy metal was born from the need for an antidote to pop music, and the lighter the pop, the darker the rock. References to the darker sides of life are largely theatrical and the myth that playing certain heavy metal songs backwards in order to contact the devil are pure nonsense. By doing so, the only outcome is a ruined stylus. Also, the sound of a cranked Marshall [guitar amplifier] and a powerful riff can shake a mortal to the core, which is largely what drew me towards heavy metal.

My brother Dave was seduced by the electric guitar when he was fourteen years old, and I was just eight. He encouraged me to play, and soon I had fallen under the spell too. I began to learn and have been learning ever since, and it's been my constant companion. As soon as I could move a barre chord up and down the neck, I began writing heavy rock riffs and jamming them with my best friend, drummer Duncan Scott. No sooner had I become a rock/heavy metal fan, I was hooked for life, and that passion for music has never abandoned me. I was always looking for heavier, faster, darker, and I think a lot of kids still look for exactly the same thing as I did.

I didn't know at that tender age that I would be fortunate enough to carve a lifelong career from playing the guitar. Diamond Head signed to MCA in 1982 but were dropped in 1984 after making our 'difficult third album'. Some people really dug it, and others found it too different from what had gone before. We naively presumed we could experiment with different styles, but in the world of heavy metal, that's not an easy rabbit to pull from the hat. It seems punters like what they like and usually aren't prepared to indulge a band's trial and error, and so bands often end up playing safe and sticking to one style. I totally get it now, but when I was twenty-two, my co-writing partner and I were idealistic, still believing we could do whatever we liked.

The NWOBHM scene covered a vast array of different styles with an infusion of the DIY punk attitude. The bands at that time were listening to a much wider range of musical styles in the 1970s than perhaps the current metal bands do. This wide choice of music made each band sound unique, whereas now metal seems more formulated and carefully aimed by the record companies at a target audience. Without a very acute ear, it's hard to tell some bands apart.

I had no idea that metal would still be around fifty years after its creation, and it seems to get bigger each year. It has a very loyal fan base from ten-year-old kids to old guys and gals in their sixties; it's a way of life to a lot of people all over the world. Metal is tribal, and people get so passionate about their favourite music and bands it becomes their escape from the normality of modern life.

When Metallica first recorded a Diamond Head song ('Am I Evil?') in 1984, it was on a B-side, and they were signed to a small independent label called Music For Nations. At that point, Diamond Head were still bigger than Metallica. It was very flattering, and it had never happened to us before, but I did not see the huge significance, nor the potential, of Metallica. It was still 'Lars's band have covered "Am I Evil?"' I did not think, 'OMG! They're going to become not only the biggest metal band of all time but the biggest live act in the world'. I had no clue.

I think one of the important aspects of music is to influence the next generation. The history of heavy metal goes back to the Black Sabbath's debut album in 1970. Black Sabbath influenced me, my band Diamond Head influenced Metallica, Metallica influenced 50,000 metal bands, and on it goes. This style of music is still evolving and splitting off into sub-genres even after fifty years. In the 1970s, no one had done fast double kick drums with guitars de-tuned to low B and A, nor had anyone done the growly, aggressive vocals that are now commonplace. Heavy metal is sometimes dismissed as simple and one-dimensional, but when you are a real fan, and you get into it, you realise there are all these different styles within the genre and a host of brilliant musicians. It's actually an increasingly difficult genre for writing songs and avoiding clichés, sounding fresh and being original. There are still the obvious references to the dark side that belong to heavy metal, and so the devil is given his due. But he can keep his filthy hands off my royalties.

The music business is tough; there are a lot of sharks out there. It's hard to keep a band together and everybody happy. It's rare for a band to make it to a professional level and then even rarer to sustain that level of success for many years. I'm very proud of the fact that Diamond Head are still making albums and touring and that I still love writing heavy metal songs. I still got the devil in me.

Brian Tatler, guitarist of Diamond Head

Mesopotamian Metal

Learning from the Past through Metal Music?

PETER PICHLER

Today, history is institutionalised as an academic discipline in its own right.[1] Mainly starting from universities in Germany and Europe, the institutionalisation and professionalisation of the discipline encompass a history of more than two hundred years. Throughout this history, there has been a key question: can we learn from the past through professional historical research? To this day, this is a key question in historical theory and the philosophy of history.[2] Many answers to the question have been presented, but there is no consensus until today. Perhaps it is logical that no agreement exists yet because the discourse surrounding this question remains unfinished. History is itself an open-ended process of culture. Repeatedly, arduously and in small steps, our shared knowledge of the past must be linked to our changing vantage points in the present. As time moves on, the past moves on as well.

These brief remarks on historical theory were intentionally placed at the beginning of this chapter on the metal sub-discourse of 'Mesopotamian metal', which includes bands like Absu, Agga, Arallu, Bohema, Decimation, Melechesh, Svartsyn and Tiamat.[3] Mesopotamian metal is a sub-discourse and substyle of metal music, specifically extreme metal music, which deals with the history of ancient Mesopotamia mainly thematically. Sometimes labels like 'Sumerian metal' are also used. Crucial here is the reference to ancient times in this region of the Middle East. There is no strict separation from other substyles of Middle Eastern-themed metal music by bands like Orphaned Land, Myrath, Salem, Distorted and Nile.[4] Rather, this is a network of thematically closely linked discourses in which Mesopotamian metal is embedded. This chapter focuses on Mesopotamian metal because it is a lucid example for studying the role of history in metal. The question of learning from the past is at its centre.

Thematically, this metal sub-discourse is about the politics of history, of which value-oriented historical storytelling is a fundamental part. Trying to learn lessons from the culture of ancient Babylonia, this sub-style of metal proposes solutions to current conflicts, such as the conflicts in Israel or

Syria. For instance, Melechesh, as a paradigmatic band in the field, discuss the past and glean insights into present conflicts in Israel.

The first section of this chapter introduces the concept of Mesopotamian metal. The most relevant bands are discussed, with Melechesh serving as our paradigmatic example, as well as their views on their focal lyrical topics and musical styles. The next part focuses on the role of history, analysing how the construction of history is undertaken in Mesopotamian metal. It is shown that this discourse promotes a certain brand of historical politics to help solve problems in the present, most of all in the conflict-rich region of the Middle East. The third part of this chapter deals with the regional and global contextual linkages of Mesopotamian metal. Connecting the linkages to two other discourses on history in metal ('Oriental metal' and 'Viking metal') adds clarity to the general role of history in metal. In summing up this argumentation, the conclusion argues that we can possibly learn from the past through metal music.

The Concept of Mesopotamian Metal

> Mesopotamian metal is the style of music that we play. That is what I call it . . . That is the only real thing that we are making a conscious effort to do with the music of Melechesh. We want it to have a real Mesopotamian metal sound. It is not really about paying tribute to our ancestors, but rather to just create a sound that we can call our own and be proud of.[5]

The quote was part of an interview conducted with Murat 'Ashmedi' Cenan in 2001 and explains the concept behind Mesopotamian metal from an artist's point of view. Cenan is the singer and guitar player for Melechesh, a black metal band formed in Jerusalem in 1993. He is the band's lead protagonist and songwriter, the most prominent Mesopotamian metal band. Melechesh's concept is paradigmatic of this discourse. Musically, a 'Mesopotamian metal sound' is a defining marker of this metal subgenre.[6] According to an interview with Cenan, his aim is to create such a sound by integrating 'Phrygian scales, which are pretty much Middle-Eastern sounding' into his songwriting.[7] However, a thorough musical analysis of the sound of Mesopotamian metal, in general and of Melechesh in particular, is missing in research. It is important to note that Mesopotamian metal not only has its own sound, but it also has its own semiotic sphere of distinct images and textual elements. This semiotic reference to ancient Mesopotamia is defining of the subgenre. Mesopotamian metal is a subcultural discourse in which a unique paradigm is constructed, including a distinct concept of how to compose, write, perform and narrate metal music.

To give an impression of how relevant this concept is on a global scale, searching for relevant lyrical themes on the *Encyclopaedia Metallum*, the biggest online database of metal bands, provides a heuristic indication. Advanced searches for relevant bands worldwide in this encyclopaedia resulted in 63 band entries for the keywords 'Sumerian' (as in Sumerian mythology), ten for 'Babylonian' (as in Babylonian mythology) and nine for 'Mesopotamia' (as the region to which the concept refers). Hence, it is a globally relevant discourse in metal. As already stated, there is a fluidity of boundaries between Mesopotamian metal and other discourses in which historical topics are equally relevant. The concept of Mesopotamian metal is not fully fixed yet, but it has reached a general level of stability. It has cemented its distinct inventory of sounds, narratives and images of 'Mesopotamian-ness'.

Originally hailing from Jerusalem, the extreme metal band Melechesh combine black metal, death metal and thrash metal with the mentioned Mesopotamian sounds, which in fact are sounds from Near Eastern music.[8] Once more, one must note that a thorough analysis of this strand of metal music still represents a gap in research. Still, when listening to their tracks, a sensation and aural impression of Mesopotamian-ness is produced.[9] This impression mainly comes from the use of folkloristic instruments. So far, Melechesh have released six full-length albums: *As Jerusalem Burns . . . Al'Intisar* (1996), *Djinn* (2001), *Sphynx* (2003), *Emissaries* (2006), *The Epigenesis* (2010) and *Enki* (2015). In particular, the releases in the new millennium and touring activities made the band the paradigmatic artist of Mesopotamian metal. Keith Kahn-Harris labelled the band an 'exception' in the Israeli extreme metal scene of the 1990s because its 'members were of Syrian, Armenian and Palestinian Christian origin', in contrast to the majority of this regional scene, which predominantly consisted of 'secular Israelis of Jewish origin'.[10]

For Melechesh, the Near Eastern region and its history are the central topics the band addresses. Their music is a discussion of the region's conflict-rich past and present.[11] Even the band's name integrates two words of Hebrew and Aramaic origins: *melech* can be translated into English as 'king'; *esh* means 'fire' – thus, the band's name means 'king of fire'. Cenan comes from Syrian and Armenian ethnic backgrounds. So, as is the case with many artists from the regions, multiculturalism and migration experiences are parts of his biography.[12] Although the band left Jerusalem for Western Europe in 1998, the city, the wider region and its history are still the main sources of inspiration for their metal music.

Melechesh are a fitting example to study the concept behind Mesopotamian metal because all the characteristic elements of the concept appear in their music. The concept consists of the classical sounds of extreme metal, the particular sounds of Mesopotamian-ness as described by Cenan, as well as distinct images and text elements supporting the feeling of Mesopotamian-ness. Blending different languages, the lyrics to the song 'Sacred Geometry' (2010) illustrate the paradigmatic semiotics of 'Mesopotamian-ness':

Sons of Sumer, open your eyes
Awake, discover maze of the sublime
Born within the cradle
Voices of the essence
Curious Enlil's legions forever watchful
As we transcend plural psyche banishing
The essence speaks to us
In every cell in every stone and space
Meen fee hali ou bali
Meen bis'aal il wali il fee
Blessed be the cosmic dust
We are all of Enlil's plan
Meen fee hali ou bali
Meen bis'aal il wali il fee
Blessed be the cosmic dust
We are all of Enlil's plan
Submit to the grace of chaotic order
With his hands, he molded us
Find the hidden meanings
Facets inseparable from his plan
Frequencies, pulsation, voices of the world
Magickal stains vaporize from
(The) proverbial, cosmic energy spheres
Doorway to the other will unlock
Neo-spiritualism
Arcane arts' interpretations
Sons of Sumer open your eyes
Intrinsic unity of creation

The track's historical protagonist is 'Enlil', who was the chief deity of ancient Sumer, and who became a major influence on the whole region's religious discourses.[13] The images in these intentionally fully quoted lyrics are those of mysterious ancient gods and their will for the people of the Earth. In combination with the sounds described by Cenan, this makes the concept of Mesopotamian metal complete. It is constructed as a 'bricolage' concept that includes an inventory of images, tales, narratives and sounds referring to ancient Sumer.[14] It is held together by the mental associations between the various elements. Melechesh being only the best-known example, bands such as Absu (the United States), Agga (the United States), Arallu (Israel), Bohema (Georgia), Decimation (Turkey), Svartsyn (Sweden) or Tiamat (Sweden) are also major contributors to the subgenre. It is worth listening to some of their music to fully grasp the concept. There is a certain variety in the approaches to the topic of ancient Sumer, but as a rule, the politics of history and learning from the past form the framework of the subgenre.

The Construction of the Past and the Politics of History in Mesopotamian Metal

So far, we have considered what Mesopotamian metal is as a set of conceptual ideas. For this concept, the distant past of ancient Sumer as a supposed cradle of civilisation between 6,000 BC and 2,000 BC provides the defining theme.[15] It is not possible to give a broader picture of the respective history in this chapter, but the notion of 'Mesopotamian' is a marker for a time more than four thousand years ago. In the subgenre, historical storytelling is the core mechanism. This means that Mesopotamian metal, or Sumerian metal, is a discourse in which the very distant past is constructed in a specific way in the present. The past becomes part of the present. Historical storytelling in metal is always 'presentist' in this way. Through this construction process, it is connected to the values and perspectives of the modern world we live in. Similarly, Mesopotamian metal also encompasses the politics of history.[16] The history of ancient Sumer is told under the auspices of an ethos that is promoted through it. On the one hand, this is the classical ethos of metal. On the other, these are liberal social values, which promote the peaceful coexistence of different ethnic groups in the Near East in particular and in the whole world in general. This brand of the politics of history comes with the specific methods of historical construction in Sumerian metal, analysable in the case of Melechesh.

The construction of the past takes the form of a culturally 'hybrid' method of historical storytelling. 'Hybridity' is a key concept of recent cultural history and postcolonial studies.[17] Research in these fields has shown that any forms of identities, including the Mesopotamian-ness identity in Mesopotamian metal, are constructed from different sources. They are always hybrid combinations of cultural facets from various sources, and hence they are not natural. They change over time. Being aware of this fact, Cenan uses and combines different narratives of Middle Eastern history to create and construct a distinctive version of history.

Hailing from the conflict-rich cultural landscape of Israel and Jerusalem, his specific construction of the past and his politics of history reflect these conflicts. In all of this, Cenan's main strategy is to put the local elements into the framework of 'Western' extreme metal music. How exactly does this happen in Mesopotamian metal?

Mesopotamian metal employs the imagination of historical distance to create a new cultural sphere. In the concept of Sumerian metal, sounds, images, texts and practices from 'Western' and Near Eastern sources are combined to build up such a hybrid construction. This only works because these fragments are being presented as historical – they refer to the long-ago past of Sumer. This is what the Mesopotamian-ness is all about. The construction of the past in this metal subgenre is the imagination of a distant past, and this enables the construction of the promoted kind of politics of history – a suggested peaceful coexistence of 'multiple truths', as in a Melechesh song with the eponymous title 'Multiple Truths' (2015):

Arrogant vain, Nephilim
They delegate the agents of chaos
Assassins of thought,
Shroud minds
These savant theological impostors
Shipwrecked in the sea
Of confusion
Adam's language
Enochian paradox
Sons of Enki,
Daughters of Ninma
Owners of methodical absolution
Agents of chaos make order
Induce one truth for all
Shipwrecked in the sea
Of confusion
Abstract of religion
It's all lies,
Multiple truths
Heterodox dissident
Sons of Anunnaki
Tear the chrysalis around the spirit
May it grow, defy these chambers
Deny the absolutes
Shipwrecked in the sea of Apzu
Adam's language, shroud DNA

Words from the soil
Enochian paradox
Enochian paradox.

In these lyrics, we see the full scope of the semiotics of Mesopotamian-ness. The crucial lines for the imagination of historical distance are: 'Shipwrecked in the sea, Of confusion, Abstract of religion, It's all lies, Multiple truths'. Melechesh use the setting of ancient Sumer in a critique of the religious sphere as experienced in Israel and Jerusalem. According to Melechesh, the tolerance inherent in the acceptance that there are generally always multiple truths perfectly encapsulates their brand of politics of history. They promote liberal social values in metal music. This type of politics of history and its relevance in metal music can be evaluated better if we compare them to other discourses on history in metal.

The Bigger Picture: Related Discourses on History in Metal

Mesopotamian metal is not the only discourse in metal grounded in history. On the contrary, since the first days of metal, historical topics have been popular with fans and musicians alike.[18] Several classic metal songs from the 1980s like Iron Maiden's 'Alexander the Great' (1986) (about the historical figure) and 'Invaders' (1982) (dealing with the Nordic invasion of Britain in the Middle Ages), or even earlier from the 1970s, such as Judas Priest's 'The Ripper' (1976) (about 'Jack the Ripper'), are meant to transport their listeners into the past. History and the construction of the past are a staple of metal culture, and in many cases, also the politics of history. Yet, a more comprehensive perspective on the role of history is a desideratum in metal studies. The articles on history in this Companion illustrate the need for further research. For the consideration of the role of history in metal, the interdisciplinary engagement in metal music studies with specific research by historians trained on metal is needed.[19] Such forms of academic dialogue must be encouraged.

In order to broaden the perspective, it is instructive to place Mesopotamian metal in the context of other discourses dealing with history in metal. In the following, two other relevant discourses that relate to Mesopotamian metal, the roles of history, the construction of the past and the politics of history in them, will thus be considered.

The first discourse is 'Oriental metal'. It comprises bands and music that deal with the Middle East. In academia, the debates on the term 'Orient' and whether this notion is a purely 'Western' construction coming from racism and colonialism are still ongoing.[20] There is an academic discourse on Oriental metal and on metal music in the Near East from a broader perspective, but there is still no consensus. Most of all, the works by Keith Kahn-Harris, Pierre Hecker and Mark LeVine are noteworthy.[21] In these works, 'Oriental metal' is interpreted in relation to the dynamics of 'localising metal' in the Near East.[22] Today, it is clear that very much like the Mesopotamian-ness in Sumerian metal, the 'Middle Eastern-ness' in the music of bands such as Amaseffer (Israel), Distorted (Israel), Myrath (Tunisia), Nile (the United States), Orphaned Land (Israel) and Salem (Israel) is also a discursive construction. Musically and semiotically, the label 'Oriental metal' describes an even more diverse and broader spectrum of bands than Sumerian metal. Basically, it means any kind of metal music in which a hybridisation of 'Western' and Middle Eastern sounds, folklore or topics is palpable. Once more, we see how important it is to be aware of the generally heterogeneous and constructed character of metal identities. If one looks at the function of history in 'Oriental metal', one discovers a rather broad spectrum of approaches. Some of the bands like Nile, or even Iron Maiden in some of their classic songs, use history as a sort of escapism. Historical settings like Sumer, Egypt or others are presented as entertaining landscapes for metal lyrics. But in some cases, such as in the case of Orphaned Land, the band exploit history in exactly the same way as Melechesh. History is used to promote a rather liberal politics of history. Not all bands' values and perspectives are in this vein, but as a general trend, the plea for an inclusive resolution of current conflicts is dominant. History here seems to be a way to learn from the past.

Another discourse related to Mesopotamian metal is 'Viking metal'. As the title of the subgenre indicates, the past of the Scandinavian Viking era in the Middle Ages is the central theme. Viking metal has gained broader attention in academic research.[23] Not all studies explicitly label the subfield Viking metal. Sometimes it is treated under the auspices of an analysis of folk metal and pagan metal, which blends various styles of folk music and heathen ideologies with metal, or the study of 'Northern-ness' in metal culture.[24] In this, history has quite a broad range of functions and purposes. As a source of inspiration for groups as diverse as Manowar (the United States), and to some extent Iron Maiden (UK), Enslaved (Norway) or Amon Amarth (Sweden), the Viking period is a semiotic source for identities of adventurism, escapism, heathenism, naturalism and, in some cases, also of hetero-normativism and nationalism.[25] The decisive point is that also in Viking metal, the construction of the past is connected to the present in terms of values and thus becomes the source of a range of politics of history.

In Viking metal, the association with progressive values is not as clear as in Mesopotamian metal and Oriental metal. Often, rather conservative or even nationalist values are promoted.

If we consider the bigger picture of these three interconnected discourses on history in metal, the general function of history in metal becomes clearer. As a rule, history is constructed in the present and linked to current sets of social and political values. In Mesopotamian and Oriental metal, a distant past has the role of serving as a historical utopia or a social role model for the resolution of current problems. Also, it is often a source of escapism or, simply, entertainment. The deep connection between Oriental and Mesopotamian metal comes from their alliance in terms of the promotion of liberal social values. Finally, the question of whether we can learn from history through such constructions of an idealised past today is connected to this realm of morality and values.

Conclusion

This chapter on Mesopotamian metal explored whether we could learn from the past through listening to metal music in general and this brand of metal in particular. We now have the necessary elements at hand to give an answer to the question, though perhaps not a fully satisfying one.

Considering Mesopotamian metal (or Sumerian metal) as a unique artistic paradigm within the global network of metal cultures and scenes, as a *first* point, it was concluded that this concept is a set of unique sounds and semiotic sources (pictures, texts, narratives) of how metal should be. The concept is stabilised but open to adaption. At its heart are sense-making resources of references to the remote past of ancient Mesopotamia. Thus, as a *second* point, how the construction of this past happens in this subfield of metal was analysed. As a core mechanism, this construction happens via the imagination of historical distance. Ancient Sumer is a temporally distant place. The remoteness of this culture enables bands like Melechesh to present it as a historical utopia of peace and tolerance. Such a kind of liberal politics of history is at the concept's centre. As a *third* aspect, we reflected on discourses on history in metal, which are closely interrelated with Sumerian metal. In this, 'Oriental metal', which in many cases strongly overlaps with Mesopotamian metal, was a logically related discourse. In it, the construction of the past and the politics of history have analogous qualities. Also in Viking metal, the imagination of historical distance is crucial. But here, the role of the construction of the past and the politics of history are less homogenous. In several cases, conservative or even intolerant views are promoted. What all three concepts have in common is a shared discursive logic in their approaches to history. The construction of the past in the present has the function of taking an ethical standpoint in the current world of metal, and sometimes even providing answers to crucial problems in this world.

The fact that the construction of the past in the present has the purpose of enabling us to reflect on the present, and sometimes even address current problems, is the central finding. For the question of learning from the past in metal music through dealing with history, this is essential. In Mesopotamian metal, the attempt to learn from the past is clear now. This attempt happens through presenting the past of ancient Sumer as the significant Other, a world of tolerance and self-reflection. This is the good side. To be sure, the attempt to promote tolerance and peace in this way can have positive effects on listeners. However, we clearly note that this has a constructed and imagined character, of which metal listeners are usually aware. The same holds true for the other discourses on history, such as Oriental and Viking metal and the role of historical topics in metal in general. In a nutshell, Mesopotamian metal creates a cultural sphere in which possible answers to current problems are constructed. These are imagined suggestions. Thus, metal fans can *potentially* learn from the past via critically reflecting upon these suggestions.

The act of listening to metal music itself would also need more scholarly attention. There is some phenomenological and other research on it, but it is not fully clear how metal music is taken in by listeners.[26] So, also from this point of view, it is important to take the 'potentially' seriously in the answer. In metal music studies as a growing academic field, more interdisciplinary engagement with the specific expertise of historians promises new insights. History as an established academic discipline has at its disposal the methodological and theoretical tools to understand the function of history in metal discourse. Integrating this expertise into research on how the act of listening actually occurs seems to be the next step forward.

Notes

1. See Martha Howell and Walter Prevenier, *From Reliable Sources: An Introduction to Historical Methods* (Cornell University Press, 2001).
2. See Jouni-Matti Kuukkanen, *Postnarrativist Philosophy of History* (Palgrave Macmillan, 2015).

3. For a first analysis of the subgenre with the paradigmatic band Melechesh, see Peter Pichler, 'The Power of the Imagination of Historical Distance: Melechesh' "Mesopotamian Metal" as a Musical Attempt of Solving Cultural Conflicts in the Twenty-First Century', *Metal Music Studies* 3/1 (2017): 97–112. In the following, my interpretation of Melechesh's art refers to this article.

4. See 'The Best Oriental Metal Band', *Ranker* (2019). www.ranker.com/list/oriental-metal-bands-and-artists/reference (accessed 25 August 2021).

5. Adrian Bromley, 'Mesopotamian Hunger', *Chronicles of Chaos* (2001). www.chroniclesofchaos.com/articles.aspx?id=1–365 (accessed 24 August 2021).

6. On the way culture can affect sound, see for the case of 'Teutonic Metal': Jan-Peter Herbst, 'Teutonic Metal: Effects of Place- and Mythology-Based Labels on Record Production', *International Journal of the Sociology of Leisure* 4 (2021): 291–313.

7. Raymond Westland, 'Interview: Ashmedi from Melechesh', *Echoes and Dust* (2015). https://echoesanddust.com/2015/04/interview-ashmedi-melechesh (accessed 24 August 2021).

8. For scholarship on metal music from Israel, see Keith Kahn-Harris, '"You Are from Israel and that is Enough to Hate You Forever": Racism, Globalization and Play within the Global Extreme Metal Scene', in Jeremy Wallach, Harris M. Berger and Paul D. Greene (eds.), *Metal Rules the Globe: Heavy Metal Music Around the World* (Duke University Press, 2011), pp. 200–26; and Keith Kahn-Harris, 'How Diverse Should Metal Be? The Case of Jewish Metal', in Niall Scott (ed.), *Reflections in the Metal Void* (Interdisciplinary Press, 2012), pp. 39–48; for scholarship on metal from Middle Eastern, Turkish and 'Oriental' sources, also see Pierre Hecker, 'Taking a Trip to the Middle Eastern Metal Scene: Transnational Social Spaces and Identity Formations on a Non-National Level', *Nord-Süd aktuell* 19/1 (2005): 57–66; and Pierre Hecker, *Turkish Metal: Music, Meaning, and Morality in a Muslim Society* (Routledge, 2012).

9. See Bromley, 'Mesopotamian Hunger'; Herbst, 'Teutonic Metal'.

10. Kahn-Harris, 'Racism, Globalization and Play', p. 202.

11. For an introduction to Near Eastern history, see Arthur J. Goldschmidt and Ibrahim Al-Marashi, *A Concise History of the Middle East* (Routledge, 2018).

12. See Markus Endres, 'Interview mit Ashmedi zu "Enki"', *Metal.de Webzine* (2015). www.metal.de/interviews/melechesh-interview-mit-ashmedi-zu-enki-60255 (accessed 25 August 2021).

13. See Marc Van de Mieroop, *A History of the Ancient Near East, ca. 3000–323 BC* (Blackwell, 2004); Daniel C. Snell, *A Companion to the Ancient Near East* (Blackwell, 2005).

14. For the notion of 'bricolage' as a concept of metal cultural sociology, see Deena Weinstein, *Heavy Metal: The Music and its Culture* (Da Capo Press, 2000).

15. See Susan Pollock, *Ancient Mesopotamia: The Eden that Never Was* (Cambridge University Press, 1999); Roger Matthews, *The Early Prehistory of Mesopotamia: 500,000 to 4,500 BC* (Brepols, 2005).

16. See the classic by Howard Zinn, *The Politics of History* (University of Illinois Press, 1990); for a more recent discussion, see Charles Tilly, 'Why and How History Matter', in Robert E. Goodin (ed.), *The Oxford Handbook of Political Science*. (Oxford University Press, 2009), pp. 521–541https://doi.org/10.1093 /oxfordhb/9780199604456.013.0026; in a broader perspective, see Andy R. Brown, 'A Manifesto for Metal Studies: Or Putting the "Politics of Metal" in its Place', *Metal Music Studies* 4/2 (2018): 343–63.

17. See 'Hybridity', in Bill Ashcroft, Gareth Griffiths and Helen Tiffin (eds.), *Postcolonial Studies: The Key Concepts* (Routledge, 2013), pp. 135–9; Homi K. Bhabha, *The Location of Culture* (Routledge, 1994); Peter Burke, *What Is Cultural History?* (Polity Press, 2004).

18. See Peter Pichler, *Metal Music, Sonic Knowledge, and the Cultural Ear in Europe since 1970: A Historiographic Exploration* (Franz Steiner, 2020); Peter Pichler, 'Metal and History w/ Peter Pichler', *ISMMS* (2021). https:// metalstudies.org/mms101/history (accessed 27 August 2021).

19. See Pichler, *Metal Music*.

20. For the academic discussion on 'Orientalism', see Urs App, *The Birth of Orientalism* (University of Pennsylvania Press, 2010).

21. See Kahn-Harris, 'Racism, Globalization and Play'; Kahn-Harris, 'Jewish Metal'; Hecker, 'Taking a Trip to the Middle Eastern Metal Scene'; Hecker, *Turkish Metal*; Mark LeVine, *Heavy Metal Islam: Rock, Resistance, and the Struggle for the Soul of Islam* (Three Rivers Press, 2008).

22. See Hecker, 'Taking a Trip to the Middle Eastern Metal Scene'.

23. See Imke von Helden, 'Barbarians and Literature: Viking Metal and its Links to Old Norse Mythology', in Niall Scott (ed.), *Reflections in the Metal Void* (Interdisciplinary Press, 2012), pp. 257–64.

24. See Imke von Helden, *Norwegian Native Art: Cultural Identity in Norwegian Metal Music* (LIT, 2017); Ross Hagen, *A Blaze in the Northern Sky* (Bloomsbury, 2020); Karl Spracklen, '"To Holmgard . . . and Beyond": Folk Metal Fantasies and Hegemonic White Masculinities', *Metal Music Studies* 1/3 (2015): 359–77.

25. See Hagen, *A Blaze in the Northern Sky*; Spracklen, 'Folk Metal Fantasies'.

26. For a phenomenological approach, see Harris M. Berger, *Metal, Rock, and Jazz: Perception and the Phenomenology of Musical Experience* (University of New England Press, 1999); and Francesca Stevens, 'Blackened Audiotopia: Privatized Listening and Urban Experience', *Metal Music Studies* 6/2 (2020): 161–74.

8 | Sparta and Metal Music's Reception of Ancient History

JEREMY SWIST

He came from the city of Sparta
Some say he's the best
He bears one thing on his mind
To free all the rest

Sound Barrier, 'Gladiator'

1986 was a watershed for metal's reception of ancient history. While the French bands Sortilège and ADX had released the songs 'Gladiateur' and 'Caligula' in 1983 and 1984, respectively, it was Iron Maiden's 'Alexander the Great' (1986) that demonstrated and popularised the congeniality of antiquity to metal.[1] Alexander has since become a prolific figure therein, an archetypal 'metal king' and talisman of power, masculinity and tradition for artists throughout Greece and the European diaspora.[2] His reception was also examined by the first scholarly analyses of the appropriation of ancient Mediterranean history and culture by hundreds of metal bands across the globe.[3]

1986 also saw the release of the song 'Gladiator' by the US-American band Sound Barrier, and with it the inception of another popular ancient topic in metal, the Greek city-state of Sparta. As one of the first metal bands to consist of all Black musicians, Sound Barrier sought to disrupt the white hegemony of the genre. In 'Gladiator', they trace their spiritual ancestry to Spartacus, the archetypal rebel slave who challenged Rome. Ancient sources identify Spartacus as Thracian, but Sound Barrier derive his name from Sparta. Such an ethnic origin, the song suggests, explains not only Spartacus' status as a consummate warrior but also his drive to liberate those like him from imperial oppression.

Metal's reception of Sparta is overwhelmingly inspired by and filtered through the products of Laconophilia – the admiration of Sparta – in popular media and culture. Sparta's symbolism of strength and defiance appeals to the traditional ethos of metal and its (counter-)culture. While many bands appropriate Sparta to celebrate their Greek or European heritage – some harnessing it for political agendas – the majority arguably see in Spartan warrior-citizens a reflection of the metal scene: the few united against the many, fighting for liberty and tradition against the forces of modernity. Spartan metal is an instructive representative of the genre's reception of antiquity at large.

Laconophilia from Antiquity to the Metal Ages

Laconophilia in metal is but a recent example of 'love of the Laconian', specifically Sparta, the militarist city-state that dominated much of southern Greece from the seventh to fourth century BCE.[4] It was during the decline and fall of Spartan supremacy that Laconophilia entered Greek intellectual thought when the Athenian Xenophon authored the earliest extant account of Spartan society at home, of not only its political constitution but also its rigorous state-run education system that forged all males who survived the eugenic scrutiny of their infancy into a citizen class of professional soldiers.[5] Plato, who, like Xenophon, had no love for Athenian democracy, took inspiration from Sparta's authoritarian society in his political philosophy.[6] Four centuries later, Plutarch indulged a nostalgia for Greek glory under the Roman Empire with works on Spartan society such as the *Life of Lycurgus* and *Sayings of Spartan Women*.[7] Laconophilia was at its origin a reaction to these authors' respective political establishments. Such agendas should provoke scepticism of how real the Sparta of these non-Spartan admirers was, separated by space and at least a century's time from the men who fell at Thermopylae, and there is tantalisingly little written or archaeological evidence from the Spartans themselves to paint a more accurate picture.[8]

These ancient accounts from non-Spartans form the basis of what moderns call the 'Spartan mirage', which spellbound philosophers, statesmen and artists throughout modern history, including Niccolò Machiavelli, Jacque-Louis David and Adolf Hitler.[9] Most beloved by modern Laconophiliacs is the battle of Thermopylae in 480 BCE, as recounted by Herodotus, another non-Spartan. This was an infantry engagement with the massive taskforce of Xerxes, king of the vast, multinational Persian Empire.[10] In the face of his impending conquest of Greece, all but 31 city-states pre-emptively capitulated. Sparta took command of this Hellenic alliance, which designated the pass of Thermopylae as the most suitable choke-point to halt the Persian army from advancing into central Greece. Exaggerating numbers to enhance the Greek achievement, Herodotus counts Xerxes' infantry at 1.7 million, though modern historians reduce it to around 200,000.[11] The Hellenic alliance sent to Thermopylae a force of 7,000. Leonidas, one of Sparta's two kings, was constrained by religious reasons to take only his royal bodyguard of 300 Spartiates, though he also brought 1,000 hoplites of *perioikoi*, that is the second-class free citizens of Laconia, plus as many helots, enslaved Greeks who were regularly humiliated and even terrorised by public decree.[12] For two days, the narrowness of the pass, combined with the determination of the more heavily armed Greeks, converted Xerxes' numerical advantage into heavy casualties. On the third day, however, the Greeks found themselves outflanked after a local Greek traitor, Ephialtes, informed Xerxes of a path through the mountains to the Greek rear. Leonidas dismissed the majority of his forces but stayed behind with the Laconian contingent plus a few hundred Thespians and Thebans, looking out for the safety of the retreating force, but perhaps also his own glory. So, they made their last stand until all perished, taking many enemies down with them. The retreating Greek forces regrouped and, with their full complement of men and ships, dealt the Persians decisive defeats at Salamis and Plataea. Greece was liberated, and the Persians never returned.

Thermopylae was remembered by ancients and moderns alike as not only a sacrificial holding action that inspired subsequent Greek victories but also a symbolic defence of liberty against tyranny, or more accurately, of political self-determination against foreign imperialism. The Spartans' valour was first immortalised in the epitaph attributed to the poet Simonides inscribed at the battlefield: 'Stranger, tell the Spartans that here we lie, obeying their words'.[13] These words have been taken to be that of their law governing conduct in battle: 'not to retreat from the battlefield even when outnumbered, to maintain formation, and to either win or die'.[14]

The memorialisation of this battle brought Sparta into the popular imagination in the aftermath of the Second World War. The 1940s saw Greece suffer first a Nazi occupation and then a devastating civil war that ended in the victory of the American-backed Greek Government Army over the Soviet-backed Democratic Army of Greece. The United States helped symbolise this halting of the advance of communism by funding a memorial to Leonidas and the 300 at the site of Thermopylae in 1955. In 1962, at the time of the Cuban Missile Crisis and erection of the Berlin Wall, the Rudolph Maté film *The 300 Spartans* similarly suggested an analogy of Greece and Persia to NATO and the Warsaw Pact.[15]

For the popularisation of Thermopylae in the twenty-first century, the groundwork was laid in 1998 by Steven Pressfield's bestselling novel *Gates of Fire* and Frank Miller's comic *300*.[16] The latter was adapted to the silver screen by Zack Snyder in 2006, following Ridley Scott's *Gladiator* (2000) and Wolfgang Petersen's *Troy* (2004) in inaugurating a renaissance of cinematic antiquity. Like the Cold War *300 Spartans*, *300* (2006) was quickly contextualised in a post-9/11 America embroiled in wars in the Middle East.[17] Iranians understandably condemned its orientalising and dehumanising portrayal of their Persian ancestors.[18] Globally, the film was a box-office hit grossing over 450 million dollars. Its CGI-heavy bringing-to-life of the graphic novel influenced subsequent cinematography and metal music videos, such as Firewind's 'Ode to Leonidas' (2016) and Ex Deo's 'The Final War (Battle of Actium)' (2010). Laconophilia in popular culture has maintained its momentum in the years since *300*'s premiere, including in political discourse, with American conservatives adopting the phrase *molōn labe* ('come and take them'), which Leonidas allegedly replied to Xerxes' demand that the Spartans lay down their weapons, in defence of gun rights.[19]

Likewise, *300* impacted Sparta's reception in metal both profoundly and measurably. At the time of writing, a search of the *Encyclopaedia Metallum* for lyrics and song titles that include the words 'Sparta', 'Spartan(s)', 'Thermopylae' and 'Leonidas' renders 143 songs. The distribution by date of release strongly correlates with *300*'s premiere in 2006: 24 were recorded in the decade prior to the premiere, 70 in the decade after, 22 in 2008 and 2009 alone.[20] *300*'s influence on metal, especially its depiction of hypermasculine warriors, is not without precedent. The 1982 film *Conan the Barbarian* starring Arnold Schwarzenegger directly inspired the hegemonically masculine imagery and sword-and-sorcery lyrics of the American band Manowar and myriad bands that followed in their footsteps.[21] *300*'s predominant and even exclusive influence in many of these songs is evident not only in album artwork, such as Sparta's *No Retreat No Surrender* (2016) and Sacred Gate's *Tides of War* (2013) but even more so in direct quotations of the film and deviations from the historical record. Like Manowar, Spartan metal's focus on hypermasculinity frequently has a hypersexual and misogynistic dimension present in either film. In contrast to Manowar's depiction of women as sexual objects, however, Spartan women, though noted for their strength and independence in the ancient sources, are almost completely invisible in Spartan metal, re-entrenching metal's chronic exscription of women.[22]

As metal is at its core a reaction to the mainstream, its appropriation of the classical world often follows suit. In recounting how he pioneered the sub-genre of 'Viking metal', Quorthon of the Swedish band Bathory explained his preference for popular over more historically accurate accounts of the past, adopting the imagery of

proud and strong nordsmen, shiny blades of broadswords, dragon ships and a party-'til-you-puke type of living up there in the great halls … an image of my ancestors and that era not too far away from the romanticised and, to a great extent, utterly wrong image most people have of that period in time through countless Hollywood productions.[23]

Bathory, which until 1987 had been devoted to Satanic themes, set the precedent for harnessing popular conceptions of ancient and medieval history and folklore, especially elements tied to themes of masculinity, violence, sensuality and freedom, for proud expressions of cultural and national heritage.[24] Bands in Greece, Italy and throughout the European diaspora have also fixated on Greco-Roman antiquity as a locus of identity and as a supposedly real world where their core values as metalheads were validated and celebrated.[25] Much as Viking metal exchanged Satanic for historical themes, so 'Mediterranean Metal' channelled antipathy to Christianity by appeal to pre-Christian roots.[26] As was also arguably the case with Bathory, appeals to antiquity to transgress contemporary zeitgeists can also extend from concerns for the preservation and revivification of national and European heritage in the face of immigration, multiculturalism and globalism.[27] Spartan metal often assimilates Spartan soldiers into the very legacy of nineteenth-century Romantic nationalism that Bathory prolonged.

Chaos and Dionysus, Ares and Hades

Metal does not simply recycle popular images of antiquity but repurposes and recreates antiquity in its own image and in line with its own spirituality. In religious terms, Deena Weinstein theorises metal as a virtual ditheism of Chaos and Dionysus.[28] Chaos is the antithesis of order, symbolising metal's inherent opposition to systems of social, political, religious and economic conformity and control. Dionysus, in turn, is the god of spiritual liberation of the self from the control of rationality and socially prescribed behaviours and identities, and thus the freedom to gratify one's animal instincts.[29]

The first metal song devoted exclusively to Sparta is the American band Stormtroopers of Death's 'Moment Truth', released in 1999, a year after Pressfield's *Gates of Fire* and Miller's *300* were published. The lyrics integrate metal's chaotic and Dionysian themes into the Herodotean narrative of Thermopylae:

steel and flesh clash in battle, blood stains the fields
bodies burst, limbs are severed still they don't yield
300,000 adversaries dressed in their best
300 Spartans stand as one they're not so impressed
the moment of truth is finally here
it's better that you make a stand, war is near
hold your ground, never plead, They'd rather
die on their feet than live on their knees
Go! Fight! F**k! Kill!
Spartans!

The song advocates dying for liberty over submitting to slavery, reflecting the Greek belief that such was the nature of Persian rule. The will to defend personal autonomy in defiance of authority channels homicidal and suicidal instincts. The Spartans transcend bodily mutilation in their resolve, while the Persians exchange their embodied humanity for exotic dress, perpetuating ancient stereotypes of eastern men draping their bodies in 'feminine' dress in contrast to the Greeks, who celebrated the male body in heroic nudity.[30] The Persians' superficiality negates their numerical superiority of 300,000 to 300, a figure bereft of helots and Greek allies that highlights the shared identity of the Spartans as the few against the many. The exhortation 'Fight! F**k! Kill!', finally, advocates the total release of irrational bestial and sexual passions.

Stormtroopers of Death were only the first to view Thermopylae as a context for performing masculinity and indulging violent animal instincts to disrupt the forces of control. This is frequently illustrated not merely by appeals to the ecstasy of violence and bloodlust but also by comparisons of Spartan hoplites to animal predators, especially lions. This choice of animal may draw in part from the name of Leonidas, whom various songs call 'Son of the lion' (Firewind, 'Ode to Leonidas', 2016), 'the Lion of Sparta' (Holy Martyr, 'The Lion of Sparta', 2008) and 'the Lion King' (Sacred Blood, 'Gates of Fire', 2008). Such analogies recast this historical battle in the mould of Homeric poetry: as numerous warriors in the *Iliad* such as Diomedes (*Il.* 5.134–143), Hector and Ajax (*Il.* 7.255–257) are likened to lions hunting their prey on the battlefield, so the Spartans in metal to '[w]ild lions seeking their prey' (Axe Battler, 'Marching Phalanxes', 2014) and '300 lions' (Arrayan Path, 'Molon Lave', 2010), while in Sacred Blood's 'Gates of Fire' (2008), they resemble 'raging lions' in their zeal to recover the corpse of their fallen king, much as Aeneas in the *Iliad* is compared to a lion, as he guards that of Pandarus (*Il.* 5.297–303).

Identifying the Spartans as predators also draws from metalheads' common equations between themselves as wolves and the mainstream as sheep.[31] The Persians, accordingly, and matching their depiction in *300*, are not only orientalised and effeminised by their attire but also dehumanised by their own animalisation.[32] They are not like the sheepish Trojans slaughtered by the leonine Diomedes, however – not prey for predators, but livestock for human butchers: '[s]lay them like sheep and like cattle' (Validor, 'To the Last Man', 2016); '[w]ave after wave, butchering the pigs' (Necronomichrist, 'Tree of Doubt', 2009); '[b]utchered like cattle' (Battlecry, 'Hot Gates of Hell', 2006). The Persians also become animals that threaten humans, often reduced to a singular 'serpent' (e.g., The Monolith Deathcult, 'Demigod', 2008) or 'beast' (e.g., Dragony, 'Sparta (Elegy of Heroes)', 2011).

That more than one band rhymes 'beast' with 'east' also plays into the ancient Greek othering of eastern barbarians. According to Hippocrates and Aristotle, the subjects of the Persian kings were natural slaves, who preferred their slavery, while the Greeks were natural masters.[33] Such a dichotomy between Greek, and by extension, western liberty versus eastern slavery, is evident throughout this catalogue of songs, and even whole albums. The 2010 album *Obsessed by War* by the Greek band Unholy Archangel uses as its cover art a classical vase painting of a long-haired Greek hoplite subduing an exotically dressed Persian soldier (Figure 8.1). The band frequently writes songs about the superiority of Greeks in war, not only of the Spartans but of those who conquered the peoples of Asia, namely Alexander and Dionysus. True to their name, Unholy Archangel also intersperse anti-Christian themes more typical of black metal, forming a thematic unity where Christianity is seen, like the Persians, as a foreign nemesis of Hellenic culture. Like Scandinavian bands nostalgic for Vikingdom, and Italian bands for Roman glory, Greek bands like Unholy Archangel often seek to recover authentic national identity from times before, and in spite of, Christianity.[34]

Greek patriotism, moreover, is often expressed through the unity of the Greeks, whereby the war against Persia anticipates a Greek nationhood not achieved until the nineteenth-century war of independence against the Ottomans. The 2006 song 'Η τὰν ἢ ἐπὶ τᾶς' by Zemial is a notable example. Its lone mention of helots fighting at Thermopylae suggests the inclusion of Greeks of all classes, while the song ends with a quotation from Aeschylus' play *Persians* (472 BCE), the famous battle exhortation taken out of the context of the battle of Salamis: 'On you now Sons of Hellas! Free your native land; free your people, the fanes of your Fathers' Gods and the tombs

Figure 8.1 Cover artwork to Unholy Archangel's album Obsessed by War (Kill Yourself Productions, 2010), featuring an Attic red-figure kylix from c. 460 BCE (National Museum of Scotland) (© Elias Siatounes / Unholy Archangel)

of your Ancestors. Now you battle for ALL!'.[35] These lines are often cited as one of the earliest expressions of panhellenism and calls for Greek unification.[36]

Like its people, the geography of Greece is also adapted to the metal ethos. Local hot-springs gave Thermopylae its name, 'Hot Gates' or, more loosely, 'Gates of Fire', that in the Christianised paradigm within which metal traditionally operates become the gates of Hell. Indeed, the Plutarchian apophthegm 'tonight we dine in Hades' or, more often, 'Hell', is often quoted, matched in frequency to the Herodotean mention of Persian arrows blotting out the sun (both quoted in *300*), thereby enshrouding the battlefield in a Stygian darkness.[37] Several bands play with this notion of Thermopylae as the gates to the underworld. Hollywood quotations such as 'into Hell's mouth we march' communicate the Spartans' dutiful embrace of an honourable death. In hindsight of the result of both the battle and the war, the Persians' entry through Thermopylae symbolises both their own death and that of the Spartans guarding it. As the Greek band Macabre Omen puts it in 'Man of

300 Voices' (2015), 'I shall fall into the Kingdom of Hades / And ensure I take with me, / Worthless lives of those, / Who stand in between . . . / The past, the present and the future'. As Thermopylae are its gates, so Greece is the underworld itself, and the Spartans are its infernal sentinels: '[m]any have sung / about the Gates of Fire / About the narrow way / which leads to Hell' sings the Finnish band Lord Vicar ('The Spartan', 2008); '[n]ow they're standing at the gates of fire, three hundred men with blood desire / Ready to die and make a stand, no one will pass through the gates of hell' writes the Greek band Tex ('Leonidas', 2011). Only in death may the Persians descend to Hades, and so the Greeks symbolise death itself. The German band Sacred Gate sing, '[t]he Persians want to send us to Hell / But they don't know / we are already the Styx, / a river of blood / We are Hades, / we are home now' ('Path to Glory', 2013).

Contrary to realms of eternal gloom and punishment supplied by a Greek and Christian mythology, the glamorisation of Hell has been a fundamental theme in metal since the 1980s. The antithesis of chthonic and celestial gods mirrors metal's contrariety to the social, political and religious mores of the mainstream.[38] In this paradigm, the Kingdom of God, with its demands of moral austerity and obedience, amounts to a system of tyranny and enslavement. The Kingdom of Satan, often syncretised with Hades, in contrast, represents the liberation from the bonds of morality and authority. It is with this mindset that several bands buy into Hollywood's distortion, itself drawing from ancient Greek misconceptions, of Xerxes as a god-king.[39] In metal, Spartans are the legions of Hell fighting not merely for political liberty but also personal autonomy against the tyranny of religion. Greece as the 'Kingdom of Satan' thus fits into its traditional symbolism in the context of the Persian Wars as the so-called bastion of freedom.

Thermopylae is not always a conflict between atheism and theism *per se*, but a struggle to defend European culture from eastern gods, be they Zoroastrian or Abrahamic. In the Iliadic tradition of divine intervention on the battlefield, Zeus, Ares and Heracles are all called upon as both the allies and ancestors of the Spartan race. 'Thunder from the sky, Gods of the Olympus / Marching by my side, Zeus Soter Nike / Ares God of War with Phobos and Deimos' sings the Italian band Holy Martyr ('Lakedaimon', 2008). Like Homeric warriors in prayer, the Greek band Sacred Blood plea 'Almighty ZEUS of eternal Olympus! / Send your thunderbolts to your sons! / Grant us with wrath to eradicate our enemies! / Crimson eyed God Ares! / Clang your sword on your shield, and let us / hear your roar!' ('The Defenders of Thermopylae', 2008). The berserker Ares is elevated from the buffoonish and seldom-worshipped god of the *Iliad* to a patron god of metal. Such preferment signals a key conversion of the Spartans into metal warriors, with a near-total absence of the discipline, austerity and tactical cunning that was the basis of Sparta's military success.[40] The strategy of Athena and the rationality and order of Apollo, two of Sparta's chief gods, are exchanged for the bloodlust and madness of Ares.

Much like their counterparts who glorify the anarchic individuality of Vikings and other 'barbarian' warriors fighting to preserve their land and culture,[41] Spartan metal songs often place Spartan strength and bloodlust in the service of something beyond the individual. The most quoted or paraphrased ancient source is the Simonidean epitaph, invariably following Cicero's influential translation of 'words' (*rhēmasi*) as 'laws' (*legibus*).[42] Echoing Herodotus' words, 'they are free but not totally free, for the law is their master', the Spartans here place their law higher than any human authority, even that of Leonidas, who while presented as the ideal Spartan and inspiration to his men, is not the reason they chose to fight and die.[43] In this respect, Leonidas is different from Alexander or Caesar, who in metal songs are often the sole focus.

The epitaph, delivered in the first-person plural, plays into another prevalent theme: the achievement of *kleos aphthiton*, of 'undying fame', by being sung about first by poets and now by metal bands.[44] 'Then and again sing of 300 men' runs the chorus to the Swedish band Sabaton's 2016 song 'Sparta'. From the very first song about Spartans by Stormtroopers of Death, these warriors followed Achilles in his choice of a short life with glory over a long life in obscurity, yet through its glamorisation of Hell, they reject Achilles' later regret that it was better to be a serf on earth than a lord in Hades.[45]

Spartan Metal and the Political Right

Umberto Eco wrote that 'the Ur-Fascist hero craves heroic death, advertised as the best reward for a heroic life'.[46] Metal originated as a white, working-class phenomenon and built its identity by an antipathy to mainstream establishments. Since the mainstream is now perceived by many as globalism and multiculturalism, Laconophilia in metal may express the desire to defend a sense of heritage from these forces as an extension of an artist's right-wing politics. One such artist is the guitarist of the American band Iced Earth, Jon Schaffer, who participated in the 2021 attack on the US Capitol. A decade prior, his side project Sons of Liberty recorded

'Molon Labe' (2011), which narrates Thermopylae as a thinly veiled manifesto against big government and restrictions on firearms. The Belgian band Ancient Rites provide a more subtle example. Their lead songwriter, Gunther Theys, has expressed Eurocentric views and plays in right-wing nationalist bands.[47] Ancient Rites' song 'Thermopylae' is part of their 2006 album *Rvbicon*, whose songs combine the Spartans with the Crusaders, Julius Caesar and Arminius as touchstones of European heritage and defiance. Similarly, the German-Swiss-Austrian band Warkings embody this pan-European collective in their stage dress, under the pseudonyms Viking, Crusader, Spartan and Tribune, the latter two resembling *300*'s Leonidas and *Gladiator*'s Maximus, respectively.

Bands with formal and sympathetic ties to the resurgence of fascism in the twenty-first century have followed the Third Reich in emulating Sparta as an ancestral and model society.[48] Two such bands, Naer Mataron and Der Stürmer, are members of the Greek far-right party Golden Dawn, which gathers annually at Thermopylae, welding torches and renewing their anti-immigrant resolve. Naer Mataron express such sentiments in their 2000 song 'Wolf of Ions': 'I hold the heart and soul of an Ancient Spartan! Destroy now, the Plague from the east … I hear the voice of Leonidas, standing in the Thermopylae'. Der Stürmer reference Sparta in several songs and use a photograph of the statue of Leonidas in modern Sparta as the artwork for their 2002 EP *Iron Will & Discipline*. Beyond Greece, the Polish band Kataxu parallel the 1938 anti-Jewish pogrom of *Kristallnacht* with the Spartans' alleged practice hurling criminals and disabled infants off of Mt. Taygetus in 'The Manifesto of the Unity' (2005), while the British band Spearhead promote their social Darwinist worldview by embodying the Spartans' ritual murder of helots in 'Wolves of the Krypteia, We' (2018).[49] Far-right bands' appropriation of Sparta, along with Alexander and the Roman Empire, situate metal's congeniality to a romanticised antiquity within the wider ecosystem of right-wing groups throughout the world who remake classical civilisation in their own image.

Conclusion

Sparta in metal music, as in its reception throughout history, persists and thrives because of its adaptability. While historically rooted in Greece and adopting a peculiar system of laws, education and economics, the Spartans, and especially their last stand at Thermopylae, have a significance that, while often tied to ideology and claims of heritage, easily transcends those things and resonates with the core of metal. Though centred on musical performance, the metal scene treats feelings of social alienation and disempowerment by instilling a sense of belonging. That sense of power inspired by the music can take the form of a heroic individual or a group of heroes who overcome challenges and define their very identity as the adversary of the dominant society. With their long hair, defiant spirit and quest for immortal fame, the Spartans live on as metal heroes.

Notes

1. For a musicological discussion of this song's lyrics, see Lauro Meller, *Iron Maiden: A Journey through History* (Appris, 2018), pp. 46–53.
2. Iain Campbell, 'From Achilles to Alexander: The Classical World and the World of Metal', in Gerd Bayer (ed.), *Heavy Metal Music in Britain* (Ashgate, 2009), pp. 120–1; Osman Umurhan, 'Heavy Metal Music and the Appropriation of Greece and Rome', *Syllecta Classica* 23 (2012): 133–40; Christian T. Djurslev, 'The Metal King: Alexander the Great in Heavy Metal Music', *Metal Music Studies* 1/1 (2015): 127–41.
3. These now include Eleonora Cavallini, 'Achilles in the Age of Steel: Greek Myth in Modern Popular Music', *Conservation Science in Cultural Heritage* 9/1 (2009): 113–41; Campbell, 'From Achilles to Alexander'; Umurhan, 'Heavy Metal Music'; Djurslev, 'The Metal King'; K. F. B. Fletcher and Osman Umurhan (eds.), *Classical Antiquity in Heavy Metal Music* (Bloomsbury, 2019); Jeremy Swist, 'Satan's Empire: Ancient Rome's Anti-Christian Appeal in Extreme Metal', *Metal Music Studies* 5/1 (2019): 35–51; Helen González Vaquerizo, 'Κλέα ἀνδρῶν: Classical Heroes in the Heavy Metal', in Rosario López Gregoris and Cristóbal Macías Villalobos (eds.), *The Hero Reloaded: The Reinvention of the Classical Hero in Contemporary Mass Media* (John Benjamins, 2020), pp. 51–72.
4. For an introduction to Spartan history and society, see Nigel M. Kennell, *Spartans: A New History* (Wiley-Blackwell, 2010).
5. For Xenophon's reception of Sparta, see Anton Powell and Nicolas Richer (eds.), *Xenophon and Sparta* (Classical Press of Wales, 2020).
6. See Fritz-Gregor Herrmann, 'Spartan Echoes in Plato's *Republic*', in Paul Cartledge and Anton Powell (eds.), *The Greek Superpower: Sparta in the Self-Definitions of the Athenians* (Classical Press of Wales, 2018), pp. 185–214.
7. See Hugh Liebert, *Plutarch's Politics* (Cambridge University Press, 2016), pp. 77–146, 189–218.
8. On the 'Spartan mirage', see Paul Cartledge, *Spartan Reflections* (University of California Press, 2001), pp. 169–84.

9. For Sparta's reception from the Early Modern period to the present, see Stephen Hodkinson and Ian Macgregor Morris (eds.), *Sparta in Modern Thought* (Classical Press of Wales, 2012).

10. For Thermopylae and its legacy, see Chris Carey, *Thermopylae* (Oxford University Press, 2019).

11. *Ibid.*, pp. 48–9.

12. Matthew Trundle, 'The Spartan *Krypteia*', in Werner Riess and Garrett G. Fagan (eds.), *The Topography of Violence in the Greco-Roman World* (University of Michigan Press, 2016), pp. 60–76.

13. Herodotus, *Histories*, 7.228.2.

14. *Ibid.*, 7.105.4.

15. Carey, *Thermopylae*, pp. 194–5.

16. See Lynn S. Fotheringham, 'The Positive Portrayal of Sparta in Late Twentieth-Century Fiction', in Stephen Hodkinson and Ian Macgregor Morris (eds.), *Sparta in Modern Thought* (Classical Press of Wales, 2012), pp. 393–428.

17. Carey, *Thermopylae*, p. 196.

18. Paul Burton, 'Eugenics, Infant Exposure, and the Enemy Within: A Pessimistic Reading of Zack Snyder's *300*', *International Journal of the Classical Tradition* 24 (2017): 308–9.

19. Sarah Bond, 'This Is Not Sparta', *Eidolon* (7 May 2018). https://eidolon.pub /this-is-not-sparta-392a9ccddf26 (accessed 12 July 2021).

20. The global increase in metal bands over this 20-year period was also a factor, as well as the recent resurgence of traditional and power metal, subgenres that most often treat historical themes. Nonetheless, there are Spartan-themed songs in nearly every subgenre.

21. Karl Spracklen, *Metal Music and the Re-imagining of Masculinity, Place, Race, and Nation* (Emerald, 2020), pp. 80–1.

22. On women's exclusion in metal, see Jasmine H. Shadrack, *Black Metal, Trauma, Subjectivity and Sound: Screaming the Abyss* (Emerald, 2020), pp. 25–31.

23. Sleeve-notes to the album *Blood on Ice* (Black Mark Production, 1996).

24. Simon Trafford and Aleks Pluskowski, 'Antichrist Superstars: The Vikings in Hard Rock and Heavy Metal', in David W. Marshall (ed.), *Mass Market Medieval* (McFarland, 2007), pp. 57–73; Spracklen, *Metal Music*, p. 92.

25. See Peter Pichler, 'The Power of the Imagination of Historical Distance: Melechesh' "Mesopotamian Metal" as a Musical Attempt of Solving Cultural Conflicts in the Twenty-First Century', *Metal Music Studies* 3/1 (2017): 107–10.

26. K. F. B. Fletcher, 'Introduction', in K. F. B. Fletcher and Osman Umurhan (eds.), *Classical Antiquity in Heavy Metal Music* (Bloomsbury, 2019), pp. 1–26.

27. K. F. B. Fletcher, 'Classical Antiquity, Heavy Metal Music, and European Identity', in Fernando Lozano Gómez, Alfonso Álvarez-Ossorio Rivas and Carmen Alarcon Hernandez (eds.), *The Present of Antiquity: Reception,*

Recovery, Reinvention of the Ancient World in Current Popular Culture (Presses universitaires de Franche-Comté, 2019), pp. 240–2.

28. Deena Weinstein, *Heavy Metal: The Music and its Culture* (Da Capo Press, 2000), pp. 35–43.

29. The Dionysian inheres in Weinstein's claim that 'anything goes' for women in metal. See Deena Weinstein, 'Playing with Gender in the Key of Metal', in Florian Heesch and Niall Scott (eds.), *Heavy Metal, Gender, and Sexuality* (Routledge, 2016), pp. 11–25. For a critique of this claim, see Amanda DiGioia and Lyndsay Helfrich, '"I'm Sorry, but It's True, You're Bringin' on the Heartache": The Antiquated Methodology of Deena Weinstein', *Metal Music Studies* 4/2 (2018): 368–9.

30. Mireille M. Lee, *Body, Dress, and Identity in Ancient Greece* (Cambridge University Press, 2015), pp. 41–2.

31. Amanda DiGioia, 'A Cry in the Dark: The Howls of Wolves in Horror and Heavy Metal Music', *Metal Music Studies* 7/2 (2016): 293–306.

32. Jeroen Lauwers, Marieke Dhont and Xanne Huybrecht, '"This is Sparta!": Discourse, Gender, and the Orient in Zack Snyder's *300*', in Almut-Barbara Renger and Jon Solomon (eds.), *Ancient Worlds in Film and Television* (Brill, 2013), pp. 79–94.

33. Hippocrates, *Airs, Waters, Places*, 16; Aristotle, *Politics*, 1252b.

34. Fletcher, 'Introduction', pp. 11–12.

35. Aeschylus, *Persians*, lines 402–405.

36. This unity is interpreted to be under Athens' leadership. See David Rosenbloom, 'The Panhellenism of Athenian Tragedy', in D. M. Carter (ed.), *Why Athens? A Reappraisal of Tragic Politics* (Oxford University Press, 2001), pp. 361–4.

37. Plutarch, *Spartan Sayings*, 225d; Herodotus, *Histories*, 7.226.

38. Weinstein, *Heavy Metal*, pp. 41–2.

39. Richard Stoneman, *Xerxes: A Persian Life* (Yale University Press, 2015), p. 72: 'the Persian king was never a god, even to his own people'.

40. The characterisation of Spartiates as 'professional' soldiers is often overstated. See Stephen Hodkinson, 'Professionalism, Specialization and Skill in the Classical Spartan Army', in Edmund Stewart, Edward Harris and David Lewis (eds.), *Skilled Labour and Professionalism in Ancient Greece and Rome* (Cambridge University Press, 2020), pp. 335–61.

41. Simon Trafford, '*Nata vimpicurmi da*: Dead Languages and Primordial Nationalisms in Folk Metal Music', in Riitta-Liisa Valijärvi, Charlotte Doesburg and Amanda Digioia (eds.), *Multilingual Metal Music* (Emerald, 2021), pp. 236–7.

42. Cicero, *Tusculan Disputations*, 1.43.101.

43. Herodotus, *Histories*, 7.10.4.

44. González Vaquerizo, 'Κλέα ἀνδρῶν', p. 65.

45. Homer, *Iliad*, 9.410–9.416; *Odyssey*, 11.489–11.491.

46. Umberto Eco, 'Ur-Fascism', *New York Review of Books* (22 June 1995). www
    .nybooks.com/articles/1995/06/22/ur-fascism (accessed 30 March 2023).
47. 'Interview mit Ancient Rites', *Metal.de* (6 December 2006). www.metal.de
    /interviews/ancient-rites-36374 (accessed 12 July 2021).
48. For the Nazis' emulation and claims of racial ties to Sparta, see
    Johann Chapoutot, *Greeks, Romans, Germans* (University of California Press,
    2016), pp. 92–109, 216–24.
49. The literary sources for Spartan infanticide are not supported by historical or
    archaeological evidence. See Debby Sneed, 'Disability and Infanticide in
    Ancient Greece', *Hesperia* 90 (2021): 749–51.

9 | Viking Metal

Obsessed with the Past?

IMKE VON HELDEN

Out of emptiness
Out of Ginnungagap
Came Yggdrasil
Came life
Out of emptiness
Out of Ginnungagap
Came all of what is today

Einherjer: 'Out of Ginnungagap', *Odin Owns Ye All* (1998)

Viking metal is one of the few varieties of metal music defined by the songs' contents and visual elements rather than sonic aspects. While a band's music can be affiliated with folk metal, death metal or black metal, the lyrics and visual elements are clearly centred around the Viking Age, Old Norse mythology and the portrayal of Nordic nature. Time is an important feature in Viking metal lyrics and imagery and appears in the shape of a 'past' that can be identified as the Viking Age (793–1066 AD) or as a past that lacks a time stamp. Often without a specific description of the underlying idea, the past is frequently attributed with wisdom and continuity. It appears in song lyrics and is depicted in various scenes from a seeming past or with direct reference to the Viking Age in the cover artwork of Viking metal bands. Why is the past such an important feature of Viking metal? What other aspects are deemed important? What ideological aspects do the references to the past entail? To answer these questions, I will identify defining features of Viking metal to then analyse the connotations of 'the past' in Viking metal.

Features of Viking Metal

Viking metal became popular during the 1990s. Instead of dealing with Satan and the occult in their lyrics and cover artwork, numerous bands turned their focus to Norse or Nordic topics and made this idea popular. Many of the early bands were of Scandinavian origin, including the Swedish band Bathory, who, as early as 1988, released their album *Blood Fire Death*, which is regarded today as one of the most influential Viking metal albums and the precursor to Viking metal.[1] The album cover, lyrics and music combined Romantic nationalism with the Viking Age in the form of metal music by showing the painting *Asgardsreien* (1872) by the Norwegian painter Nicolai Peter Arbo, which was a novelty. Emerging from or strongly influenced by black metal,[2] other bands chose the same lyrical focus, which was displayed in the cover artwork of their albums and sometimes in their clothing as well: the Norwegian band Enslaved released their EP *Hordanes Land* (1993) and their debut album *Vikingligr Veldi* (1994), and were joined by other Norwegian bands such as Einherjer[3] and Helheim.[4] Swedish Unleashed[5] and Amon Amarth[6] added to Viking metal's sonic dimension by introducing death metal with a focus on Viking motifs. Even though the term was not widely used during the 1990s, Enslaved labelled their music 'Viking metal' in the sleeve notes of their album *Frost* (1994).

Well before the Scandinavian extreme metal Vikings, others matched rock and metal music with lyrics on Vikings: Led Zeppelin's 'Immigrant Song' (1970) is frequently mentioned as a precursor of Viking motifs in metal music, as is Yngwie Malmsteen's *Rising Force*'s song 'I am a Viking' (1985). Other bands deployed these themes without being deemed Viking metal, including Manowar on their 1983 album *Into Glory Ride* and their more recent *Gods of War* (2007) or, to name a more recent example, Burning Witches with their album *The Witch of the North* (2021). Today, bands such as Amon Amarth or Týr have a huge fan base and play concerts worldwide. Despite the numerous bands coming from Northern Europe, bands from other countries came into play by the end of the 1990s. Viking metal, one of the 'place-based metal labels full of mythology',[7] became a global phenomenon, and today there are, for example, Viniir from Malaysia, Thorvald from Egypt or Jörmundgandr from New Zealand. Apart from Old Norse mythology, other mythologies such as references to ancient Mesopotamia also emerged.[8] The early 2000s saw the rise of Pagan metal, with bands mixing folk and metal music with lyrics about pre-Christian eras or other religious or historical backgrounds.[9]

Viking metal as a name of a metal subgenre is highly contested. While it is certainly a genre featured in metal magazines[10] and the *Encyclopaedia Metallum – The Metal Archives*, many bands such as Amon Amarth reject the term for their own music because it refers to the textual instead of the sonic dimension.[11] Sometimes, even atmospheric bands that do not indulge in metal music are included in the genre. One of them is Wardruna, a band that are partially made up of (former) metal musicians but do not use electric guitars, which is an indicator of metal music for many. The question of why some bands are deemed part of the Viking metal genre while others, whose lyrics also take up Viking and Norse mythology, are not, shows the complexity of the manifold genres of metal music.[12] In order to understand the features that define Viking metal, one has to turn to the history of black metal. Many of the 1990s Viking metal bands moved away from the nascent Norwegian black metal scene[13] when realising Satanism and the occult were based on the same Christian beliefs they were trying to avoid. With the Viking Age, bands focused on an era before the Christianisation of Norway or Scandinavia – or, as some of the musicians I interviewed[14] argued, 'the authentic religion of Scandinavia'. Sometimes, musicians from the respective countries even extend the geographical focus to Germany, the United States and others.

One can only make assumptions about the music of the Viking Age, as there are no written sources on music from this era. Today's knowledge derives from sagas,[15] Eddic and Skaldic poetry, various Latin chronicles, illustrations and archaeological findings.[16] The sources mention music-making frequently[17] and suggest that musicians were of importance during the Viking Age.[18] The little information that exists on the horns, lures and rattles[19] may have inspired bands such as Wardruna. Having said that, some sonic characteristics appear in Viking metal, which may have derived from popular images of the Vikings. As a seafaring population, they are often depicted as chanting in a sort of choir, an image reflected in more epic passages, such as in songs like Skálmöld's 'Gleipnir' (2012) or Helheim's 'Rignir' (2019). Another feature is horn sounds, which are perhaps intended to resemble a Gjallarhorn, a horn instrument associated with the god Heimdallr, as in Helheim's 'Yme' (2000) or King of Asgard's 'The Nine Worlds Burn' (2012). Simon Trafford also suggests that bands try to make their sound more 'Viking' and highlights instruments such as violin (for example, in the Swedish band Månegarm) and accordion (for example, in the Finnish band Ensiferum). He further mentions sea shanties[20] or, in the case of Týr, traditional Faroese folk songs collected in the eighteenth and nineteenth centuries.

An important feature of both the sound and the lyrics is the language. Many Viking metal bands use their respective native language exclusively or add some English lyrics. Some bands include local variants, such as the Sognamål dialect used by Windir from Norway. Often, a translation is available in the album booklet by the bands themselves or in online sources such as Darklyrics.com, usually provided by fans.

Apart from a 'Viking sound', the visual elements of Viking metal in the cover artwork of albums, on various merchandise and in stage props are also crucial to the overall concept. These references to a Viking past in popular culture are usually dominated by male figures: 'indeed the Viking is hyper-masculine. They are big and strong with blond or red hair, and equipped with swords or axes and winged or horned helmets'.[21] Without the winged helmets, this image could be applied to Viking metal as well: strong bearded with long, wild hair and beards, apparently ready to climb onto their longboats and sail to their next battle. The martial appearance can include women, but it usually does not. In terms of musicians, the impression is similar: in a cursory review of the first twenty of 486 entries in the *Encyclopedia Metallum* for the music genre 'Viking metal', 54 musicians are male, while only six are female. A comprehensive study including cis- or transgender women musicians in Viking metal is still lacking,[22] as is a comprehensive analysis of Viking metal outside of Europe and North America.[23]

Focus on the Past

History and mythology have often been addressed in metal music: From references to the colonialisation of the Americas (Iron Maiden: 'Run to the Hills', 1982) to Greek myth (Iron Maiden: 'Flight of Icarus', 1983) and the history of the Middle East[24] (Melechesh: *Enki*, 2015), history has always been a part of metal music and is certainly not restricted to Viking metal. And yet, the Vikings were the first to establish their own metal subgenre. What is it that renders the topic so suitable for metal music? Simon Trafford and Aleks Pluskowski state that

[i]t is in heavy rock and metal that enthusiasm for the Vikings has been most evident, largely because the characteristics typically attributed to the Vikings – machismo, chaos, freedom, irreverence for authority and so on – correspond closely to those most lauded by heavy metal culture.[25]

With respect to the rebellious character of metal music, Catherine Hoad argues that the Viking in Viking metal is 'frequently configured as oppositional',[26] that is, the figure is characterised in opposition to Judeo-Christian religion like Satan is in black metal, or, in the case of Týr from the Faroese Islands, in opposition to the Celts. Yet, while this might be the reason the Vikings became popular in metal culture, I argue that this is only one of many reasons why the Vikings and Norse mythology have infiltrated metal music. It does not explain, for instance, why references to the past in general play such an important role for the musicians and fans and, more importantly, what the meaning of this past could be. In order to understand this phenomenon, it is necessary to analyse the elements of the Viking era and Norse mythology in Viking metal and the contexts in which they appear.

With a focus on the Viking Age and Norse mythology at the heart of the definition of Viking metal, the phenomenon raises questions as to the reason for applying Norse motifs, the sources considered and, looking back at the history of the use of Viking motifs, what ideological aspects this use in Viking metal entails. The following analysis is an extension of my earlier work on cultural identity in Norwegian metal music. In an attempt to grasp the character of 'Norse-themed metal music', I conducted qualitative analyses of outputs by Norwegian metal bands and identified five main categories that mattered within this frame: nature, religious elements, representations of history, references to metal music and aesthetics, as well as Nordic and Norwegian aspects of cultural identity.[27] The categories overlap in some aspects: when Amon Amarth's vocalist Johann Hegg sings about Thor in 'Twilight of the Thunder God' (2008), he does so by referring to the Christianisation (and a Vikings' battle against Christian invaders) in 'Where is Your God?' (2008) on the same album (*Twilight of the Thunder God*, 2008), setting the mythical thunder god in direct relationship to the Christianisation and a possible defence against an intruding force. The study included many representations of history and considered references to battles and fighting without concrete historical contexts (including imagery of past battles, weaponry and wounds, but also personal struggles and peace), mentions of historical practices, and some literary, sonic and visual sources. It is interesting that most of the battles are mentioned in the context of the fight against Christianity and the emotions of hate, grief and wrath connected to a force perceived as colonial. Another big group in this category are mythical battles, often specified as *Ragnarök*, the mythological end of the world.

The second biggest sub-category are references to 'time and the past'. Even when the Viking Age is not mentioned explicitly, the analysis suggests a connection to the era due to references to Norse mythology, for example, in Helheim's 'Det Eteriske Åndevesenes Skumringsdans' (1997): 'I edle tider og døde stormenns land, hvor myter ble skrevet av norrøn mann' (In noble times and the land of the dead lords, where myths were written by Norse man). Specific historical events such as the Lindisfarne raid in 793 are mentioned in Enslaved's '793 (Slaget om Lindisfarne)' (1997) or the

Battle of Stamford Bridge in 1066 in the case of Amon Amarth ('The Berserker at Stamford Bridge', 2019), among others. It is striking that the 'past' in general, as well as 'timelessness', are mentioned often, sometimes connected to words such as 'ancient' and 'eternal'. Even though the past is presented as a lost one in most cases, it is a time of primordial power that is lingering and waiting for its return. Some ancient elements are connected to sound(s). For example, Einherjer mention sounds that suggest a force that connects warriors to their roots: 'Gamle tonar, djupe tonar' (Ancient sounds, deep sounds) in their song 'Norrøn Kraft' (2011). In the same song, ancient elements are related to wisdom, which affects the people involved: 'Eg står støtt på norrøn grunn/I kraft av tanken på vår tid' (I'm standing supported on Nordic ground/strengthened by the thought of our time).

The Vikings in the lyrics usually show certain characteristics and are portrayed as very masculine in their strength and endurance, and hard-working 'men' and 'sons'. They are intimidating, tough and brutal, for example, in 'Svart Visdom' (1995) by Helheim. Time has left a mark on these men: Vikings are 'Menn tæret av tidens tann' (Men marked by time) and, in the same song, one is also described as old and possibly marked by many battles: 'Hans hår er grått og hans sinn er likeså/Hans øyne speiler bare sverd' (His hair turned grey, just like his mind/His eyes mirror only the sword). A certain fixation on wisdom and age is shown by referring to ancient knowledge and ideas, which might be superior to those of the present world and transmit powers to people relating to their antique roots, such as in Glittertind's 'Svart Natt' (2005). In their song 'Jotunblod' (Blood of Giants) (1994), Enslaved present a primaeval force alongside mythical references: 'Vår Urkrafts dype røtter/med energi fra treets fire elver' (The deep roots of our primaeval power/with energy from the tree's four streams), the tree being a reference to the gigantic ash tree Yggdrasil, which in itself is a reference to the cosmos. Further Viking characteristics are glory: 'Let's drink to the sons of glory!' and seafaring skills (Glittertind: 'Longships and Mead', 2009).

Ancestors are a vital factor in establishing a connection to the past: They are 'sønner av den norrøne ætt' (sons of the Norse tribe; Helheim: 'Svart Visdom', 1995) and 'sviklause ættar' (authentic dynasties; Einherjer: 'Balladen om Bifrost', 2011). They are immortal in spirit, as described by Helheim's 'Fra Ginnunga-gap Til Evig Tid' (1997): 'Den norrøne ætt vil aldri dø!' (The Norse lineage will never die!). In 'Jotunblod' (1994), Enslaved connect to mythology and primordial forces: 'Om en søker all Midgards viten/Om den kloke Volve svinger sin stav/En unngår ei sitt opphav/Urkraftens kaos, Jotunblod' (If one seeks all Midgard's knowledge/If the wise woman swings her staff/One cannot avoid one's origin/The chaos of the primitive force/ Jotun blood). Outside of Viking metal, the Vikings were farmers and seafaring people, but especially in Viking metal's early days, very few bands included this aspect of Viking life.

Another vital aspect connected to the bands' lyrics, cover artwork and interviews are sources, yet the information gathered from interviews with musicians is certainly a limited one. While musicians are able to provide information on specific sources and material they gathered for writing a particular song or album, we can never know what other elements may have subconsciously influenced their way of portraying Vikings, which might include elements from popular culture, such as films and books that are often consumed at a young age. However, some of the material is referenced in album booklets and, in the case of Norwegian metal bands, often points to Old Norse literature, such as quotations from and references to the Poetic Edda. Many bands refer to 'Hávamál' (for example, Helheim's 'Viten og Mod', 2011) and other sources such as the 'Völuspá' (for example, Ásmegin's 'Vargr i Véum', 2003) or 'Lokasenna' (for example, Solefald's 'Lokasenna', 2003).

The question remains why musicians (and fans) spend so much energy on members of a people who lived and raided more than a thousand years ago and are often associated with ideologies of right-wing extremists. The answer to why bands devote their band concept to the Vikings and what they aim to achieve with their work is complex and, of course, invariably depends on the person writing the lyrics and the band concept in question. Both have been analysed by scholars in various academic disciplines, focusing on the role of authenticity in Viking metal and other metal styles with 'country- or place-of-origin references'.[28] Catherine Hoad calls this phenomenon with reference to Týr's music a 'practice of symbolic (Nordic) ethnicity' and describes the band's work as a fight against Christianity as a 'foreign, slave religion' in order to prepare the 'return to their "true" gods' and describes it as 'hegemonic representation of ethnicity'.[29] Toni-Matti Karjalainen, in his work on Finnish metal bands, observes 'country-specific characteristics and stereotypes' appearing in media coverage on such bands, including 'features of the local scenes and cultures, natural environments, geography and weather, cultural mentality, and other contextual portrayals', set to connect with the musical style.[30] Jan-Peter Herbst sheds light on the economic perspective and perceives the bands' efforts in presenting their heritage, and thus authenticity, as a marketing principle.[31]

In my previous research, I have found that the musicians indeed strived for authenticity, but also to connect to their very own, personal level of how they perceive the world and emotions. I asked Norwegian musicians about their motivation and intention when writing about Norse themes and what they wished to express with their work. Enslaved's guitarist Ivar Bjørnson explained that one way of writing lyrics for him meant historical and mythical references with a poetic take on Nordic history, for example, an interpretation of runes, which Enslaved have been well known for since their album *Isa* (2004) or even earlier in the case of single songs (for example, 'Ansuz Astral', 1998). In order to make sure fans from across the world would understand the lyrics, the band switched from Norwegian to English lyrics. In contrast, a member of a band, which I will call band A in the following to grant their wish to remain anonymous, connects their lyrics to their life phases and refers to the Vikings, especially in an early period, when they were in search of identity and belonging. The project led them to Norwegian history and specifically Romantic nationalism and the (forceful) Christianisation of Norway. The person described their music as heavily inspired by Viking rock, which is decidedly ideological and revered by right-wing extremists, especially in Sweden. When moving to another city and becoming less isolated, however, they began working with other musicians and widened their lyrical focus, turning away from potentially right-wing ideas. Another band, here referred to as band B, explained to me that they imagined their music as a view into the Norse with a dark take on mythology and interpretation of runes. It is interesting that this band's bassist studies languages and is fascinated by the diachronic aspect of the Norwegian language. So, rather than presenting a Viking image with longships and the likes, this band aims at finding meaning in the language itself. For a band that I call C, the concept behind their music was a reverence to their roots with an emphasis on nature, Norse mythology and belief. Another band in the study, here called band D, focused on history, mythology and Norwegian roots, but without too much focus on the exact words. Their idea of making music was to transport moods and tell stories while making it sound as Norwegian as possible.

While there is a lot of literature on the role of religion in metal music studies, the role of religion in Viking metal – or, for that matter, pagan metal – has been surprisingly rarely studied in academia. In 'Antichrist Superstars', Simon Trafford and Aleks Pluskowski draw a link between Ásatrú and the evolving Viking metal phenomenon during the 1990s. They describe the turn from Satanism and the occult in favour of Norse gods as the opposers of Christian followers and Scandinavia's conversion to Christianity as a 'wrong that needs to be righted'.[32] My 2017 study suggests that religion plays a surprisingly limited role in the opinion of musicians.[33]

In her research focusing on the visual and textual representation of Celtic and Germanic mythology by Pagan metal bands, Serina Heinen concludes that Pagan metal bands may seem like a religious movement to outsiders, while musicians seldom refer to religious aspects.[34]

As mentioned above, ideological aspects are certainly a part of Viking metal. While many bands claim, '[w]e're not even political in any way',[35] the focus on Norse themes is influenced and informed by studying Vikings and runes in Europe in the past. Romantic nationalism in Northern Europe adapted the Viking (and rural depictions) as a means of connecting with their past, especially in Norway, a country that was under Danish and Swedish rule until independence in 1905. European history also referred to strong male and blonde Viking warriors prior to and during World War II in Nazi Germany and beyond. While the representations of Vikings in Viking metal are certainly martial, the ideology behind the music is, in most cases, not connected to ideas of a supreme race. However, there are subgenres called National Socialist Black Metal, or the aforementioned Viking rock, which have a distinct right-wing extremist and racist agenda. Yet, it is important to include the etic perspective by people not involved in metal, who view the music and culture as problematic, which may not correspond to the musicians' emic perspective. Additionally, there are racist or right-wing extremist bands that use (Viking) metal aesthetics, so Viking metal becomes adaptable by people following this ideology or is being used by bands from this spectrum.

Having said that, some bands change their way of dealing with the past. While in the 1990s, bands such as Helheim can certainly be perceived as referring to 'mean' and brutal Vikings conquering and taking in terms of 'narratives of nationhood and liberation',[36] the band Helheim in the 2010s is one that focuses on different perspectives of the topic, taking a more personal approach to the Norse. The same can be said about Enslaved, who, rather than describing Viking or mythical battles, analyse and explore the inherent meaning of runes, trying to interpret them in a way that fits into their personal and today's world (for example, on the albums *Riitiir* (2012) and *E* (2017)). In a recent interview with a German metal magazine, Johann Hegg of Amon Amarth, a band that write about battles and fighting on the majority of their eleven albums, talks about lyrics with different themes: On *Jomsviking* (2016), he wrote about a Viking burial rite ('One Thousand Burning Arrows') and included a duet of a man and a woman, in which the woman perceives the changed character of the man, who wants to take her by force, and refuses to let him 'take her with him' ('A Dream That Cannot Be').[37]

Conclusion

Viking metal is part of a growing phenomenon in metal music. Instead of focusing purely on sonic characteristics, as is the case with black or folk metal, a focus on the Vikings is the defining feature. It is interesting that some bands do not wish to label their music Viking metal and instead refer to the style of music as death, black or progressive metal. Regardless of the debate on subgenres, the aspects of time and the past play a crucial role in defining the Viking genre and are closely related to questions of religion, mythology and ideology, but they also serve very different purposes and for very different reasons, such as a means of placing oneself within a tradition and heritage, telling stories and exploring Norse mythology, among others.

Scholars have pointed out the role of authenticity in metal in general and Viking metal in particular, which can be perceived as problematic in terms of the politics of belonging but can also be a way to engage with heritage, tell stories or be a means of marketing for labels. Viking metal has been widely regarded from the musicians' perspectives. A comprehensive study of the fans' perceptions of Viking metal in general, ideology in particular, and the way Viking metal culture works (for example, at festivals such as *Midgardsblot* in Norway and *Ragnarök* in Germany) is still missing and would contribute to understanding the way the 'products' rendered by Viking musicians are received and what the interaction between both parties is like.

Notes

1. Simon Trafford, 'Viking Metal', in Stephen C. Meyer and Kirsten Yri (eds.), *The Oxford Handbook of Music and Medievalism* (Oxford University Press, 2020), pp. 564–85.
2. Ross Hagen, 'On Horseback They Carried Thunder: The Second Lives of Norwegian Black Metal' in this volume.
3. Einherjer released their first album, *Aurora Borealis*, in 1994, including the song 'Einherjer' about the fallen warriors in Norse mythology, and have been writing lyrics about mythology and stories from a Norse past ever since.
4. Helheim is a Norwegian band with a clear focus on Norse mythology. The band released their first album, *Jormundgand*, in 1995.
5. Unleashed released their first album, *Where No Life Dwells*, in 1991. The early lyrics are not exclusively about Vikings or Norse mythology but include songs that refer to topics like legal injustice (for example, 'Legal Rapes', 1995). The more recent albums focus on a martial take of Norse mythology and Vikings.

6. Their first album, *Sorrow Throughout the Nine Worlds* (1996), already pointed to the band concept, which Amon Amarth still apply today.

7. Jan-Peter Herbst, 'Teutonic Metal: Effects of Place- and Mythology-Based Labels on Record Production', *International Journal of the Sociology of Leisure* 4 (2021): 291–313.

8. *Encyclopaedia Metallum: The Metal Archives*, the most comprehensive online archive on metal bands, currently lists 474 bands that are labelled 'Viking metal', with 152 bands from outside Europe.

9. Serina Heinen, *Odin Rules: Religion, Medien und Musik im Pagan Metal* (Transcript, 2017).

10. Metal Hammer UK lists '10 Essential Viking Metal Albums' that are 'known to man and Valkyrie', *Metal Hammer* (2020). www.loudersound.com/features/10-essential-viking-metal-albums (accessed 24 June 2021).

11. Stef Lach, 'Amon Amarth: Don't Call Us Viking metal', *Metal Hammer* (2014). www.loudersound.com/news/amon-amarth-don-t-call-us-viking-metal (accessed 14 August 2020).

12. The 'bricolage of heavy metal' has been addressed in many instances, for example, in Deena Weinstein, *Heavy Metal: The Music and its Culture* (Da Capo Press, 2000) and Sam Dunn's documentary *Metal Evolution: The Series* (Banger Films, 2011). For his series, Sam Dunn developed a 'Heavy Metal Family Tree' with 26 subgenres.

13. During the 1990s, the Norwegian black metal scene became notorious for arson and murder. In the name of black metal, a group of young people set fire to stave churches, and some of them were convicted for murder. The story of Norwegian black metal is featured in many books, journalistic works, documentaries and movies, for example, Sam Dunn's documentary *Metal: A Headbanger's Journey* (Warner Bros. Home Entertainment, 2005), Harald Fossberg, *Nyanser av svart: Historien om norsk Black Metal* (Cappelen, 2015) and the controversial Michael Moynihan and Didrik Søderlind, *Lords of Chaos: The Bloody Rise of the Satanic Metal Underground* (Feral House, 1998).

14. Imke von Helden, *Norwegian Native Art: Cultural Identity in Norwegian Metal Music* (LIT, 2017).

15. Trafford, 'Viking Metal'.

16. Nils Grinde, *Norsk musikkhistorie: Hovedlinjer I norsk musikkliv gjennom 1000 år* (Musikk-Husets Forlag, 1993).

17. Trafford, 'Viking Metal'.

18. Grinde, *Norsk musikkhistorie*, p. 11; von Helden, *Norwegian Native Art*, p. 58.

19. Cajsa S. Lund, 'People and Their Soundscape in Viking-Age Scandinavia: Critical Reflections in a Music-Archaeological Perspective', in Ellen Hickmann, Ricardo Eichmann and Lars-Christian Koch (eds.), *Studien zur Musikarchäologie* (Verlag Marie Leidorf, 2000), pp. 235–41.

20. Trafford, 'Viking Metal', p. 574.

21. Simon Trafford and Aleks Pluskowski, 'Antichrist Superstars: The Vikings in Hard Rock and Heavy Metal', in David W. Marshall (ed.), *Mass Market Medieval* (McFarland, 2007), pp. 57–73.
22. There are studies focusing on female metal fans, for example, Rosemary Lucy Hill, *Gender, Metal and the Media: Women Fans and the Gendered Experience of Music* (Palgrave Macmillan, 2016), and gender aspects in metal music, for example, Florian Heesch and Niall Scott, *Heavy Metal and Gender: Interdisciplinary Approaches* (Routledge, 2016), as well as on queer metal fans, see Amber R. Clifford-Napoleone, *Queerness in Heavy Metal Music* (Routledge, 2017).
23. Viking metal outside of Europe is addressed in various papers, for example, Catherine Hoad, 'Hold the Heathen Hammer High: Viking Metal from the Local to the Global', in Oli Wilson and Sarah Attfield (eds.), *Shifting Sounds: Musical Flow* (IASPM, 2013), pp. 62–70.
24. Peter Pichler, 'Mesopotamian Metal' in this volume.
25. Trafford and Pluskowski, 'Antichrist Superstars', p. 71.
26. Hoad, 'Hold the Heathen Hammer High', p. 2.
27. von Helden, *Norwegian Native Art*, pp. 59–129.
28. Toni-Matti Karjalainen, 'Tales from the North and Beyond: Sounds of Origin as Narrative Discourses', in Toni-Matti Karjalainen (ed.), *Sounds of Origin in Heavy Metal Music* (Cambridge Scholars Publishing, 2018), pp. 1–40.
29. Hoad, 'Hold the Heathen Hammer High', p. 1.
30. Karjalainen, 'Tales from the North and Beyond', p. 5.
31. Herbst, 'Teutonic Metal', pp. 294–6.
32. Trafford and Pluskowski, 'Antichrist Superstars', p. 63.
33. Heinen, *Odin Rules*, confirms this view the role of religious ('Pagan') elements in Viking and Pagan metal, p. 210.
34. *Ibid.*
35. Statement by Moonsorrow and Týr on the occasion of accusations against the bands at the music festival *Paganfest* in Germany in 2008 on YouTube (2018). www.youtube.com/watch?v=HRsSamI1MLs (accessed 31 August 2021).
36. Hoad, 'Hold the Heathen Hammer High', p. 4.
37. Wedekind Gisbertson, 'Amon Amarth: In der Ruhe liegt die Kraft', *Legacy: The Voice from the Dark Side* 123 (2021): 20–3.

PART III

Metal and Identity

Personal Take III – Jasmine Shadrack

Music for Rebels: The Sounds of Our Perseverance

I was a fan first. I discovered metal when I was seventeen years old, and it immediately offered me something special; a place of belonging, a home for the underdog, sonic textures and compositions that satisfied me and an aesthetic that I felt mirrored how I already felt. I forged my identity through metal, and I have been in love with it ever since. It is how I engage with the world, how I listen to it, and how I negotiate my place within it. Sometimes, metal offers you everything you need – warmth, security, belonging – and sometimes it gives you a slap in the face (sometimes warranted, sometimes not).

After a while, being a fan was not enough. I needed to be part of its cultural production as well as its consumption, so I bought a guitar and amplifier, slowly started to change my appearance (so many band shirts!) and got to work. Since 2000, when I started playing, trying my best to play the right-hand triplets of Dino Cazares (Fear Factory), I have been completely hooked. Over the course of the last twenty years, I have been in gradually heavier and heavier bands, until my last band, Denigrata, where I decided to take up vocals too. Suddenly, I was a frontwoman, playing a BC Rich 1989 class axe series Warlock and screaming down a mic; it was perfect.

I have committed much of my academic research to exploring the ways in which metal and metal performance aids trauma recovery, specifically healing from grief and domestic abuse. I wrote my PhD dissertation and my first monograph on this subject: *Black Metal, Trauma, Subjectivity and Sound: Screaming the Abyss.*[1] I don't know what I would have done without metal, and I know I am not alone.

Metal, as a music form and subculture, however, is not perfect. We love to think of it as this separate bubble where everyone is equal and treated fairly. After twenty years in the scene as a performer, this was only true some of the time. It has its problems with race, class and gender, and it is easy to forget that metal, whilst rebellious, is an extension of the dominant discourse; we cannot fully divorce ourselves from it, even though we try.

I became a feminist through metal, and I was able to identify those engagements at gigs that were self-affirming and those that were deeply problematic, when I was safe to make music and when I wasn't. I have come to understand that nothing got in the way of my relationship with the music, between me and my guitar, even if sometimes at shows, experiences could have led me to think otherwise. I persevered. And that is something metal expects of you as a listener and as a performer. You have to stick with it. For example, the first time I ever heard Strapping Young Lad's *City* (1997), my ears felt utterly overloaded, but as I started to unpick and unravel what each instrument was doing, how the riffs moved in conjunctive motifs, I soon realised what a masterpiece it was and still is. As a woman guitarist playing extreme metal, it was the pinnacle of technicality, fluidity of playing and brutality of songwriting that I aimed for.

I have played in metalcore, death metal, black metal, blackened death and grind bands over the years, I've been in signed and unsigned bands, got to play with some of my heroes (Napalm Death, Morbid Angel, Arkhon Infaustus), and had moments when the only money we had was from merch sales at gigs! But none of this would have been possible without my love for metal, in all its glory.

I am therefore immensely proud to introduce Part III of this book that examines notions of identity and mental health, the rebellious spirit of metal, feminist fury and metal and the aesthetics of metal's uniform. I will leave you, if I may, with some of my all-time favourite metal lyrics that offer me hope and strength in difficult times; a gift from Sepultura's Max Cavalera to us all: 'under a pale grey sky, we shall arise . . . ' (*Arise*, 1991).

Denigrata Herself

Note

1. Jasmine H. Shadrack, *Black Metal, Trauma, Subjectivity and Sound: Screaming the Abyss* (Intellect, 2020).

 # Metal Identities and Self-Talk

Internal Conversations of Belonging, Empowerment, Well-being and Resilience

PAULA ROWE

Contrary to decades of speculation about the poor mental health of heavy metal fans, newer research conducted with metal people has begun to reveal some of the more positive and nuanced connections between heavy metal music, metal culture and mental health.[1] In this chapter, I build on new understandings of metal and wellness by examining three domains of well-being through a lens of heavy metal identity formations. Specifically, I will discuss: (1) belonging and acceptance by like-minded others; (2) stress and coping in the social world; and (3) building resilience in uncertain times. Ultimately, I will explore ways that being metal can facilitate good outcomes in these three spaces.

Note the term 'being metal' that is used here, rather than listening to metal or enjoying metal music. Yes, the music is vitally important in any discussion of metal, but this chapter focuses on those who take the next step of declaring a metal identity – whether verbally by saying things like 'I'm a metalhead', or maybe in more visual ways like embodying a metal identity that can be seen and read on the body by others.

Identity studies have a long history of looking at well-being outcomes associated with identity choices. It is widely accepted that identity and well-being are tightly bound, for better or worse. It is also clear that metal identities are highly valued by their 'owners', so it makes sense to examine the nexus of metal identity formations and the mental health of metal fans and artists.

The arguments throughout this chapter are drawn from my previous research,[2] critical identity studies and my own life in metal. I conclude by proposing that the identity self-talk of metalheads, and its interplay with the embodiment of metal identities, has significant value for steeling oneself against some of the most pervasive social and emotional threats of modern life.

Identity Making and the Internal Conversation

There are many different theories surrounding our identity formations, or put simply, what makes us who we are in terms of how we define ourselves in the world. As an academic discipline, psychology has certainly been dominant in theorising self and identity. However, this chapter takes a sociological view of identity-making, particularly social-relational perspectives that view identity-making as something that happens *between* people.

Whether we realise it or not, our interactions with others give us new information or affirm existing information about who we are and what is possible for us in life. This includes our interactions at the micro level in our personal relationships and immediate contexts like work, school and community, through to institutional interactions at the meso and macro levels of our social system (like housing, employment, health and justice systems).

We all construct identity biographies, or the story of who we are, based on past experiences, present circumstances and future predictions. Think of it as a screenplay: we craft the story of our lives with ourselves in the leading role, and we make rolling revisions to the script as other actors enter and exit the scene, often throwing the plot into chaos. Sometimes we 'write' our identity narratives with a lot of effort and overthinking, and sometimes without even realising it, but we are all doing it, albeit in different ways, and we are testing our identities out and revising them based on the feedback we get and how we process it.

For example, let us say I am teaching a class and pose a question to students. If everyone looks at me blankly and no one answers, I might process that as negative feedback about my teaching capabilities. I might think, 'I'm a terrible teacher, I couldn't get the key points across, no one understood what I was trying to say, I'm a fraud, I don't belong here'. Despite students not actually saying that to me, that might be my interpretation based on the interaction, and consequently, my teacher identity is likely to suffer a blow. Some identity 'injuries' are minor and easily healed, but some can be major injuries that may take a very long time to repair, if at all. It also depends on the importance we place on the portion of identity that has been harmed because we have many different moving parts to our identities. For example, teacher is only one of my identities; I also identify as a woman, a mother, a daughter, an activist and a metalhead, to name a few.

We 'discuss' and strategize our identity components in an ongoing internal dialogue we have with ourselves – how we are regarded by others is a crucial factor for shaping these internal conversations through which we come to understand 'ourselves, our lives, the meaning of our actions and our biographical narratives'.[3] This idea is critical for analysing how metalheads construct a sense of self in everyday life, particularly what we come to 'learn' about ourselves through interactions with others, and how this shapes our self-talk.

Of course, we all wear multiple identities, as mentioned above, but the focus here is squarely on metal identity formations and ways they play out in everyday life because being in the world as a metalhead often embodies a clear and compelling social identity that others can see and recognise. And furthermore, not everyone likes it! Metal identities have been negatively characterised as deviant and delinquent, apathetic and demotivated, socially undesirable or mentally unwell, to outright dangerous (think stereotypes of school shooters and Satan worshippers). So why then would people sign up for this? And why make such a point of embodying an (often) unmistakeable metal identity that is subject to negative stereotyping?[4]

If you believe metal's detractors, it is because there is something clearly wrong with us. But if you start asking serious questions of metal people in respectfully curious and non-judgemental ways, you might get some interesting answers that challenge myths and stereotypes about metal fans and artists.

That is precisely what I did; I spent five years talking to (the same) metal youth as they left school, moved out of home, started playing gigs and touring, and got jobs. I got to know them well, and I watched them adapt to many different curve balls that life threw at them. The constant thing in their lives was their passion for metal, but the enjoyment consisted of so much more than just the music, although that was clearly the primary drawcard. Their metal identities were incredibly important for helping them cope with all sorts of things – things that, in one way or another, could fit into three key areas of well-being: namely, belonging and acceptance; stress and coping; building resilience. Further, the wellness factors participants described were crucial for supporting optimal well-being in everyday life, not just in metal contexts.

The metal identity narratives I collected were largely very positive, which of course mounts a significant challenge to the deficit constructions of metal fans as being more likely to be depressed or suicidal than fans of other genres. To be clear though, I am not attempting to present a utopian view of the metal landscape as being carefree and untouched by mental health concerns. Like *all* areas of society, metal too is touched by mental health concerns and suicide within the fold. But here, I argue that our understanding of metal identities has been skewed by uninformed stereotyping for a very long time, and for this reason, this chapter unapologetically presents a positive line of dialogue to redress the imbalance somewhat.

Self-Talk of Belonging and Acceptance in the Metal World

Building an identity and attaining a sense of belonging and acceptance are complex human pursuits. As social beings, we spend a lot of time and effort constructing a social identity that we can shop around until we find the right fit. In one way or another, it is generally a sense of community we are looking for, or at least communion with like-minded others whose approval reflects and affirms that our lives are somehow worthwhile, and our ideas are valued. Identity transactions like this are going on all the time, all over the world, among all age groups, as we all try and find our place in the world. Even those who consider themselves to be outsiders or against the social grain are forging their 'uniqueness' in solidarity with other outsiders, with a lot of metal people in this category. And so begins the entanglement of identity and well-being, which explains why we spend so much time trying to fit in to whatever we deem as important *to fit in with* – we intrinsically know that it is good for our well-being to feel accepted – a sense of belonging tells us 'We're okay, it's okay, I'm okay'.[5]

Heavy metal communities make for fascinating case studies of belonging and acceptance. On one hand, there is the more obvious sense of acceptance that is possible for metalheads in their local scene or in face-to-face metal communities. The separation between artists and fans is usually rather minimal in metal communities because it is common for numerous metal bands to regularly play together in local scenes, and the musicians *are* fans too, and vice versa, even if fans are at the pre-contemplative stage of writing and performing.

Also common to artists and fans alike is the embodiment of metal identities. Not only are metalheads often visible to each other in local scenes and face-to-face communities, but complete strangers can know and accept each other.[6] My young adult research participants described some of the more fleeting ways this can occur, such as seeing someone on a bus or in a coffee shop and having a sense of 'just knowing where they're coming from' because of the band T-shirt they are wearing or a particular metal aesthetic. Of course, we would critically question the validity of statements like this, but the symbolic significance is real in the eyes of the perceiver, and that is the key point in terms of fostering a sense of belonging.

On a more practical note, some participants in my research in Australia had travelled internationally to attend music festivals in Europe and the United States, and to explore death metal scenes in South-East Asia.

For them, travel experiences were opportunities to test out the perceived sense of metal kinship that they had forged from a very early age, long before they ever met another metal person or went to shows. They had some language barriers to navigate in the countries they visited, but the language of the metal shirt was indeed universal. They were instantly recognisable as metalheads and were welcomed into local scenes, and I am sure this will resonate with seasoned metal people reading this, who have been embraced by other local scenes when travelling (as I have).

In sum, the universal acceptance of being metal by other metal people[7] is a legitimate phenomenon, and metal folks know it. But the interesting thing, from a well-being perspective, is the surrogate sense of belonging and acceptance that imagined community membership can also provide for those who are isolated and cannot access face-to-face communities, whether by choice or circumstance.

My research findings showed that establishing a sense of collective metal identity was the first step to feeling like a member of a global metal community. The metal youth I interviewed achieved this by watching metal media, participating in metal forums online, learning to embody metal identities and decorating their rooms with metal posters and various other pieces of metal paraphernalia and artefacts.

Long before they ever met another metalhead in person, their collective identity narratives fostered a deep sense of connection to a global metal community – albeit imagined. It was common to hear them say things like 'that sense of community is great', 'we take care of our own' and 'we're a tight-knit community', despite the fact they did not know any other metalheads at that point in time. Crucially, this imagined sense of community was a significant protective factor for mental health challenges associated with experiences of bullying, bereavement, family breakdown and the social isolation of moving around (or changing schools) and not knowing anyone.

Based on the consistency of my findings and lived experience, it is plausible to suggest that the positive benefits of imagined metal community membership are transferable across the lifespan and in any number of socially marginalised contexts. Loneliness and isolation are universal; anyone is susceptible. But 'being metal' can go a long way towards re-authoring the stories we tell ourselves about being alone in the world – just pulling on a metal T-shirt can give us an instant sense of belonging and acceptance that can get us through the day. Further, this alternate belonging and acceptance can be seen and known by others, which can be enormously therapeutic for those who have been socially rejected by dominant cultural groups and norms, and even protective in social contexts, as I will discuss next.

Deploying Metal Identities to Manage Stress in the Social World

While participating in metal community life, real or imagined, is widely regarded by metal fans and artists as a positive experience, the broader social world is not always as uplifting. Family, school and work are three pivotal environments that many of us must navigate at some stage, as well as various social systems and institutions that make up our social landscape (think health, justice, housing, banking, transport, welfare systems, to name a few). Within these contexts, there are many social interactions to work through as well; some friendly, some hostile.

Hostile social relations can range from being mildly uncomfortable, to a feeling of vulnerability that something bad could happen, through to outright rejection and exclusion, and even a sense of imminent physical or emotional danger. Regardless of the nature or severity, the common denominator is power, and if we are the ones feeling hard done by, it is probably because we have been disempowered in some way – by either a person, a group, a process or a system that seems stacked against us because they are holding the power.

Feeling disempowered and disrespected amounts to a moral attack on our identity. When our sense of self is attacked and injured, it can leave us feeling hurt, angry and generally disappointed that we do not measure up in some way, or are not quite good enough, or worthy enough, of respect and inclusion (at school, at work, in peer groups or in any number of social settings).

Feeling disrespected can spark an intense desire for recognition and justice that is not being met, and it can be very stressful trying to reclaim power and recognition in alternate ways. When we talk about stress management and music, it is usually in terms of the listening experience and the calming (or motivating) effect that music can have on us.[8] However, looking beyond the music reveals interesting ways the metal culture can intersect with identity and well-being to remediate social conflicts. Resistance against dominant groups as an exercise in self-care might not be a new idea, but it certainly offers a fresh way of looking at metal identities and stress management in the social world.

Think of it this way, if metal identities can create a sense of belonging and acceptance by like-minded others (or keeping the right people in), they can also be used for protection in socially vulnerable situations (or keeping the wrong people out). And this is where those long-standing negative stereotypes about metalheads can prove quite useful for some.

Most readers will be familiar with the 1985 US Senate hearings into lyrical content of (mostly) heavy metal and rap music. In short, the key arguments for censoring lyrics rested on the unsubstantiated claims that such music would send people off the rails, particularly impressionable youth. Conservative detractors opined that metal was 'outrageous filth' portraying and glorifying rape, incest, sexual violence, perversion and suicide.[9] The testimonies were based on opinion, not evidence, but they had an enduring influence on moral and religious commentary – including the Catholic Archbishop of New York, who drew on 'evidence' from the hearings when claiming some years later that heavy metal music is spiked with Satanic lyrics that disposed listeners to devil worship and demonic possession.[10]

In 1988, journalist Geraldo Rivera seized an opportunity to capitalise on metal's bad press by producing a documentary called *Devil Worship: Exposing Satan's Underground*,[11] in which he tried to infer links between metal, murder and Satanism. Rivera highlighted several murders carried out by people who also liked heavy metal music. In the absence of any evidence showing that metal played any part in planning or carrying out the murders, the programme instead relied on sensational accounts of blood-drinking and human sacrifice to fuel the 'Satanic Panic' surrounding metal that was sweeping the United States at that time. In the decade or so after, metal was a ready-made scapegoat for numerous high-profile prosecutions – and was pounced on by prosecutors and media alike. School shootings kept metal at the forefront of moral panics too. For example, even though the shooters were not into metal, all school outcasts came under scrutiny after the Columbine High School shootings in 1999, and metalheads were put forward by media commentators as prime examples of 'outsiders' and 'loners' in school settings.

I revisit these rather well-known cultural time stamps to set the context for exploring why people would sign up for a recognisable identity that could stigmatise and stereotype them in such negative and disparaging ways. We all do things for a reason, so what can be gained by being misrepresented as a dangerous, devil-worshipping deviant who should be avoided at all costs? The hint is in the last statement there, the potential for *being avoided by others*.

We have all felt socially vulnerable at times, whether that is a case of not fitting in, feeling rejected (or at risk of rejection) or being outright bullied, harassed or victimised in some way. This can occur at any time throughout the lifespan, but these things are often felt acutely during high school years.

My research with metal youth showed a clear pattern of feeling socially vulnerable during high school – some just felt like outsiders, whereas others were overtly bullied by popular students.

But the one thing participants had in common was the sense of social protection they felt after they started embodying metal identities; they enjoyed being stereotyped as the dangerous kid who *might* be capable of shooting the school up because people finally stopped picking on them and left them alone. Some said that it 'feels good to know they [the bullies] are the ones afraid of you now' and that 'you get instant respect in a metal shirt'. Others reported the well-being aspect of being left alone, saying that 'it feels good to have space' and like 'you can finally breathe and relax a bit'.

The politically transformative properties of social movements and sub-cultural groups are not new.[12] However, many metal people describe themselves as loners or outsiders, and my research affirmed that political transformation tended to occur at the level of the individual for partici-pants, which makes metal rather unique in its political capacity for redress-ing individually experienced power relations.

On one hand, being left alone and labelled an outsider does not sound promising for making friends and building networks. But if they are not your type of people anyway, then keeping bullies at bay without having to get in a fistfight with them can be quite a good and clever option. As it turned out, the metal youth I interviewed were all very introverted and non-confrontational by nature. They did not want any trouble, they did not want to fight, they just wanted to go about their business in peace and be left alone, which is a far cry from the stereotype of dangerous and violent metal youth. They were able to recalibrate power relations on their own terms.

During our teenage years, identity-making is vitally important for estab-lishing ourselves, although we tend to have a rather limited pool of options to choose from. As we make our way through adulthood, more identity oppor-tunities usually start to open for us: as workers, lovers, spouses, scholars, artists or members of leisure groups. But these can also give rise to new opportunities for hostile relations to emerge, including social exclusion from systems like housing and labour markets. The frustration of exclusion can present itself in complex ways throughout the lifespan; therefore, future research with more senior metal people could provide fascinating insights into the emotionally protective factors of metal identities throughout the life course. Anecdotally, the well-being factor of maintaining a metal identity feels true for me and other 'older' metalheads I talk to about this. However, empirical data from metal scholars is long overdue, given that metal elders are now approaching anywhere up to five decades of embodying a metal identity.[13]

Arguably, there is always an 'edge' to pulling on a metal shirt and keeping the world at bay when needed, regardless of how old we are. Finding retreat and respite are important mechanisms for refuelling our energy to meet life's challenges and the resilience we need to forge ahead.

Metal as a Building Block for Resilience in Uncertain Times

The concept of resilience is no stranger to discussions of well-being; indeed, it is widely regarded as a significant protective factor for mental health.[14] But the contours of building resilience in the context of being metal are especially intriguing and multi-faceted.

At its core, resilience is the ability to cope and bounce back from adverse life events. Our mental and emotional capacity to navigate life stressors also depends on how flexible and adaptable we are or need to be when facing uncertainty. Those of us who hang on too tightly to 'what ought to be' often have trouble going with the flow and accepting 'what is'. Being too rigid about ideas and opinions only serves to make us stuck and hold back our progression through new ideas and learning, even when they are thrust upon us and not of our choosing, like having to re-skill after losing a job or learning to date again after a long-term relationship ends.

But when everything around us is in flux, like work, education, housing, relationships and so on, sometimes we need an anchor point to steady us in rough seas, and metal identities can provide a comforting sense of certainty and reliability. We may not always know how things will turn out, and we may not be able to control some things, but we can know who we are as a metalhead.

But metal is more than a fixed anchor point for resilience building. It can be a significant emotional resource for finding a way back from bereavement, family breakdown, health issues, unemployment and various types of victimisation or social vulnerabilities – but finding a way forward, in a tangible way, requires some skills and resources that metal can also provide, along with the confidence and motivation to deploy them.

Skill Building, Future Proofing

Around the time the 'Satanic Panic' was sweeping across America and beyond, researchers, most notably from psychology, were becoming preoccupied with 'proving' the problem of metal for youth development.[15]

Some authors took the suicide and mental health angle, while others started speculating that metalheads were pretty much pre-destined for low-educational attainment and low-achieving futures.[16] The bleak picture of metal youth was one of dropping out of school, smoking pot all day, and barely being able to string a coherent sentence together, despite any rigorous research evidence to substantiate such ideas.[17]

In contrast, more recent studies have found metal youth to be rather gifted students with spirited aspirations.[18] Whether or not they can achieve them, however, depends on a predictable set of social, economic and domestic factors that can impact all people, regardless of the music they listen to. This should not be surprising, but more interesting is the role that metal can play in skill development and confidence building, both of which are crucial building blocks for resilience and future-proofing the self in an ever-changing social world.

Metal is known from within as a DIY (do it yourself) culture which encompasses all aspects of musical production and scene maintenance. Indeed, participation in local scenes can provide extensive opportunities to build a diverse complement of both hard and soft skills – hard skills being teachable and measurable in nature like learning to write, play, record and perform music, engineering live performances and producing artwork and promotional materials; and soft skills capturing desirable attributes like good communication, effective time management, problem-solving, mentoring, organisational skills and teamwork required to maintain and sustain local metal scenes. The acquisition of these skills might originate in the metal context, but crucially, once learned, they are transferable to other environments.

Other (less obvious) opportunities for skill development are metal-inspired life choices like undertaking international travel to attend metal festivals. Participants in my research documented the important life skills they learned by embarking on international travel, such as saving money, budgeting, organising, communicating in other languages, and generally having to be self-sufficient in a foreign country. These young adults in Australia had never travelled abroad (nor had they travelled anywhere alone). However, metal was the motivating force 'to save up and live the dream', hence it motivated them to undertake further study and 'get better jobs' to fund future trips.

This is a good example of ways we reflexively incorporate new experiences into the identity stories we tell ourselves. These trips, inspired by a love of metal, had imbued these people with a new sense of purpose, capabilities, aspirations and visions for where they could set the bar in life more broadly. Importantly, their biographies of growth and empowerment had a significant impact on their positive outlook and overall well-being.

These outcomes might not be the same for everyone, but they should encourage us to rethink metal as a potentially positive developmental tool rather than a problem. Metal scenes and communities clearly provide numerous opportunities to road-test ideas and acquire skills and confidence that underpin well-being under the tutelage of good metal mentorship.

Conclusion

Outside of the metal fold, metal had a bad reputation for a long time. Discourses of deviancy, Satanism, suicide ideation, violence and generally poor life outcomes for metalheads were common in mainstream media and public sentiment. This chapter, however, has drawn on sociological research *with metal fans and artists* to present a more detailed understanding of the positive benefits of forging a metal identity.

No desire exists to convince the reader that all metal people are perfectly well adjusted, but there *is* sufficient evidence to drive an alternate discourse of metal music and culture as protective factors for mental health and well-being. In an era of unprecedented spikes in mental health diagnoses across the lifespan, it is crucial that we widen our scope for understanding ways that people deploy coping tools that might be considered against the grain by normative standards. If heavy metal identities are serving their owners well, that should be the most compelling evidence of all.

Notes

1. For examples of newer research that rethinks metal as a positive coping tool, see: Paula Rowe and Bernard Guerin, 'Contextualizing the Mental Health of Metal Youth: A Community for Social Protection, Identity and Musical Empowerment', *Journal of Community Psychology* 46/4 (2018): 429–41 and Leah Sharman and Genevieve A. Dingle, 'Extreme Metal Music and Anger Processing', *Frontiers in Human Neuroscience* 9/272 (2015): 1–11. https://doi .org/10.3389/fnhum.2015.00272.
2. Paula Rowe, *Heavy Metal Youth Identities: Researching the Musical Empowerment of Youth Transitions and Psychosocial Wellbeing* (Emerald, 2018).
3. Ian Burkitt, 'Emotional Reflexivity: Feeling, Emotion and Imagination in Reflexive Dialogues', *Sociology* 46/3 (2012): 458–72.

4. The following is a good example of unsubstantiated stereotyping of metal fans in the 1990s and lack of critical engagement with social constructions of 'looking like a behaviour problem': 'Those who reported higher commitment to heavy metal dressed not unlike the stereotypical juvenile delinquent: They wore torn jeans, black t-shirts bearing the name of one of many popular heavy metal bands (*Metallica* was the most prevalent), black leather jackets, long hair, and one earring worn in the left ear (often a skull or another symbol associated with heavy metal music). It is possible that these students were singled out more often as behaviour problems because they looked like the type of student who would be a behaviour problem', in Jonathon Epstein, David Pratto and James Skipper, 'Teenagers, Behavioural Problems, and Preferences for Heavy Metal and Rap Music: A Case Study of a Southern Middle School', *Deviant Behaviour* 11/4 (1990): 381–94.

5. Attaining a sense of identity and belonging will be shaped by many different social factors and will intersect with multiple categories of gender, race, class and cultural norms that will be experienced very differently around the world. It is beyond the scope of this chapter to address global diversity and identity formations.

6. I say 'usually' visible to each other based on long-standing metal styles. That said, diversity within metal continues to grow rapidly and not all subgenres have defining visible aesthetics, nor do all metalheads take up the aesthetic of their preferred genre even if it does have a recognisable style.

7. In the main this is true; however, some metal subgenres are less accepting of others. For example, black metallers have a reputation for rejecting more mainstream metal artists and fans.

8. This is widely accepted in most genres, and more recent findings have found the same to be true of metal – despite long-held beliefs that metal music might agitate people and make them violent, the opposite seems to be true. There is good evidence of metal music having calming and therapeutic benefits. See Rowe, *Heavy Metal Youth Identities*, pp. 31–48.

9. Deena Weinstein, *Heavy Metal: The Music and its Culture* (Da Capo Press, 2000), pp. 249–50.

10. *Ibid.*, p. 251.

11. *Devil Worship: Exposing Satan's Underground*, talk-show documentary (1988); *The Geraldo Rivera Show* aired October 1988, National Broadcasting Company, USA.

12. Ross Haenfler, Brett Johnson and Ellis Jones, 'Lifestyle Movements: Exploring the Intersection of Lifestyle and Social Movements', *Social Movement Studies* 11/1 (2012): 1–20.

13. Here I refer to ageing, internal conversations and wellbeing, rather than external resources and care provisions for ageing metal fans that Kahn-Harris has previously raised in Keith Kahn-Harris, 'Care and the Limitations of Metal

Community', in Nelson Varas-Diaz and Niall Scott (eds.), *Heavy Metal Music and the Communal Experience* (Lexington Press, 2016), pp. 171–84.

14. Steven M. Southwick, Brett T. Litz, Dennnis Charney and Matthew J. Friedman (eds.), *Resilience and Mental Health: Challenges across the Lifespan* (Cambridge University Press, 2011).

15. Andy R. Brown, 'Heavy Genealogy: Mapping the Currents, Contraflows, and Conflicts of the Emergent Field of Metal Studies, 1978–2010', *Journal for Cultural Research* 15/3 (2011): 213–42.

16. For examples of studies investigating musical preferences and educational attainment (including metal fans) see Keith Roe, 'Different Destinies, Different Melodies: School Achievement, Anticipated Status and Adolescents' Tastes in Music', *European Journal of Communication* 7/3 (1992): 335–58 and Julian Tanner, Mark Asbridge and Scott Wortley, 'Our Favourite Melodies: Musical Consumption and Teenage Lifestyles', *The British Journal of Sociology* 59/1 (2008): 117–44.

17. In lieu of empirical evidence, the social constructions of metal youth have largely been a production of conservative commentary, media stereotypes and/or lampooning of metal in popular culture, as per Rowe, *Heavy Metal Youth Identities*, pp. 8–12.

18. Stuart M. Cadwallader, *The Darker Side of Bright Students: Gifted and Talented Heavy Metal Fans* (National Academy of Gifted and Talented Youth, 2007).

  Metal in Women

Music, Empowerment, Misogyny

ROSEMARY LUCY HILL

'Metal is really inclusive' – Let's stop right there, my friend, and think: who are the most famous or influential metal bands you can think of? Chances are you have a list of men there. So, let's reflect on the fact that the canon of metal is mostly white men from the UK and USA, with a few coming from Northern Europe and Australia. Heavy metal is a male-dominated genre, and it has long been reported to have issues with women, femininity and misogyny. What happens if we look at heavy metal and centre women in that history? Let us start by asserting that 'woman' is a socially constructed category rather than a stable or biologically rooted certainty.[1] That category, 'woman', is expansive and includes heterogeneous experiences of living in a gendered, classed and raced world. Let us, then, put women at the heart of our story about heavy metal and see what new aspects of the music and culture it reveals. Let us discover what new connections across musical and cultural contexts can be made. And let us glimpse the future for metal.

Heavy Metal Origins

Who was the first heavy metal band? Jinx Dawson (USA) could make the claim that her band, Coven, were the first to blend the occult with hard rock.[2] Their first album, *Witchcraft Destroys Minds and Reaps Souls* (1969), features a Satanic Mass and other devilish themes. Musically, it is similar to Jefferson Airplane, and Black Sabbath were compared to Coven on the release of *Black Sabbath* (1970).[3] Dawson also arguably invented the devil horns sign now synonymous with metal.[4] The 1960s was a difficult time for women making rock music, with numerous barriers of sexism, including sexual assault, hindering women's achievements.[5] A minority of women were able to break through into the mainstream, but Coven's opportunities for success were further impeded by anti-Satan sentiment in the USA.

Coven are rarely given their place in the canon of metal,[6] an omission that contributes to the impression of metal (and rock) as a masculine genre.

That there were few women musicians who were successful in contributing to the early development of heavy metal does not mean that women were not present and important. In her fan autobiography, Pamela Des Barres[7] describes the late 1960s West Coast US rock and early metal scene as an environment in which women were ever-present. They supported men in financial, practical, domestic and sexual aspects of their lives, which enabled those men to concentrate on making music. She also argued that women acted as muses, inspiring great love songs. Furthermore, they *were* involved in the production of the music, supporting, cheerleading, giving feedback: Des Barres writes of sitting with Jimmy Page and Robert Plant of Led Zeppelin as they wrote songs. These roles are rarely regarded as being important in the history of metal, but in enabling great music to be made, they are as essential as the role of the producer.

However, this already raises questions about what 'counts' as metal and who is able to define the boundaries of the genre. As Laina Dawes[8] argues, the origins of metal are in rock and the blues and, therefore, to consider the origins of metal means we need to ask who is important in blues rock? The received history of rock and metal is not only typically a male history, but also a *white* history that omits to take the contribution of Black women into account. For example, Big Mama Thornton's hit song 'Hound Dog' (1952) pioneered the vocal style that was later similarly employed by Elvis Presley on his cover of the song. But Presley was white, and his song marketed to white audiences, so his version became *the* version, preventing Thornton from capitalising on *her* success, from which she never saw the profits. Sister Rosetta Tharpe's guitar technique and distortion were influential on British musicians such as Led Zeppelin's Jimmy Page and John Paul Jones;[9] Odetta, Billie Holiday and Aretha Franklin, via Janis Joplin, influenced Robert Plant. Indeed, early reviews of Plant referred to him as 'the male Janis Joplin', raising the question of whether it is not Plant who is the authoritative look and sound of a (1970s) heavy metal vocalist, but Janis.[10]

These Black blues women can be considered as important to the evolution of metal as artists such as Chuck Berry, Muddy Waters and Screamin' Jay Hawkins. We should be mindful that histories of popular music have typically written out the contributions and influence of all but a few women and people of colour.[11] Such histories are never apolitical. They serve the ends of those who would seek to reinforce the white male hegemony of rock and metal, part of a tradition which saw Led Zeppelin famously attribute authorship of songs written by Anne Bredon, Howlin' Wolf, Jake Holmes and Willie Dixon to themselves.

Exclusion of Women from Music-Making

Despite the inclusion of a minority of women (for example, Maggie Bell of Stone the Crows), early heavy metal was regarded as a worryingly misogynistic genre, an extension of rock music. It came in for criticism from various feminist groups for articulating sexist and dangerous views about women. In the UK and USA, feminists set up their own alternatives to sexist rock in the form of Women's Liberation rock bands. These bands reclaimed rock music and took innovative approaches to their sounds, including, for example, using horn sections. Their lyrics were about things that were happening to them as women, such as too much bad sex with men. These innovative women's scenes did not really break into the mainstream or have much impact on metal; metal remained resolutely male-dominated and concerned with male issues as the New Wave of British Heavy Metal (NWOBHM) exploded in the late 1970s. But there was (and still is) Girlschool, the all-women NWOBHM band, who toured with Motörhead and released a joint single under the moniker 'Headgirl' (1980). However, for women, being in a rock band in the 1970s and 1980s was very challenging for a number of reasons.

Mavis Bayton's[12] interviews with rock musicians, including members of Girlschool, identified issues such as a lack of disposable income to purchase instruments, equipment or lessons, or difficulties accessing rehearsal spaces and transport. A lack of personal space and time were also barriers caused by expectations of increased domestic workload for young women. Furthermore, women's time and leisure activities were regulated by family members, boyfriends and husbands, problems compounded for the budding female metal musician due to sexist ideas about what kinds of music and instruments are suitable for women, and proscriptions on making *loud noises*. Not to mention the fact that men often did not want to play with women, that they did not value women's contributions, that they hogged equipment and networked with other men to the exclusion of women. This suggests the significant value of finding other women to play with, a situation that enabled Girlschool to sidestep some of the issues that arose in mixed-gender groups. On top of all that, the music industry was (and remains) full of gatekeepers with sexist attitudes about what sells, attitudes that push women down particular musical routes, into the role of singer rather than instrumentalist, or which leave them out in the cold altogether. As Girlschool were told more recently when being turned down for a festival slot, 'Oh no, we've already got our female band'.[13] For women of colour, these constraints on music-making are compounded by racist sexual objectification and the idea that Black women should not play rock music.[14]

The Myth of Equality

Some argue that things have improved for women in rock music[15] and that metal is somehow magically immune to the sexism present throughout most societies.[16] The presence of artists such as Tatiana Shmailyuk of Jinjer or Rob Halford of Judas Priest is often rolled out as an argument in favour of metal's equality and inclusivity. But the presence of exceptions does not prove the rule: as Pauwke Berkers and Julian Schaap's[17] analysis of the *Encyclopædia Metallum* shows, since the late 1970s, 97 per cent of metal musicians have been men, a figure which blows the 'myth of equality'[18] in metal out of the water. The 'myth of equality' is the persuasive idea that metal is a culture that sits outside of general societal problems such as sexism, racism, classism, ablism: all that matters is the music. If you like heavy metal, you are *in*, regardless of your gender, sexuality, race etc. (ignoring obvious exceptions such as National Socialist Black Metal here). Such a myth serves to reassure metalheads that they are already on the right team and that they do not have to do anything to challenge misogyny, racism, homophobia etc. However, this kind of magical thinking hinders feminist and anti-racist work and obstructs attempts to improve the conditions for making and enjoying metal. Speaking out means risking one's place with the 'in crowd' of metal.[19]

Nevertheless, although there may be only a minority of women making metal, they do exist. And we might want to ask if they are represented adequately in the *Encyclopædia Metallum*: maybe there are more than the 3 per cent identified by Berkers and Schaap? We should ask questions of *Encyclopædia Metallum*'s criteria for inclusion when a very successful mainstream all-male metal band like Avenged Sevenfold are excluded. What are we to make of this exclusion? One answer to this may lie in the perception of the fans of metal, and in particular those bands or subgenres that have a predominantly female audience. Girls and women who love rock music are typically not taken seriously, perceived as girlfriends of male metal fans, only interested in sexual relationships with musicians rather than the music – the 'myth of the groupie'.[20] They are considered to be unable to move beyond the dailiness of their lives in order to understand the transcendent qualities of the music.[21] These myths and discourses interact with broader societal sexism that besmirches the culture of girls and women. The result is that not only are the girls and women regarded as second-class fans, but the music they love is disparaged and excluded from the definition of 'metal'.[22] Thus, what 'counts' as metal is not just an entertaining conversation, but a serious political debate about gender and race, with serious implications.[23]

Gendering Genre

As a genre, heavy metal has long been theorised as 'masculine' or even hypermasculine, as it has built on the existing gendering of rock music. Writing in 1978, Simon Frith and Angela McRobbie's feminist-informed article 'Rock and Sexuality' set the tone for discussions about heavy metal and hard rock. They examine what they call 'cock rock', as exemplified by Robert Plant, Phil Lynott, Mick Jagger, Roger Daltrey:

Cock rock performers are aggressive, dominating, and boastful, and they constantly seek to remind the audience of their prowess, their control. Their stance is obvious in live shows; male bodies on display, plunging shirts and tight trousers, a visual emphasis on chest hair and genitals.[24]

This characterisation continued in the 1980s when glam metal became a staple of MTV (although thrash and death metal bands sought to distance themselves from such imagery). The emphasis on lustful male heterosexuality was one of the reasons that heavy metal was the focus of a moral panic in the 1980s, led by the Parents Music Resource Center (PMRC). The PMRC was founded by influential women whose husbands were US politicians. They were concerned that metal (and some other popular music) was a bad influence on children and that it encouraged them to take part in sexual behaviour, drinking, drug-taking, Satanism and violence, including sexual violence. W.A.S.P.'s 'Animal (F**k Like A Beast)' (1984) and AC/DC's 'Let Me Put My Love Into You' (1980) were two of the 'Filthy Fifteen' songs particularly identified for censure. The PMRC sought to put labels on records to warn parents of the content of the lyrics and were successfully granted a Senate hearing in 1985. The PMRC have been widely traduced by the metal media, fans and even pro-metal academics,[25] to the point that the idea that the PMRC were entirely wrong and completely humourless has become an unquestioned orthodoxy. But in many ways the PMRC made a good point about the sexism and sexual violence in heavy metal.[26] The moral panic funded a number of psychological studies to show the impact of metal, which concluded that listening to it did not encourage children to commit crimes.[27] But studies do not stretch to understanding the impact on girls and women listening to the music, how the sexual violence and oppressive relationships in a number of the songs may make them feel, nor how such themes may normalise sexual violence.[28]

Queering Metal

Whilst these are important considerations, heavy metal is a broad church, and in its many subgenres can be found songs that do not glamourise sexual violence. Indeed mainstream rock and metal songs tend to be much less likely to depict 'degrading sex' than rap,[29] although the moral panic around rap has an additional nasty layer of racism.[30] Robert Walser argued that heavy metal tried to create a fantasy world where women were literally written out, or 'exscripted'.[31] This form of 'exscription', if it exists, is a different kind of musical sexism, but the contradiction between Walser's appraisal of heavy metal and that of the PMRC reveals that something more complex is going on with metal.

Sheila Whiteley[32] and Susan Fast[33] argue that heavy metal and rock are more complex in terms of their gender significations than Simon Frith and Angela McRobbie claim. Signifiers of long hair, high voices and makeup (especially in glam metal) challenge the idea that 'cock rock' is all about masculine performance. Amber Clifford-Napoleone[34] goes further, arguing that whilst previous work on metal has understood it as masculine and heterosexist, it is better understood as a many-layered scene in which different marginalised identities – including that of 'metal' – can be layered together. Within these layers, there is a space in which queerness exists through BDSM, leather and the style-setting fashions of Rob Halford, Susie Quatro and Joan Jett.

In a further upset of the gender binary, Arch Enemy's first female singer Angela Gossow sprang into the metal limelight in 2001 and shocked many metalheads by *being able to growl*. The growl is created by the vibration of the false folds above the larynx. It is low-pitched with a rough timbre. The shock was that a woman was physically capable of performing the growl, which was perceived to be too low for women's biology. But, since there is no sex difference in the way the false folds work, there is no difference in men's and women's ability to growl.

Instead, many gender conventions align to give growling the cultural ascription of 'masculine': low pitch, rough timbre, association with aggression (gendered masculine), and that men's use of the style is more well-known than women's.[35] Women have been growling in metal since the early 1990s, yet their vocals are still met with surprise and expressions of being 'very good for a chick', thus showing that in spite of positive evaluations by metal fans, the style itself is deeply gendered.[36]

Women making metal are more likely to be making symphonic or 'goth' metal than other subgenres.[37] In this subgenre, they are typically singers using an operatic style. We can celebrate the inclusion of more women making metal, but we should question how the over-representation in this genre, as opposed to other genres, relies on restrictive and racist ideals of white femininity. The 'female-fronted' or *metal à chanteuse* genre name, which is often applied to symphonic metal, is often accompanied by pejorative media coverage, and it treats the genre as homogenous.[38] The 'marking' of some bands by the gender of its members indicates that women making metal are seen as outsiders[39] – after all, Iron Maiden are never referred to as 'male-fronted metal' or as an all-male band.

Empowerment for Women

Women metalheads *do* face sexism within the genre, for example, requirements that they 'prove' their fandom to men;[40] exclusion by male fans in group settings;[41] male-dominated concert spaces character-ised by groping and sexual harassment from men; exclusion from mosh pits and stage diving. Yet, for all that, metal *can* provide an 'escape' from everyday oppressions outside metal[42] as well as alternative routes to self-presentation that do not rely on burdensome strictures of femininity.[43] And although metal is very often gendered as masculine, this is a problematic construction: the idea of gender itself is a social construc-tion, and we should therefore be wary of reading gender onto music.[44] Taking a Butlerian approach, metal is not essentially masculine, but can rather be read more like drag in which masculinity is performed[45] without there being an original: the music itself is the reiteration or copy of previous performances of gendered music.[46] Indeed, metal supplies multitudinous pleasures for women metal fans: aural pleasures of enjoying the riffs and beats; visual pleasures of enjoying the spectacle of metal; erotic and romantic pleasures in watching musicians; enjoying the feel of the music in the body;[47] embodied experiences of gender transgression in the mosh pit;[48] identities which do not rely on physical attractiveness.[49]

Metal as a Vehicle for Feminist Fury

Indeed, during the 2010s and 2020s, a space within metal culture has arisen for feminist musicians to scream and growl their discontents at patriarchy. Anger is a staple emotion of heavy metal, and as women have increasingly become more exasperated with sexism, misogyny and male violence, metal's toolkit to convey fury looks increasingly attractive.[50] Not veering too far from metal's conventions, some bands such as Castrator sing violent revenge fantasies against rapist men through 'vigilante feminism'.[51] Such bands draw inspiration from riot grrrl and place their rage centre stage. For others, metal is seen as the perfect vehicle for exploring experiences of violence, such as the victim/survivor's experience of gendered-based violence in which the abused body of earlier metal portrayals screams back. Jasmine Shadrack[52] argues that black metal is the perfect vehicle for purging the trauma of domestic abuse, as the genre is a way to look at the darkness inside ourselves. Similarly, Kristin Hayter, aka noise/metal musician Lingua Ignota, argues that noise/metal is a good genre for representing the experience of trauma suffered in domestic abuse.[53] There is a white privilege in being able to employ anger, however, because stereotypes of Black women as inherently angry make rage an unwieldy weapon for them. Nevertheless, Black women are making angry metal[54] and drawing on African heritage in the same ways that Nordic black metal might draw on Viking heritage and archaeological instruments. For example, Vodun (UK) use feminist lyrical themes related to Vodun religion and Afrobeats to create heavy Afro doom metal.

This exciting new movement, however, does not yet have the inter-band organisation of riot grrrl, the feminist punk movement that begun in Olympia, USA, in the early 1990s. Riot grrrl was successful because of the centrality of feminist solidarity and practical support systems.[55] Feminist metal has a little way to go before becoming a movement that extends beyond Western countries, although feminist solidarity in metal has the potential to raise consciousnesses and create empathy for survivors of gender-based violence.[56] That said, the internet and social media are facilitating new ways of being involved in metal, enabling women who previously lacked access to musical networks to get feedback on their music[57] and to come together to write and perform in women-only groups. The Chaos Rising collective is one such example, drawing in musicians from Europe, Iran and South America.

Chaos Rising release a song a month, written and performed by any members of the collective, rather than being an unchanging unit of band members. The members highlight their different kinds of experiences and the need to be respectful of these differences, rather than locating their commonality in essential characteristics.[58] The collective is not an overtly feminist collective, but a space where women can come together to make music without some of the tensions and discriminations that they sometimes experience in working with men.

Conclusion

Metal is a genre that is often *thought* to be inclusive, but it exists in a sexist world, and so sexism is written into the genre. In many ways, the sexisms within metal are the same as in other genres (for example, the barriers to music-making), but the extreme masculinity of some subgenres presents additional challenges (for example, viciously misogynistic lyrics). Such misogyny has profound effects on women's participation. And yet metal provides much for its female fans and musicians to get excited about. The new trends towards collectivity and feminist themes, alongside greater recognition for women like Jinx Dawson, provide an opportunity for metal culture to shift towards a more feminist consciousness, to work towards really being inclusive.

Notes

1. Judith Butler, *Gender Trouble: Feminism and the Subversion of Identity* (Routledge, 1990).
2. Addison Herron-Wheeler, *Wicked Women: Women in Metal from the 1960s to Now* (Self-published, 2014).
3. Pauwke Berkers and Julian Schaap, *Gender Inequality in Metal Music Production* (Emerald, 2018).
4. Leonie Cooper, 'The Unsung: Jinx Dawson Invented Rock's Devil Horns – But a Man Took All the Credit', *The Forty-Five* (2021). https://thefortyfive.com/opinion/jinx-dawson-coven/?amp (accessed 22 February 2021).
5. Sini Timonen, 'Sexual Misconduct in the Music Industry: Then and Now', *Crosstown Traffic: Popular Music Theory and Practice* (2018). www.youtube.com/watch?v=8Rr7NLTbuQA (accessed 22 February 2021).
6. Berkers and Schaap, *Gender Inequality*.
7. Pamela Des Barres, *I'm with the Band: Confessions of a Groupie* (Helter Skelter, 2005).

8. Laina Dawes, *What Are You Doing Here? A Black Woman's Life and Liberation in Heavy Metal* (Bazillion Points, 2012).

9. Chris Long, 'Muddy Waters and Sister Rosetta Tharpe's "Mind-Blowing" Station Show', *BBC News* (2014). www.bbc.co.uk/news/uk-england-manchester-27256401 (accessed 7 May 2021).

10. Tracy McMullen, '"Bring it on Home": Robert Plant, Janis Joplin, and the Myth of Origin', *Journal of Popular Music Studies* 26/2–3 (2014): 368–96.

11. Lucy O'Brien, *She Bop II: The Definitive History of Women in Rock, Pop and Soul* (Continuum, 2002).

12. Mavis Bayton, *Frock Rock: Women Performing Popular Music* (Oxford University Press, 1998).

13. Berkers and Schaap, *Gender Inequality.*

14. Dawes, *What Are You Doing Here?*

15. Mary Celeste Kearney, *Gender and Rock* (Oxford University Press, 2017).

16. Eleanor Goodman, 'Does Metal Have a Sexism Problem?', *Metal Hammer* (2020). www.loudersound.com/features/does-metal-have-a-sexism-problem (accessed 6 March 2020).

17. Berkers and Schaap, *Gender Inequality.*

18. Rosemary Lucy Hill, *Gender, Metal and the Media: Women Fans and the Gendered Experience of Music* (Palgrave Macmillan, 2016).

19. Sonia Vasan, 'Gender and Power in the Death Metal Scene: A Social Exchange Perspective', in Andy R. Brown Karl Spracklen, Keith Kahn-Harris and Niall Scott (eds.), *Global Metal Music and Culture: Current Directions in Metal Studies* (Routledge, 2016), pp. 261–76.

20. Hill, *Gender.*

21. Holly Kruse, 'Abandoning the Absolute: Transcendence and Gender in Popular Music Discourse', in Steve Jones (ed.), *Pop Music and the Press* (Temple University Press, 2002), pp. 134–55.

22. Rosemary Lucy Hill, 'Is Emo Metal? Gendered Boundaries and New Horizons in the Metal Community', *Journal for Cultural Research* 15/3 (2011): 297–313.

23. Ben Hutcherson and Ross Haenfler, 'Musical Genre as a Gendered Process: Authenticity in Extreme Metal', in Norman Denzin (ed.), *Studies in Symbolic Interaction* (Emerald, 2010), pp. 101–21; Catherine Hoad, 'Whiteness with(out) Borders: Translocal Narratives of Whiteness in Heavy Metal Scenes in Norway, South Africa and Australia', *Medianz* 15/1 (2015): 17–34.

24. Simon Frith and Angela McRobbie, 'Rock and Sexuality', in Simon Frith and Andrew Goodwin (eds.), *On Record: Rock, Pop, and the Written Word* (Routledge, 1990 [1978]), pp. 371–89.

25. See books by Weinstein and Purcell for defences of the genre: Deena Weinstein, *Heavy Metal: The Music and its Culture* (Da Capo Press, 2000); Natalie J. Purcell, *Death Metal Music: The Passion and Politics of a Subculture* (McFarland, 2003).

26. Rosemary Lucy Hill and Heather Savigny, 'Sexual Violence and Free Speech in Popular Music', *Popular Music* 38/2 (2019): 237–51.

27. American Academy of Pediatrics Committee on Communications, 'Impact of Music Lyrics and Music Videos on Children and Youth', *Pediatrics* 98/6 (1996): 1219–21.

28. Rosemary Lucy Hill, Daisy Richards and Heather Savigny, 'Normalising Sexualised Violence in Popular Culture: Eroding, Erasing and Controlling Women in Rock Music', *Feminist Media Studies* (2021): 1–18. https://doi.org /10.1080/14680777.2021.1902368.

29. Brian A. Primack Melanie A. Gold, Eleanor B. Schwarz and Madeline A. Dalton, 'Degrading and Non-Degrading Sex in Popular Music: A Content Analysis', *Public Health Reports* 123/5 (2008): 593–600.

30. Kimberle Crenshaw, 'Beyond Racism and Misogyny: Black Feminism and 2 Live Crew', *Boston Review* (1991). https://bostonreview.net/race-gender-sexuality/kimberle-w-crenshaw-beyond-racism-and-misogyny (accessed 5 May 2021).

31. Robert Walser, *Running with the Devil: Power, Gender, and Madness in Heavy Metal Music* (University Press of New England, 1993), p. 110.

32. Sheila Whiteley, *Women and Popular Music: Sexuality, Identity, and Subjectivity* (Routledge, 2000).

33. Susan Fast, 'Rethinking Issues of Gender and Sexuality in Led Zeppelin: A Woman's View of Pleasure and Power in Hard Rock', *American Music* 17/3 (1999): 245–99.

34. Amber Clifford-Napoleone, *Queerness in Heavy Metal Music: Metal Bent* (Routledge, 2015).

35. Florian Heesch, '"Voice of Anarchy": Gender Aspects of Aggressive Metal Vocals: The Example of Angela Gossow (Arch Enemy)', *Criminocorpus: Rock et violences en Europe/Metal et violence* (2019). https://journals .openedition.org/criminocorpus/5726 (accessed 5 May 2021).

36. Schaap and Berkers, 'Grunting Alone?'. Online Gender Inequality in Extreme Metal Music', *IASPM Journal*, 4/1: 101–16.

37. Berkers and Schaap, *Gender Inequality*.

38. Charlene Bernard. '"Female Fronted Metal?" "Women" and "Symphonic Metal" in the French Metal Press of the 2010s', paper presented at the *4th International Society for Metal Music Studies Biennial Research Conference* (ISMMS, 2019).

39. Berkers and Schaap, *Gender Inequality*.

40. Susanna Nordström and Marcus Herz, '"It's a Matter of Eating or Being Eaten": Gender Positioning and Difference Making in the Heavy Metal Subculture', *European Journal of Cultural Studies* 16/4 (2013): 453–67.

41. Keith Kahn-Harris, *Extreme Metal: Music and Culture on the Edge* (Berg, 2007).

42. Leigh Krenske and Jim McKay, '"Hard and Heavy": Gender and Power in a Heavy Metal Music Subculture', *Gender, Place & Culture* 7/3 (2000): 287–304.

43. Jamie Patterson, '"Getting My Soul Back": Empowerment Narratives and Identities among Women in Extreme Metal in North Carolina', in Andy R. Brown, Karl Spracklen, Keith Kahn-Harris and Niall Scott (eds.), *Metal Studies: The Music, the Culture, the Fans, the Future* (Routledge, 2016), pp. 245–60.

44. Hill, *Gender.*

45. Clifford-Napoleone, *Queerness.*

46. Jasmine Shadrack, *Black Metal, Trauma, Subjectivity and Sound: Screaming the Abyss* (Emerald, 2020).

47. Hill, *Gender.*

48. Gabrielle Riches, 'Re-Conceptualizing Women's Marginalization in Heavy Metal: A Feminist Post-Structuralist Perspective', *Metal Music Studies* 1/2 (2015): 263–70.

49. Patterson, 'Getting My Soul Back'.

50. Melissa Arkley, 'Feminist Anger in Extreme Metal Music', paper presented at *Feminism and Metal: An Academic Workshop* (online, 2021).

51. Joan Jocson-Singh, 'Vigilante Feminism as a Form of Musical Protest in Extreme Metal Music', *Metal Music Studies* 5/2 (2019): 263–73.

52. Shadrack, *Black Metal.*

53. J. Bennet, 'On Dismantling Systems and processing Trauma through Art', *The Creative Independent* (2019). https://thecreativeindependent.com/people/ musician-lingua-ignota-on-dismantling-systems-and-processing-trauma- through-her-art (accessed 8 August 2021).

54. Dawes, *What Are You Doing Here?*

55. Marion Leonard, *Gender in the Music Industry: Rock, Discourse and Girl Power* (Ashgate, 2007).

56. Jesús Antonio Córdoba and Karen Ortiz Cuchivague, 'Female Participation in Colombian Metal: An Initial Approach', *Metal Music Studies* 7/1 (2021): 159–70.

57. Schaap and Berkers, 'Grunting Alone?'.

58. Keith Kahn-Harris, 'The Greatness Beyond: How Chaos Rising Are Breaking Metal's Boundaries', *The Quietus* (2021). https://thequietus.com/articles/ 30299-chaos-rising (accessed 25 September 2021).

12

Refuse/Resist

What Does It Mean for Metal to Be Transgressive in the Twenty-First Century?

CATHERINE HOAD

There is a wonderful Calvin & Hobbes comic published in March of 1992, where Calvin begs his mother to buy him a heavy metal album. She refuses accordingly: 'The fact these bands haven't killed themselves in ritual self-sacrifice shows they're just in it for the money like everyone else. It's all for effect'. There is disillusion writ across Calvin's features – 'Mainstream commercial nihilism can't be trusted?!'[1]

Bill Waterson's comic dismissal of metal's lack of sincerity in its provocation was not, even in 1992, a particularly new jibe. Theodor W. Adorno's scathing critiques[2] of the popular music industry mourned the revolutionary possibilities and dulling of art as it is produced within capitalist contexts. Adorno had further extended this argument by the 1960s, where he was dismissive of the notion of a popular music 'counterculture': for Adorno, popular 'protest music' was 'doomed from the start', given the relationship of popular music to the same culture industry that manufactured and disseminated advertising and propaganda. The apparent inability of music to both entertain and transgress represents a longer, and much-debated, tension for performers, audiences and researchers of popular music alike. This chapter discusses what this particular tension represents for heavy metal music, performers and fans. Metal is a genre that has often spurned the 'popular', yet is nonetheless entrenched within, and has often benefitted from, the commercial operations of the contemporary music industry. Waterson's comic is a helpful starting point for unpacking what it means to be rebellious in a genre that has long seen itself as 'outsider' music, yet whose transgressions are limited by both the realities of the commercial music market and the wider political contexts that it circulates through.

This chapter considers what it means for heavy metal and its fans to identify as 'outsider' music in the 2020s. Resistance and rebellion[3] have long been central to metal's identity and fandom, where metal has long traded on its reputation as 'outsider' music, a genre populated by proud pariahs that exist on the edge of acceptability.[4] However, the true potential of such transgression has been troubled by metal's commercial success, its diversification across different geographic locales and generational shifts amongst fans, where 'resistance' takes on different meanings and forms. Through considering how some of metal music's most well-known scholarship has framed this 'transgression', this chapter explores how metal's politics of rebellion and resistance have played out in fragmented ways as metal fandoms worldwide negotiate shifting ideologies, contexts and markets, calling into focus questions of the pop music spectacle and commodified dissent. Such a discussion points to a central tension for metal's self-image: where the genre has seen itself as a site of transgression and liberation, I then want to probe how metal communities consolidate the prizing of transgression with the realities that metal texts, scenes and practices have often replicated many of the same older, conservative orthodoxies that circulate in wider socio-political contexts.[5] This chapter thus leads with a central provocation: is it still possible for metal to be transgressive in the twenty-first century? And, to that end, has it ever really been?

This idea of transgression has been central to the ways in which metal imagines its own politics and discourses. However, as Chris Jenks notes, transgressions are 'manifestly situation-specific and vary considerably across social space and through time'.[6] In starting from a position that acknowledges transgressions are never stable, and are always context-dependent, this chapter begins with an overview of how 'transgression' has been framed in scholarly and popular accounts of heavy metal, before proposing three fragmented ideological positions that metal has found itself straddling as it exists in the 2020s: conservativism, progressivism and apolitical individualistic misanthropy.[7] These are not exhaustive of metal's ideological outlets for transgression, but rather I think these are tangibly indicative of tensions and extremities that emerge within and between metallic discourses of identity, community and resistance. Mapping these positions is useful to think through how metal confronts, enables or ignores the encroachment of wider socio-cultural phenomena into its scenic structures. The chapter concludes by considering metal's position within the commercial operations of the contemporary music industry, and how the genre increasingly redresses its own communities and histories, and remaps the politics of metal itself.

Horrible Histories: Transgression as Metallic Capital

In talking about 'transgression', I draw on Chris Jenks' work, where he states that 'to transgress is to go beyond the bounds or limits set by a commandment or law or convention, it is to violate or infringe'.[8] For Jenks, transgression is that conduct which breaks rules or exceeds boundaries. However, he also reminds us that analysing transgression also invites analysis of its situatedness and 'the character of the cultures ... and contexts that provide for the appreciation or receptability of such behaviour'.[9] Transgression was a core theme of the ways in which metal's cultures and contexts were discussed in the earlier years of subcultural studies[10]: Paul Willis linked hard rock music to the countercultural 'motorcycle boys'; Dick Hebdige defined metal as 'a curious blend of hippy aesthetics and football terrace machismo'; Will Straw argued that metal had been positioned within a 'genealogy of bad-boy currents' in rock history. Such gendering of metal's ostensible 'rebelliousness' carried on through the moral panics that surrounded heavy metal in the mid-1980s and early 1990s[11]: Tipper Gore argued that heavy metal was a vehicle for countercultural rebellion that urged adolescent boys to go to 'new extremes'; Carl Raschke argued that 'the yowling and bellowing of the metal groups' encouraged young men to adopt 'a lifestyle of swagger, brutality, theft and sexual excess'.

This sense of metal existing on the 'edge' of, or as a response to, the cultural mainstream has informed much of the genre's own self-image and scholarship.[12] Metal and its fans are positioned on the fringes of acceptability, the very 'edge of music'; Weinstein then characterises metal fans as 'proud pariahs', who relish in their 'outsider' status. Nonetheless, she argues that this 'outsiderness' was also underscored by an absence of, and often antipathy towards, women, LGBT+ communities and people of colour. It is then vital to consider how metal's response to the 'mainstream' might also function as a response to what was seen as the ostensible decentring of certain identities from the 1960s onwards. Much of metal's generic cohesion, Robert Walser argued in 1993, has been dependent upon the 'desire of young white male performers and fans to hear and believe in certain stories about the nature of masculinity',[13] where 'true' masculinity was taken to be under threat, and thus aggressively asserted within the 'rebellious' spaces offered by metal.

Metal, Masculinities and the Mainstream

Any discussion of metal's 'rebellion' should then start with a consideration of how such narratives have protected certain boundaries, just as often as they seek to transgress others. Weinstein goes so far as to say that heavy metal subculture represents a 'preservationist and conservative tendency', where white, working-class male youth found an 'ideological home in a nostalgic utopia'[14] in response to their apparent 'de-centering' in the cultural zeitgeist from the 1960s onwards. Such an argument, however, assumes that metal's 'core' audience is and always has been white, straight and male, limiting an understanding of the diversity of metal fans, and furthermore, how different contexts produce different forms of transgression. Nevertheless, this is a useful starting point for considering the tensions that surround metal's claims to 'transgression'.

One of metal discourse's most time-honoured myths is that heavy metal music and culture is not only 'anti-mainstream', but furthermore, represents a space in which 'true' masculinity can be 'reclaimed'.[15] This narrative, which suggests masculinity is in crisis, or under attack, is a continuous theme across multiple decades. This perspective, Niall Scott notes, 'perpetuate[s] the view that masculinity for the metal fan and metal musician alike is both hegemonic and in a state of crisis'.[16] Metal, in this way, is understood as an assertive, masculinist response to the supposed disempowerment of masculinity, and particularly blue-collar disenchantment of white, working-class masculinity amidst deindustrialisation, which then becomes a key context for theorising heavy metal transgression.[17] For Weinstein, such aggressive masculinity is a defensive response to the ostensible 'weakening' of male hegemony: 'heavy metal music celebrates the very qualities that boys must sacrifice [freedom, individuality, power] in order to become adult members of society'.[18]

Much discussion of metal's transgression has hence been largely framed through the symbolic figures of alienated young white men navigating the intersecting crises of masculinity and deindustrialisation, albeit in the West throughout the latter decades of the twentieth century. Kyle Kusz argues that alternative rock, in which he situates metal, represented a '1990s popular music context in which we hear a number of songs by white male artists who express a desire for alterity and make claims of being disadvantaged and victimized'.[19] These politics of 'alienation' within metal have been subject to sophisticated critiques, not least because of what Karen Bettez Halnon argues is a heterogeneous audience for metal, which disrupts any notion of consistently articulated, and hence alienated, identities.[20] Nevertheless, metal's masculinist, 'anti-mainstream' critique remains a steady feature of scholarly work[21] on its transgressive potential, where metal is positioned as a response to an 'inauthentic', 'hyper-commercialised society'. Sanna Fridh takes this critique further in her discussion of black metal, arguing that metal operates as a response to 'consumerist society and how it emasculates men through the feminization of masculinity . . . [metal works as a tool for] men to free themselves of the metrosexual shackles and experience themselves as authentic in a world where everyone is supposed to be the same'.[22]

Fridh's invocation of an 'authenticity' that transgresses consumerist, capitalist society invites further consideration, not least because of an approach to gender, which assumes that 'authentic' masculinity unfolds in largely hegemonic, and heteronormative, ways. This notion of metallic 'authenticity' in response to a consumer mainstream nonetheless permeates discussions of its transgressive possibilities. The 'highly transgressive, for-the-music-only spirit of heavy metal culture', Halnon argues, 'has served as a boundary between itself and the dis-authenticating forces of commercialism'.[23] Metal's more spectacular forms of transgression (namely blood, gore, carnage and Satanism) are thus characterised by Halnon as a particular form of the 'carnivalesque' that she then brands 'heavy metal carnival':

Heavy metal carnival breaks through the noise of commercial culture by raising the transgression ante to the extreme and challenging nearly every conceivable social rule governing taste, authority, morality, propriety, the sacred, and, some might say, civility itself. For fans, the freaky, bizarre, outrageous, and otherwise extreme aspects of the performance are important indicators of a band's dedication to the music and rejection of the forces of commercialism (even sometimes amid commercial success).[24]

Halnon's caveat of the rejection of commercialism, amidst commercial success, is hence a core consideration for metal's transgressive potentialities. Nonetheless, while she argues against a 'reductive understanding' of heavy metal carnival as 'the commodification of dissent',[25] it remains important to consider how metal's shock politics may be read as a purely spectacular rebelliousness within a wider consumer context.

Metal's fascination with the spectacular and abject has been extensively documented elsewhere,[26] and certainly, this work offers sophisticated and valuable analyses of the politics and uses of bodily horror as an affective response to the 'inauthentic' nature of consumer capitalism. How political positions become entangled within and represented through such transgressions, however, is an ever-evolving and complex issue within metal. As such, where Halnon cautions against seeing heavy metal carnival as 'ultimately a conservative phenomenon that restores and rejuvenates the status quo',[27] it remains that many of metal's most obvious images of transgression have been seen as reinstatements of deeply ingrained forms of social power.[28] The 'horror' of Norwegian black metal, oft considered one of metal's most 'notorious' subgenres, is read by Laura Wiebe-Taylor as extending a tradition of cultural nationalism relying on the construction of a homogenised Nordic heritage;[29] metal more generally, as Scott Wilson has explored, has become a site for articulations of discontent 'in the face of the expansion of the EU and its borderlands'.[30] Such analyses immediately temper the idea that heavy metal is not political; what's more, as the remainder of this chapter discusses, they reveal how metal acts as a space for developing political critique. As metal's audiences, performers, cultures and contexts have evolved, so too have its transgressions, and its potential to disrupt, reinforce and reimagine the status quo.

Discursive Transgression, Fascism and Conservativism

Keith Kahn-Harris' notion of 'discursive transgression'[31] is an immediately valuable concept to consider the ways in which metal rebellion is asserted through political ideology. While Kahn-Harris notes that metal's 'transgression' also emerges sonically and bodily, such a concept emerges alongside other work[32] acknowledging the central role that political discourse plays in connoting 'transgression'. There are, Niall Scott argues, a diverse range of positions and outlooks under a political heading to be found in metal culture; for Harris Berger, metal texts and fantasies are thus attempts to deal with various socio-political anxieties in complex and coded ways. However, such fantasies can play out with violent and extremely problematic realisations: this context hence informs metal's relationship with what Kahn-Harris refers to as 'the pre-eminent transgressive symbol in the modern world' – Nazism.[33] Appropriation of Nazi and wider fascist symbolism has long been a feature of discussions of heavy metal scenes, and examples from an array of fairly mainstream metal bands such as KISS, Slayer and Motörhead are fairly well-trodden territory in the wider documentation of such imagery.[34]

Such instances are oft-located within what Kahn-Harris calls 'reflexive anti-reflexivity'[35] – i.e., playing with the symbolism in a performative manner, exploiting its shock value, without actively subscribing to the ideology.

To position appropriations of fascist symbolism as purely performative rebellion nonetheless undercuts the very real power structures that accompany such signs. Attempts to depoliticise fascist symbolism, for Kahn-Harris, masks a highly efficient protection of the workings of power, where appropriations enabled the (c)overt incorporation of fascist ideologies into the operations of scenes. Fascist scenes are often taken to be isolated from metal itself; Hochhauser argues that fascist metal is a product of the white supremacist industry more so than anything else.[36] Nonetheless, this approach can overlook the ways in which fascist rhetoric can circulate in more covert ways in metal – Spotify took down 37 white supremacist and neo-Nazi bands in 2017,[37] but left many acts not overtly marked as 'fascist' bands. Playing off a fascination with fascist symbolism as simply 'taboo' items can also mean ignoring that such signs can and have been translated into scenic texts and practices which openly embrace virulent kinds of racism, sexism and homophobia – forms of oppression that are entrenched by large-scale power-structures.

Responding to Power: Liberalism, Progressivism, Anti-fascism

Situating metal's engagement with fascism as purely a form of discursive rebellion is a complicated endeavour given the material consequences of fascist rhetoric, and the actual transgressive possibilities of such discourse. From this perspective, metal merely looks like 'a self-consciously shocking dramatization of deeply ingrained forms of power'.[38] Following this, it is necessary to consider the ways in which metal asserts a resistant position in response to institutionalised forms of oppression, particularly through declarations of progressivism, liberalism and anti-fascism. Such rhetoric invokes the 'anti-mainstream' narrative, which shapes much early work on metal: just as much as metal's mythology has focused on symbols of violence, horror and excess, it has also been concerned with resisting institutional oppression and control. In this way, metal's transgression is asserted as a resistance to dominant forms of power and authority, oft-realised in quite broad terms. Gojira, in articulating their environmentalist position, argue that '[i]t's a chaotic world, with an economy based on fraud, and politics based on corruption, but as ugly as the world is, we can change it'.[39] Positions such as this, Niall Scott claims, often emerge under the guise of metallic unity, of a unified 'we' who can use metal to protest the ugliness of the world.[40]

This notion of a 'metallic unity' is particularly pertinent in light of the response of the metal community to the Black Lives Matter movement, particularly as it gained momentum in 2020.[41] Many reactions from some of metal's better-known public figures, Laina Dawes notes, have been disappointing. Dawes points to the sharing of racist conspiracy memes on social media by high-profile artists and their partners. Such actions reveal how, as Dawes' earlier work has noted, metal scenes are 'regularly thought of as inclusive spaces and centred on a community spirit' but, in reality, fail to block out raced and gendered issues that exist in wider contexts.[42] It has, then, been encouraging to see large portions of the metal world react to the Black Lives Matter protests with a commitment to anti-racist action. A particularly high-profile example emerges in Black Sabbath selling shirts with their *Master of Reality* logo changed to read 'Black Lives Matter', with all profits supporting the movement. To a more cynical eye, these actions may be read as a superficial attempt by bands to attach themselves to an enormously influential social movement; such arguments can, however, overlook the material reality of the funds raised in service of anti-racist movements by metal communities. Moreover, such a clear stand by metal's much-mythologised originator, Black Sabbath, is a vital rejoinder to claims that metal and politics be 'strange bedfellows'.[43]

Such anti-racist stances are, of course, not new in metal: bands and scene members have long asserted anti-fascist, anti-colonialist, anti-racist, anti-homophobic and anti-misogynistic positions. There are myriad examples of this worldwide, from which I draw on only a few recent examples: the collective *Crushing Intolerance* has, across multiple releases, condemned bigotry and fascism; in Australia, Hazeen have used metal's love of horror to respond to and mock Islamophobia; Hawai'i's Kūka'ilimoku dedicated their music to the 'children of Hawai'i ... Death to all missionaries and rotten politicians'.[44] Metal's anti-fascist, anti-racist and anti-colonial politics have themselves unfolded in complex and multisited ways. There is, on one hand, the British folk/black metal band Dawn Ray'd, who see metal as an extenuation of folk's roots in revolutionary narratives of a unified working class. As they argue, to be both metal and anti-fascist go hand-in-hand.[45] Nonetheless, such anti-authority positions are subject to criticism in that they can be easily appropriated into metallic fascinations with cruelty and bodily brutality, and thus may be limited in their transgressive potentiality. In her work on the self-described 'emasculating death metal' band Castrator, Joan Jocson-Singh responds to such charges by arguing that vigilante feminism manifesting as bodily violence acts as a form of empowerment that enables women to coexist in a liminal space so often dominated by their male counterparts.[46] This tension nevertheless demonstrates some of the persistent issues with metal's attempts to take political stands – that often such positions potentially end up reinforcing the same forms of power they seek to destabilise and commodify dissent within the maintenance of the metallic status quo: *Metal Hammer*'s 'Metal Takes a Stand' issue,[47] which salutes 'the bands out there who have seen their music as an instrument of social and political change for the better', serves as a timely reminder of this tension. Of the twenty-five bands featured, only four featured women as members, and only four were from non-Western countries.

Apolitical Misanthropy

Such polarising ideological positions hence lead to the third potentiality for metallic transgression that I want to explore here: apolitical misanthropy. Within this position, metal rejects the notion of politics, and instead articulates frustration and disillusionment, which calls for the misanthropic destruction of all humanity. This misanthropy is often expressed in extreme ways – Niall Scott looks to black metal's obsession with self-loathing, misery and the void as examples of such 'subversive discourse'.[48] Within this third space, there emerges a conscious rejection of the 'political' itself, and instead a 'determined effort to set oneself apart from the world'.[49] Misanthropic discourses are therefore often accompanied by a self-conscious elitism and contempt for humanity. Wolves in the Throne Room declare, '[o]ur culture has failed, we are all failures. The world around us has failed to sustain our humanity, our spirituality'.[50] These apolitical positions are nevertheless filled with tensions: when metal asserts itself against politics, it often does so with the understanding that 'politics' refers to affairs that concern the government and the state. As such, what ostensibly emerges as a rejection of any kind of political stance – what Niall Scott has referred to as 'heavy metal's great refusal'[51] – may nonetheless amount to its reaffirmation.

Metal's wider desire to be seen as apolitical can often mean that problematic material is allowed to flourish under the guise of free speech, or what Berger has called 'radical tolerance'[52] – of permitting even the most offensive of statements so as not to be seen as taking a side or not to engage in censorship of the music. However, as Dawes argues, 'the things that the artists say *outside* of their music are the most problematic'.[53] For Dawes, this raises particular questions about the ways in which these 'insides' and 'outsides' of metal's transgressions can be navigated: 'Can you separate the musician's personal views from the music? . . . How do we react to offensive personal views of musicians [we] enjoy? Do we simply chalk everything up to free speech?'.[54] This question – of whether a musician's personal actions can be separated from their music – is an ongoing tension for music communities and scholars alike. Moreover, metal's desire to appear apolitical can often mean that the boundaries between 'freedom of expression' and purposeful hate messages become blurred; or that wider issues of bigotry go unaddressed in communities. This apolitical misanthropic position thus can and has been used to cloak problematic discourse in scenes, precisely by refusing to label it as such due to concerns that such overt politicisation will take away from the music.

Conclusion

Struggles over the role of the '(a)political' in metal point to the ways in which scenes, and their expressions of transgression, continue to be caught up in relations of domination and power. Metal both reinforces and ameliorates power in its production of transgression. As Kahn-Harris argues, much of metal's transgression might simply reinforce forms of oppression, which are produced by state apparatus. The transgressive logics of scenes, for Kahn-Harris, are limited in two key ways. The first is destruction; to fully experience misanthropic, antisocial nihilism, he argues, would be to kill oneself or to kill another. The second, he says, is when transgression involves a challenge to one's own self-interest.[55] The above examples of metal's commitment to confronting racism, sexism and fascism show the fruits to be born from such challenges to self-interest, yet also reveal the potential limits of such transgression. Metal's ability to be truly 'transgressive', in this way, has often been romanticised insofar as it remains comfortable for certain groups: to call out such comfort, as Laina Dawes' work has shown, often creates uncomfortable and unsafe environments for those who do so.

There is also, of course, the reality of commerciality and consumerism. Metal has long defined itself in opposition to mass culture and other forms of popular culture. However, at the same time, metal has been sold and expressed itself through the infrastructure of mass culture. The relationship between heavy metal and the mainstream has then 'never been stable'; as Benjamin Earl argues, 'this musical form finds itself constantly crossing back and forth from the subcultural to the commercial'.[56] Metal is a commodity: it has been able to distribute itself through music, fashion and lifestyle markets. As such, as scholars such as Karen Bettez Halnon have observed, to the more cynical audience, metal has never really been apolitical, subversive and culturally dangerous, but rather is simply a component within the 'dominant spectacle ... the culture industry's commodification of dissent, rebellion being an enormously profitable, mass-marketed product of the culture industry today'.[57] Nonetheless, such cynicism could also overlook the pluralism of values and political perspectives addressed in metal, how the genre itself has responded to its own position in the culture industries, and ultimately, the affective spectacle of resistance that metal invites for its communities. Metal has offered a vital space for subaltern resistance and the articulation of anti-hegemonic discourses the world over. Perhaps a more productive future lies in continuing to re-engage with 'transgression' as it has emerged throughout metal's history, particularly in light of Karl Spracklen's argument that while metal music might be seen as a leisure space that resists the norms and values of the mainstream, it can also serve to re-affirm and construct those norms and values.[58]

To return to my leading question – is it still possible for metal to be transgressive in the twenty-first century – in offering some form of conclusion, my answer is a rather frustratingly cloudy yes, no, and maybe. I think the more productive discussion to be had is not necessarily whether metal is or is not transgressive, but rather a reckoning with what 'transgressive' actually means in any given context, and a concurrent understanding that the focus of such rebellion has never been the same thing throughout metal's history. What we are left with is a series of questions that will continue to evolve as metal itself does: how scenes themselves respond to transgression when challenging one's own self-interest is not 'comfortable', or furthermore, how many of these political divides are starting to emerge along generational and geographic axes. Continuing to question how transgression is framed and represented, and whether metal's rebellion is only permissible when it reassures privileged groups of their hegemonic power, can help us to radically reimagine the potential that metal was only ever born to be mild.

Notes

1. Bill Watterson, 'Calvin and Hobbes', *GoComics* (18 March 1992). www .gocomics.com/calvinandhobbes/1992/03/18 (accessed 27 August 2021).
2. Theodor Adorno, 'On Popular Music', *Zeitschrift für Sozialforschung* 9/1 (1941): 17–48;, Sonia Ramírez, 'Music and Protest' (2010). www.youtube.com/watch? v=-njxKF8CkoU (accessed 27 August 2021).
3. Accordingly, this chapter is named for the Sepultura track 'Refuse/Resist' from their 1993 album *Chaos A.D.*

4. Deena Weinstein, *Heavy Metal: The Music and its Culture* (Da Capo Press, 2000), p. 271; Keith Kahn-Harris, *Extreme Metal: Music and Culture on the Edge* (Berg, 2007), p. 30.

5. Karl Spracklen, *Metal Music and the Re-Imagining of Masculinity, Place, Race and Nation* (Emerald, 2020).

6. Chris Jenks, *Transgression* (Routledge, 2003), p. 2.

7. For a longer discussion of these three themes, see Catherine Hoad, *Heavy Metal, Texts, and Nationhood* (Palgrave, 2021).

8. *Ibid.*, p. 2.

9. *Ibid.*

10. Paul Willis, *Profane Culture* (Routledge, 1978); Dick Hebdige, *Subculture: The Meaning of Style* (Routledge, 1979), p. 155; Will Straw, 'Characterizing Rock Music Cultures: The Case of Heavy Metal', *Canadian University Music Review* 5 (1984): 104–22.

11. The "satanic panic" that heavy metal inspired in this period was recently drawn back in to public consciousness through the character of Eddie Munson in the fourth season of Netflix's *Stranger Things*. See also Tipper Gore, *Raising PG Kids in an X-Rated Society* (Abingdon Press, 1987), p. 50; Carl Raschke, *Painted Black* (HarperCollins, 1990), p. 274.

12. Kahn-Harris, *Extreme Metal*, p. 5; Weinstein, *Heavy Metal*, p. 93; Robert Walser, *Running with the Devil: Power, Gender and Madness in Heavy Metal Music* (Wesleyan University Press, 1993), p. 110.

13. Walser, *Running with the Devil*, pp. 111–12.

14. Weinstein, *Heavy Metal*, p. 101.

15. *Ibid.*, pp. 104–5; Walser, *Running with the Devil*.

16. Niall Scott, 'The Monstrous Male and Myths of Masculinity in Heavy Metal', in Niall Scott and Florian Heesch (eds.), *Heavy Metal, Gender and Sexuality* (Routledge, 2016), pp. 121–31.

17. Harris M. Berger, *Metal, Rock, and Jazz: Perception and the Phenomenology of Musical Experience* (Wesleyan University Press, 1999), p. 283; see also Michelle Phillipov, *Death Metal and Music Criticism: Analysis at the Limits* (Lexington Books, 2012).

18. Weinstein, *Heavy Metal*, p. 105.

19. Kyle Kusz, '"I Want to be the Minority": The Politics of Youthful White Masculinities in Sport and Popular Culture in 1990s America', *Journal of Sport and Social Issues* 25/4 (2001): 390–416.

20. Karen Bettez Halnon, 'Inside Shock Music Carnival: Spectacle as Contested Terrain', *Critical Sociology* 30/3 (2004): 743–79.

21. Karen Bettez Halnon, 'Heavy Metal Carnival and Dis-Alienation: The Politics of Grotesque Realism', *Symbolic Interaction* 29/1 (2006): 33–48; Sanna Fridh, 'Lord Satan's Secret Rites and Satanism as Self-Therapy: The Creation of a Masculinity Gender Identity within Black Metal', in Collin McKinnon,

Niall Scott and Kristen Sollee (eds.), *Can I Play with Madness? Metal, Dissonance, Madness and Alienation* (Inter-Disciplinary Press, 2011), pp. 177–84.

22. Fridh, 'Lord Satan's Secret Rites', p. 177.

23. Halnon, 'Heavy Metal Carnival', pp. 33–4.

24. *Ibid.*, p. 34.

25. Halnon, 'Shock Music', p. 750.

26. See Walser, *Running with the Devil*; Halnon, 'Heavy Metal Carnival'.

27. Halnon, 'Shock Music', p. 750.

28. Ross Hagen, 'Musical Style, Ideology, and Mythology in Norwegian Black Metal', in Jeremy Wallach, Harris M. Berger and Paul D. Greene (eds.), *Metal Rules the Globe: Heavy Metal Music Around the World* (Duke University Press, 2011), pp. 180–99.

29. Laura Wiebe-Taylor, 'Nordic Nationalisms: Black Metal Takes Norway's Everyday Racisms to the Extreme', in Niall Scott (ed.), *Metal Void: First Gatherings* (Inter-Disciplinary Press, 2010), pp. 161–73.

30. Scott Wilson, 'From Forests Unknown: Eurometal and the Political/Audio Unconscious', in Niall Scott (ed.), *Metal Void: First Gatherings* (Inter-Disciplinary Press, 2010), pp. 149–60.

31. Kahn-Harris, *Extreme Metal*, p. 34.

32. Niall Scott, 'Heavy Metal and the Deafening Threat of the Apolitical', *Popular Music History* 6/1 (2012): 224–39; Berger, *Metal, Rock, and Jazz*.

33. Kahn-Harris, *Extreme Metal*, p. 41.

34. Jon Stratton, 'KISS: Jewishness, Hard Rock and the Holocaust', *Metal Music Studies* 6/3 (2020): 277–97; Dominic Williams, '"Feel the Knife Pierce You Intensely": Slayer's "Angel of Death" – Holocaust Representation or Metal Affects?', *Genealogy* 3/4 (2019): 61; Keith Kahn-Harris, 'Engaging with Absence: Why is the Holocaust a "Problem" for Metal?', *Metal Music Studies* 6/3 (2020): 395–414.

35. Kahn-Harris, *Extreme Metal*, p. 144.

36. Sharon Hochhauser, 'The Marketing of Anglo-Identity in the North American Hatecore Metal Industry', in Jeremy Wallach, Harris M. Berger and Paul D. Greene (eds.), *Metal Rules the Globe: Heavy Metal Music Around the World* (Duke University Press, 2011), pp. 161–79.

37. See www.vox.com/culture/2017/8/17/16162146/spotify-removing-white-supremacist-neo-nazi-bands (accessed 27 August 2021); see also Benjamin Hillier and Aash Barnes, 'Wolf in Sheep's Clothing: Extreme Right-Wing Ideologies in Australian Black Metal', *IASPM Journal* 10/2 (2020): 38–57.

38. Kahn-Harris, *Extreme Metal*, p. 161.

39. Scott Munro, 'Gojira: Everyone Has a Responsibility to Change the World', *Metal Hammer* (2016). www.loudersound.com/news/gojira-everyone-has-a-responsibility-to-change-the-world (accessed 27 August 2021).

40. Scott, 'Deafening Threat', p. 237.

41. Dawes notes anti-BLM responses from the metal community accordingly; Laina Dawes, 'Fighting Against Racism in Metal is More Iimportant than Ever', *Metal Hammer* (2020). www.loudersound.com/features/fighting-against-racism-in-metal-is-more-important-than-ever (accessed 27 August 2021). However, there also emerges a myriad of positive examples, such as We Stand's *BLM Collective* collaborative album, with all profits donated to BLM-approved charities *Shut It Down*, a digital compilation to raise funds for the organisation The Movement for Black Lives and Black Sabbath's fundraising efforts; see Jasper Bruce, 'Black Sabbath Reveal "Black Lives Matter" Shirt Based on "Master of Reality" Design', *New Musical Express* (2020). www.nme.com/news/music/black-sabbath-are-selling-black-lives-matter-shirts-2689613 (accessed 27 August 2021).

42. Laina Dawes, *What Are You Doing Here? A Black Woman's Life and Liberation in Heavy Metal* (Bazillion Points, 2012), p. 21.

43. Justin Davisson, 'Extreme Politics and Extreme Metal: Strange Bedfellows or Fellow Travellers?', in Niall Scott (ed.), *Metal Void: First Gatherings* (Inter-Disciplinary Press, 2010), pp. 175–210.

44. https://kukailimoku.bandcamp.com/album/ka-hui-hawaii-aloha-ina (accessed 27 August 2021).

45. www.terrorizer.com/news/features-2/dawn-rayd (accessed 27 August 2021).

46. Joan Jocson-Singh, 'Vigilante Feminism as a Form of Musical Protest in Extreme Metal Music', *Metal Music Studies* 5/2 (2019): 262–73.

47. www.loudersound.com/features/metal-takes-a-stand-meet-the-bands-making-a-difference (accessed 27 August 2021).

48. Scott, 'Deafening Threat', p. 235.

49. Kahn-Harris, *Extreme Metal*, p. 40.

50. www.nocturnalcult.com/WITTRint.htm (accessed 27 August 2021).

51. Scott, 'Deafening Threat', p. 234.

52. Berger, *Metal, Rock, and Jazz.*

53. Dawes, *What Are You Doing Here?*, pp. 136–7.

54. *Ibid.*

55. Kahn-Harris, *Extreme Metal*, p. 162.

56. Benjamin Earl, 'Metal Goes "Pop": The Explosion of Heavy Metal into the Mainstream', in Gerd Bayer (ed.), *Heavy Metal Music in Britain* (Ashgate, 2009), pp. 33–52.

57. Halnon, 'Shock Music', p. 746.

58. Spracklen, *Metal Music.*

PART IV

Metal Activities

Personal Take VI – Richard Taylor

Enjoy the Ride

My band – Everything for Some – wasn't particularly good! In fact, we probably hold the record for the most number of gigs played to the least amount of people. Post-show overpriced service station pasties on the road at 3 am seemed to cost more than we ever got paid. Our music 'career' as a band was funded by numerous terrible minimum-wage temporary jobs. Once we split, I then got into independent promoting. On more occasions than I can remember, after preshow sleepless nights, I would inevitably be heading to the cash machine to cover the show loss and the remaining costs. Unless incredibly lucky (or compromising your passion), I don't believe there is any other industry where you would put more work in to get so little out financially. However, I still look back at those days as some of the best in my life. Music is incredible, and music is shit!

To recall a 24 hours on tour, I remember travelling to Newcastle on a tour bus, drinking on the way and blasting out music with friends. Then followed a soundcheck, backstage shenanigans and an awesome gig in front of some actual people, followed by cocaine, pills, drinks and an after-show party and then back on the bus to the next city, absolutely loving life. Five hours later, after finally getting an hour of sleep and doing the cocaine luge in the bus bunk, I awoke to no serotonin left in my body, a horrendous stink from fifteen blokes in a bus, a lost bank card, the realisation we had left merch at the venue, my mouth chewed to bits and a general overall feeling of questioning my life choices.

This rollercoaster of emotions over a 24-hour period, for me, epitomises life in the music business and the mindset you need to be able to enjoy your passion. The highs are as high as you can get: to play a killer show, promote a band you love and feel part of that creative process, manage an artist you love to a level of success, and the friendships you make with likeminded people are, I believe, as good a feeling as you can get. The competitiveness, financial requirements, sense of injustice, pressure and worry and the lack of security in what you do can be very testing. If I can give one piece of advice to anyone beginning their journey, if you have the ability to sack off the negative shit and are comfortable in taking things as they come, then just enjoy the ride.

You never know where music will take you, the lows will be lows, but the highs, when they come, will be higher. The music industry beats a lot of people down, but you can experience more in a short space of time than most would in a lifetime.

I'm currently writing this at the tail end of 2020. At the beginning of this year, I was moving forward with some considerable investment for my live music promotional and software company. This very soon evaporated with the news and spread of Covid-19, alongside the possibility of making any revenue this year (and as I write for the foreseeable future). It would be difficult to think of a more damaging period for the live music industry. However, the friendships and relationships I have made throughout my time being involved in music have provided new opportunities from the crisis, and new projects I'm now working on in the recorded sector are beginning to build momentum. I cannot emphasise enough the importance of networking and building relationships in the music business. This is one industry where things can happen quickly, and there will always be opportunities if you keep moving forward.

Positive Mental Attitude is everything.

Richard Taylor, founder and CEO of MusicPlanet Live

13

Metal as Leisure Space and Tourism Industry Destination

KARL SPRACKLEN

For 23 hours, the red-white ferry will be at the mercy of dark, or even diabolical, forces! Heavy metal energises the darkest time of the year – and the floating stage will give you both an excellent sound and the chance to relax: after all, this is not a music festival with tents and beer fences, but a cruise ferry with everything from a spa and sauna to exquisite food.[1]

The tropical cruise was once the quintessential getaway of the elderly retiree – a relaxing voyage through sun-soaked climes augmented by the soothing sounds of the open ocean. Not any more. Come Sunday evening, the vast expanse of the Caribbean Sea will echo to the altogether more riotous noise of 'Shiprocked', a heavy metal festival aboard the giant Norwegian Pearl cruise ship. Setting sail from the port of Miami, Florida, the floating concert will alight in Great Stirrup Cay in the Bahamas five days later. Pina coladas by the pool and tranquil ocean sunsets from the cabin balcony this raucous event is not . . . According to 'Shiprocked' owner Alan Koenig the event will be 'the ultimate hard rock festival at sea'.[2]

Consider what these pieces of marketing and reporting tell us about metal and its place in today's global society. *Viking Line* (who published the first quote), a great name for a tourist corporation operating in northern Europe, is trying to get metal fans on board a metal holiday cruise with them. They target metal fans with a reference to 'diabolical forces' that will endanger the cruiser ferry. But they know that the marketing will work because metal and metal holiday cruises are an acceptable part of the tourism and leisure industry. The report from the CNN website (the second quote) is an older piece that is making fun of the idea that metal fans – headbangers who drink beer – would ever be found on a cruise ship sipping cocktails and soaking up the sun. As the reporter tells us, cruises typically have attracted older people, wealthy retirees spending their pension money.[3] Now, of course, an entirely new cohort of music fans have been attracted to festivals taking place on cruise ships, not metal and rock fans but fans of every possible subgenre, who want the fun of a festival with the pleasure of sailing around in circles for a few days.[4]

In this chapter, metal as a space for leisure and tourism will be explored. I will first discuss how metal is leisure, for musicians and for fans, by exploring the meaning and purpose of leisure and leisure's relation to modern society. I will look at how metal is a part of the wider entertainment industry, and how that industry is best defined as commodified popular culture. Finally, I will discuss three specific forms of tourism and leisure industries that align with metal: tours, festivals, and the recent growth of metal holiday cruises.

Leisure and Metal

First, what do we mean by leisure spaces and leisure activities? Both are taken to be things we do in our free time, of our own free will, when we are not compelled to be in other spaces and doing other activities that are forced upon us.[5] That is, leisure activities are things that are not work activities: work, then, is the thing we have to do in workspaces. When we were hunter-gatherers, we worked to hunt and gather food. But we also worked to construct weapons, prepare and cook food, and look after our children. Our leisure was the free time we had (if we had any at all) to tell each other stories, sing and play music, or draw on the walls of our cave.[6] Of course, the reality of any culture is that work and leisure activities and spaces can be and are blurred. The hunter-gatherers in our past almost certainly chatted to each other when they were out finding food. And at night, the chores of work and the activities of free leisure often merged. But the idea that leisure is the thing we do when we are fed up with the work that pays our bills is still meaningful today. Being a metal fan is a leisure choice.[7] We put on a record or watch a video, and we are hooked, and this becomes our leisure identity as metal music and metal culture enrich our free time. Being a metal musician is also a free choice: metal musicians feel the urge to be creative because this is the music they love and feel gives them meaning and purpose.

In the preceding paragraph, we jumped back in time to a period before historical records began, then came right back to this century. It is necessary to do some more historical reflection, as it allows us to make sense of how leisure today has become constrained.[8] In the Classical Age, the time of the Greeks and the Romans, work was something done by the lower classes, women and slaves. In Greece, elite men like the philosopher Plato spent their leisure time doing physical activity, writing and speaking to their fellows, and playing music. They nurtured an ideal of a leisured life but on the blood and sweat of the toil of others. In Rome, this ideal of what elite men did was adopted, but the Romans had a society in which significant numbers of lower-class men were free and had some influence in politics. That meant elite Romans had to create entertainment for the lower classes: chariot-racing, gladiatorial combat and other spectacles in the theatres. These were the first examples we have of what became the sports and entertainment of the wider leisure industry.

Fast-forward to the start of the modern age, the period known by historians as modernity. In the nineteenth century, the United Kingdom became one of the most powerful of the imperial powers of Western Europe, but the rest of the West was outcompeting the rest of the world as well. This was because the West had new technologies such as steam engines and the new sciences of physics and chemistry that underpinned the Industrial Revolution.[9] The West had capitalism, liberalism and had seen a shift from rural to urban economies. For the rulers of the British Empire, the lessons of Classical Age were close to their hearts: they all learned Latin and Greek in the British public schools such as Eton. They believed in the Greek ideal of the healthy body and the healthy mind. They also saw the importance of bread and circuses: keeping the lower classes from rioting and rising up by giving them things to consume and things to distract them. It was no surprise, then, that in the second half of the nineteenth century, modern sports such as athletics and football emerged.[10] For elite men taking part in these sports, playing the game taught them to serve the Empire. But many of these sports quickly became entertainment, with paying spectators becoming hardcore fans in football clubs around the world wherever British imperial or commercial interests spread.[11]

Western society, at this point in time, became a site where technology and urbanisation and the interests of elites constructed the form of consumer capitalism we see today.[12] Because there were more workers who were well-off, and men and women with free time, industries emerged that targeted them: pre-prepared food and domestic appliances; restaurants; public houses; tourism facilitated by trains and steamships; and music halls.[13] Some of the elites in Britain loathed these attractions and bewailed the poor leisure choices of the working classes. Drinking alcohol in pubs was seen by many as a moral danger as well as a danger to the health of British workers. But others – the owners of breweries, for instance – defended pubs as places where hard-working men could quench their thirst.

Finally, modernity was where the divide between classical music and popular music was formalised and used as a way of controlling the meaning of culture. Popular music was at first dismissed by the elites as something simple-minded for the lower classes but increasingly co-opted by governments in the West as a means of stopping the urban working classes from taking part in morally bad leisure and politically bad activism.[14] From the music halls to the invention of recorded music and radio, popular music like sports such as football soon became a leisure form shaped by mass spectatorship. Popular music became a leisure space that was used as both a site of control and a site of resistance. Metal music has emerged from rock music, itself a form of popular music. Rock'n'roll offered young people a sense of belonging, of being different from their parents and rebelling against them. Rock music in the nineteen-sixties soon offered fans a chance to be a part of an alternative counterculture. And metal, like rock, has been created as alternative leisure space that stands against the mainstream of popular music and popular culture.

Metal has been unfashionable, situated in the margins of society and its culture, and its rules have been leisure spaces that are characterised as underground. Many metal fans spend much of their free time debating genres online, collecting vinyl and seeking out the most obscure black metal. Many metal fans revel in metal's rebel, evil, Satanic stereotypes, believing that metal is the only form of popular music that resists mainstream trends.[15] Metal fans and musicians believe they have found metal through their own free leisure choices. Metal is what we might call a *communicative leisure* choice, something found freely and entered into through our own will.[16] Metal is not the clever choice that makes a musician money, or the one entered into because one wants to be best friends with the men in Darkthrone t-shirts. Metal is not imposed on its fans and musicians by government legislation or by the government putting adverts for metal in newspapers. Metal is not sold to its fans through the round of popular music competitions on television, or through the ubiquitous social media influencers. Nonetheless, it is not wholly true to say that leisure choices made by metal fans, or the creative choices made by metal musicians, are completely free. This is because metal is part of the entertainment industry.

Metal as a Part of the Entertainment Industry

The entertainment industry is a product of modern capitalism and the successive industrial and scientific revolutions we are all still living through. The German critical theorist Theodor W. Adorno was the first person to attempt to understand its purpose, though he called it the culture industry.[17] For Adorno, modern sports and popular music in the first half of the twentieth century were intertwined with the media (at the time, newspapers, radio and films) to keep the masses believing they were free when actually they were being controlled by governments and corporations. This was hegemonic power, as Antonio Gramsci identified occurring in Fascist Italy: the working classes were fed lies in the media and sold products and fantasy stories, and were fooled into thinking the Fascists were working on their behalf.[18] People did not give away their freedom, they were distracted by the magician's sleight of hand and did not even notice they lost their freedoms. There is no doubt that totalitarian states manipulated the culture industry and used it to maintain power and keep their rivals and internal enemies in check. But Adorno saw the instrumental logic of the culture industry in totalitarian states operating to a lesser degree in liberal democracies in the West, such as the United States of America and the United Kingdom. Adorno loathed all forms of culture and leisure that were commodified, bought and sold to consumers by capitalists. He hated the rise of three-minute popular music played on radio and would have hated Instagram and TikTok if he had lived in our times for their reductive, artificial, inauthentic culture.

The culture industry grew into what we now know as the entertainment industry.[19] At its greatest extent, the industry covers the following forms of modern leisure and culture: music, music-making and music audiences; dance; theatre; performance arts; comedy; books; magazines and newspapers; spectator sports; television; digital leisure; social media; active recreation; drinking and eating out (hospitality); and some elements of active recreation and tourism. The entertainment industry is one where millions of people around the world work full-time as professionals, with millions more working part-time or unpaid. Many of the people who work are paid poorly, whether they are musicians struggling with streaming contracts or delivery drivers carrying fast food. The entertainment industry's workers are generally making things that are consumed by others in their leisure time: the 12-inch pepperoni pizza is exactly the same as the black metal vinyl; it is all a product that meets someone else's leisure needs. It is all a product that is part of a capitalist exchange that has transformed what we think of as our leisure choices.

Imagine a slightly different modern society and its popular culture. This is a thought experiment, and what follows never happened. In this alternative Earth, modernity emerges exactly like it does, and the United Kingdom is replaced by the United States of America as the political power that shapes the twentieth century. Instead of jazz, African Americans create *coastarama*, dance music played on North African tribal drums inflected with English sea shanties. Coastarama spreads around the world as a form of popular music and creates variant subgenres green, blue and pink.

Coastarama pink is adopted as the music of the middle-class countercul-ture in the sixties, then coastarama pink-brown becomes a darker version of coastarama pink. This music becomes popular among young, white, working-class men in the seventies and eighties, and was subsequently sold to them by the entertainment industry. There is no doubt that if this form of popular music actually existed, music fans and musicians around the world would believe that they had found coastarama pink-brown by their own free will. They would argue about who was an authentic coastarama pink-browner, who was a sell-out, who was a fashion victim, who was evil, who was underground. Coastarama would saturate every aspect of our lives, and its variants would be the subject of books, films, websites, blogs, television programmes and podcasts. Leaders of nations would be inter-viewed expressing their love of coastarama pink bands. Fans would be able to buy everything coastarama, spending billions of dollars every year on coastarama pink products. Transnational corporations would invest in coastarama pink festivals, tours and bands. These corporations would own recording studios, radio stations, television stations and websites, ensuring they had an economic stake in every part of the mechanical processes of the industry. Governments would be happy that their citizens were too busy arguing the merits of coastarama green (or blue or pink or pink-brown) to notice their rights were being eroded in successive waves of rationalising legislation.

Metal, then, is completely gripped in the talons of the entertainment industry. It has its own independent labels that operate as supposedly authentic voices of an underground subculture. It has bigger labels like Nuclear Blast or Earache that operate like the big transnational corporations that control mainstream popular music. And, increasingly, those large independent labels are being controlled or taken over by the transnationals. Metal music is constructed according to the templates and restrictions of popular music, using electric instruments and using recording studios to create products to sell. Metal music is sold to fans as a form of resistance and rebellion, but the labels and managers who control the bands are just replicating the business models of the wider popular music industry.[20] Metal is about albums, not singles, but that is the same as rock music, or indie music, or folk music. And metal bands rely on music that is catchy enough – or kult enough – to make some impact as musicians. Of course, the advent of illegal downloads and legal streaming means it is difficult for any bands or musicians to make enough money from metal to turn their leisure activity into a work one. Once upon a time, bands quit their jobs or left school to try to become the next Manowar or Iron Maiden. In those days, managers and labels could make huge amounts of money from the labour of their bands, but the bands themselves could live off their earnings, too. Now, though, it is almost impossible for metal musicians to become full-time professionals – they have to keep other jobs and limit the metal music-making to times when they are free. But that does not mean metal is rejecting the norms of the entertainment industry. Musicians still want their songs to be heard and still conform to those norms. Musicians make demos and send them to labels, seeking contracts. They seek out the music press, the magazines and fanzines that remain important arbiters of taste, hoping that someone in the media will endorse them. Musicians seek out managers, producers, booking agents, accountants and stylists. They use social media and the internet to reach out directly to fans, using what is currently fashionable in that virtual space to carve a metal niche that sell their music.[21] Musicians or their partners become adept at sourcing and selling their merchandise: knowing who can offer cheap rates for bulk purchase of black t-shirts; finding companies that print designs; setting up as limited companies to make sure every padded envelope is tax-deductible. Bands that build up a fanbase can get bigger deals for their merchandise or may choose to license their logo and imagery to companies that have money to advertise online and in metal magazines. Finally, metal remains part of the entertainment industry in the way it has adopted the model of selling the product through playing live.

Metal Tours, Festivals and Holiday Cruises

For metal fans, there is nothing more authentic than listening to their favourite bands live. The live performance is at the heart of the relationship between musician and fan, and that relationship is based on authenticity. Metal fans want to prove to each other that they are true fans, so they attend gigs, enter the mosh-pit, raise their horns and buy the tour t-shirt. Metal fans tell each other about the bands they have seen, and they boast about seeing bands live when they talk to each other, to show how metal they are: 'So, you saw Iron Maiden in 1985? I saw them down the pub in 1979'. Live albums and video recordings – and the infinite database that is the internet – allow fans who are unable to get to attend the gigs (or are too young, or in the wrong half of the world). Tours allow true fans to see the same band play the same set-list at different venues up and down a country. Some bands have huge, dedicated followings who meet each other when these tours happen, fans who take holidays to tour with their band. For metalheads, being a casual listener or consumer of metal is not enough. You must *love* the band and the music that you dedicate your holidays to and your free leisure time to: catching the bands live – or talking about tours. Watching bands play live is also important in metal because one of the founding ideologies is: metal is real music, played by real musicians. Popular and rock music has an infamous secret history of inauthenticity. In the sixties and seventies, many hit singles were constructed from the talent of session musicians, people not listed on the backs of the actual singles. Even pop singers would get a lot of help and were sometimes replaced altogether by someone who could sing perfectly. By the eighties, many popular music singles and albums were completely constructed from samples and artificial drums, guitars and pianos. Metal fans are fearful of fakery, so watching bands play live is a way of reassuring themselves that they are not being sold something artificial. Of course, metal bands are just as happy as pop artists to find ways of making recorded productions and live music as easy as possible. But they know their role in this part of the industry: they must try to perform as truly as possible, but as close to the album recordings as they can, even if that means a bit of fakery around the edges.

Bands tour because this is how the entertainment industry has evolved. Metal bands are like the rock bands of the sixties and seventies. They make albums, then they tour those albums. Early in their careers, many bands play support slots and do not make any money from the privilege of supporting an established band (sometimes support bands have to pay and lose money on the deal). Promoters want to ensure that they sell out the entire tour. Managers and accountants of the headline bands want to see better returns on merchandise in each new region the tour heads through. Before the internet allowed people to share music illegally, albums were the most important part of a band's portfolio, and tours were viewed as the way to sell albums: metal fans hooked in the eighties and nineties would buy the whole back catalogue if they could. Since the internet made music fans reluctant to buy the music they loved, the entertainment industry changed the way it made its money.[22] Now, the album was a new product that the bands had to play live to their fans who would not buy the album – but they would go to see their favourite metal bands play live. Touring, then, became the way already successful bands made money for themselves and their labels and managers and shareholders.[23] Touring is still a lucrative route for metal bands, as metal fans are still happy to buy tickets to see their favourite bands, to buy the merchandise and even the new album on shiny new vinyl. Touring, however, has become harder, as bands and labels make less and less money, and established suppliers and venues reduce around the world. For many metal bands who are not signed to a big or at least respected label, or who have just established their own label, there is still the problem that becoming a full-time professional is difficult, especially in the age of streaming.[24] So these bands are unable to tour extensively, tap into new markets and create media exposure because they do not have the leisure time or space. Metal musicians working as delivery drivers and raising children cannot easily abandon those commitments to go support Mastodon around South America.

Festivals have become the main space in the entertainment industry for metal bands and metal fans to reach out and find each other. Music festivals were first established for classical music – but in the post-war period, promoters and labels saw an opportunity to use the festival model for jazz, blues and popular music.[25] Festivals allow a number of bands and artists to appear one after the other in the same place. In the sixties, Woodstock demonstrated that huge numbers of popular music fans could be encouraged to pay for tickets for such events if the range of acts on the bill was sufficiently diverse. Woodstock also showed that festivals needed proper security and support facilities. In the seventies and eighties, Glastonbury and others such as Pinkpop developed the model of the modern music festival, balancing the commodification of the event (the food stalls, the toilets, the fields for tents, the big fences, the showers, the marketplaces) with the desire of the fans to catch the acts they loved.[26] Metal music, as it matured, developed its own dedicated music festivals, or became dominant in pre-existing music festivals. Wacken is probably the most famous metal music festival, though there are now metal music festivals in every part of the world. Metal festivals now have multiple stages, so fans can drift from one performance to the other. Some stages may be dedicated to extreme metal or to unsigned or local bands. Metal festivals offer VIP camping or hotel packages. They offer signing tents, beer tents and stalls selling everything a metalhead might need: burgers, chips, albums, tattoos, piercings, t-shirts. Again, metal festivals are exactly like any other modern music festival. They are sold as events, spaces to get away and get stoned, to live a liminal experience, like a pilgrim. But these liminal spaces are part of the entertainment industry and have been ever since free festivals and mass invasions of paying festivals disappeared. Instead of peace and love, there are things to buy, purchased from the businesses and corporations making huge amounts of money. Even where festivals are run by people with progressive politics, or for charity, the entertainment industry is never far away, making a profit from running ticket sales or catering or security.[27]

Metal festivals allow metal bands to play in front of fans without the need for extensive touring. Headliners can make more money from festivals than from playing multiple arenas, as festival owners know fans of the headline bands will always pay for a festival ticket even if they do not watch any band other than the one of which they are a fan. Multiple nights allow multiple headlines, so more tickets can be sold at a higher price. For bands halfway down the bill, there is not so much money as the headliners, but the fees are enough to make these bands happy and reluctant to lose money touring more extensively. Again, a carefully cultivated line-up means more dedicated fans are buying tickets just to see a band that may never come to this country again. For the bands at the bottom of the bill, there is often only the offer of a free pitch for their tents, or even a demand for money – these bands are living the dream, and festivals know there are other bands keen to share the bill if and when these bands give up.

Festivals invite fans to meet other fans and listen to their favourite bands in idyllic fields.[28] They offer fans the idea of living in a tent by a stream, or a hedgerow, or a tree, watching the sun rise. Of course, real festivals are horrible spaces, filled with other people's rubbish and excrement. Rain and wind make many festivals a nightmare of slipping knee-deep in mud and flash floods. It is no surprise, then, that some promoters developed the idea of music cruises. The cruise industry had grown at the end of the twentieth century as more and more middle-class people in the West retired early with comfortable pensions. Cruise holidays allowed these people to imagine they were authentic travellers, visiting islands in the Caribbean and the Mediterranean, but having the luxury of the all-inclusive hotel in a beach-side resort.[29] Cruises also became a way for these people to travel to places beyond the seaside resorts, to Norway or the Baltics. Cruises allowed these people to claim a higher status than the working classes who flocked to the beach resorts in Spain and Mexico. Then some of the people who normally went to those resorts all started going on cruises as well, and the cruise industry expanded even more. This meant music fans, musicians and promoters were already going on cruises and enjoying the buffets and the bars and the spas. Meanwhile, the cruise industry itself was looking at ways to maximise its profits and the return on its capital investments: the enormous cruise liners packed with fun and luxury plumbing. The worsening economic climate in the second decade of this century and the fall in the number of people with secure pension schemes meant that the industry had to find new customers.

It was not long before the first music cruises emerged as small events using spare cruise liners.[30] Metal promoters followed their rock and prog equivalents and realised cruises were a perfect, safe environment for festival-style events. Cruise-liner owners saw metal fans as being well-behaved, high-spending consumers who could become future cruise-liner regulars. Onboard ship, the fans can mix with the bands, but the bands can also get luxury cabins. Onboard ship, fans can drink all day, eat all day, soak up the sun and mosh on a floor that is not a swamp. For the bands, the same benefits and problems occur on a cruise liner as they do at a festival. But at least the problems of being low on the bill on a cruise liner is you get to be on holiday in a sunny part of the world for a few days – and you might get the chance to make new fans and sell them your new merch.

Conclusion

Metal is inextricably part of the entertainment industry. No metal fan or musician has come to metal of their own free choice. All forms of popular culture are inherited by the people who live in them. But metal still gives meaning to people's leisure lives and allows musicians to make the music they love, and for fans to be moved by that music. All leisure is constrained, but metal is less constrained than mainstream pop music, say, because it remains unfashionable to critics and uncool to trendsetters. Metal, therefore, provides a communicative leisure space in which fans and musicians can find meaning, belonging and solidarity. Musicians make the music because it gives them satisfaction and status in metal culture, and many do it in their free time alongside other things that pay their bills. Until metal becomes trendy, it retains some potential as a leisure form that resists conformity, commercialisation and control. Metal's uncompromising riffs and unfashionable themes still make it more likely to be a space for resistance rather than a way for the entertainment industry to maximise profits.

Notes

1. 'Nordic Metal Cruise', *Viking Line*. www.sales.vikingline.com/find-trip/cruises/from-turku/minicruises/nordic-metal-cruise (accessed 22 January 2021).
2. Eoghan Macguire, 'The Boat that Rocked: Heavy Metal on the High Seas', *CNN* (24 January 2014). http://edition.cnn.com/2014/01/23/sport/the-boat-that-rocked/index.html (accessed 22 January 2021).
3. Rory V. Jones, 'Motivations to Cruise: An Itinerary and Cruise Experience Study', *Journal of Hospitality and Tourism Management* 18/1 (2011): 30–40.

4. David Cashman, '"The Most Atypical Experience of My Life": The Experience of Popular Music Festivals on Cruise Ships', *Tourist Studies* 17/3 (2017): 245–62.

5. Karl Spracklen, *The Meaning and Purpose of Leisure: Habermas and Leisure at the End of Modernity* (Palgrave Macmillan, 2009).

6. Karl Spracklen, *Constructing Leisure: Historical and Philosophical Debates* (Palgrave Macmillan, 2011).

7. Karl Spracklen, *Metal Music and the Re-Imagining of Masculinity, Place, Race and Nation* (Emerald, 2020).

8. Spracklen, *Constructing Leisure.*

9. *Ibid.*

10. *Ibid.*

11. Tony Collins, *How Football Began: A Global History of How the World's Football Codes Were Born* (Routledge, 2018).

12. Spracklen, *Constructing Leisure.*

13. Karl Spracklen and Ian Lamond, *Critical Event Studies* (Routledge, 2016).

14. *Ibid.*

15. Spracklen, *Metal Music.*

16. Spracklen, *The Meaning and Purpose.*

17. Theodor W. Adorno, *The Culture Industry* (Routledge, 1991).

18. Antonio Gramsci, *Selections from Prison Notebooks* (Lawrence and Wishart, 1971).

19. Spracklen and Lamond, *Critical Event Studies.*

20. Spracklen, *Metal Music.*

21. Karl Spracklen, *Digital Leisure, the Internet and Popular Culture: Communities and Identities in a Digital Age* (Palgrave Macmillan, 2015).

22. *Ibid.*

23. Martin Cloonan, 'Steering a Review: Some Reflections on a Gig', *International Journal of Cultural Policy* 19/3 (2013): 318–32.

24. Spracklen, *Digital Leisure.*

25. Chris Gibson and John Connell, *Music Festivals and Regional Development in Australia* (Ashgate, 2012).

26. Spracklen and Lamond, *Critical Event Studies.*

27. *Ibid.*

28. *Ibid.*

29. Jones, 'Motivations to Cruise'.

30. Cashman, 'Atypical Experience'.

14 | Dance Practices in Metal

DANIEL SUER

Vignette 1: Israeli metal band Orphaned Land headlines this evening as the fourth band, and the audience seems relaxed and excited at the same time. As the song 'All is One' begins with a toned-down iteration of the main riff, the band's singer, Kobi Farhi, claps along with the $^7/_8$-time signature, emphasising the riff's 3+2+2 accent structure as heard on the studio version of the song. He animates the audience to join in, which works surprisingly well considering the unusual rhythm. As the song continues – while maintaining the rhythmic structure throughout various formal sections – people engage bodily with the music in different ways. The bass player, for example, seems to be the most avid headbanger of the band, throwing his head up and down in a slightly tilted manner in strict synchronisation with the riff's 3+2+2 structure. Meanwhile, Kobi Farhi, besides moving about on stage, performs his most expressive movements with his hands and, in part, with his shoulders. These include intricate hand gestures with minute finger actions, flowing movements and circular motions that extend to the shoulders. There is also a variety of movements among audience members, although the majority stands rather still. A few people continue clapping, others also headbang in synchronisation with the riff accents, but not as clearly as the bassist. Instead, heads are visible that are pointedly thrusting downwards on each downbeat, moving rather fluidly through the rest of the bar. Yet other audience members calmly sway from side to side, the shoulder leading the movement while slightly twisting the upper body according to the swaying direction.

Based on the author's field notes, 6 March 2018, Cologne, Germany

> Vignette 2: During Orphaned Land's rendition of 'Sapari' in Vancouver, the band is joined by belly dancer, artist and musician Mahafsoun, who contributes a dance performance throughout the entire song. She positions herself in the centre of the stage, her left leg slightly bent and her arms raised above her head. Together with the singer, she animates the audience to clap along to the intro vocals that are heard via playback. As the entire band begins to play, she starts moving her arms in a circular motion, performing intricate gestures, and she accents the musical hits with jolts of her hips and a forward-directed motion of her left leg. This complex interplay between her movements and the music – including synchronicity, ornaments and more – also incorporates a headbanging motion during a number of pronounced musical accents played in unison by the band. These are embodied by Mahafsoun as she thrusts her head from one side to the other in synchronisation with the accents. After headbanging, her movement focus shifts back to her hips, with which she continues to emphasise and embellish the musical beat.
>
> Video shot from the audience's perspective, uploaded to Mahafsoun's YouTube channel[1]

As these introductory examples illustrate, people move their bodies to metal music and interact with it – they dance. Audience members and performers on stage do so in various ways, some of which have become iconic practices of metal, such as headbanging, and others that seem rather uncommon and are not as closely associated with metal at first glance, such as belly dancing. A dance practice that is not mentioned in the vignettes, but which has attracted considerable public and arguably the most academic attention of all metal dances, is moshing. The next section therefore investigates the social organisation of mosh pits and discusses them as contested communities because they offer communal experiences while simultaneously perpetuating existent obstacles to participation, especially in relation to gender identities. Revisiting the introductory vignettes, the final section's outlook points out blind spots in research to highlight the need and possibilities for further research. This especially pertains to an extended scope of dance-related phenomena so as to account for practices beyond headbanging and moshing in extreme metal. Such an extended focus would additionally include perspectives on digital dance spaces, the global distribution of dance practices, histories of metal dance and further studies on the aesthetic relations of music and movement in metal. In this way, this chapter aims to provide an introductory overview of dance practices in metal, their social organisation and avenues for future research.

Contested Mosh Pit Communities

Moshing is one of metal culture's most common forms of movement. There is no single practice to which this term refers, as the terminology varies across metal scenes and cultures. In this chapter, moshing is understood as a conglomerate of different movement practices that are mostly, though not exclusively, performed at metal concerts, such as pushing, jumping, running or clashing into each other and more.[2] All these movements take place in the mosh pit (or just 'pit' for short), which is a performative, often circular, space that emerges in the audience, usually close to the stage. Depending on the size of the audience, there can be several mosh pits at an event, which are dynamic in that they can merge into a larger one, just as one large pit can separate into several smaller ones. Further practices that often involve the pit are 'stage diving' and 'walls of death'. In case of the latter, the pit opens up, and participants split into two halves that face each other. Following a musical and/or verbal cue by the band, the two walls run towards each other and clash into each other, often leading to further moshing. If audience members manage to get onto the stage, they jump off the stage's edge and dive into the audience below, which usually awaits them with outstretched arms, ready to catch them. Being caught by the audience opens up the possibility of crowd surfing, i.e., instead of dropping the stage diver, the audience continues carrying them and passes them on through the audience area, thereby surfing over the crowd.

Considering that pushing, running, jumping and clashing constitute a pit, moshing at first glance might make the impression to be nothing but violent chaos that happens to take place while music is playing. There is some truth to that in so far as participants might sustain injuries, and the numerous, fast-paced activities in a pit can be disorienting. Yet, research into the social workings of moshing has shown that it is more complex than that.

Mosh Pits as Communal Spaces

Moshing is indeed a regulated practice that enables experiences of communal bonding and individual identity work. The most overt means of regulating moshing is the so-called 'pit etiquette', which consists of a rather loose collection of guidelines for how to act in a mosh pit. The etiquette's specifics can vary in detail because it is part of metal's informal cultural knowledge, which can change across times, locations, scenes and situations.[3] Nevertheless, as pit etiquettes generally aim to prevent an escalation of violence and prompt moshers to be mindful of each other despite their transgressive interactions, there are basic elements that most, if not all, pit etiquettes share. These include, for example, limiting moshing to the pit so as not to involve those who do not want to participate, or the imperative to pick up moshers who have fallen down to prevent them from getting trampled and stepped on accidentally. The pit etiquette illustrates that while moshing involves violent practices, this violence is not uncontrolled. Although it might seem contradictory from an etic perspective, moshing's violent character supports bonding among moshers.

Early research on moshing from the 1990s already noted this complex interplay. Harris M. Berger, investigating mosh pits at US-American death metal shows, pointed out that there is a continuous and dynamic tension between violence and order.[4] Moshing not only enacts but also represents violence, according to Berger, and when the enactment steps into the background, the representation and portrayal of violence can bring camaraderie and friendship to the fore. In examining and comparing UK metal, punk and ska subcultures, dance scholar Sherril Dodds observes a similarly ambivalent role that violence plays for metal's dance practices in fostering communal bonds among dancers.[5] In another early ethnographic study, Katharina Inhetveen analyses movements and violence at hardcore concerts in Germany.[6] Although hardcore's and metal's dance practices are not always identical, they do share similar movements that involve violence, and they have historical points of contact.[7] Regarding the movements' violence, Inhetveen also stresses the existence of rules of moshing and identifies three different forms of violence at hardcore concerts: negative (i.e., intentionally harmful), necessary (i.e., sanctioning) and positive violence. Instead of aiming to dominate others, the latter tends towards symmetrical interactions of the participants and is rather supposed to guarantee that everyone involved has a good time.[8] Inhetveen calls this rather playful violence 'sociable violence' (*Gesellige Gewalt*).[9] In order to accommodate this positive and socially productive violence that is at odds with everyday life's conventions of bodily interactions, mosh pits have been conceptualised as 'liminal spaces'.[10] As such, they suspend rules to a certain degree that govern everyday life and temporarily replace them with other rules specific to that space, such as pit etiquette.

According to Gabrielle Riches, these liminal spaces tend to form in backspaces, as these offer participants relatively little official surveillance, the possibility to indulge in practices that may otherwise be off-limits, and a sense that these practices are generally sanctioned by other people in that space.[11] Collectively producing mosh pits as liminal spaces within shared backspaces further contributes to moshing's capacity to provide communal experiences for those involved. While engaging in these spaces, dancers must strive to maintain a balance between suspending everyday life's rules of bodily comportment and not transgressing metal's own moshing conventions. Doing so is a continuous and dynamic joint effort with its own contingencies, and therefore the participants need to be able to rely on each other, which requires and, in turn, builds trust among them.[12] This illustrates that moshing's intense and sometimes violent corporeality furthermore entails and is inseparable from its affective charge. Affective intensities are crucial to the experience of moshing and have been largely neglected in earlier research in favour of a focus on mosh pits as representational means of bonding.[13] Rosemary Overell, in her study of Australian and Japanese grindcore scenes, pursues the foundational and extensive role affect plays for moshing's ability to connect and collectivise people. When moshing, among other moments, 'scene members feel a collective sense of belonging with other fans at the event. The self, as bordered, individualised subject, is effaced via the affective intensity of the gig'.[14]

Taking the complexity of moshing as social interaction into account, it is moshing's ambivalent inclusion of violence, its liminal status and its bodily as well as affective intensity that enable the dancers' bonding experiences. Viewed from these interlaced perspectives, mosh pits are embodied manifestations of metal communality.[15]

Mosh Pits as Contested Spaces

Although the communal aspect of moshing is repeatedly emphasised by many dancers and theorised by researchers, moshing is not an all-inclusive space, and there remain obstacles to equal participation in the communal experience it can offer. Most notably, this pertains to moshing as a gendered practice. Most research on moshing's gender politics begins with the observation that far more men than women engage in moshing, thereby construing it as a male-connoted practice. For example, while Jonathan Gruzelier estimates that 70–75 per cent of moshers are male, Leigh Krenske and Jim McKay even observe a rate of 95 per cent or more male pit participation.[16]

Whatever the precise number, which is sure to vary over time, place and event, the quantitative dominance of men in the pit and their intimate interactions – including clashing, sweaty bodies – have prompted the theorisation of mosh pits as homosocial spaces.[17] As such, the image of mosh pits as inclusive spaces that are open and welcoming to everyone is differentiated by the fact that they primarily foster male bonding. Crucially, Gabrielle Riches' nuanced analyses of gendered pit experiences stress the existence and interaction of multiple instead of one monolithic masculinity within mosh pits.[18] By engaging with these competing masculinities, she is able to show that not all masculinities are unreservedly welcome in the pit, further shattering the notion of an all-inclusive space, and demonstrating that mosh pits serve as spaces for the negotiation of metal masculinities. In her research on Canadian pits, Riches proposes what she calls 'marginal metal masculinities' as those that do not have access to traditional sites of discursive power and are therefore opposed to mainstream or hegemonic forms of masculinity. These marginalised masculinities were valorised in the pit, which is why it was experienced as inclusive by the men concerned. In order to maintain this sense of inclusivity, however,

performances of a traditional hegemonic masculinity were negated in that men who used moshpits to demonstrate feats of strength, to size up other men or who intended to display their dominance over other men were considered unwanted outsiders, or what the participants referred to as 'meatheads'. These men embodied a hegemonic masculinity, which was understood as antithetical to heavy metal masculinity.[19]

As these so-called 'meatheads' exhibited what Inhetveen calls negative violence, it was legitimate for other moshers to engage in necessary violence so as to drive out the meatheads and ensure the maintenance of positive violence.

Although the predominance of men is especially striking at first glance, it is important to note that women also throw themselves into pits and engage in the transgressive whirlwind that is moshing. Riches and colleagues show that by doing so, female moshers can also inscribe themselves into this temporal metal community corporeally and experience themselves as part of a larger scene, in this specific case, the Leeds (UK) extreme metal scene.[20] What mosh pits also potentially offer women is to defy traditional gender roles and expectations by rejecting conventionally female-connoted forms of leisure and instead participating in moshing's violence.[21] This participation empowers them as committed subcultural members and heightens their visibility as such, especially in practices such as stage diving.[22]

Moshing women not only transgress norms of everyday bodily interaction but simultaneously also the metal mosh pit as a male homosocial space. Male moshers' ambivalent reactions, in turn, highlight the pit as a contested arena, as interactions range from continued moshing through especially protective behaviour – so as not to harm the women who supposedly cannot compete in a 'regular' pit – to women simply being forced out of the pit or to its margins by men in order to restore homosocial stability.[23] These attempts are not always successful because female moshers do not simply accept but defy their exclusion by re-entering the pit and claiming participation.[24] Yet, pit ejection is not the only way the moshing experiences of female moshers are undermined by men. As Riches and colleagues go on to explain, pit participation is fraught with risks for female moshers because they are potentially subject to sexual abuse due to the anonymity granted by the blurring disorientation in pits, especially during stage diving and crowd surfing.[25]

While conceptions of mosh pits as contested homosocial spaces already touch on aspects of sexuality, and Riches even suggests a (homo-)erotic perspective on pits,[26] the role moshing plays for queer metal fans has not received much academic attention so far. Yet, Amber Clifford-Napoleone's study on queer metal provides an account of how queer metalheads consume moshing.[27] About one-fifth of her survey participants claim to focus on moshing at metal concerts, and those who actually participate in the pit point out the contribution of moshing to their metal identity and sense of being part of a metal community, similar to the experiences described above. For those queer metal fans that focus on moshing without physically participating in it, mosh pits offer a spectacle that allows for queer desire because 'disorganized movements of sweaty, out-of-control bodies slamming into each other provides a way to consume bodies in physical action without being policed as a queer person in a heteronormative space'.[28]

As the various perspectives on moshing's gender dynamics highlight, mosh pits are ambivalent spaces and not simply sites of an all-encompassing metal community. They offer communality, empowerment, good times and much more to metal fans, and therefore they occupy a central place in the lives of many metalheads. Yet, mosh pits simultaneously present themselves as contested and, at times, fragile social spaces where different masculinities compete; female moshers face additional physical risks and obstacles when claiming their place in the pit; and queer fans covertly navigate the mosh pit's heteronormative terrain. In doing so, mosh pits and their conditional inclusivity mirror a gap between metal's proclaimed inclusivity and its remaining mechanisms of exclusion that have been observed in metal culture more widely.[29] While this chapter has addressed and illustrated moshing's conditional inclusivity in terms of gender, further aspects of identity and difference could and should be pursued, such as exclusions due to race or ability. These identities are likely to face similar challenges concerning pit participation as those relating to gender, although research on these issues is scarce in the realm of mosh pits.

Outlook and Avenues for Future Research

Research into metal's dance practices spans more than twenty years and provides numerous insights and sophisticated analyses, all of which further the understanding of these corporeal activities. Nevertheless, there are common foci that have established specific representations of dance and the resulting blind spots. The remainder of this chapter points beyond these representations and highlights desiderata for future research as well as first steps that have already been taken towards addressing them.

Beyond Headbanging and Moshing in Extreme Metal

When considering the majority of the literature cited so far in this chapter, one might be tempted to equate dance in metal with moshing practices and headbanging at live concerts of extreme metal bands, primarily in the Global North. As the introductory vignettes hopefully illustrate, there are more movements, cultural interactions and spaces involved in metal dance than that. Since headbanging and moshing are so prominently associated with metal, other forms of movement are easily overlooked. The intricate gestures and movements of Orphaned Land's singer or the performance of a belly dancer are striking examples and by no means the only ones. During my ongoing research on metal dance, I encountered numerous forms of movement: spontaneous circle dances during the performance of folk metal band Korpiklaani; humorous conga lines initiated and choreographed by the musicians of Trollfest; or the collective swaying of smartphones during metal ballads, to name but a few. Metal's movement repertoire is more complex than its depiction in research. Besides the prominence of headbanging and moshing, this is probably connected to the fact that the focus is mostly on extreme metal, which tends to be conceptualised as locally self-contained subcultures or scenes. The implicit depiction of moshing and headbanging as (extreme) metal's only dance forms reinforces such a conception and, in effect, contributes to an essentialist notion of 'what metal is'. By broadening the scope beyond extreme metal and viewing metal's subgenres as porous formations that interact with other music cultures, different movements come into view. Such a perspective can also better account for the movement variety, as some fans literally move through different movement cultures – physically and via media – potentially disseminating and modifying dance practices along the way. Thereby, for example, belly dancing is combined with headbanging at metal concerts, and hip hop and electronic dance music cultures have adopted mosh pits as they see fit.

Digital and Global Dances

Another blind spot concerns the spaces where dancing in metal takes place. Due to dancing's embodied, interactive nature, facilitated by the loud music, the numerous potential fellow dancers and further social conditions, live concerts are the main dancing events in metal. Research has attended to them with insightful results, as described above. Yet, dancing is not restricted to physical spaces such as live concerts but also takes place digitally. This became especially apparent when the Covid-19 pandemic forced concert venues to close down, encouraging alternative formats such as live streams of bands performing while audience members sit individually at home and simultaneously inhabit a shared digital space via platforms such as Zoom or Twitch. Although physical bodily inter-action is prevented that way – precisely the aim of these formats – audience members film themselves raising their horns, banging their heads or otherwise going wild in their homes. The workings of these hybrid dance experiences have yet to be explored, and their investigation might reveal fluid body/media constellations and contribute to dismant-ling nature/culture dichotomies. This possibility is slightly touched upon by Paula Rowe when her interviewees, some of whom have never physic-ally participated in a mosh pit but have watched recorded performances, describe feelings of care and community in mosh pits.[30]

Digital space is not the only dance environment scholars have scarcely paid attention to so far. Despite the fact that metal is heard, played and lived all over the world, metal studies have less to say about metal dance in the Global South, as significantly more of the usually ethnographic research has been conducted in the Global North, especially in English-speaking countries.[31] A simple extrapolation of these findings to the Global South would reinforce a hegemonic overgeneralisation that assumes the Global

North as the universal norm. In order to prevent this, it is necessary to take the situatedness of dance practices seriously and investigate how they figure into the lives and experiences of metal cultures and fans from the Global South. A similar argument motivated Eliut Rivera-Segarra and colleagues in their research on mosh pits in Puerto Rico.[32] Furthermore, the global circulation of metal and its movements also begs the question of how movements are consumed and how their meanings have shifted as they have travelled the globe. When Mahafsoun performs at a concert in Vancouver, as described in vignette 2, issues surrounding exoticising gazes, for example, emerge that warrant further investigation.

Metal Dance Histories

A further aspect that is crucial to dance as a cultural practice is its historical development, and a more thorough understanding entails grasping transformations and continuities throughout situated dance histories. However, since research on these embodied performances usually relies on ethnographic approaches with valid arguments, insights into metal's dance histories largely remain a desideratum. Two approaches that exemplify such a perspective are provided by Stephen Hudson and Wolf-Georg Zaddach. Hudson investigates headbanging with a focus on the US and argues that it can be viewed as a continuation and exaggeration of movements already present in earlier styles of African American rock and blues music, therefore positioning it as a legacy and not as an entirely new form that first arises in metal.[33] Zaddach's study of metal in the German Democratic Republic vividly depicts the potential consequences faced by moshers and the musicians, who instigated mosh pits, when confronted with a repressive governmental system.[34] This could include, for example, the forced break-up of bands because they were perceived to incite riot-like behaviour.

Relating Music and Movement in Metal

The last gap in knowledge to be briefly addressed in this chapter is the relation between metal music and metal dance as aesthetic and performative practices. While side notes frequently mention the central importance of music for dance, research has barely examined their relation in detail.

Stephen Hudson develops a construction-based theory of musical metre and turns to headbanging with the aim of identifying how music can invite people to headbang.[35] To this end, he investigates two of metal's most common metering constructions by which he means 'any conventional association between a specific way of moving, a specific syntactic function or rhythmic interpretation, and specific sounding musical features'.[36] The metering constructions he turns to are backbeats and 3+3+2 phrase endings.[37] Analysing these by mainly focusing on the music of Metallica, Hudson relates headbanging movements to features of sounding music, especially rhythm. In this way, he is able to position headbanging as a cultural convention among metalheads while simultaneously considering the individual freedom in feeling and interpreting musical rhythm through the body as described in vignette 1.[38] In his discussion of groove in doom metal, Jonathan Piper similarly emphasises that headbanging is not just an automatic reaction to imperious music. Instead, headbangers respond variedly to musical developments, including modifications in headbanging style, and actively embody their temporal experience of the music.[39]

A musical feature often associated with metal dance are so-called mosh parts, a term originating from fan and journalistic discourses and adopted in musicology. Generally, mosh parts designate sections in songs that seem to particularly invite moshing. According to Dietmar Elflein's extensive study of heavy metal's musical language, they are characterised by a perceived reduction in tempo, in that the pulse of at least one crucial sound layer (for example, drums or rhythm guitar) is halved or slowed down even further, and have gained in prominence, especially with the development of extreme metal in the 1980s.[40] Although it might seem like a paradox, it is the perceived slowing down of the music that is accompanied by heightened dance activity. Glenn Pillsbury, whose work Elflein partly draws on, lays out a similar notion of mosh parts, which he integrates into his description of cycles of (musical) energy that 'focus power and intensity into bodily experience'.[41] Varying combinations of musical elements such as distorted and palm-muted timbres, rhythmic intensities, the register and range of riffs, and variations in the perceived speed amount to different levels of energy throughout a song. These are, in turn, embodied by musicians and audience members through headbanging and moshing as well as through rigid postures and jerking movements, for example.[42] By considering the contribution of sound specifics and the register and range of guitar riffs, Pillsbury broadens the musical scope beyond the crucial role of rhythm and tempo for a bodily engagement with music.

Another formal section closely related to mosh parts and moshing is breakdowns. In his multifaceted analysis of breakdowns in twenty-first century metal(core), Steven Gamble observes that this musical structure stimulates moshing in a similar way to mosh parts and actually positions mosh parts as progenitors of breakdowns in recent metal music.[43] In his definition, breakdowns are characterised by a two-part pulse structure: cymbals and snare drum create a solid backbeat that establishes a regular metre. The rhythm is set against this as a second structure that consists of potentially complex patterns of kick drum hits and guitar chugs played in unison and contrasting the regularity of the metre. This relation is asymmetrical in favour of what he calls a 'metrical hegemony', as audience members are more likely to engage with the regular backbeat. Gamble relates this musical tension between metre and rhythm in breakdowns to tensions and negotiations between local pit communities and 'wider society': 'Breakdowns invite listeners to mirror perceptual properties of the music in the listening process, acting out the tension between rhythm and metre with their own imagined contest against constraints'.[44]

Despite these insightful contributions to the study of music-movement relations, further research is needed. Similar to the generally narrow focus mentioned above, a broader scope would be beneficial that extends beyond the relation of music to headbanging and moshing, beyond a focus on rhythm and tempo, and beyond 1980s extreme metal (particularly Metallica), although there is already significant work that addresses the latter two aspects. Finally, in terms of methodology, an integration of different research approaches would be a reasonable next step. While ethnographic investigations into metal dance as communities tend to neglect consideration of the music, musical analyses have tended to forego ethnographic fieldwork and rely instead on audio-visual recordings of concerts. Combining participant observation and approaches to music and movement analysis promises further insights into the interactive, embodied relationship between metal music and bodies.

Conclusion

As this introductory chapter has hopefully shown, research on dance practices in metal offers differentiated analyses and a rich understanding of these interactions. In the process, it becomes transparent that uninformed devaluations of dance and its practitioners are just as untenable as sweeping praise of aspects such as inclusivity and communality, as can sometimes be found in fan discourse. Nevertheless, considerable gaps and desiderata still need to be attended to. Although these have been described separately, they are actually intertwined, as, for example, the relationship between music and movement is not isolated from, but feeds into, the communal experiences offered by moshing and other practices. These intersections are what metal studies need to engage with if they are to further a notion of dance in metal as a heterogeneous, complex and culturally situated practice.

Notes

1. Mahafsoun, 'Orphaned Land Feat: Bellydancer Mahafsoun {Sapari} ~ Vancouver', *YouTube* (2020). www.youtube.com/watch?v=I7gX3TCyDPA (accessed 14 April 2022). More information on Mahafsoun is available at www.mahafsoun.art/about.
2. To give a contrasting example, in Germany 'moshing' can also simply denote headbanging.
3. An instance of such a 'corporeal etiquette' can be found in Sherril Dodds, *Dancing on the Canon: Embodiments of Value in Popular Dance* (Palgrave Macmillan, 2011), p. 157. Further numerous examples, provided by fans, can be found on video platforms such as YouTube.
4. Harris M. Berger, *Metal, Rock, and Jazz: Perception and the Phenomenology of Musical Experience* (Wesleyan University Press, 1999), pp. 70–3.
5. Dodds, *Dancing on the Canon*, pp. 152–9.
6. Katharina Inhetveen, 'Gesellige Gewalt: Ritual, Spiel und Vergemeinschaftung bei Hardcorekonzerten', in Trutz von Trotha (ed.), *Soziologie der Gewalt* (Westdeutscher Verlag, 1997), pp. 235–60.
7. For further early investigations on moshing practices in hardcore cultures see Bradford Scott Simon, 'Entering the Pit: Slam-Dancing and Modernity', *Journal of Popular Culture* 31 (1997): 149–76; William Tsitsos, 'Rules of Rebellion: Slamdancing, Moshing, and the American Alternative Scene', *Popular Music* 18 (1999): 397–414.
8. Inhetveen, 'Gesellige Gewalt', pp. 241–6.
9. *Ibid.*, p. 252.
10. Gabrielle Riches, 'Embracing the Chaos: Mosh Pits, Extreme Metal Music and Liminality', *Journal for Cultural Research* 15 (2011): 315–30.
11. *Ibid.*, p. 324.
12. Craig T. Palmer, 'Mummers and Moshers: Two Rituals of Trust in Changing Social Environments', *Ethnology* 44 (2005): 147–66.
13. Rosemary Overell, *Affective Intensities in Extreme Music Scenes: Cases from Australia and Japan* (Palgrave Macmillan, 2014), pp. 23–4.
14. *Ibid.*, p. 13.
15. Something that is generally acknowledged but hardly explored by the mentioned research is how crucial the music is to dance. After all, these are not groups that move randomly, but all the mentioned activities and processes take place during and interact with musical performances.
16. Jonathan Gruzelier, 'Mosh Pit Menace and Masculine Mayhem', in Freya Jarman-Ivens (ed.), *Oh Boy: Masculinities and Popular Music* (Routledge, 2007), pp. 59–76; Leigh Krenske and Jim McKay, '"Hard and Heavy": Gender and Power in a Heavy Metal Music Subculture', *Gender, Place, and Culture* 7 (2000): 287–304 .

17. Gruzelier, 'Mosh Pit Menace'; Gabby Riches, 'Brothers of Metal! Heavy Metal Masculinities, Moshpit Practices and Homosociality', in Steven Roberts (ed.), *Debating Modern Masculinities: Change, Continuity, Crisis?* (Palgrave Macmillan, 2014), pp. 88–105.

18. Riches, 'Brothers of Metal!'.

19. *Ibid.*, p. 99.

20. Gabrielle Riches, Brett Lashua and Karl Spracklen, 'Female, Mosher, Transgressor: A "Moshography" of Transgressive Practices within the Leeds Extreme Metal Scene', *IASPM Journal* 4 (2014): 87–100.

21. Riches, 'Embracing the Chaos', p. 327.

22. *Ibid.*; Gruzelier, 'Mosh Pit Menace', p. 67; Riches, Lashua and Spracklen, 'Female, Mosher, Transgressor', pp. 90, 96.

23. Riches, Lashua and Spracklen, 'Female, Mosher, Transgressor', pp. 94–5.

24. *Ibid.*, p. 95. Riches' interview partners all reported such resilient behaviour on their part. Yet, it should be noted that they seem to be experienced fans, who are more likely to be located at the core of the scene, as they 'engage in everyday scene activities' (p. 92). It is hard to tell whether less experienced novices who relate to the scene more casually might find it more difficult to insist on their participation.

25. *Ibid.*

26. Riches, 'Brothers of Metal!', pp. 96–8.

27. Amber R. Clifford-Napoleone, *Queerness in Heavy Metal Music: Metal Bent* (Routledge, 2015), pp. 123–4.

28. *Ibid.*, p. 124. As described above, moshing does not only consist of 'disorganized movements' and 'out-of-control bodies' but is constituted by a more ambivalent interplay of social regulation and experiential disorientation.

29. Rosemary Lucy Hill, *Gender, Metal and the Media: Women Fans and the Gendered Experience of Music* (Palgrave Macmillan, 2016), p. 4.

30. Paula Rowe, '"We're in this Together and We Take Care of Our Own": Narrative Constructions of Metal Community Told by Metal Youth', in Nelson Varas-Díaz and Niall Scott (eds.), *Heavy Metal Music and the Communal Experience* (Lexington Books, 2016), pp. 85, 87, 96, n7.

31. As a reminder: Berger: USA; Dodds: UK; Gruzelier: UK; Inhetveen: Germany; Krenske/McKay: Australia; Overell: Australia, Japan; Riches (et al.): Canada, Germany, UK.

32. Eliut Rivera-Segarra, Sigrid Mendoza and Nelson Varas-Díaz, 'Entre el orden y el caos: El papel del mosh en la comunidad metalera de Puerto Rico', *Revista de Ciencias Sociales* 28 (2015): 104–21.

33. Stephen Hudson, 'Metal Movements: Headbanging as a Legacy of African American Dance', in Toni-Matti Karjalainen and Kimi Kärki (eds.), *Modern Heavy Metal: Markets, Practices and Cultures: International Academic Research Conference, June 8–12 2015, Helsinki, Finland: Conference Proceedings* (Aalto University, 2015), pp. 445–53.

34. Wolf-Georg Zaddach, *Heavy Metal in der DDR: Szene, Akteure, Praktiken* (Transcript, 2018), pp. 195–7.
35. Stephen Hudson, *Feeling Beats and Experiencing Motion: A Construction-Based Theory of Meter*, doctoral dissertation (Northwestern University, 2019).
36. *Ibid.*, p. 54.
37. Hudson defines backbeats as a rhythmic pattern with snare drum accents on beats 2 and 4 of a 4/4 bar that simultaneously implies beats 1 and 3 as strong beats. His notion of a 3+3+2 phrase ending entails an accent pattern at the end of a musical phrase that is played in unison by guitars and drums, and which arranges groups of 3-pulses into phrase durations that are powers of 2 (*Ibid.*, pp. 57, 62–4).
38. *Ibid.*, pp. 54–65.
39. Jonathan Piper, *Locating Experiential Richness in Doom Metal*, doctoral dissertation (University of California San Diego, 2013), p. 60.
40. Dietmar Elflein, *Schwermetallanalysen: Die musikalische Sprache des Heavy Metal* (Transcript, 2010), p. 282f.
41. Glenn T. Pillsbury, *Damage Incorporated: Metallica and the Production of Musical Identity* (Routledge, 2006), p. 10.
42. *Ibid.*, pp. 10–14.
43. Steven Gamble, 'Breaking Down the Breakdown in Twenty-First-Century Metal', *Metal Music Studies* 5 (2019): 338, 347. On a terminological note, Elflein and Gamble define breakdowns differently, as they base their definitions on songs from different points in time. While Elflein engages with burgeoning 1980s extreme metal, Gamble develops his notion with respect to twenty first century metal and metalcore. The difference becomes tangible as both coincidentally analyse the same section of Slayer's *Raining Blood* for illustrative purposes: Gamble denotes a section as proto-breakdown which is a mosh part to Elflein, while the immediately preceding iteration of the riff in question without the drums is described as breakdown by Elflein (Elflein, *Schwermetallanalysen*, p. 285; Gamble, 'Breaking Down the Breakdown', pp. 342–3).
44. *Ibid.*, p. 349.

15 | Battle Jackets

Wearing Metal Identity

THOMAS CARDWELL

For anyone who has attended a heavy metal concert, or seen fans congregating outside one, the particular aesthetics of metal style will be familiar. Metal clothing is famously characterised by the fabrics denim and leather, to such an extent that the British band Saxon even named a song and album, *Denim and Leather* (1981), after this combination. The de facto uniform of the concert crowd is the band t-shirt, usually black, adorned with bold graphics and logos announcing the wearer's band of choice. Paired with jeans and boots or trainers, the band t-shirt is the staple of most metal wardrobes. For the committed fan, the outfit is often completed by a customised 'battle jacket' uniquely configured to the wearer's preference (see Figure 15.1). A battle jacket – also variously known as a battle vest, patch jacket, cut-off or *Kutte* – is a denim jacket, usually with the sleeves removed, decorated with patches, badges, studs, festival bands, handmade artworks and various other embellishments added by the owner to display their musical taste and allegiances.[1]

Battle jackets are an important expression of metal identity for many fans and musicians and allow individuals to demonstrate commitment to metal subcultures and signify difference from mainstream styles and values. This chapter discusses the history and origins of battle jackets as a key component of metal style and considers the meanings and significance of these garments for those that make and wear them. The following argument makes reference to a series of interviews conducted by the author with jacket makers between 2014 and 2020.

Heavy Metal Style

As with the music itself, heavy metal style evolved in large part from the 1960s counterculture, as well as bringing influences from blues culture via 1950s rock 'n' roll,[2] both of which had connections with working class and manual labour, with the prevalence of denim as a workwear fabric giving rise to the term 'blue collar'.[3] Motorcycle culture also had a significant impact on the development of metal style, with the leather jackets, jeans and boots favoured by bikers becoming commonplace in rock and metal wardrobes by the 1970s.[4] The historically masculinist codes of such working-class cultures, along with connections to military traditions, have caused many to view heavy metal clothing as at best nostalgic and at worst reactionary,[5] with limited stylistic options available for women. Writing in 1985, Philip Bashe identified two alternatives for female metal fans when it came to clothing, either dressing like 'the boys' or else adopting the looks of the 'goddesses they see in their heroes' videos'.[6] Whilst possibilities for more nuanced negotiation of gender identities through metal clothing arguably exist in today's scenes (more on which later), these connotations ostensibly persist.

One of the key functions of heavy metal style is to mark the wearer as part of the 'community of all metalheads'[7] and to differentiate them from the perceived mainstream.[8] As one fan I interviewed, Emily, put it when talking about her jacket: 'You tend to exclude the mainstream from your insider [culture]. I call it "outsider/insider" because you're an outsider, but you're inside of this outsider culture'. This sense of distinction from wider culture is reinforced through the challenging and sometimes extreme nature of the images and texts that feature on metal clothing.[9] The 'insider' or community aspect of metal fandom is expressed through individuality negotiated within the stylistic structures of the wider subcultural group. A sense of the tribal is apparent in metalhead style, for example, in the prevalence of long hair, beards, tattoos and DIY customisation of clothing.[10] In these respects, the battle jacket is emblematic of many aspects of metal culture through its distinctiveness, connection to subcultural structures and traditions and personal construction.

Key Features of a Battle Jacket

Although individually customised, most battle jackets adhere to a set of tacitly agreed conventions amongst makers. The majority of jackets are based on the classic denim jacket epitomised by the 'type III' jacket created by Levi Strauss in the USA in the early 1960s;[11] other popular garments are leather jackets, military jackets and workwear shirts. This includes a large rectangular area on the back of the jacket formed by the borders of the yoke, side panels and waistband. This area provides a prominent location to display patches or other artwork and is usually the site of a 'backpatch' – a large patch featuring detailed artwork and band logo, which is generally chosen to foreground a band that the wearer favours above most others. Around the backpatch, smaller patches can be displayed, often in closely-tessellated rows and columns (see Figure 15.2). The yoke area across the shoulders provides another large space but on a narrow landscape orientation, making it suited for large text-based logo patches, or a series of smaller patches. The area at the base of the back of the jacket is often populated by one or more 'superstrip' patches – wide horizontal patches, which usually bear a text logo appended by small artworks.[12]

The front of the jacket can be adorned with small patches as well as pin badges, studs and festival wristbands sewn on as strips (giving an effect similar to military rank colours) and other chosen additions (see Figure 15.3). Unlike the back of the jacket, the front does not afford any ideal spaces for bigger patches, as it is interrupted by fastenings (for example, buttons and buttonholes), collar, pockets and vertical seams. Nonetheless, some fans manage to feature large patches or artworks on the front, perhaps by changing the orientation of the patch, or cutting the patch in half and sewing half on each side of the front, so that the image is unified when the jacket is closed. Most battle jackets have the sleeves removed, allowing them to be worn over another garment (hence the popular term 'battle vest' used interchangeably with 'battle jacket'), although some choose to retain them, in which case further patches can be added.

Amongst jacket makers like those interviewed, there are variously acknowledged 'rules' about how a jacket should be composed and what type of patches these should feature. These rules are rarely universal but may be upheld as important by certain groups of makers or fans of particular genres of metal. Perhaps the most commonly held view is that a jacket should only feature patches relating to bands that the wearer has a sincere appreciation for. Some extend this to a qualification that one should own physical music (vinyl, cassettes, CDs) by the featured band, and others argue that they must have attended live concerts by each artist. Another common 'rule' is that a jacket should not be 'double patched', that is, feature only one patch by any particular band. There are many exceptions to this rule, however, notably in the genre of 'tribute jackets' that exclusively feature patches representing a favourite band.

Some fans maintain that a jacket should be genre-specific, featuring only patches for 1990s death metal bands or black metal bands, for example.

Figure 15.1 Tom Cardwell, Moonsorrow, 2020, watercolour painting on paper, 38 × 26 cm (© Tom Cardwell)

Many jacket makers emphasise the importance of personal choice above genre conformity, however. As a maker called Pete put it:

Because this is documenting my life and my taste in music, and consequently, there's a lot of non-metal stuff on here as well, which *really* f**ks people off! The 'true metal heads' go, 'How can you have *that* next to *that*?!', and I say, 'Because I like 'em!'.

For all the credence extended to various rules by some, a common rejoinder to this attitude is expressed by Simon Springer, founder of Pull the Plug patches: 'The overarching theme is (that) there should be no rules! It's metal, it's supposed to be rebellious'.[13]

History and Development of Battle Jackets

Whilst it is difficult to say for certain when battle jacket-making first started, it seems to have been well established by the time heavy metal music became widely popular in the 1970s.[14] Methods of customisation around this time included hand embroidery, which was practised by fans as a way of rendering band logos on their jackets in the absence of readily available commercial patches.[15] Once bands began to cater to the demand for patches, these became a way of commemorating particular gigs and tours, with unique editions sold at merchandise stands in concert venues. This means of distribution lent a sense of authority to the patches, as possessing a particular patch would usually indicate that the wearer had attended the concert it had been sold at. The battle jacket thus became a garment that testified to lived experience, with a heavily patched vest marking its wearer as someone who was deeply invested in the subculture.

The sense of a battle jacket as a marker of subcultural status owes much to the heritage of motorcycle jackets, and particularly the denim or leather 'cut-offs' worn by members of 'outlaw' bike clubs, which feature patches bearing logos of club affiliation and rank.[16] The quasi-military order of the patches on bikers' jackets is arguably linked to the formation of such clubs by returning veterans after World War II and the Vietnam War in America.[17] Military uniforms themselves have been highly influential in heavy metal style, just as themes and imagery of war and conflict feature regularly in metal music. Some bands produce artworks and merchandise that directly reference military insignia and patches,[18] and items of combat gear such as camouflaged clothing and army boots are staples of metal fans' attire. Indeed, the term 'battle jacket' directly connects the garments to such traditions. During World War II, bomber crews wore leather flying jackets (most popularly the A2 type), which were often custom painted with the nose artwork from the plane they operated, as well as tally markings that enumerated missions flown or targets destroyed.[19]

Going back even further in history, early antecedents for metal fans' jackets might be found in the heraldic tabards and armour worn by combatants in the Middle Ages.[20] The tradition of heraldry has continued in folk costumes, such as those worn by Morris dancers, which are customised with badges, bells, coloured fabrics and small objects,[21] in a parallel of the customisation of battle jackets. Like battle jackets, these costumes are worn in a performative context and play a key role in marking the wearer as part of the group and a participant in the festivities at hand.

Amongst twentieth century youth subcultures, there are many examples of customised clothing that compare directly to the jackets of heavy metal fans.[22] During the 1950s in Britain, informal motorcycle subcultures such as the 'rockers' and 'ton-up boys' customised their leather jackets (often based on the famous 'Perfecto' style popularised by Marlon Brando in the 1953 movie *The Wild One*) with bike logos, club badges and 'run patches', which commemorated particular rides, in much the same way as metal band patches commemorated concerts.[23] During the 1970s and 1980s, punks re-appropriated leather biker jackets, which were decorated with hand-painted logos and slogans, studs, chains and other additions.[24] A number of post-punk subcultures, such as goths and crustpunks, also used hand-painting on leather jackets as a key mode of individuation.

Whilst battle jacket-making has remained an important part of metal subcultures since the practice was first established, there have been periods and genres of metal in which it has been particularly popular. The early 1980s was one such period when genres such as the New Wave of British Heavy Metal (NWOBHM) in the UK and thrash metal in the USA both saw an emphasis on battle jackets amongst musicians and fans. During the 1990s, battle jackets were perhaps less common, as the genres of nu metal and grunge changed the style and expression of metal fans,[25] although even during this period, jacket customisation practices persisted in extreme genres such as black metal[26] and death metal. After the turn of the millennium, the popularity of previous styles of metal grew once more, and battle jacket-making enjoyed a renaissance, which has continued until now.[27] Today, battle jackets are very much in evidence in many metal scenes, with a large online community that post images of jackets and trade patches.[28] Part of the present popularity may be driven by the nostalgic interest of veteran fans, who wish to revive the jacket-making of their younger days. Louis, a jacket maker who sells patches and jackets through an online store, comments: 'I do get a lot [of customers] who are older ..., and they had their own jackets back in the day, and they've either sold them or lost them, and now they see that they can get another one'.

Global Jacket Scenes

If battle jackets, like heavy metal music and culture more broadly, were once considered predominantly Western, today they are increasingly globalised.[29] Metal fans and musicians in Australasia, Africa, Asia and South America, as well as Europe and North America, have taken up jacket customisation as part of their identification with metal culture.

In Malaysia, Marco Ferrarese found that fans placed great importance on obtaining authentic patches of death and thrash metal bands from the 1980s and 1990s to populate their jackets, with Western bands being particularly sought after.[30] In Indonesia, patch collecting is also a big part of metal culture, with fans using social media to showcase their densely patched jackets.[31] For fans in Nepal, the prohibitive cost of metal merchandise compared to local wages can be a limitation for fans, although many will use DIY methods to customise various items of clothing.[32] For the 'cowboy metalheads' of Botswana,[33] leather clothing is more common than denim, although some fans there sew band patches onto their jackets or waistcoats, with bands such as Iron Maiden and Cannibal Corpse being particularly popular.[34]

Whilst the exact expression of battle jacket practices varies from place to place, reflecting geographic and cultural specificities, in many ways, battle jackets can be considered a globally observed marker of metal fandom, with the universalising effects of online discourse allowing fans everywhere to post and view jackets and obtain patches. Like the ubiquitous band t-shirt,[35] the battle jacket is an overt way for fans everywhere to stand out from the crowd and fit in with metal subcultures.

'They Should Represent Your Life': Personal Meanings and the Subcultural Significance of Battle Jackets

Within most subcultures, negotiating personal identity within the tacitly agreed structures of the subcultural community is important. In her research into club cultures in the UK during the 1990s, Sarah Thornton emphasised the importance of gaining and maintaining 'subcultural capital' for members of these scenes.[36] In relation to metal, Nicola Allett looked at the 'connoisseurship' exhibited by extreme metal fans, expressed through distinctions of taste and esoteric knowledge of metal music and culture.[37] David Muggleton has written extensively about the conditions of subcultural engagement in a postmodern context, highlighting the importance of 'insider/outsider' distinctions and individual negotiation of a personal sense of subcultural identity.[38] Authenticity is key for many subcultures and is especially important in heavy metal. J. Patrick Williams summarises some of the important debates on this in subcultural literature.[39] Niall Scott discusses ways in which resistance is demonstrated amongst metal fans, whether on a literal or symbolic level, and the importance of symbolism in this regard.[40] Metal fans continue to signify differences from mainstream culture and allegiance to metal through their clothing and appearance, as Rosemary Overell[41] and Paula Rowe[42] both testify in their research.

As I have demonstrated through my own research,[43] the making and wearing of a battle jacket represents a serious investment (of both time and money) in metal culture by the fan. Lauren O'Hagan also emphasises this point in her interview study of a broad group of metal fans who post and discuss their jackets online.[44]

Identity

For many fans, a sense of personal identity is closely bound up with the meanings of their battle jacket. As one interviewee called Eleanor remarked: 'It's expressive. It is who you are. It's definitely important. I think we ... find style quite an important thing'. Another fan, Alex, put it this way: 'This is a *personal* thing. You can't go and *buy* a jacket like this. And why would you, if you could? Because it doesn't make sense'. For Alex, the meaning of the jacket is fundamentally tied to its uniqueness, and the fact that she made it herself.

The choice of patches, as well as their arrangement on the jacket, are some of the most important factors for any wearer, with the selection of bands to feature indicating a fan's taste and showing others within the subcultures which genre(s) of metal they identify with.

Whilst there may be a sense in which the wearer is conscious of peer approval in this selection,[45] many claim that it is important to show their personal taste, even if others may consider this idiosyncratic. Pete, a long-time jacket maker and metal musician, emphasised the importance of authentic expression in his choice of band patches. In a view that is characteristic of many in metal subcultures, Pete would only feature patches on his jacket from bands that he had a strong liking for, and in most cases, had seen in concert:

They should represent your life. And in this case, my life in bands. Like the bike jackets. You only get a patch if you've done something to get it . . . you have to earn them by being there and getting it and saying, 'I was there and here's the proof!' And that's how I treat this jacket. I only put on patches of bands that I have seen live, and that's a rule.

In this sense, the jacket acts as a document of lived experience, a form of externalised autobiography for the metal fan. In a broader popular culture landscape in which style is often chosen over substance, the battle jacket wearer values genuine investment in the music and culture they are

Figure 15.2 Metal fan photographed at Bloodstock Festival, UK, August 2014.
Photograph by Jon Cardwell (© Jon Cardwell)

displaying on their clothing. Authenticity is a fundamental value for metalheads,[46] and this is visually communicated through the DIY construction of the battle jacket[47] – the handmade aspects testifying to personal investment through its making and a lack of concern for 'slickness' or refinement – as well as through patch choices.

Patches may also carry personal meanings. For Tony, some reminded him of his changing musical tastes, whilst a particular patch was connected to a life change when his girlfriend moved in with him:

The Almighty patch is off my old jacket. So that patch is over twenty years old, as is the Wolfsbane one. The Skid Row one's off my old jacket. The Volbeat one's new, Airbourne one's new. But the Slash one, I actually found that one, I've just had my girlfriend move in with me, and I was clearing out a load of drawers, and I found it at the bottom of the drawer.

Battle Jackets and Gender Identities

As has been previously mentioned, the prevalence of denim and leather in metal style can often be thought of in terms of working-class masculinities.[48] For early metal scholars writing in the 1980s and 1990s, these styles, and the subcultures they represented, were interpreted as masculinist and even misogynistic.[49] Whilst a 'traditional' white male audience is still predominant in many genres of metal,[50] increasingly, academic research testifies to growing diversity in heavy metal.[51] Feminist and queer perspectives bring new interpretations to metal and metal style.[52]

Niall Scott suggests that metal masculinity 'is in a confident state of flux and diverse in its expression',[53] offering a range of expressive options for men that do not necessarily conform to traditional gender representations. In her study of female metal fans in Canada, Jenna Kummer argued that these women resisted patriarchal meanings through the active choices they made with their clothing, responding in personal ways to challenge or subvert masculinist expectations.[54] A queer perspective on metal culture is expounded by Amber Clifford-Napoleone, who suggests that metal culture, in general, can be read as a 'queerscape' that does not necessitate the reinforcing of traditional gender norms.[55] Clifford-Napoleone points to the influence of queer BDSM (Bondage, Domination and Sado-Masochism) clothing on metal style.[56] Perhaps the most famous example of this is Rob Halford, frontman of Judas Priest and arguably the most prominent openly gay metal musician.[57] The prominence of hand sewing, and even embroidery, in battle jacket-making offers a contrast to common gender expectations, as in many other areas of culture, needlework is still thought of as a feminine occupation, which is less likely to be embraced by men.[58]

Whilst many who make battle jackets are male, an increasing number of women are taking up jacket-making on their own terms. Some suggest that female fans bring different approaches to their jackets, as this excerpt from my interview with two jacket makers, Eleanor and Jemima, indicates: 'A lot of the guys actually tend to have really laid-out ... regimented structured jackets. Boys do it. But I prefer things to be a little bit out-of-place and a little bit ... wonky and stuff like that'. Others discuss bringing particular design agendas to their jacket-making, and all view it as an important means of self-expression. Yasmin, a British Pakistani woman, who is a prolific jacket maker, emphasises the growing possibilities for expressing diversity through metal styles: 'It's nice to see [people from] other backgrounds with battle jackets or people who are into metal, as metal is mostly male, or a white audience'. As a deeply personal garment that offers connections to wider subcultural norms and discourses within metal, a battle jacket provides scope for the individual to express their own identity and values in ways that an 'off-the-peg' item would not.

Conclusion

Worn in various guises by fans for around the last fifty years, battle jackets are firmly established as a key element of heavy metal style. Whilst perhaps not as ubiquitous as band t-shirts, battle jackets epitomise serious metal allegiance in a way that no other garments do. The personal customisation and DIY ethos of these jackets allow them to function as unique expressions

Figure 15.3 Tom Cardwell, Aidan's Jacket (Front), 2015, watercolour painting on paper, 38 × 26 cm (© Tom Cardwell)

of individual identity, as documents of lived experience and as an external-isation of the wearer's musical taste. The collecting and trading of patches, as well as the posting and responding to images of jackets online, are key aspects of the international battle jacket community.

Like heavy metal itself, whilst battle jacket-making might have started in Europe, Great Britain and North America, it is an increasingly globalised practice which connects fans in disparate locations. Battle jacket-making offers the individual fan the opportunity to negotiate and express their personal identity whilst also connecting them to wider metal subcultural communities. This interface of the personal and the communal is reflected in the material structure of the battle jacket, as the common form and framework facilitate personal configuration. As one fan put it, '[t]hey should represent your life!'.

Notes

1. Tom Cardwell, 'Battle Jackets, Authenticity and "Material Individuality"', *Metal Music Studies* 3/3 (2017): 437–58.
2. Deena Weinstein, *Heavy Metal: The Music and its Culture* (Da Capo Press, 2000), p. 100.
3. John Fiske, *Reading the Popular* (Routledge, 1990), p. 5.
4. Weinstein, *Heavy Metal*, pp. 127–8.
5. See, for example, Robert Walser, *Running with the Devil: Power, Gender and Madness in Heavy Metal Music* (Wesleyan University Press, 1993), pp. 108–36.
6. Philip Bashe, *Heavy Metal Thunder: The Music, Its History, Its Heroes* (Dolphin, 1985), p. 8.
7. Ana Baka, 'The Forming of a Metalhead: Constructing a Subcultural Identity', in Toni-Matti Karjalainen and Kimi Kärki (eds.), *Modern Heavy Metal: Markets, Practices and Cultures* (Aalto University Press, 2015), pp. 55–63.
8. David Muggleton, *Inside Subculture: The Postmodern Meaning of Style* (Berg, 2000), pp. 63–4.
9. See, for example, Bryan A. Bardine, 'Metal and Gothic Literature: Examining the Darker Side of Life (and Death)', in Toni-Matti Karjalainen and Kimi Kärki (eds.), *Modern Heavy Metal: Markets, Practices and Cultures* (Aalto University Press, 2015), pp. 572–81.
10. Weinstein, *Heavy Metal*, p. 129.
11. Alexander Ramos, 'Levi's Denim Trucker Jacket Overview: Type I, II and III', *Heddels* (2013). www.heddels.com/2013/03/levis-denim-trucker-jacket-review-type-i-ii-and-iii (accessed 24 June 2021).
12. Tom Cardwell, *Still Life and Death Metal: Painting the Battle Jacket*, doctoral dissertation (University of the Arts London, 2017), pp. 127–33. https://

ualresearchonline.arts.ac.uk/id/eprint/12036/1/Thesis%20TC%20final%20PV
%20edit%20(2)%20Web%20version.compressed.pdf (accessed 22 June 2021).

13. Sarah Kitteringham, *Fabric of Metal*, episode 2 (Banger TV, 2021). www
.youtube.com/watch?v=E35-J5Viq_0 (accessed 24 June 2021).

14. Cardwell, 'Battle Jackets', p. 439.

15. *Ibid.*, p. 454.

16. Steven Alford and Suzanne Ferriss, *Motorcycle* (Reaktion, 2008), pp. 86–7.

17. Karl Vick, 'Roots of a Biker Battle', *Time* (1 June 2015), p. 10. https://time.com
/3892040/roots-of-a-biker-battle/ (accessed 28 June 2021)

18. See, for example, the artwork for Megadeth's *So Far, So Good . . . So What!*
(1988) or Watain's 'Black Metal Militia'.

19. Lisa Hix, 'WWII War Paint: How Bomber-Jacket Art Emboldened Our Boys',
Collectors Weekly (6 December 2012). www.collectorsweekly.com/articles/
wwii-war-paint-how-bomber-jacket-art-emboldened-our-boys (accessed
22 June 2021).

20. Cardwell, *Still Life and Death Metal*, pp. 104–7.

21. Chloe Metcalfe, *The Full English: Beginners Guide English Folk Costumes*
(English Folk Dance and Song Society, 2015), p. 7. http://media.efdss.org.uk
/resourcebank/docs/RB025BeginnersGuideEnglishFolkCostume-
ChloeMetcalfe-Revised-May-2015.pdf (accessed 22 June 2021).

22. Ted Polhemus, *Street Style: From Sidewalk to Catwalk* (V&A, 1994).

23. See Horst Friedrichs, *Pride and Glory: The Art of the Rockers' Jacket* (DAAB
Media, 2012); Johnny Stewart, *Rockers! Kings of the Road* (Plexus, 1989).

24. Monica Sklar, *Punk Style* (Bloomsbury, 2013).

25. Weinstein, *Heavy Metal*, pp. 56–7.

26. See Jørn Stubberud, Svein Strømmen and Christian Belgaux, *Death Archives:
Mayhem 1984–94* (Ecstatic Peace Library, 2016).

27. Cardwell, 'Battle Jackets', p. 443.

28. See, for example, https://tshirtslayer.com (accessed 22 June 2021).

29. See Jeremy Wallach, Harris M. Berger and Paul D. Greene (eds.), *Metal Rules
the Globe: Heavy Metal Music Around the World* (Duke University Press, 2011).

30. Marco Ferrarese, 'Heavy Metal Nothingness: Alluring Foreignness and
Authenticity Construction in Early 2010s Malaysian Metal', in Toni-Matti
Karjalainen and Kimi Karki (eds.), *Modern Heavy Metal: Markets, Practices
and Cultures* (Aalto University Press, 2015), pp. 195–205.

31. Battle Vest Assault (2020). www.instagram.com/battlevestassault.official
(accessed 22 June 2021).

32. Michael Hann, 'Himalayan Headbangers: In the Moshpit with the Metalheads of
Kathmandu', *The Guardian* (12 January 2020). www.theguardian.com/music/
2020/jan/12/nepal-metal-silence-festival-kathmandu (accessed 22 June 2021).

33. Keith Kahn-Harris and Frank Marshall, 'Botswana's Cowboy Metalheads',
Vice (31 March 2011). www.vice.com/en_uk/article/3b5pp3/atlas-hoods-
botswanas-cowboy-metalheads (accessed 30 July 2020).

34. Bill McGrath, 'The Othering of Botswanan Metal', in Toni-Matti Karjalainen and Kimi Karki (eds.), *Modern Heavy Metal: Markets, Practices and Cultures* (Aalto University Press, 2015), pp. 206–18.

35. Paula Rowe, '"We're in this Together and We Take Care of Our Own": Narrative Constructions of Metal Community Told by Metal Youth', in Nelson Varas-Díaz and Niall Scott (eds.), *Heavy Metal and the Communal Experience* (Lexington Books, 2016), pp. 89–92.

36. Sarah Thornton, *Club Cultures: Music, Media and Subcultural Capital* (Polity Press, 1995).

37. Nicola Allett, 'The Extreme Metal "Connoisseur"', in Titus Hjelm, Keith Kahn-Harris and Mark LeVine (eds.), *Heavy Metal: Controversies and Countercultures* (Equinox, 2013), pp. 166–81.

38. Muggleton, *Inside Subculture*, p. 63.

39. J. Patrick Williams, *Subcultural Theory* (Polity Press, 2011).

40. Niall Scott, 'Heavy Metal as Resistance', in Brenda Gardenour Walter, Gabby Riches, Dave Snell and Bryan Bardine (eds.), *Heavy Metal Studies and Popular Culture* (Palgrave Macmillan, 2016), pp. 19–35.

41. Rosemary Overell, *Affective Intensities in Extreme Music Scenes: Cases from Australia and Japan* (Palgrave Macmillan, 2014), pp. 16, 80.

42. Rowe, 'We're in this Together', pp. 89–92.

43. Tom Cardwell, *Heavy Metal Armour: A Visual Study of Battle Jackets* (Intellect, 2022).

44. Lauren O'Hagan, '"My Musical Armor": Exploring Metalhead Identity through the Battle Jacket', *Rock Music Studies* 9/1 (2022): 34–53.

45. Ferrarese, 'Heavy Metal Nothingness', p. 200.

46. Keith Kahn-Harris, 'Coming Out: Realizing the Possibilities of Metal', in Florian Heesch and Niall Scott (eds.), *Heavy Metal, Gender and Sexuality* (Routledge, 2016), pp. 26–38.

47. Cardwell, 'Battle Jackets', pp. 453–6.

48. Ryan Moore, 'The Unmaking of the English Working Class: Deindustrialisation, Reification and the Origins of Heavy Metal', in Gerd Bayer (ed.), *Heavy Metal Music in Britain* (Routledge, 2016), pp. 143–60.

49. Walser, *Running with the Devil*; Weinstein, *Heavy Metal*.

50. Kahn-Harris, 'Coming Out', p. 27.

51. See, for example, Laina Dawes, *What Are You Doing Here? A Black Woman's Life and Liberation in Heavy Metal* (Bazillion Points, 2012); Laura Wright, 'Transcending the Form, Advancing the Norm: Queer Post-Structuralism in Post-Metal', in Toni-Matti Karjalainen and Kimi Kärki (eds.), *Modern Heavy Metal: Markets, Practices and Cultures* (Aalto University Press, 2015), pp. 247–56.

52. See Amber Clifford-Napoleone, *Queerness in Heavy Metal Music, Metal Bent* (Routledge, 2015); Rosemary Lucy Hill, 'Using Women's Listening Pleasure to Challenge the Notion of Hard Rock and Metal as "Masculine" Music', in

Toni-Matti Karjalainen and Kimi Kärki (eds.), *Modern Heavy Metal: Markets, Practices and Cultures* (Aalto University Press, 2015), pp. 240–6; Catherine Hoad, 'Slashing through the Boundaries: Heavy Metal Fandom, Fan Fiction and Girl Cultures', *Metal Music Studies* 3/1 (2017): 5–22.

53. Niall Scott, 'The Monstrous Male and Myths of Masculinity in Heavy Metal', in Florian Heesch and Niall Scott (eds.), *Heavy Metal, Gender and Sexuality* (Routledge, 2016), pp. 121–31.

54. Jenna Kummer, 'Powerslaves? Navigating Femininity in Heavy Metal', in Brenda Gardenour Walter, , Gabby Riches, Dave Snell and Bryan Bardine (eds.), *Heavy Metal Studies and Popular Culture* (Palgrave Macmillan, 2016), pp. 145–66.

55. Clifford-Napoleone, *Queerness.*

56. Amber Clifford-Napoleone, 'Metal, Masculinity and the Queer Subject', in Florian Heesch and Niall Scott (eds.), *Heavy Metal, Gender and Sexuality* (Routledge, 2016), pp. 39–53.

57. Moore, 'The Unmaking', p. 153.

58. Cardwell, *Heavy Metal Armour*, p. 46.

PART V

Modern Metal Genres

Personal Take V – Arne Jamelle

Metal Labels and the Shift towards Digital

Perhaps the most important job a record label has nowadays is showing artists why they would need a record label, to begin with. In that regard, metal labels, in catering to a narrowly defined audience and working in more or less clear-cut structures, do have an advantage compared to their competitors in most other genres. At its core, metal as a genre is still very much album driven, as opposed to putting out a vast number of standalone digital singles like pop or rap artists would, and thus its loyal fans still show a strong affinity towards the physical product. Digital singles have gained significance for metal bands as well, but for most, they are just promotional assets leading up to an album release.

For a standard album release that contains a variety of physical formats (at least CD and LP) in addition to the full digital treatment, it's very advisable to have a team of experts looking after the various aspects of financing, product management, layout, production, physical and digital distribution and sales, as well as marketing and promotion. This all depends on the individual band's ambitions, of course. Most bigger labels offer all of these services under one roof, and you don't have to hire third-party companies to take care of the aspects you're lacking expertise in. To be honest, with a little effort, a lot of the aforementioned can be handled in a do-it-yourself-fashion by devoted and well-organised artists, but it's both time-consuming, virtually a full-time job in its own right, and potentially quite expensive to outsource occasional jobs that could pop up along the way. The costs involved in kicking off a proper album campaign have led to many bands seeking labels for the sole purpose of using them as credit banks to cover their studio costs and for contractually agreed additional advances for negotiable assets such as separate budgets for videos, album artwork and band photos.

While digital streaming is vastly on the rise for metal, in some territories faster developing than others, buying and listening to CDs and LPs is still being considered the 'normal' way of consuming music for fans of the genre because the purchase of an album or band merchandise is believed to be the gold standard of showing support for an artist. The fixation on a physical product within metal circles could be ascribed to a strong sentiment of nostalgia that has always played a huge part in the musical socialisation of the first generations of metal fans, who grew up with the early waves of proper heavy metal in the 1980s and 1990s and still represent a majority in the scene as a whole. In Germany, one of the biggest markets for metal worldwide, even CDs are still a thing, and some experts already predict a major resurgence of the CD due to the current shortage of raw materials that has led to a ridiculous price increase for vinyl.

In terms of marketing and public relations for metal bands, from a label's perspective, there have been significant changes over the last decade. While you would spend at least 80 per cent of your campaign budget for advertisements in printed press and other analogue formats about ten years ago, today it is the other way around. Most of the money is being spent online nowadays for a much wider potential reach, customisable targeting options on various platforms, more creative ideas to be implemented, as well as for transparency and subsequent evaluation. The shift towards digital has also led to much longer campaigns because you're not only trying to get as many people as possible to buy an album during pre-order or in the first week of release; you also try to build and keep up the momentum of the digital product as a steady source of income. While a decade ago, you would basically spend all of your marketing budget during the two months leading up to an album release for the biggest possible impact and visibility within a relatively short timeframe, modern campaigns can easily stretch out over six months, including several singles, music videos, teasers or other audio-visual assets serving as constant reminders on social media platforms.

In this professional respect, the shift in metal has happened significantly slower than in other popular musical genres, which can partly be attributed to a degree of gatekeeping deeply rooted in the scene's self-conception. Many of the older metal fans have an inexplicable aversion to anything modern and will react allergically to what they perceive as intrusions from outside of their scene, while on the other hand embracing scene integrity and cherishing everything that reminds them of their musical upbringing. Yet again, nostalgia seems to be a huge factor for metal fans, who would trust their favourite magazine writer more than a random person on the internet or a sponsored post that is showing up in their social media feed. This is one of the reasons why some of the established and well-known printed metal magazines still have a decent number of dedicated readers while at the same time maintaining social media accounts with decent interaction, or even video formats and podcasts, transitioning their role as trusted opinion leaders and tastemakers into the world wide web, and thus retaining their relevance as valuable media partners and marketing vehicles, both online and offline. The metal scene seems to be so obsessed with its many dinosaurs and artefacts that even the recording industry is unlikely to be turned upside down or steer in a completely different direction. And maybe that's not a bad thing at all.

Arne Jamelle, Nuclear Blast Records

  On Horseback They Carried Thunder

The Second Lives of Norwegian Black Metal

ROSS HAGEN

Since its first moments of relatively widespread visibility in the 1990s, black metal has become one of the most artistically fruitful styles within extreme metal, as well as one of the most contested. Its emergence into wider public consciousness was occasioned by a rash of serious crimes committed by black metal musicians and fans in Norway in the early 1990s, including a number of arson attacks against historic churches and several murders. These events, coupled with the genre's penchant for neo-fascist political extremism, provided a wealth of lurid material for tabloid journalists, cultural critics, and eventually academics. Although Norway was undoubtedly the crucible in which the black metal aesthetic was forged, the intervening decades have seen it spread across the globe, with some bands finding significant commercial success. The broader musical style itself has also become more eclectic, although many bands continue to devotedly adhere to a narrower and more rigid definition of the style. However, one aspect that has remained constant within black metal's existence as a musical practice is the foregrounding of geographic location and local cultures within both the music and the bands' visual presentation. Although black metal's aesthetic is tied to the Nordic regions in some respects, this notion has inspired bands around the globe to this day. This chapter focuses particularly on black metal as it is currently being cultivated in the Mountain West in the United States, where the musical and ideological conventions of Norwegian black metal are recontextualised into forms that honour this new location while still retaining key points of Norwegian black metal's aesthetic and worldview.

Up North

Black metal's self-actualisation as a coherent musical genre depended on a fairly insular circle of young Norwegian musicians in the late 1980s and early 1990s, who self-consciously determined to chart a path away from the increasing professionalism in underground metal production and musicianship. Instead, the members of bands like Mayhem, Darkthrone and Immortal preferred the rougher-sounding recordings and relatively simplistic music of 1980s bands like Venom, Bathory and Celtic Frost. Although these earlier bands predated the codification of 'black metal' as a musical style and genre, they have been adopted into its history as founders. In general, the musical style is less formally complex than death metal, prizing relentlessness and atmosphere instead of rhythmic dynamism and guitar pyrotechnics. The guitar parts frequently employ tremolo-picking, a technique that involves non-stop rhythmic subdivision, while the harmonies typically change at a much slower pace. Black metal guitarists also regularly employ full triads (usually in minor) in addition to power chords, creating a much denser sound. Drummers in black metal bands also make extensive use of 'blast beats', which involves intense rhythmic subdivision akin to tremolo picking, resulting in an unrelenting torrent of sound without much sense of groove. Black metal musicians and fans tend to value DIY production aesthetics; low-fidelity or otherwise unorthodox recording qualities are typically interpreted as markers of authenticity rather than incompetence. Although in some ways this conception of black metal was riven with the sorts of rigidities that often plague retro-minded musical endeavours, it also opened the field for new conceptions of black metal in more cinematic, symphonic and avant-garde modes.[1] However, all of these developments ran alongside Norwegian black metal's brief history as a vector of borderline-terroristic criminality, which necessarily colours its legacy.

This side of black metal's history also makes it difficult to strike a balance between dutifully rehashing the genre's violent history or essentially pushing it under the rug. Although this chapter mostly concerns later developments in black metal, it is important to acknowledge that the genre's global popularity rests at least partly on the graves of Per 'Dead' Ohlin, Øystein 'Euronymous' Aarseth and Magne Andreasson. Ohlin was the singer for Mayhem from 1988 until his suicide in 1991, which Aarseth subsequently used as a way to promote the band's evil image. Aarseth himself was murdered in 1992 by Varg Vikernes, sole musician of the band Burzum and session bassist for Mayhem. Vikernes and Aarseth, along with other black metallers, had also been involved in a number of arson attacks against Norwegian churches, most infamously burning the Fantoft stave church near Bergen. Magne Andreasson was stabbed to death in 1992 by Bård 'Faust' Eithun, who was then the drummer of Emperor, after propositioning him in a park. With a few exceptions, overt criminality of this sort has been a rarity in black metal in the decades since, but this violent introduction also provided a uniquely powerful kind of publicity and notoriety.

After all, there are very few musical genres with an origin story that would be right at home on a true-crime podcast.

In the intervening decades, black metal became a relatively normalised presence within the Norwegian music industry, in marked contrast to its earlier pariah status. Black metal musicians are regularly nominated for music industry awards and sometimes receive commendations from government institutions. To take one recent example, Darkthrone's 1992 album *A Blaze in the Northern Sky* was included by the National Library of Norway in an exhibition featuring 'significant pieces of Norwegian cultural history', taking a place alongside objects like handwritten scores by the composer Edvard Grieg and a manuscript of *Magnus Lagabøtes landslov*, a thirteenth-century book of comprehensive national legislation. The Norwegian popular music museum Rockheim has an entire room dedicated to black metal, and the Norwegian government also subsidises international tours by black metal musicians through Music Norway, a programme funded by the Royal Norwegian Ministry of Culture and the Ministry of Foreign Affairs. Although black metal is far from the only style of popular music to become respectable after initially being considered disreputable and dangerous, it is nonetheless striking that it has been so embraced by official cultural institutions in Norway.

Yet the official promotion of black metal as a distinctly 'Norwegian' style of music also makes a certain amount of sense, given many of the musicians' intense investment in their own Norwegian-ness. Their black metal lyrics and album covers are full of rugged Norwegian landscapes, wolves, trolls, figures from Norse mythology, and Vikings, mirroring many of the touchstones of nineteenth-century 'national romantic' artists, writers and composers, who shaped conceptions of Norwegian national identity during its drive for independence from Sweden. Although many Norwegians certainly found black metal music and musicians off-putting at best, its brand of nationalistic sentiment involves many familiar themes, particularly its focus on Norway's spectacular landscapes. Similarly, and unfortunately, the xenophobia and racism sometimes found in black metal are also regular features of Norway's political discourse, although they are generally expressed in more polite terms.[2] In any case, black metal relied on these existing discourses of Norwegian-ness, often intensifying them in the process, which also gave black metallers a foundation for their reputation and aesthetic that did not necessarily rely on criminal activity.

As a result, black metal's appeal beyond Scandinavia has often relied on conjuring an exotic, dangerous and magical North for international listeners, many of whom likely have few other points of contact with Norwegian culture. This exoticised fantasy remains important even for the vast majority of listeners, who understand that Norway is not actually populated with bloodthirsty wolves and savage Vikings. The Nordic environment even infiltrated the discourse of black metal musicians, as particular types of guitar riffs and recording aesthetics are regularly described by black metallers as 'cold' or 'frosty', sometimes in a playful manner but often also with complete seriousness.[3]

A 2017 episode of the Norwegian talk show *Trygekontoret* provides a few illuminating moments demonstrating how these exoticised conceptions of black metal have resonated abroad. In this particular episode, the program's host Thomas Seltzer (himself a musician in the rock band Turbonegro) joins the Norwegian black metal band Mayhem on a tour through Latin America, including stops in Colombia, Costa Rica, El Salvador and Mexico. The episode focuses mostly on Mayhem's bassist, Jørn 'Necrobutcher' Stubberud, who was a childhood friend of Seltzer. While the episode does make some jokes at the expense of these fans, including one who confidently states that 70 per cent of people in Norway are metalheads, some of them also seem well aware of the fantasy aspect. When Seltzer asks some Salvadoran fans what they think Stubberud's house looks like, one man enthusiastically replies that he probably lives in a cave with candles. Seltzer riffs on the idea by suggesting that Stubberud probably also wears a cape and plays a pipe organ, to much laughter. Metal is not always these fans' only interest in Norway either, as another Salvadoran fan notes that he enjoys the works of Henrik Ibsen and finds parallels between the play *An Enemy of the People* and the country of El Salvador. The people at Music Norway and the Ministry of Foreign Affairs would likely be pleased.[4]

The *Trygekontoret* episode also highlights how difficult it can still be for Norwegian black metal to escape the violence of its past, particularly for bands like Mayhem, who were directly affected by it. At one point, Seltzer notes that some fans treat Mayhem concerts like a travelling crime scene, tied inextricably to the violent deaths of Per Ohlin and Øystein Aarseth. For his part, Stubberud seems to have resigned himself to the fact that his international musical career necessarily involves bootleggers selling unauthorised t-shirts featuring pictures of his long-deceased bandmates. These include a particularly grisly photograph of Per Ohlin's corpse (taken by Aarseth when he discovered the body) that wound up on a live bootleg released by a label in Colombia.[5]

However, black metal has also evolved in various ways beyond Scandinavia, even as many black metal musicians continually return to its initial stylistic well. Along these lines, it is possible to speak of a 'late' black metal style or constellation of styles, following Dominic Fox's conception of 'late' or 'belated' black metal that turns towards introspection, and in which the genre is defined by aesthetics instead of actions. Even though the earlier violence becomes mythologised and even hallowed, there is no desire to return to it.[6] The music of 'late' black metal musicians, particularly those from outside Scandinavia, has further potential to be reflective and self-aware since the genre's history may not hang over them in the way it does the genre's progenitors. To be sure, many black metal bands around the world continue to adhere to the original musical aesthetic, with stylistic mimicry becoming almost like a cycle of tribute and renewal. As with genre fiction and cinema, the repetition of familiar materials with only slight alterations is a significant and lasting part of the appeal. Yet black metal has also proved to be quite elastic, allowing it to reflect the cultures and concerns of fans and musicians around the world and to foster individual and idiosyncratic musical explorations.

Black Metal in the Mountain West

One of the hallmarks of black metal music globally is that the musicians regularly foreground their geographic location and specific local cultures and histories in their lyrics, visual themes and musical style, no matter where in the world they are from. The Norwegian bands provided a model of sorts, and their interactions with mythology and folklore, languages and local dialects, historical events, landscapes and traditional rural ways of living proved to be quite adaptable for use in a variety of new circumstances. Some black metal bands go so far as to include traditional instruments as a part of their ensemble, a kind of fusion that is often categorised separately as 'folk metal'. The intentions behind the bands' interests in local culture vary from place to place. In some instances, the emphasis on local culture has an undercurrent of chauvinistic xenophobia, but it can also signal resistance to commercial and political forces of globalisation or support for indigenous communities.

Black metal's fascination with and even reverence for locality and associated customs and cultural memories also frequently intersects with modern neopagan and animist religions, in which physical environments are imbued with sacredness as opposed to locating the sacred in an unreachable heavenly realm.[7] This reification of nature is at least partly an echo of nineteenth-century Romanticism, itself a reaction against Enlightenment rationalism, but the assertion of local identities in black metal often also involves conjuring visions of a (mostly imagined) pre-Christian past. Black metal's customary antipathy towards Christianity then often invokes its suppression of ancient local customs in addition to the acrimonious history between mainstream Christianity and rock music more generally. Specific attributes of the local landscape and its flora and fauna also figure heavily in these traditions. In the United States, however, this abiding interest in local identity and cultural memory necessarily involves more recent concerns, as seen in examples of black metal from the Mountain West region, particularly the Colorado band Wayfarer.[8]

Black metal is a relatively recent arrival to the music scenes in this region. Although American black metal bands existed in the 1990s, they were few in number and generally toiled in extreme obscurity, with the possible exception of the California band Von, whose 1991 demo cassette *Satanic Blood* became legendary in the tape-trading underground (due in part to the fact that it was so hard to find). It was not until the latter half of the 1990s that a dedicated. black metal scene began to coalesce in the San Francisco Bay Area, revolving around the eclectic record stores Aquarius Records and Amoeba Records, and the record label tUMULt, run by Aquarius Records owner Andee Connors. This scene cultivated an initial crop of American black metal bands like Weakling, Leviathan, Xasthur and Ludicra, all of which departed from the Scandinavian model in various ways. Lyrically and thematically, many of these American bands had little interest in the Satanic, Nordic or mythological conceits of their European forebears, writing instead on 'real-life' topics like alienation, mental distress, philosophical despair, self-harm and suicide.[9] Most also tended to eschew the elaborate theatricality, costumes and stage names common in European black metal, at least in part because many of the musicians first cut their teeth in DIY punk scenes.[10]

In the wake of the San Francisco scene, a small coterie of younger black metal bands formed in the Pacific Northwest. The Portland band Agalloch, in particular, crafted a musical aesthetic that revolved around long and drawn-out songs and influences from post-rock bands and art-house cinema. Their lyrics often continued to mine the wilderness themes of Scandinavian bands, with a thread of Romantic-era melancholy that finds solace, refuge and healing in the wilds.[11] Other 'Cascadian' black metal bands like Wolves in the Throne Room and Fauna underscored this wilderness aesthetic with references to animist spiritualities and shamanism. Wolves in the Throne Room often explicitly connect their music with their local forests, such as when the drummer Aaron Weaver describes synesthetically hearing an orange-red 'vibrational frequency' during recording, which he connects with the colour of decomposing cedar stumps and a feeling of literal 'rootedness' within the forest.[12] The California band Botanist, notable also for relying on a distorted hammered dulcimer rather than guitars, invokes similar themes along a quasi-Lovecraftian path, tracing a concept across multiple albums involving semi-sentient plants reclaiming the earth from humanity.[13] A number of philosophers, theorists and other scholars have also made connections between black metal and deep ecology, an anti-anthropocentric current of thought that posits revoking any special moral consideration for humanity (as opposed to more traditional environmentalism) and disavowing the philosophical divide between human and non-human.[14] But painting black metal's love of natural environments as idyllically pastoral is too simplistic; the distorted, frenzied and irrevocably industrialised modern music also speaks to feelings of alienation from nature and the impossibilities of utopian idealism.[15]

Given that Cascadian bands' geo-musicological focus often resembles that of Scandinavian black metal, it is worth noting that the landscapes of Scandinavia and the Pacific Northwest can be quite similar. Both regions are renowned for spectacularly rugged wildernesses full of forbidding mountains and misty forests. John Haughm of Agalloch has mentioned that the evocations of Northwestern forests and landscapes in their album artwork were initially interpreted by fans as an attempt to mimic European black metal bands, which, to be fair, seems like a reasonable first impression.[16] Their artwork may not be a direct copy, but it is clearly a variation on the theme. However, in both cases, these landscapes are also conceived as largely devoid of human civilisation and cultivation, with survival requiring rugged self-sufficiency and an individualistic, even misanthropic, temperament. However, this Edenic conception of the American West as 'virgin wilderness' conceals the fact that the region was purposefully emptied of its original American Indian inhabitants through government campaigns of genocidal settler colonialism. Indeed, this kind of rhetoric has been a crucial part of those campaigns, as land cannot be considered to have been stolen if nobody was living there.[17]

Wayfarer and Cowboy Mythology

While the Cascadian bands tend to focus more broadly on ecology and environment, the Colorado band Wayfarer explores this more specific regional history of colonial exploitation and national myth-making. These themes run through their recorded output, particularly the albums *Old*

Souls (2016), *World's Blood* (2018) and *A Romance with Violence* (2020), and are evident in their album art, lyrics and musical styles.

The artwork on these three albums engages with this history in varied ways. The cover for *Old Souls*, by the Las Vegas artist Adam Gersh, is a sepia-toned black-and-white lithograph of a mountainous landscape featuring a figure emerging from the lower corner pointing at the distant mountains. He has a pair of feathers tied around his bicep, and instead of a head, there are two branches growing from his neck, forming a wooden frame for the web of a dreamcatcher. The dreamcatcher also features a profile of a mountain range within its design. Feathers figure heavily in American Indian design and religious symbolism, as well as serving as cultural markers of honour and bravery. The dreamcatcher likewise is a protective charm with connections to the mythological Spider Grandmother, a benevolent Earth goddess who figures in numerous traditions across American Indian cultures.[18] Gersh's artwork for posters and merchandise for Wayfarer and their Fire in the Mountains festivals typically involve similar iconography. Given that feathers and dreamcatchers are regularly appropriated by non-Natives in fashion and home décor, it is perhaps worth noting that none of the members of Wayfarer nor Mr Gersh claim indigenous heritage to my knowledge, or, at least if they do, it is not part of their public artistic presentation. Since their use of these symbols is fairly non-specific and highlights their connection to Native cultures rather than divorcing them from their context, they perhaps sidestep potential concerns over cultural appropriation, although opinions might vary. Wayfarer's last two album covers are derived from historical photography. Their 2018 album *World's Blood* uses the photo *The Scout in Winter, Crow* (1908) by Edward S. Curtis (Figure 16.1), a photographer and ethnologist whose work focused on American Indians. Curtis produced a massive and valuable corpus of arresting and haunting photographs, along with other accounts of American Indian life in the early twentieth century, even though his work definitely fed into the narrative of American Indians as a vanishing people. Finally, the cover art for *A Romance with Violence* uses the photo *Temporary and Permanent Bridges and Citadel Rock, Green River, Wyoming* (1868) by the railroad photographer Andrew J. Russell. The photo features a steam locomotive on a raised trackbed, with the butte Citadel Rock in the background. On Wayfarer's cover, the original is given a dark red tint, with gold filigree patterns in the corners.

The artwork also reflects the broader lyrical content of these albums. *World's Blood* (2018) conjures visions of a haunted landscape in which ghostly riders meld with thunderstorms, while the closing track, 'A Nation of Immigrants', explicitly channels the violence and death of

Figure 16.1 The Scout in Winter, Crow (1908) by Edward S. Curtis. Library of Congress, Prints and Photographs Division, Edward S. Curtis Collection [LC-USZ62-1206] (© Edward S. Curtis)

the West's subjugation and exploitation. *A Romance with Violence* (2020) shifts the perspective to the settlers and, in particular, a lone gunslinger figure, the Crimson Rider, murderously paving the way for the railroad's Iron Horse. The final tracks on the album, 'Masquerade of the Gunslingers' and 'Vaudeville', invoke the way in which historical violence becomes the stuff of entertainment, thus obscuring its brutality. With a little squinting, it is possible to see parallels between these American colonisation narratives and Nordic black metallers' obsessions with pre-Christian Nordic cultures and religious practices. Indeed, some Nordic black metallers regularly depict the region's conversion to Christianity as a colonisation. The analogy is not perfect by any stretch of the imagination, however, since Native communities continue to suffer real deprivation and marginalisation in the Americas while the Norwegian metallers sometimes seemed to be searching for a form of 'grievance authenticity'. But both cases propose a drastic re-evaluation of their regions' respective national mythologies.

Wayfarer's musical references to the American West are somewhat more elusive, as they often rely heavily on lyrical themes and visual presentation rather than obvious 'Western' musical tropes. The general musical style across their albums is heavily indebted to the Cascadian models of Agalloch and Wolves in the Throne Room in their mixture of intense black metal sections, meditative 'post-rock' excursions and instrumental interludes. Yet there are points of reference with musical traditions associated with the American West, although tracing them requires a trek through the worlds of mid-twentieth-century film music and the Rocky Mountains' alternative country music scene.

The music of the American West has a tangled history, including musical pieces that evoke the West (like Aaron Copland's 1942 ballet *Rodeo*) and the songs and scores of Hollywood Westerns. There's little doubt that current conceptions of the 'Wild West' were profoundly influenced by television and film in the mid-twentieth century, particularly concerning the much-mythologised cowboy or outlaw figure.[19] The films of the actor John Wayne, whose cowboy characters were typically taciturn loners uncomfortable with regular society, were particularly influential. Wayne's run of successful Westerns and war epics made him an enduring American icon, who embodied for many a certain strain of ruggedly individualistic and politically conservative masculinity.[20] Beyond Wayne, the American cowboy embodied a mythic and heroic stereotype standing in for closeness to nature, freedom of movement, and nationalistic sentiment while also operating as a law unto himself, dispensing violent individual justice as he sees fit.[21] Further, the view of history promoted by classic Westerns provided rationales for America's expansionist foreign policy in the 1950s while also promoting American exceptionalism, white superiority and male dominance.[22] The allure of these films has also clearly not faded in the intervening generations and continues to be regularly called upon by politicians and other public figures.

While *A Romance with Violence* (2020) explores this mythology in its lyrics, the music itself also employs several references to cinematic music, particularly the short introductory track 'The Curtain Pulls Back'. This piece functions as a prelude for the album while also providing a sonic *mise en scène*, somewhat akin to a radio drama. Such tracks are a common inclusion on black metal albums, often involving sounds of medieval battle, wolves, whooshing wind, and sometimes choral or instrumental music in a more 'classical' mode. However, the convention is put to slightly different use on *A Romance with Violence* because its title suggests an audience watching a theatrical performance, rather than a literal setting. This framing implies a sense of distance from the subject, like a metaphorical proscenium arch. The track is produced to sound like it is being played from an antique phonograph, beginning with a few seconds of vinyl noise, transporting the listener to the past by invoking the sonic materiality of old records. The main instrument is a slightly out-of-tune piano, which conjures not only the stereotypical saloon pianist but also the piano accompaniment often found on releases of silent movies. The final seconds before the band enters on the next track include a few record 'skips', again highlighting the imagined phonograph while also implying fragility, malfunction, and possibly a measure of artifice.

'The Curtain Pulls Back' also subtly interfaces with music used to depict American Indians across generations in American films and other media. Its main musical theme begins with a short descending motif on the scale degrees 1 – ♭7 – 5, invoking the minor pentatonic mode, along with a prominently dissonant tritone later in the theme. Descending minor pentatonic motifs like this one, along with increased dissonances, were regular tropes employed by twentieth-century film composers for scenes involving American Indians, almost always accompanied by tom drums played in a four-beat 'THUMP-thump-thump-thump' rhythm. The title sequence of the 1948 John Wayne movie *Fort Apache* portrays this music's function clearly. Cowboys, cavalrymen and other white characters are accompanied by peppy, patriotic-sounding music, but whenever a group of Natives are onscreen, the music shifts to a minor-key descending melody with blaring horns, high trilling strings that seem to invoke war whoops, and the requisite thumping drums.[23] It creates a marked contrast and clearly identifies the Natives as the film's villains (even though at this point they are just trotting leisurely across the prairie on horseback). While 'The Curtain Pulls Back' is only played by a piano trio, its minor pentatonic theme bears more than a passing resemblance to these earlier film music tropes, and its main motif is also nearly identical to the beginning of the controversial 'tomahawk chant' sung by fans of the Atlanta Braves baseball team.[24] It is unclear if this was an intentional choice by Wayfarer, but it certainly aligns with the album's concern with how colonial violence gets repackaged as entertainment.

However, other 'Western' musical touchstones employed by Wayfarer in the album reference a more complicated conception of the West with roots in Italian composer Ennio Morricone's iconic scores for Italian 'spaghetti westerns' like *A Fistful of Dollars* (1964) and *Once Upon a Time in the West* (1968). These films featured distinctive twangy, jangling electric guitars that quickly became a new musical signifier for a much bleaker and more ambiguous vision of life in the West. This side of Western film music also became a key sound for 'alt-country' or 'Americana' bands beginning in the 1990s, with Denver, CO, in particular hosting notables like 16 Horsepower, Wovenhand, Slim Cessna's Auto Club and Jay Munly. Their music often employs guitar sounds reminiscent of Morricone's scores, with lots of twangy baritone guitars and spring reverb, along with various mixtures of traditional country music and alternative rock. As opposed to the anodyne country-pop music from Nashville, these bands often inflected their songs with sombre tales of religious apocalypticism, mental illness, violence and gothic weirdness. Such country influences are less overt in Wayfarer's music, but their softer and more meditative moments feature guitar licks and flourishes reminiscent of country styles. For example, the beginning half of 'Vaudeville' from *A Romance with Violence* (2020) features minor-key acoustic slide guitar licks and handclaps that would fit neatly in an alt-country context.

Wayfarer are also not the only American black metallers to take an interest in traditional American folk music styles like bluegrass, blues and country and to utilise it to reflect on local histories. Probably the most well-known American black metal band to explore what might be called 'Americana' black metal is Panopticon, a one-man project by multi-instrumentalist Austin Lunn. His 2012 album *Kentucky* famously mixed black metal with traditional Appalachian folk music, archival recordings and strike songs like Pete Seeger's 'Which Side Are You On' (1940) to portray the history of labour and environmental exploitation related to mining in the Appalachian Mountains. Lunn continued this artistic trajectory on *The Scars of Man on the Once Nameless Wilderness* (2018), which includes several songs in the style of Appalachian folk music. As with bands in the Western region of the country, Lunn's music unearths hidden and suppressed regional histories that have left deep and enduring psychological and ecological scars that continue to echo in the present.[25] Also, beginning in 2014, the Swiss-American musician Manuel Gagneux began experimenting with combining black metal with African-American spirituals, Delta blues and work songs in his band Zeal and

Ardor. Thematically, his music mixes occult religiosity with poignant references to racist violence and murder, both historical and contemporary.

Finally, it is worth highlighting that several American black metal bands with indigenous members are also writing music exploring Native identities and history, notably Nechochwen from West Virginia, Pan-Amerikan Native Front from Illinois, and Yaotl Mictlan from Salt Lake City. Nechochwen are a duo whose music calls to mind the expansive songs of Opeth and Agalloch, with extensive classical guitar sections, and deals primarily with the histories of Eastern tribes such as the Shawnee and Seneca.[26] Their song 'He Ya Ho Na' from the album *OtO* (2012) also includes a brief interlude featuring sung vocables, non-lexical (but not meaningless) syllables that are used extensively across many Native music traditions.[27] Pan-Amerikan Native Front play fairly traditional black metal with a low-fidelity aesthetic, but with album art and lyrical themes referencing the history of Native warfare against colonial expansion. Yaotl Mictlan are focused more on pre-Christian Mexican and Mesoamerican cultures, and their music employs a number of traditional instruments and indigenous chants. But as Nechochwen's eponymous songwriter has noted, this kind of specificity honours the fact that the history of indigenous cultures in the Americas is entirely too vast and diverse to be reduced to any generalised representation.[28]

Conclusion

These specific invocations of the troubled past of the American frontier and the 'Wild West' also fulfil a fundamental role common across metal music of all stripes. Metal music often aims to transport the listener to other places and to imagine other lives, whether based in reality or not. Whether taking cues from fantasy literature, science fiction, biker subcultures, ancient mythology or historical events, metal has always been fascinated with evoking 'elsewhere'. Music often provides both a window into other time periods and cultures while also acting as a mirror reflecting one's own culture. These American black metal bands, however, attempt to briefly open a sliding door into perspectives on American history that have been deliberately neglected and suppressed. Panopticon unearth ongoing histories of class struggle and environmental destruction, while Nechochwen et al. use black metal to celebrate and explore their own Native heritage, in the process reminding listeners that they are not a conquered or vanished people.

However, an important aspect of this lingering myth of indigenous 'disappearance' is that American Indian cultures have also long been used by mainstream American culture as symbolic stand-ins representing closeness to nature, an echo of the Enlightenment-era 'noble savage'. These notions turn up variously in the ceremonies of the Boy Scouts of America, off-road vehicles named after American Indian tribes, famous environmental advertisements, and the numerous new-age movements that have liberally borrowed from indigenous traditions. Given black metal's general fascination with the natural world, pre-Christian traditions and romanticised pasts, it would perhaps be unsurprising to find non-Native black metal musicians unconsciously reproducing these tropes. In the case of Wayfarer's albums, though, there is thankfully a deliberate anti-romanticism at work that mitigates against such trite (and premature) eulogies, pulling back the curtain on the way the American West's founding mythologies have been carefully curated in order to appear appropriately heroic, just and innocent.

Notes

1. Ian Reyes, 'Blacker than Death: Recollecting the "Black Turn" in Metal Aesthetics', *Journal of Popular Music Studies* 25/2 (2013): 240–57.
2. Laura Wiebe Taylor, 'Nordic Nationalisms: Black Metal takes Norway's Everyday Racisms to the Extreme', in Niall Scott (ed.), *Reflections in the Metal Void* (Inter-Disciplinary Press, 2012), pp. 185–98.
3. Ross Hagen, *Darkthrone's A Blaze in the Northern Sky* (Bloomsbury, 2020), p. 6.
4. NRK, 'Los Bambinos del Satan: On the Road with Mayhem'. https://youtu.be /5RF3B-RjWDg (accessed 29 August 2021).
5. Mayhem, *Dawn of the Black Hearts: Live in Sarsborg, Norway, 28/2, 1990* (Warmaster Records, 1990).
6. Dominic Fox, *Cold World: The Aesthetics of Dejection and the Politics of Militant Dysphoria* (Zero Books, 2009), pp. 50–4.
7. Rupert Till, 'Paganism, Popular Music, and Stonehenge', in Donna Weston and Andy Bennett (eds.), *Pop Pagans: Paganism and Popular Music* (Acumen, 2013), pp. 24–42.
8. The Mountain West of the United States refers to the portion of the country defined by the Rocky Mountains, including Arizona, Colorado, Idaho, Montana, Nevada, New Mexico, Utah and Wyoming.
9. Owen Coggins, 'Distortion, Restriction and Instability: Violence against the Self in Depressive Suicidal Black Metal', *Metal Music Studies* 5/3 (2019): 401–18.
10. A number of band profiles and interviews can be found in Daniel Lake, *USBM: A Revolution of Identity in American Black Metal* (Decibel Books, 2020).

11. Julian Knox, 'Ashes against the Grain: Black Metal and the Grim Rebirth of Romanticism', in James Rovira (ed.), *Rock and Romanticism: Post-Punk, Goth, and Metal as Dark Romanticisms* (Palgrave Macmillan, 2018), pp. 235–57.

12. Gregory Adams, 'Wolves in the Throne Room on "Powerful Plants," Transcendence, *Primordial Arcana*', *Revolver* (8 July 2021). www.revolvermag.com/music/wolves-throne-room-powerful-plants-transcendence-primordial-arcana (accessed 29 August 2021).

13. Olivia Lucas, '"Shrieking Soldiers . . . Wiping Clean the Earth": Hearing Apocalyptic Environmentalism in the Music of Botanist', *Popular Music* 38/3 (2019): 481–97.

14. Niall Scott, 'Blackening the Green', in Scott Wilson (ed.), *Melancology: Black Metal Theory and Ecology* (Zero Books, 2014), pp. 66–8.

15. Owen Coggins, 'Ecology, Estrangement and Enchantment in Black Metal's Dark Haven', *Green Letters* 24/4 (2021): 1–13.

16. Lake, *USBM*, p. 348.

17. David Treuer, 'Return the National Parks to the Tribes', *The Atlantic* (May 2021). www.theatlantic.com/magazine/archive/2021/05/return-the-national-parks-to-the-tribes/618395 (accessed 19 August 2021).

18. Mardith K. Schuetz-Miller, 'Spider Grandmother and Other Avatars of the Moon Goddess in New World Sacred Architecture', *Journal of the Southwest* 54/2 (2012): 283–435.

19. Richard Slotkin, *Gunfighter Nation: The Myth of the Frontier in Twentieth-Century America* (University of Oklahoma Press, 1998).

20. See Gary Wills, *John Wayne's America* (Simon & Schuster, 1997).

21. Marshall W. Fishwick, 'The Cowboy: America's Contribution to the World's Mythology', *Western Folklore* 11/2 (1952): 77–92; Tristram P. Coffin, 'The Cowboy and Mythology', *Western Folklore* 12/4 (1953): 290–3.

22. Stanley Corkin, 'Cowboys and Free Markets: Post-WWII Westerns and U.S. Hegemony', *Cinema Journal* 39/3 (2000): 66–91.

23. Hollywood composers of the time regularly used music with similar qualities as a shorthand for 'savages' of all ethnicities, as in Max Steiner's score for *King Kong* (1933). The music in *Fort Apache* and other Westerns also predictably bears little resemblance to actual American Indian music.

24. There is a long history of American sports teams whose names reference Native tribes and cultures, including slurs like 'redskin', along with stereotyped caricatures as mascots. Some of them have been changed in recent years, but significant resistance remains in other cases.

25. Olivia Lucas, '*Kentucky*: Sound, Environment, History: Black Metal and Appalachian Coal Culture', in Toni-Matti Karjalainen and Kimi Kärki (eds.), *Modern Heavy Metal: Markets, Practices and Cultures* (Aalto University Press, 2015), pp. 555–63.

26. Matt Solis, 'The Serpent Tradition: An Interview with Nechochwen', *Decibel* (15 October 2015). www.decibelmagazine.com/2015/10/15/the-serpent-tradition-an-interview-with-nechochwen (accessed 20 August 2021).

27. Charlotte J. Frisbie, 'Vocables in Navajo Ceremonial Music', *Ethnomusicology* 24/3 (1980): 347–92; David P. McAllester, 'New Perspectives in Native American Music', *Perspectives of New Music* 20/1–2 (1981): 433–46.

28. Solis, 'The Serpent Tradition'.

17

Subgenre Qualifiers and Prescribed Creativity in Technical Death Metal

LEWIS F. KENNEDY

Pay attention to metal discourse in print, online or in person, and a simple fact becomes evident: genre labels abound. A cursory glance at almost any metal studies text, metal album review, or comment section on a metal music video reveals a diverse genre vocabulary about which metal participants routinely disagree. One person's symphonic death metal is another person's post-black metal, or so it would seem. The present chapter is concerned with how participants interact with these genre names in their practice, focusing on how writers position artists (and artefacts) as well as how artists position themselves in relation to genre and subgenre.

Drawing on metal's extensive genre discourse, both academic and otherwise, this chapter explores the significance and effects of subgenre qualifiers. After demonstrating the prevalence of genre and subgenre terms in metal, I outline how subgenre qualifiers function to both describe and prescribe participants' conceptions of metal music culture. Technical death metal acts as a case study of how these qualifiers can be utilised by musicians, critics and fans to variously focus or limit one's approach to producing and receiving music. For some, 'technical' serves as a descriptive term that expresses a general attitude toward music-making and listening, while for others, it demarcates a series of relatively finite rules within which one must operate. Finally, I discuss how artists variously reject or embrace technical death metal in their creative practice.

Conceptions of Genre and Subgenre in Metal

As aforementioned, genre terminology is ubiquitous in metal discourse, 'academic' or otherwise. Throughout this book and almost any other metal studies text, readers will find numerous examples of genre names, some widely encompassing and well-known, others ostensibly specific and novel. Moreover, such genre discourse pervades non-academic discussions of metal in newspapers, magazines, press releases, blogs, social media and, of course, in conversations among metal fans of all stripes. Building on the work of Pierre Bourdieu and Sarah Thornton, Keith Kahn-Harris elucidates one of the main drivers behind metal's apparent obsession with genre: 'mundane subcultural capital and transgressive subcultural capital'.[1] Metal fans may claim mundane subcultural capital 'by knowing the complex histories of the scene and by having heard the music of its vast number of bands',[2] and given that '[n]ew (generally young) members entering the scene are frequently disparaged',[3] there is a clear incentive to accrue subcultural capital in order to be accepted by other genre participants. To this end, innumerable books, magazines and websites (including blogs and online forums) construct extensive histories of artists and artefacts grouped within genres or scenes of varying specificity. It is this notion of (varying) specificity with which this chapter is most concerned, but exploring how we might understand sub-genre qualifiers requires a brief overview of how these genre histories are constructed.

Whether communicated through prose or illustrated taxonomies, metal historiography is often presented in a broadly chronological manner, and sometimes further arranged by genre. This mode of presentation tends to result in constructions of metal history as con-sequential; that is, individual genres are regularly characterised as developing in a unidirectional, linear and fixed fashion, separate from one another, and demarcated by an apparent generic lifespan. Most salient for present purposes are those taxonomies that seek to illustrate both the links between various metal genres and the artists or artefacts proffered as representative of those genres.[4] Sam Dunn's 'Heavy Metal Family Tree' – an arborescent model of metal history displaying genres and relevant example artists alongside inter-generic familial relationships – is perhaps the archetypal exemplar of this model.[5] Comprising a series of genre titles with lists of representative artists as well as links between genres designed to illustrate their genealogical lineage (for example, 'grindcore' is begotten by 'first wave of black metal' and 'thrash metal'), subsequent revisions to the family tree commonly focus on individual genres. Here we locate the significant tension between generality and specificity, an issue most frequently addressed through the notion of subgenres.[6]

Despite this chapter's title, I have thus far sought to avoid using the term 'subgenre' if for no other reason than to circumvent the obvious linguistic problem of relative scale: if metal is a genre, and death metal a *sub*genre of metal, then technical death metal must be a *sub-sub*genre of metal (a subgenre of death metal). Moreover, while it is accurate to suggest that 'death metal' denotes a smaller grouping than 'metal', referring to the former as a subgenre connotes, to my mind, a much smaller, less varied construct than one finds in death metal (or black metal, etc.). Consequently, I refer to metal as a genre as well as exploring metal genres (for example, death metal), perhaps suggesting a designation more akin to Roy Shuker's 'meta-genre'.[7] In essence, this is a recognition of what David Brackett calls 'different *levels* of genre',[8] and while his usage of the term generally refers to more broad musical categorisation,[9] it highlights a number of key points regarding the relationship between genres and subgenres. Most obviously, each level corresponds to some notion of specificity, from the general (metal) to the specific (technical death metal), but (sub)genre labels may also be relatively arbitrary and contingent in the sense that an artist might be referred to as death metal by one observer and technical death metal by another. Benjamin Hillier seeks to 'propose a means for categorizing the different "levels" of subgenres in metal' through a taxonomy that favours a synchronic view of the relationships between metal genres.[10] In Hillier's framework, death metal is deemed a major subgenre of extreme metal, while technical death metal is a minor subgenre, thereby avoiding a model wherein genres 'fragment into sub-subgenres' and even 'endless permutations of sub-sub-subgenres that become almost farcical'.[11] Absurdity notwithstanding, how might we understand these terms productively?

Subgenre Qualifiers

In literal terms, subgenre qualifier refers to a word or affix added to a genre title that 'qualifies' or modifies some element of the genre: if death metal is a genre and technical death metal a subgenre, then 'technical' functions as the subgenre qualifier. While the connotations of 'technical' are more circumscribed and convoluted than one might assume upon first reading (see below), the term 'technical death metal' is nonetheless relatively straightforward insomuch as one can clearly identify qualifier and qualified. This distinction is deliberately blurred in terms like 'death doom' or 'deathcore' such that the genre titles are most productively understood as an explicit amalgam of two distinct genres – death metal and doom metal in the former instance, death metal and hardcore in the latter. Perhaps, then, the simplest way to identify a *sub*genre is to identify a clearly recognisable subgenre qualifier – *technical* death metal – while those terms without clear distinction are more indicative of genres. Even when easily identifiable, subgenre qualifiers do not carry obvious connotative meaning: what does it mean to speak of 'blackened' death metal? Does 'symphonic' mean the same thing when prefixing death metal as it does prefixing black metal? Most immediately, these qualifiers are describing something about the artist or artefact to which they are being ascribed (much like a genre title) but also describing something about the genre itself. At the same time, however, subgenre qualifiers can be interpreted as prescribing something about the artist or artefact and, indeed, the genre. Principally, therefore, subgenre qualifiers function as a way to account for the variety encompassed not only by metal but by metal genres themselves.

In developing a 'musical syntax' of heavy metal comprising a 'set of codes based on musical elements', Andrew L. Cope utilises a 'core and periphery model, identifying and situating "key" codes that appear to be present in all forms of metal (the core) and the peripheral codes that become important in the formation of sub-genres; for example, the use of synthesisers in black metal and symphonic metal'.[12] In one respect, then, we might interpret subgenre qualifiers as dictating which codes are deemed core and peripheral within a given subgenre. As such, subgenre qualifiers may function as 'a sort of "hyper-rule" which establishes [a subgenre's internal] hierarchy' or even the '"ideology" of that [sub] genre'.[13] In other words, qualifiers like 'technical' and 'brutal' not only imply the core or peripheral status of given codes but also (seek to) establish a hierarchy or system of organisation of those codes. Technical and brutal death metal may share many compositional devices, for instance, but ways in which these devices are employed – frequency, function, position in a song, etc. – alongside other devices provide points of departure between the two subgenres.

Having outlined some of the ways we might conceptualise subgenre qualifiers in abstract, we can now turn our attention to how these qualifiers are applied in practice. Death metal provides particularly fertile ground when exploring subgenre qualifiers, including but not limited to melodic death metal, technical death metal, old school death metal, brutal death metal, slam, deathcore and deathgrind. Technical death metal generally refers to death metal bands that play at faster tempos than regular death metal and make heavier use of techniques like sweep-picking and blast beats, while melodic death metal is used to describe death metal bands that play at a slower pace, utilising melodies closer to those found in New Wave of British Heavy Metal than in standard death metal. Prefixes like 'technical', 'progressive' and 'melodic' are also used when referring to subgenres of metalcore and hardcore, while 'old school' and 'neo' have been applied to thrash metal, and 'symphonic' or 'post' regularly accompany black metal. Similarly, goregrind utilises human autopsy-inspired imagery, and electro- or cybergrind integrates electronics, specifically including digital drum machines rather than physical drummers, into the wider genre of grind-core. Despite the seemingly arbitrary subgenre qualifiers, each has come to denote a relatively specific meaning in metal discourse.

Some qualifiers are affixed to multiple genre titles, suggesting that such meaning may be transferrable. When prefixing genres like death-core, metalcore or, simply, metal, 'progressive' connotes relatively specific small-scale details: the use of keyboards and/or clean vocals, less reliance on verse-chorus song form, deliberate incorporation of non-metal genres, and a propensity for concept albums. In short, the progressive prefix suggests that the band in question are drawing influence from the lineage of progressive rock, albeit remaining within the boundaries of their particular genre. Progressive metalcore might include '[s]ampling, peculiar structures or the introduction of unexpected genres (like jazz, for example) [that] seek to modify the basic metalcore formula', clearly combining elements of progressive rock without compromising too many elements deemed fundamental to metalcore.[14] Here, 'progressive' connotes the incorporation of elements from outside the genre's normal boundaries. In a similar vein, symphonic black metal introduces new elements into black metal by combining keyboards (regularly utilising orchestral string patches), a more polished production style and clean vocals (solo or choir) with standard black metal genre traits, not too dissimilar from the qualifier's function in symphonic death metal.[15]

While some qualifiers represent the integration of 'outside' elements within a genre, others signify a deliberate focus on certain internal elements. Both 'neo' and 'old school' bands aim to uphold older genre standards, largely eschewing overt stylistic changes that have occurred since the genre first became popular. While 'neo' usually refers to bands forming since a genre's supposed heyday but emphasising older aspects of that genre, most 'old school' bands have continued to make music in a certain genre past its initial period of popularity and have avoided straying too far from the original incarnation of that genre. Interestingly, some newer artists are also ascribed the old school qualifier if their music is deemed to carry a similar essence or attitude toward the genre without actively sounding like older artists.[16] Hence, subgenre qualifiers can be understood as circumscribing both the datable, locatable elements of style (for example, riff types, song form, etc.) *and* the more abstract concept of approach or attitude towards a genre.

Technical Death Metal

As a subgenre qualifier within the title 'technical death metal', 'technical' functions foremost as an adjective *describing* a certain version of death metal. On one hand, this descriptor is relatively broad and connotes an approach to death metal that privileges 'technicality', 'a frequently used word roughly meaning "complicatedness"', as the primary facet of the music (as opposed to 'melody', as in melodic death metal, for instance).[17] On the other hand, however, through consistent usage by critics, fans and musicians, technical death metal has come to describe a comparatively narrow set of stylistic markers. In this guise, 'technical' routinely connotes death metal that utilises fast tempos, irregular metres, unconventional song structures and the recurrent employment of instrumental techniques that are less frequent in other forms of death metal (to say nothing of the non-sonic implications of the qualifier).[18] These discrete readings are at play when commentators construct lists of the best, greatest or essential technical death metal bands that include artists like Atheist, Death and Cynic (representative of the broad conception of the qualifier), alongside artists like Cryptopsy, Necrophagist and Spawn of Possession (representative of the narrow conception).[19] Readers familiar with these artists will note that the former three bands are older than the latter and, significantly, these older bands might also be deemed representative of other metal subgenres, while the newer bands are almost universally recognised as representative of technical death metal. One of the reasons for this discrepancy, and that between the two readings of 'technical' as descriptor, is what I have elsewhere termed 'generic codification': a recognisable period (or series of periods) during which certain, specific elements of style come to be identified with a genre or subgenre.[20] While some artefacts by the older bands might be accurately described as technical death metal, they do not necessarily include all of the specific stylistic elements connoted by the qualifier, whereas the newer bands mentioned above incorporate most if not all of these elements in their music as a matter of course. Over time, through the ongoing processes of generic codification, technical death metal has become a term both descriptive and prescriptive; that is, in order to be deemed technical death metal, a band must adhere to the unwritten rules of that subgenre by consciously displaying their technical ability at the fore-front of their music and do so by utilising a circumscribed variety of compositional and performance techniques.

Read as prescriptive, 'technical' carries connotations of constraint, as evidenced when technical death metal band Rings of Saturn were accused of recording parts of *Dingir* (2013) at half-tempo before speeding them up digitally.[21] Regardless of their veracity, claims that the band had digitally manipulated their recordings in a presumed bid to sound more technically advanced harmed the artist's credibility with some participants due to the nature of the subgenre. Rings of Saturn guitarist Lucas Mann is 'part of a technical metal band; he's part of a scene which is supposed to value musicianship', and since his 'is a band that sells itself on dizzying technicality, breakneck speed and little else. If those two traits are proven inauthentic, nothing is left'; thus, the specific connotation of 'technical' is connected directly to the way in which the composition and performance of this music are judged.[22] Tellingly, Brad Sanders notes that if 'the same accusation [was] leveled against Cannibal Corpse, whose chief aim is brutality rather than technicality. Doubtless, the same outrage would ensue, but in this case, it wouldn't be warranted', as Cannibal Corpse are not a technical death metal band, when understood in this prescriptive sense.[23] Marcus Erbe notes a similar phenomenon in relation to metal vocalists who uphold an 'ideal of a voice that remains as unspoiled as possible, either onstage or in the studio', observing that this concept seemed most prominent among 'people from technical death metal bands, which is to say by vocalists who place a high value on very controlled ways of growling and/or pig squealing'.[24] While the notion of technicality is present in many forms of metal, technical death metal prescribes fastidious attention to displays of a specific *version* of technicality.

Given the additional level of specificity entailed by subgenre qualifiers, it is unsurprising that artists or albums may become difficult to accurately classify. Some commentators decide, therefore, to avoid ascribing such artists a subgenre at all, while others simply stack multiple qualifiers; thus, Simon Handmaker describes Rivers of Nihil as 'technical progressive blackened death metal juggernauts'.[25] This positioning of Rivers of Nihil suggests a very specific oeuvre that does not correspond neatly to any one death metal subgenre, but neither is it captured by the more general title of death metal. In combining three subgenre qualifiers, Handmaker attempts to marry the descriptive and prescriptive aspects of subgenre titles, describing the amalgam of different subgeneric traits while also implying the flexibility with which the artist uses these traits to avoid prescription. This tension between description and prescription leads to inevitable disagreements when attributing (sub)genres to a given artist or artefact. For example, Hillier classifies Cannibal Corpse as 'slam/brutal death metal' while Eric Smialek and Méi-Ra St-Laurent consider them a technical death metal band.[26] Likewise, while I have described Rings of Saturn as technical death metal in relation to

Dingir, Andrew Rothmund expresses some reservations about the band's apparent move from deathcore to technical death metal on their later album *Ultu Ulla* (2017), 'an okay deathcore album because it's a pretty great tech-death album'.[27] These examples of contested subgeneric affiliation are a direct result of subgenre qualifiers that simultaneously describe the music in general terms while prescribing it in specific terms.

Artist Perspectives on Prescription

Not only the preserve of the fan or critic, but metal artists are also often conscious of these (sub)generic terms. Although members of Rivers of Nihil do not necessarily identify with such a specific subgenre title as Handmaker ascribes them above, both generic label (death metal) and subgeneric qualifier (technical) are clearly known to the band. Hence, former guitarist Jon Kunz contends that '[a]t the end of the day, we are a death metal band. We may have some technical stuff going on, but it's never tech for the sake of tech'.[28] Kunz is aware that some may refer to his band as technical death metal, or some variant thereof, but his assertion that any 'technical' elements the band employ are not done so in order to be considered technical death metal suggests that he understands the sub-genre as prescriptive. Acknowledging the band's common categorisation as technical death metal, Obscura vocalist and guitarist Steffen Kummerer suggests that 'it doesn't matter if a riff or an idea is technical or easy to play [since] [t]he song itself is most important'. Moreover, echoing Kunz, Kummerer contends that '[t]here is no need to write a technical song just for the sake of being technical!'.[29] In other words, these artists seek to convey both that the term 'technical death metal' is too limited to accommodate their musical expression and that while parts of their music might be described as 'technical', those parts were not written and performed specifically in order for the artist to be described as such. Nile vocalist and guitarist Karl Sanders goes one step further when stating that for the band's eighth album, *What Should Not Be Unearthed* (2015), he 'decided we were going to be anti-technical death metal'. Sanders explicitly recognises his band's common subgeneric categorisation as well as their consequent affiliation to artists he may not wish to be associated with: 'A lot of people call us tech-death, but when I hear tech-death nowadays, there's lots of amazing playing in those records, but sometimes it gets hard to hear a f**king song'.[30] In wanting to be 'anti-technical death metal', Sanders is rejecting an overtly prescriptive reading of the subgenre as privileging a notion of technicality above all else, even songwriting.

There are, however, some artists who actively seek to create technical death metal. According to bassist Þórður Hermannsson, Ophidian I formed 'due to shared affinity for technical death metal, and bands like Spawn of Possession and Necrophagist. . . . The original plan was simple – to spend time together, party and play technical music'.[31] Unlike those bands for whom technical death metal is constraining, Ophidian I took direct inspiration from the subgenre and wanted to compose and perform in a style similar to artists who are widely heralded as archetypal of technical death metal. Perhaps no other artist is more emblematic of this positive approach to technical death metal than Archspire. Appropriating and championing a label that other artists seek to avoid, Archspire employ 'stay tech' as what vocalist Oliver Rae Aleron calls the band's 'catchphrase', emblazoned on merchandise, used to sign-off social media posts and displayed prominently in album liner notes.[32] Indeed, Archspire's affiliation to a prescribed notion of technicality leads some to suggest the 'band is a gimmick . . . they are technical, some may say, to a fault'.[33] But Aleron conceptualises the band's approach in a more positive light: 'taking a subgenre of a subgenre of music and elevating it and making it even more obscure, but just really trying to break it down and focus on each individual element to create something that's more complex and more orchestrated as a total'.[34] Rather than feeling constrained by the prescribed nature of technical death metal, Archspire use this perceived limitation in a creative way to explore further those musical elements that seem to dictate subgeneric affiliation.

Insofar as their music is prescribed, Archspire are often regarded as emphasising common technical death metal tropes. Thus, the band are 'held up as an example of Technical Death Metal at its most outrageously and enjoyably OTT' thanks, in part, to showcasing a 'shameless dedication to ludicrous speed'.[35] Similarly, the use of 'compound' riffs that combine disparate, sometimes contradictory time feels and riff types, 'requires a high level of proficiency, on which musicians in the technical death metal subgenre (which includes Archspire) pride themselves'.[36] Suggestions that the band's third album, *Relentless Mutation* (2017), might best be understood by 'someone who gives it a few careful listens back-to-back' is evocative of Smialek's concept of technical death metal's 'pleasurable disorientation' that encourages and 'reward[s] repeated listenings' wherein a listener focuses on different elements and their interaction to better comprehend the music's dense texture.[37] Moreover, recalling accusations about Rings of Saturn's supposed inability to perform their music at tempo, Aleron suggests that Archspire's 'goal is that somebody will listen to the album and be like, "Oh, they can't play that live, there's no way", and then they come and see it live, and like, "Oh, you guys can play it live".[38] In each of these cases, Archspire deliberately embrace components (and criticisms) of technical death metal and utilise them as creative impetus rather than limitation.

Not content to simply accentuate the subgenre's extant tropes, Archspire have also sought to develop the range of musical expression *within* technical death metal. According to Aleron, the members of Archspire 'wanted every element of the band to be as impressive as possible to try to make us stand out a bit'. Whereas 'in a lot of death metal the vocals are a bit more simple and slower, and then the drums are going hyper-speed and the guitars are crazy', the members of Archspire 'wanted the vocals to match the music'. To this end, Aleron studied 'speed rappers like Tech N9ne and Busta Rhymes and Twista', focusing specifically on their 'really interesting vocal patterns'.[39] Notably, rather than incorporate rap vocals directly, Aleron utilises a distorted growl vocal tone and builds intricate vocal patterns through a process wherein he 'count[s] the amount of snare hits on some sections and I'll try to match my syllables to those snare hits'.[40] The influence of speed rappers is demonstrated most literally during the introduction to 'Calamus Will Animate' (2017) when Aleron matches his syllables to the rhythmic patterns of sampled gunfire, which, according to the band, they 'blatantly ripped off' from Tech N9ne's 'Stamina' (2001).[41] While this influence clearly emanates from beyond the traditional purview of technical death metal, Aleron's integration of the compositional technique – 'applying this principle of phrasing and of speed to death metal' – is done in such a way as to support and perhaps further Archspire's avowed commitment to technical death metal. Rather than draw inspiration from genres outside metal and display those elements prominently as originating from elsewhere as one might encounter in, say, progressive or experimental subgenres, Archspire's assimilation of a specific type of rap-derived vocal delivery seems motivated by a drive to be more 'technical'. Aleron developed this technique in order to remain within the confines of technical death metal, to 'stay tech', but also 'to try to give ourselves a unique sound' in a subgenre that is markedly prescribed.[42]

Conclusion

This chapter has sought to explore some of the ways in which generic and subgeneric terminology functions in relation to metal participants' experience of the music culture. In the twenty-first century, genre and subgenre terms are ubiquitous in metal discourse, with participants seeming to employ increasingly esoteric vocabulary to categorise their musical experiences. The accrual and demonstration of subcultural capital offer a compelling motivation for the prevalence of genre in metal discourse, not to mention the variety of genre histories and taxonomies from which participants may become enculturated within this discourse. The ostensibly highly-stratified nature of contemporary metal is achieved through the use of what we might call subgenre qualifiers – those words or affixes that denote a particular version of a given genre. Qualifiers function to circumscribe genre both broadly, referring to a general approach or attitude, and narrowly, connoting relatively specific elements of style as well as the potential arrangement of those elements.

In technical death metal, we encounter a qualifier that generally signifies an approach to death metal that privileges technicality while simultaneously delimiting the forms within which that technicality may be expressed. In this formulation, technical can be understood as variously descriptive and prescriptive. Unsurprisingly, some artists move to reject this apparent constraint and attempt to position themselves as something other than technical death metal. By contrast, a few artists are not only comfortable with this affiliation but, in Archspire's case, actively situate themselves within the ostensible confines of the subgenre. For Archspire, death metal provides a space in which to interrogate the broad ideology of 'technical' through an exploration of the very limits of the subgenre, scrutinising the supposed constriction of stylistic elements to produce something conventional and innovative, a prescribed creativity.

Notes

1. Keith Kahn-Harris, *Extreme Metal: Music and Culture on the Edge* (Berg, 2007), p. 121. Kahn-Harris draws this concept, in part, from Pierre Bourdieu, *Distinction: A Social Critique of the Judgement of Taste* (Routledge, 1986), and Sarah Thornton, *Club Cultures: Music, Media, and Subcultural Capital* (Polity Press, 1995).
2. Kahn-Harris, *Extreme Metal*, pp. 122–3. 'Mundane subcultural capital is accrued through a commitment to the collective. In contrast, transgressive subcultural capital is claimed through a radical individualism, through displaying uniqueness and a lack of attachment to the scene' (p. 127).
3. *Ibid.*, p. 130.

4. For thorough analyses of metal genre taxonomies see Eric Smialek, *Genre and Expression in Extreme Metal Music, ca. 1990–2015*, doctoral dissertation (McGill University, 2015), pp. 29–64, and Lewis F. Kennedy, *Functions of Genre in Metal and Hardcore Music*, doctoral dissertation (University of Hull, 2018), pp. 40–52.

5. Sam Dunn, *Metal: A Headbanger's Journey* (Banger Productions, 2005).

6. These revisions began in Sam Dunn, *Metal Evolution: The Series* (Eagle Rock Entertainment, 2012), and continue in the YouTube-based *Lock Horns* series beginning in 2015, see BangerTV, 'Metalcore Bands Debate with Liam from Cancer Bats' (2015). www.youtube.com/watch?v=69bJiqfpJk4 (accessed 31 August 2021).

7. Roy Shuker, *Understanding Popular Music Culture* (Routledge, 2008).

8. David Brackett, '(In Search of) Musical Meaning: Genres, Categories and Crossover', in David Hesmondhalgh and Keith Negus (eds.), *Popular Music Studies* (Arnold, 2002), pp. 65–83; original emphasis.

9. Brackett's model distinguishes between labels used by different participants within the music industry: 'marketing category', 'chart name', 'radio format', and 'media-fan genres' (p. 69). It was explored further in David Brackett, *Categorizing Sound: Genre and Twentieth Century Popular Music* (University of California Press, 2016).

10. Benjamin Hillier, 'Considering Genre in Metal Music', *Metal Music Studies* 6/1 (2020): 5–26.

11. *Ibid.*, p. 8.

12. Andrew L. Cope, *Black Sabbath and the Rise of Heavy Metal Music* (Ashgate, 2010), pp. 3–4.

13. Franco Fabbri, 'A Theory of Musical Genres: Two Application', in David Horn and Philip Tagg (eds.), *Popular Music Perspectives* (IASPM, 1982), pp. 52–81.

14. Heavy Blog, 'Heavy Blog Is Heavy's Best of: Progressive Metalcore' (2014). www.heavyblogisheavy.com/2014/08/07/heavy-blog-is-heavys-best-of-progressive-metalcore (accessed 31 August 2021).

15. Richard Street-Jammer, 'Dimmu Borgir's *Stormblast* Turns 20', *Invisible Oranges* (2016). www.invisibleoranges.com/dimmu-borgirs-stormblast-turns-20 (accessed 30 August 2021).

16. Langdon Hickman, 'Blood Incantation's "Hidden History of the Human Race" is Death Metal Infinite, Incarnate', *Invisible Oranges* (2019). www.invisibleoranges.com/blood-incantation-hidden-history-review (accessed 26 October 2021).

17. Jose Manuel Garza, Jr., *Adapt and Prevail: New Applications of Rhythmic and Metric Analysis in Contemporary Metal Music*, doctoral dissertation (Florida State University, 2017), p. 57. https://diginole.lib.fsu.edu/islandora/object/fsu%3A604968 (accessed 30 August 2021).

18. For instance, technical death metal bands are well-known for frequently utilising a variety of blast beats on drums, sweep-picking on guitar and tapping

on bass, to name only a few techniques ubiquitous in technical death metal but less common elsewhere.

19. See, for instance: Heavy Blog, 'Heavy Blog Is Heavy's Best of: Technical Death Metal' (2015). www.heavyblogisheavy.com/2015/05/05/best-of-technical-death-metal; Loudwire, '10 Greatest Technical Death Metal Bands' (2017). www.youtube.com/watch?v=LBXmdtLW4bE; BangerTV, 'Tech Death Essential Bands Debate' (2017). www.youtube.com/watch?v=JkRLexEjKOQ (all accessed 30 August 2021).

20. See Kennedy, *Functions of Genre*, pp. 237–47. Uses of the more recent term 'tech-death' are as much a product of referring to a more strictly delimited technical death metal post-codification as they are an attempt to shorten the subgenre name.

21. Vince Neilstein, 'Did Rings of Saturn Record Their New Albums at Half-Speed?', *MetalSucks* (2012). www.metalsucks.net/2012/11/05/did-rings-of-saturn-record-their-new-album-at-half-speed (accessed 31 August 2021).

22. Axl Rosenberg, 'Video: Rings of Saturn Guitarist Lucas Mann's Criminal Abuse of Guitar Pro', *MetalSucks* (2013). www.metalsucks.net/2013/10/08/video-rings-saturn-guitarist-lucas-manns-criminal-abuse-guitar-pro (accessed 30 August 2021); Brad Sanders, 'Metal's Physical Bias', *Invisible Oranges* (2013). www.invisibleoranges.com/metals-physical-bias (accessed 30 August 2021).

23. Sanders, 'Metal's Physical Bias'.

24. Marcus Erbe, 'By Demons Be Driven? Scanning "Monstrous" Voices', in Eric James Abbey and Colin Helb (eds.), *Hardcore, Punk, and Other Junk: Aggressive Sounds in Contemporary Music* (Lexington Book, 2014), pp. 51–71.

25. Heavy Blog, 'Singled Out (7/4 – 7/10): New Music from Soilwork, Scale the Summit, Coheed and Cambria, and More!' (2015). www.heavyblogisheavy.com/2015/07/10/singled-out-74-710 (accessed 31 August 2021).

26. Hillier, 'Considering Genre', p. 15; Eric Smialek and Méi-Ra St-Laurent, 'Unending Eruptions: White-Collar Metal Appropriations of Classical Complexity, Experimentation, Elitism, and Cultural Legitimization', in Ciro Scotto, Kenneth Smith and John Brackett (eds.), *The Routledge Companion to Popular Music Analysis: Expanding Approaches* (Routledge, 2018), pp. 378–99.

27. Andrew Rothmund, 'Not (Really) Deathcore: Rings of Saturn's "Ultu Ulla"', *Invisible Oranges* (2017). www.invisibleoranges.com/not-really-deathcore-rings-of-saturns-ultu-ulla (accessed 31 August 2021).

28. Jon Kunz in Kevin Stewart-Panko, 'Upfront Profile: Rivers of Nihil', *Decibel* (January 2014), p. 22.

29. Steffen Kummerer in Rich Taylor, 'The Sound of Perseverance', *Terrorizer* 267 (January 2016): 46.

30. Karl Sanders in José Carlos Santos, 'How the Gods Kill', *Terrorizer* 262 (August 2015): 24.

31. Dom Lawson, 'New Noise: Ophidian I', *Metal Hammer* 351 (Summer 2021): 30.

32. Oliver Rae Aleron in Lingua Brutallica, 'Episode 11: Oliver Aleron of Archspire (Canada)' (2021). https://linguabrutallica.podbean.com/e/lingua-brutallica-episode-11-oliver-aleron-of-archspire-canada (accessed 31 August 2021).

33. Bradley Zorgdrager in BangerTV, 'Archspire Relentless Mutation Album Review | Overkill Review' (2017). www.youtube.com/watch?v=PFwv3rHEVzs (accessed 31 August 2021).

34. Aleron in Lingua Brutallica, 'Episode 11'.

35. Andy Synn, 'Archspire: "Relentless Mutation"', *No Clean Singing* (2017). www.nocleansinging.com/2017/09/18/archspire-relentless-mutation (accessed 31 August 2021).

36. Jose Manuel Garza, Jr., 'Transcending Time (Feels): Riff Types, Timekeeping Cymbals, and Time Feels in Contemporary Metal Music', *Music Theory Online* 27/1 (2021). https://doi.org/10.30535/mto.27.1.3.

37. Kronos, 'Archspire: Relentless Mutation Review', *Angry Metal Guy* (2017). www.angrymetalguy.com/archspire-relentless-mutation-review (accessed 31 August 2021); Smialek, *Genre and Expression*, pp. 193, 164–94.

38. Aleron in Beth Roars, 'Oli Peters (Archspire) – Fun & Frenzy – The Roarcast Podcast' (2020). www.youtube.com/watch?v=rUr7JPuyl4Q (accessed 31 August 2021).

39. *Ibid.*

40. Aleron in Archspiremetal, 'Archspire "Ludic Collective Somnambulation" Vocal' (2014). www.youtube.com/watch?v=LTOxsbyEHmM (accessed 31 August 2021).

41. www.facebook.com/Archspireband/videos/10155395606047090 (accessed 31 August 2021).

42. Aleron in Beth Roars, 'Oli Peters (Archspire)'.

18

From 'Stereotyped Postures' to 'Credible Avant-Garde Strategies'

The Alchemical Transformation of Drone Metal

OWEN COGGINS

Metal has often been derided for a supposed lack of sophistication, with such criticism frequently betraying undercurrents of snobbery at music perceived to be by and for young, working-class, white men. Metal musicians, audiences and researchers in the 1980s and 1990s responded by comparing metal's complex structures and musical virtuosity to the more culturally prestigious baroque music.[1] More recently, the extreme subgenre of drone metal, characterised by extremes of slowness, repetition and amplified distortion, has also attracted classical connotations from minimalism, twentieth-century avant-gardes and non-Western art musics. This chapter examines how drone metal and its experimentalism grounded in metal tradition has influenced external perceptions, not just about that subgenre but about metal in general. Evidence for this transformation can be found in the monthly music magazine *The Wire*, a publication based in the UK and with global coverage and audience. First published in 1982, it covered jazz and improvisation, expanding to consider experimental and global avant-garde music in a serious critical and intellectual manner. Since 2013, largely complete archives have been available online to subscribers.

This chapter traces the magazine's changing attitude to metal, influenced by its coverage of drone metal, through the straightforward method of searching for and analysing all mentions of the term 'metal' in 437 issues from 1982 until July 2020. Throughout the 1980s and 1990s, *The Wire* frequently and explicitly denigrated metal as stupid, this disdain often seeming to relate to prejudices about class and education. Any positive discussions of metal were legitimated through association with more acceptable jazz or experimental musicians or by appeals to exotic and even racialised difference. From the early 2000s, however, drone metal musicians such as Earth, Boris, and especially SunnO))), garnered more approving responses. While sometimes *The Wire* still painstakingly distanced drone metal from the rest of metal, gradually the overall tone towards metal shifted. After drone metal had been judged worthy of coverage as avant-garde music, metal itself could be retrospectively recognised as having always been experimental. Drone metal, via its links to classical and experimental musics, thereby influenced the perception and treatment of metal more broadly, even prompting revisionist rewriting of historical bias against it in this particular publication. This case study therefore shows how marginal subgenres can affect how the broader genre and its cultural status and value are perceived beyond metal.

Drone Metal

Music that would become known as drone metal emerged in the 1990s, with the 1993 album *2: Special Low Frequency Version* by Earth widely regarded as the landmark early recording of what would develop into a loosely defined subgenre featuring extremes of extension, slow repetition and distortion. Drone metal extends beyond the atmospheric slow riffs of doom metal to present more radical abstractions of genre tropes while still grounded in metal's heavily amplified noise.

Contrasting with other extreme metal subgenres, drone metal did not develop in a local scene but through isolated bands influenced by recordings of other similarly unusual bands. Versions of Boris' 1996 debut album *Absolutego*, for example, bore the same subtitle 'Special Low Frequency Version' and showed a clear influence from Earth in the extended repetition of extremely slow, distorted metal riffs. Sleep's *Jerusalem* (1996, later rereleased as *Dopesmoker* in 2003) extended their earlier Black Sabbath worship to a single hour-long dirge. When Sleep split, the rhythm section formed the band Om to explore sparse doomy meditations on bass riffs and mysticism. The band SunnO))) emphasised their commitment to amplification by taking their name from amplifier manufacturer the Sunn Musical Equipment Company, even reproducing typographically the company logo, which itself visually signifies sound waves. SunnO))) began playing smoke-filled shows in black cowls in the late 1990s and have continued to develop their massively amplified droning sound. Less well-known drone metal bands lurk at the edges of metal and experimental scenes: Bong's weird-literature-inspired heavy drones sometimes feature Indian instrumentation; Corrupted alternate between short sludgy hardcore pieces and vastly extended drone doom tracks embellished with piano or harp; Nadja and Black Boned Angel build slow swirls of harsh ambience towards abrasive, cutting riffs; Menace Ruine combine haunting vocals with odd folk-infused distortion. Drone metal musicians claim influence from both metal tradition and experimental avant-gardes: guitarist Dylan Carlson named his band Earth after an early incarnation of Black Sabbath and wore a Morbid Angel t-shirt in the back cover photograph on their best-known record, while in interviews mentioned the minimalism of Terry Riley and La Monte Young as conceptual inspirations.[2] As the most critically and commercially successful drone metal band, SunnO))) perform at both metal festivals and prestigious classical concert venues; they pay tribute to metal in collaborations with black metal vocalists Attila Csihar, Wrest and Xasthur, while also working with contemporary artists Banks Violette and Richard Serra, and experimental musicians beyond metal.

Finding Metal in *The Wire*

Having previously enjoyed occasional issues, I subscribed to *The Wire* in April 2013. Reading every monthly issue since then, I became familiar with the music covered, the writing style, the magazine's values, and, as with any such publication, the implied projection of those values onto its readership. I noticed a distinctly ambivalent attitude to metal music, even in positive treatments of examples of what I considered to be metal. Some writers were and are more generously disposed to metal, but in the editorial voice and across the magazine in general, metal stood out, needing to be excused or justified in ways that other genres did not. A searchable online archive of past issues provided an opportunity to historically examine *The Wire*'s discussions of metal. My approach was simply to search this archive for all instances of the term 'metal' and, where it referred to the music genre, analyse how metal was presented.[3] As expected, the search garnered many false positives, for example, where 'metal' described the material, as in 'direct metal mastering' in advertisements for recordings, or regarding instruments such as saxophones or the unusual creations of industrial musicians Test Dept, Z'ev or Einstürzende Neubauten. The word 'metal' also appeared in song or album titles rather than referring to the music genre; though interestingly, several were examples that influenced drone metal: Coil's occultist drone *Gold is the Metal (With the Broadest Shoulders)*; PiL's atmospheric post-punk *Metal Box*; and especially, the relentless distortion of Lou Reed's *Metal Machine Music*. It is likely that some remarks about metal music in the magazine were not discovered by this method if band names like Black Sabbath or Slayer or subgenres like thrash, grindcore or doom were mentioned without using the word 'metal'. Some of the scanned magazine pages had been damaged or obscured, and automated text processing sometimes rendered text incorrectly, so some mentions of metal may have been lost. However, the method found many examples over nearly four decades of publication, revealing historical changes in metal music's presentation in the magazine.

Extraction

Metal's first mention sets the tone for its early treatment in *The Wire*. A 1982 review reports that free jazz band Catalogue 'ape the stereotyped postures of Western rock music (the heavy-metal axe-hero, the screaming banshee, etc.). Yet their stance is perhaps more serious'.[4] Here, metal represents a rock cliché, which can, among other tropes, be mastered by experimental musicians for loftier goals. Bobby Previte is described in 1992 as possessing 'accumulated wisdom of almost a century of jazz with influences as diverse as Gamelan, minimalism, heavy metal and King Sunny Ade',[5] while Branford Marsalis in 1994 plays a 'mix of everything from jazz with dancehall rhythms, Heavy Metal riffs with blues improvisations to country twang over HipHop beats'.[6] Metal is one among many options available to the masters of an umbrella music, jazz or an unnamed 'everything'. In the 1980s and 1990s, some metal-related music is appraised positively, but only if noted jazz or experimental musicians are involved. Projects involving John Zorn and Bill Laswell are mentioned favourably,[7] though metal is presented as a part-time foray by musicians whose credentials are guaranteed by their contributions to proper jazz and experimental music elsewhere. In one review, Laswell and Zorn are literally 'traffic cops' overseeing collisions between metal and other styles.[8] Musicians who just play metal, or worse, identify with it, are ignored or scorned.

As early as 1992, there appears an article arguing that 'heavy metal is at last ready for credibility' and that it 'essentially experiments with the outer limits of sound'.[9] But the article cannot resist distancing itself from metal's 'inherently reactionary nature', its 'endemic sexism' and the 'presumed chauvinism of its audience'.[10] Metallica, Iron Maiden, Deep Purple and Diamond Head are mocked, and the only group pictured is, incongruously, grunge band Nirvana. Metal is commended for providing samples for use in rap, for (again) the involvement of Laswell and Zorn, and for production techniques used outside metal: Rick Rubin 'shouldn't be forgiven for Slayer' but is praised for his work with The Beastie Boys.[11] Metal is valued only for aspects that have been extracted for use elsewhere.

Reclaimed Metal

Music that resembles metal must be rescued by associations with more prestigious music. Any worth in the Stooges' classic 1970 proto-punk album *Fun House* derives from its 'trans-spectrum overblow of free jazz', because 'without that, it would have indeed been the "fast heavy metal" its detractors deplored'.[12] The magazine's writers criticise what they think metal is trying to achieve, positioning experimental musicians as having casually mastered not only the musical style but its entire aims as well. Peter Brötzmann's aggressive 1985 saxophone-led free jazz album reportedly out-muscles guitar music: 'Rock's supposed "threats" – for example, Heavy Metal or Punk – were just so much fairy cake for *Machine Gun* people'.[13] Also trumping metal's apparent goals is Brötzmann's son Caspar in 1992, whose music is able to 'wade through dense gastric sludge to emerge into the implacable clarity of The Riff. Well, if only heavy metal was really like that'.[14] Experimental rock group Zeni Geva are commended with a comparison to the latter musician for doing metal better than metal bands, as their 'improvisational, Brötzmann-esque guitar fills' lift them 'out of the death metal swamp'.[15] Whatever metal tries to do, jazz musicians – especially ones called Brötzmann and ones who play like them – can do better, and they can do more besides.

Metal's audiences need saving from metal. Describing a noisy 1994 guitar record by Ascension, the reviewer (after yet another reference to a Brötzmann) benevolently hopes for metal (and indie) fans to be saved from the music that is somehow misleading them: 'This guitar noise desperately needs to reach all those currently being fobbed off with indie jangle and "Heavy Metal"'.[16] Conversely, readers of *The Wire* can listen to metal sounds if protected from metal audiences. A 2004 review of Kayo Dot approves of the band's transcendence of everything that is wrong with metal culture:

It's heartening that so much of what purportedly has its roots in the 'Metal scene' nowadays is leaving behind the ancient trappings, the effete machismo, the hair, the tattoo parlour drivel and the Teutonic fonts and monikers associated with the genre, bringing with it only . . . the Metal.[17]

Disdain for audiences is evident, but there is relief that the metal sounds can be safely removed from them. Zeni Geva reportedly 'recycled the power and density of death metal as it should have been played, and rebroadcast it to audiences who wouldn't have listened to a group such as Death'.[18] That review implicitly approves of those who do not listen to death metal since they are able to hear that style played properly by musicians not defined by metal. The text does suggest that the writer has listened to or is at least aware of the metal band Death, showing a similar mastery in listening or critical writing that the jazz musicians are purported to have in playing.

Claims to mastery in listening are, however, betrayed by obvious errors. At first, Napalm Death are from Norwich;[19] then they are from Ipswich;[20] before a reader's letter correctly points out they are 'Birmingham born-and-bred'.[21] The nationalities of two notorious Nordic black metal entities are mistakenly reversed: Abruptum described as from Norway[22] and Euronymous of Mayhem as from Sweden.[23] In 2008, the magazine describes 'Leicester's outlandish Black magic rock group Coven, the nearly men of heavy metal', mistaking the Californian proto-doom group Coven for the British band Black Widow.[24] The magazine portrays itself as knowledgeable, but carelessness about details suggests it wishes only to show that it knows enough about metal to dismiss it.

Stupid Reactions

The problem with metal is openly stated: it is stupid. A 1992 review of a metal compilation makes a striking comparison to the music that was then the magazine's more usual territory: 'Metal – stupid jazz, jazz for intimidated teens – shelters unwitting Coltrane's countless unwitting children'.[25] The musicians do not 'know how or when to end a solo', they 'indulge themselves', the music is 'clueless', 'histrionic' and 'insane', but in the end is described, with benign condescension, as 'not as totally brainless as all the speed and weight would imply'.[26] Elsewhere, metal is fundamentally young and dumb: it is rock's 'aesthetically-challenged baby brother'.[27] A reviewer observes that '[m]etal short-circuits informed opinion-makers and sells directly to unformed kids'.[28] Young people are problematically ignoring cultured, educated gatekeepers like *The Wire*. Instead, in the same piece, a 'working class-ish' audience is depicted as attracted to the 'macho vocal preening' and 'arrogant, slag-fluid virtuoso guitar' of Deep Purple's 'idiot pretensions'.[29] Here stupidity, as lack of education, is really about class. An article in a themed issue titled 'In Praise of the Riff' bemoans that

Legions of hard rock halfwits have used riffs to bludgeon their audience into dazed submission, using noise and repetition to muffle thought processes and boil music down to the reductively physical. . . . Exhibitionists like Clapton, Page and Beck all missed the point, paving the way for heavy rock and the tedious, denim-clad cul de sac of Metal.[30]

Hard rock is bad enough; music for halfwits which actually makes you stupid. But metal's dead-end associations with manual labour (evoked especially by the mention of denim) make it even worse.

Inverse Others

Some metal is treated positively. One of the first examples of an encouraging review mentioning metal is in 1991 for the band Oxbow: 'mogadon metal submerged in volcanic lava . . . a bizarre fusion of psychotic flamenco and thrash'.[31] Managing to be complimentary despite referencing mental instability and a sedative drug, the review again situates the music as a mixture rather than just metal. Other than John Zorn or Bill Laswell projects, the earliest band with multiple approving mentions tied to the term 'metal' is Body Count, described in positive write-ups as speed metal in 1993,[32] thrash metal in 1994,[33] and rap/metal in 1996;[34] the first metal band awarded a full feature article were Living Colour in March 1993.[35] The song 'Super Stupid' by Funkadelic is described as akin to Black Sabbath;[36] as featuring one of the greatest riffs of all time,[37] and as 'the greatest Heavy Metal song ever'.[38] It is fitting that *The Wire* considers the best example of metal to be a song with the word 'stupid' in the name. Even Michael Jackson's songs 'Black or White' and 'Beat It' are 'disco-metal'.[39] The common factor is striking: the most prominent musicians praised in *The Wire* for playing metal are Black. It is commendable that these musicians received positive coverage, particularly since, as Kevin Fellezs has observed, musicians of colour are often subject to racist exclusion from metal and hard rock institutions.[40] However, given *The Wire*'s open disdain for metal, valuing these specific metal musicians and almost no others remains troubling. In a short review contrasting two bands who combine elements of metal and hip hop, when readers are told that 'New York's Biohazard, work from within metal [and] LA's Rage Against the Machine work from without',[41] it is difficult to avoid the implication that this is because the former band features all white members, while the latter comprises mixed race Black Latino and white musicians. Rage Against the Machine's album is described as 'absolutely flawless',[42] yet this recognition is tempered by the magazine's inability to accept them as primarily a metal band. While the term 'metal' is mentioned, the review aligns them more with rap, funk and Flavor Flav; 'their funk discipline is even more honed than their hardcore chops'.[43] In a kind of inverse othering, *The Wire* in the 1990s covers musicians of colour who play metal, but disassociates them, and itself, from metal. In doing so, it colludes from the outside in constructing metal as an essentially white space by rhetorically undermining the 'metalness' of non-white musicians in order to situate them as acceptable for discussion in the magazine.

Metal can therefore be commended if distanced from an imagined white working class. A 1999 editorial is intrigued by 'Maghreb Metal', thinking that a 'collision of speed Metal and Berber culture sounds like a real headfuck'.[44] The same piece expresses curiosity about 'death Metal units from Cuba and Colombia' before yet again mentioning Bill Laswell and Funkadelic's 'Super Stupid'.[45] A 1995 feature discussing 'Malaysian speed metal kids' and 'the Black Rock Coalition' displays its exoticising nature in the article title 'Lost in Translation'.[46] Zeni Geva, mentioned earlier in relation to death metal, are categorised in 1994 as 'Japcore', reducing them to a juxtaposition of heaviness with national/ethnic identity, and further stereotyped as 'turning the old Japanese trick of replicating an American model better than its original makers'.[47] A 1993 article about Islam and metal even highlights how both Muslims and metalheads are stigmatised as exotic.[48] *The Wire* in the 1990s fetishizes otherness, rejecting metal that is implicitly white, working class, young and stupid, and considering metal only if it displays non-white or non-Western signifiers.

Enter Drone Metal

Drone metal, as experimental music and then as metal, gradually gains acceptance in *The Wire* over the two decades since its first mentions in the early 2000s. Initially, drone metal is treated according to the pattern established by *The Wire*'s previous treatment of metal, where heavy music is worthwhile if it can be rhetorically distanced from metal. By the mid to late 2010s, drone metal becomes accepted as a form of metal music and prompts retrospective revisionism where the magazine, despite its earlier denigration of metal, acknowledges that metal has always been an experimental tradition.

In the early 2000s, qualifications still need to be attached to anything metal-related for it to be presented to *The Wire*'s readers. SunnO))) and Earth are called 'Metal method actors', suggesting that their connection with metal must be role-play rather than sincere.[49] A 2003 editorial disapprovingly states that metal 'has remained hidebound by subcultural constraints',[50] but views 'the "meta-Metal" of artists like SunnO)))' as palatable because it is apparently 'Metal played by people who aren't Heavy Metal people, who have no investment in satisfying that audience'.[51] Metal sounds are acceptable if removed from unacceptable metal people. The claim that SunnO))) and others are not 'Heavy Metal people' is obviously ideological because it is obviously wrong: SunnO))) members have played in multiple metal bands, performed at metal gigs and metal festivals, run metal fanzines and metal record labels, collaborated with metal musicians and consistently expressed commitment to metal scenes.

An early feature on SunnO))) from 2002 begins with a quote from the band's guitarist: '"I'm a headbanger, what can I say?" announces an unapologetic Stephen O'Malley',[52] the interviewer's added adjective hinting at an unspoken convention that metal should be apologised for, and that refusing to do so is daring. The article describes

Heavy Metal's contentious border regions, where diehard believers cast an untrustworthy eye on anyone crossing back and forth too often between Metal and its aesthetic near-neighbours such as avant rock, noise, industrial and power electronics[53]

an ironic statement, given *The Wire*'s stern policing of exactly that border from the other side. The initial quote joins a long tradition: in 1987, musician Nigel Manning was evidently conscious of the expectation that shame should be attached to metal: 'I've never lost my heavy metal roots. I still listen to Black Sabbath albums – and you can print that'.[54] In a 2005 interview, Cambell Kneale of drone metal projects Black Boned Angel and Birchville Cat Motel is treated similarly, his enthusiastic words about metal editorially framed with disdain:

'I was always into metal' insists Kneale, 'It just so happens through the syncronicity of the universe that other people of an underground inclination are timidly raising their hands to say, I was a teenage bogan [Australian white trash Metal troglodyte] too'.[55]

The reporting verb 'insists' works in a similar underhanded way to the description of O'Malley as 'unapologetic'; these terms are used to describe the musicians' words, but it is the writer who is smuggling in hints that perseverance with metal is somehow contrarian. Then, when Kneale reports a tentative solidarity between metal fans known in antipodean slang as 'bogans', the author or editor interjects a translation of this colloquialism, introducing aggressive class prejudice which is not present in Kneale's use of the term (see, for example, Dave Snell's work on this term).[56] Three years later, as if returning to a nagging, unresolved concern, a review of one of Kneale's projects refers back to this same piece incredulously:

Not once but twice does Campbell proclaim 'I was always into Metal', during an interview ... If we are to take Kneale at his word that Metal is a legitimate musical foundation and not a red herring of post-ironic posturing for camp value or retro-garde trendiness, then the Birchville Cat Motel allusions to Metal are found not in structural references to the music. Rather, Kneale taps into Metal's pursuit of extremes through the sheer velocity of sound and a singleminded, expressionist intensity.[57]

Even by 2008, the magazine seems unwilling to take at face value the words of a musician who straightforwardly professes that metal is important. Nevertheless, the last sentence of the quote suggests the route to metal's rehabilitation.

Alchemical Transformation

Anti-metal sentiment still appears in *The Wire*, but acceptance of metal through drone metal reaches a turning point in 2005. An eight-page 'guide to the core recordings' of metal features far more drone metal examples than might be expected from its marginal status in the metal world. Of thirty-six featured albums, the first three are by Earth, ten are by SunnO))) or directly related projects, with another four by Boris, two by Corrupted and two by Sleep; the remainder are by black metal musicians, two of whom have since collaborated with SunnO))), or by industrial metal/noise artists.[58] Drone metal's centrality to *The Wire*'s view of metal is consolidated further in 2009 when SunnO))) became the first metal band to feature on the cover.[59] To date, the only metal bands ever pictured on the front of the magazine are SunnO))), Earth[60] and Boris,[61] all of whom played drone metal for at least significant parts of their careers. SunnO)))'s cover story coincided with the release of their 2009 album *Monoliths & Dimensions*, perhaps their most self-consciously avant-garde recording, with a song named after Alice Coltrane, horn players with jazz and experimental histories, and cover artwork by contemporary artist Richard Serra. On this record, *The Wire* considered SunnO))) to 'have provided the catalyst for Metal's recent emergence as a credible avant garde strategy', after Earth had laid the groundwork in taking their sound 'some distance from the lewd phantasmagoria of mainstream Metal'.[62]

Metal now can appear as always having been experimental. By 2013, '[m]etal has long been a testing lab for vocal techniques' for Ronnie James Dio, Bruce Dickinson and Rob Halford,[63] vocalists from an era when metal was routinely described by the same magazine as stupid. Two years later, *The Wire* has completely reversed its previously scornful position: 'It's not so much that there is a rich tradition of experimentalism in heavy metal; more that heavy metal is, at its core, an experimental form'.[64] In 2020, there is room for serious discussion of a 'death metal avant garde';[65] and in 2018, Celtic Frost's *Into the Pandemonium* from 1987 is recognised as having 'helped carve out a space in metal for the kind of avant garde experimentation that is now taken for granted'.[66] There is even a complaint printed in the letters page, also in 2018, that in the magazine now 'only metal is appreciated as a proper avant rock form'.[67] Denigration of metal does still appear, and some writers were already more open-minded towards metal. But drone metal, and specifically SunnO)))'s *Monoliths & Dimensions*, changed perceptions and prompted a reappraisal of metal in the magazine.

Metal thus emerged from waste to become something of value. It is no surprise, then, to find that writers have often reached for the metaphor of alchemical transmutation. Movement from disdain to qualified acceptance to revisionist approval can be traced through these magical reference points. Godflesh in 2001 are 'working with superheavy base Metal',[68] implying a lumpen material requiring transformation. Such work is successful in 2008 for drone metal band Nadja whose 'alchemical process transforms ponderous Metal into abstract grandeur'.[69] By 2009, sludge/drone metal band Gore can also be found 'transforming leaden Metal into heavy instrumental gold'.[70] Again it is SunnO))), who are awarded the most extravagant praise in esoteric terms, for their 'extraordinary alchemical feat of turning base Metal into an open, richly resonating musical platform incorporating spectralist, cosmic jazz and heavy drone influences'.[71] When in 2014 Earth guitarist Dylan Carlson released a solo album entitled *Gold*, the trope was impossible to avoid, with *The Wire* even referring in a passive-tense generalisation to the kind of prejudice that had previously been common in its own pages:

Earth helped transform metal from something that was seen as base and generic into something that was revealed as having a central relationship with vanguard 20th century musical thought. The transmutation of lead into gold, or metal into minimalism, if you like, was always at the heart of the alchemical work.[72]

Drone metal's experiments thus initiated a magical, revisionist transformation of perspective for *The Wire*. The precious value of metal finally dawned on learned gatekeepers of the experimental avant-garde. Metal audiences – the aesthetically-challenged kids, the stupid intimidated teens, the denim-clad halfwits – had known that secret all along.

Notes

1. Robert Walser, *Running with the Devil: Power, Gender and Madness in Heavy Metal Music* (Wesleyan University Press, 1993), see especially pp. 57–107.
2. Dylan Carlson quoted in Edwin Pouncey, 'Earthshifters', *The Wire* 261 (2005): 26.
3. For transparency, I should note my own involvement in two of the results that arise: a 2016 article I wrote for the magazine about drone metal for a special issue on religion and music (Owen Coggins, 'Are You Experienced?', *The Wire* 394 (2016): 38–9) and a review of my 2018 book also about drone metal (Abi Bliss, 'Mysticism, Ritual and Religion in Drone Metal; Owen Coggins', *The Wire* 411 (2018): 74) that otherwise do not significantly impact on the analysis.
4. David Ilic, 'Cecil Taylor', *The Wire* 3 (1983): 36.
5. Stuart Nicholson, 'Bobby Previte', *The Wire* 100 (1992): 29.
6. Laura Connelly, 'Bad Young Brother', *The Wire* 123 (1994): 14.
7. Mark Sinker, 'Old', *The Wire* 93 (1991): 56–7.
8. Biba Kopf, 'Blind Idiot God', *The Wire* 64 (1989): 59–60.
9. Ben Thompson, 'Aaaaaaaaarrrrrrrrrrrrrggggggghhhhhh!!', *The Wire* 100 (1992): 32, 34.
10. *Ibid.*, p. 35.
11. *Ibid.*
12. Ben Watson, 'Punk Jazz', *The Wire* 93 (1991): 44.
13. Steve Lake, 'The Peter Brötzmann Quartet', *The Wire* 13 (1985): 45.
14. Jonathan Romney, 'Caspar Brötzmann Massaker', *The Wire* 97 (1992): 59.
15. Jakubowski, 'Strange Cargo', *The Wire* 129 (1994): 41.
16. Ben Watson, 'Ascension', *The Wire* 128 (1994): 54.
17. David Stubbs, 'Kayo Dot', *The Wire* 239 (2004): 60.
18. *Ibid.*
19. Sinker, 'Old', p. 57.
20. Edwin Pouncey, 'Subterranean Metal', *The Wire* 252 (2005): 38.
21. Jamie Stephenson, 'Metal Matters', *The Wire* 253 (2005): 6.
22. Byron Coley, 'Engine of Industry', *The Wire* 220 (2002): 12.
23. Pouncey, 'Subterranean Metal', p. 42. Mayhem were based in Norway, and it was their early singer 'Dead', not 'Euronymous', who was Swedish.
24. Andy Sharp, 'Supersonic Festival', *The Wire* 296 (2008): 82.
25. Hopey Glass, 'Various', *The Wire* 100 (1992): 95.
26. *Ibid.*
27. Kean Wong, 'Metallic Gleam', *The Wire* 110 (1993): 18.
28. Hopey Glass, 'Deep Purple', *The Wire* 120 (1994): 56.

29. *Ibid.*
30. Chris Sharp, 'Renegade Sound Waves', *The Wire* 250 (2004): 47.
31. Biba Kopf, 'Oxbow', *The Wire* 93 (1991): 71.
32. Laura Connelly, 'Cutting No Ice', *The Wire* 110 (1993): 34.
33. Jake Barnes, 'The New Beats', *The Wire* 124 (1996): 46.
34. Mike Barnes, 'Invisible Jukebox', *The Wire* 149 (1996): 42.
35. Ben Watson, 'Colour (Un)Coded', *The Wire* 109 (1993): 46–8.
36. Peter Shapiro, 'Epiphanies', *The Wire* 167 (1998): 74.
37. *Ibid.*
38. Peter Shapiro, 'The Primer', *The Wire* 172 (1998): 50.
39. Hopey Glass, 'Michael Jackson', *The Wire* 98 (1992): 40.
40. Kevin Fellezs, 'Black Metal Soul Music: Stone Vengeance and the Aesthetics of Race in Heavy Metal', in Eric James Abbey and Colin Helb (eds.), *Hardcore, Punk, and Other Junk: Aggressive Sounds in Contemporary Music* (Lexington Books, 2014), pp. 121–38.
41. Nick Terry, 'Rage Against the Machine', *The Wire* 108 (1993): 59.
42. *Ibid.*
43. *Ibid.*
44. Tony Herrington, 'Editorial', *The Wire* 184 (1999): 8.
45. *Ibid.*
46. Peter Shapiro, 'Lost in Translation', *The Wire* 136 (1995): 42.
47. Jakubowski, 'Zeni Geva', *The Wire* 122 (1994): 71.
48. Wong, 'Metallic Gleam', p. 18.
49. Jim Haynes, 'Black Boned Angel: Supereclipse', *The Wire* 254 (2005): 54.
50. Rob Young, 'Editor's Idea', *The Wire* 238 (2003): 4.
51. *Ibid.*
52. Jim Haynes, 'Thieves of Fire', *The Wire* 218 (2002): 16.
53. *Ibid.*
54. Nigel Manning quoted in Ben Watson, 'Feel Like a Sax Machine', *The Wire* 44 (1987): 20.
55. Cambell Kneale quoted in Bruce Russell, 'Angelic Upstart', *The Wire* 260 (2005): 16.
56. Dave Snell, *Bogan: An Insider's Guide to Metal, Mullets and Mayhem* (Penguin, 2013).
57. Jim Haynes, 'Birchville Cat Motel', *The Wire* 290 (2008): 52.
58. Pouncey, 'Subterranean Metal', pp. 36–43.
59. *The Wire* 302 (2009).
60. *The Wire* 337 (2012).
61. *The Wire* 385 (2016).
62. Joseph Stannard, 'The Gathering Storm', *The Wire* 302 (2009): 43.
63. Phil Freeman, 'Gnaw: Horrible Chamber', *The Wire* 358 (2013): 57.
64. Joseph Stannard, 'Liturgy', *The Wire* 374 (2015): 53.

65. Phil Freeman, 'Chaos Motion', *The Wire* 433 (2020): 46.
66. 'Archive Releases of the Year', *The Wire* 407 (2018): 6.
67. Dimosthenis Miliaras, 'Metallic KO', *The Wire* 409 (2018): 6.
68. Mike Barnes, 'Godflesh', *The Wire* 213 (2001): 57.
69. Tom Ridge, 'Nadja', *The Wire* 289 (2008): 57.
70. Edwin Pouncey, 'Gore', *The Wire* 299 (2009): 53.
71. Chris Bohn, 'The Masthead', *The Wire* 302 (2009): 6.
72. David Keenan, 'Drcarlsonalbion', *The Wire* 365 (2014): 57.

19 | Djent and the Aesthetics of Post-Digital Metal

MARK MARRINGTON

This chapter considers djent, a subgenre of metal whose emergence in the late 2000s reinvigorated metal practice while simultaneously reigniting debates concerning metal's identity in the post-digital era. Djent did not begin to come to the attention of metal scholars until relatively recently, mainly due to its having been pigeonholed as an informal, hobbyist activity whose origins as an online phenomenon made it appear somehow remote from the mainstream of metal music practice. Djent's reputation has also not been aided by the often tongue-in-cheek and sometimes disparaging approach of bloggers and journalists (see later in this chapter) to evaluating it, which has tended to obscure the seriousness of intent of its individual practitioners as well as the importance of the music in its own terms. A particular benefit of the increased scholarly focus on djent is that key lines of enquiry have now begun to emerge that highlight important themes for research. Robert Burns and Allan Moore and Remy Martin, for example, have focused on djent's progressive musical characteristics, while Steven Gamble, in the vein of much previous metal scholarship, has considered the scene context, here in reference to the online community that congregated around djent during its early period.[1] Another significant line of enquiry, which is also a focus of this chapter, concerns the technological circumstances of djent's emergence, particularly the post-1990s digital production environments, which were integral to both its creation and dissemination. Djent's reliance upon digital tools to construct its guitar timbres has been the focus of Matt Shelvock, for example, while Mark Marrington and Robert Strachan have commented more broadly on the importance of digital production environments to the musical aesthetics of the subgenre.[2]

This chapter aims, firstly, to provide some background to djent's emergence, focusing upon its musical provenance as well as the technological factors underlying its creation and production and the digital aesthetics these bestowed upon the music's sound and character. Following this, an overview is provided of djent's stylistic features, including its progressive musical leanings and gravitation towards electronic and popular music influences. The final part of the chapter considers the polarised critical reception surrounding djent, providing a backdrop from which to consider the subgenre's position in relation to modern metal, particularly regarding its technological stance, which, it is argued, aligns it with recent trends for situating metal in ever-closer proximity to the aesthetics of post-digital musical practice.

The Emergence of Djent and the Technological Circumstances of its Production

Djent initially began life as an underground internet phenomenon during the early-mid-2000s, becoming recognised as a subgenre of metal music around 2010–11. It is generally accepted that the word 'djent' was coined by Misha Mansoor of Periphery as an onomatopoeic reference to the Swedish band Meshuggah's distinctive palm-muted staccato riffing style, which had a particular influence on his own playing.[3] This trope became so closely identified with djent thereafter that Meshuggah are now commonly recognised as the progenitors of djent even though they themselves have tended to downplay this role.[4] Djent artists also acknowledge the influence of Meshuggah's guitarists' (Mårten Hagström and Fredrik Thordendal) use of down-tuned seven-string (and later eight-string) instruments, and the band's celebrated rhythmic innovations – namely, their superimposed polymetres and juxtapositions of odd time signatures.[5] Another frequently cited influence on djent is the band SikTh, hailing from Hertfordshire in the UK, who pursued the progressive paradigm into what might be best described as postmodern territory on their seminal early recordings *The Trees Are Dead & Dried Out Wait for Something* (2003) and *Death of a Dead Day* (2006). Their work, which owed much to earlier technical metal, was characterised by rapid time changes, vocals that are part-rapped, part death-metal screaming and part clean-sung, altered guitar tunings and advanced guitar techniques.[6] The band's eclectic musical outlook, synthesising frenetic mathcore with ballad-style material and even piano-led classical-style instrumentals, anticipated the pronounced contrasts of style found in djent.

SikTh were also notable for producing their own albums, which reflected the growing importance of the DIY aesthetic within metal production in the early 2000s. This attitude was built upon by djent artists, whose emergence coincided with the explosion of the bedroom producer phenomenon, a movement catalysed by the increased availability of Digital Audio Workstation (henceforth, DAW) software, which was now beginning to substitute for the 'real-world' studio. With this democratisation of technology came the decentralisation of music production practice to the home environment, affording musicians the freedom to evolve their music in a situation of relative autonomy from commercial industry trends. A number of djent artists initially began their musical activities as solo 'projects', a term commonly associated with solo DIY set-ups during this period, using DAW software as a collaborative substitute for the full-band line-ups they initially lacked, before morphing, in the majority of cases, into full-band outfits.[7] Among the more notable djent practitioners who emerged from the bedroom producer nexus were Misha Mansoor, initially operating under the pseudonym Bulb, before co-founding the band Periphery, Acle Kahney, guitarist in Fellsilent (and later TesseracT), and one-man operation Chimp Spanner (Paul Ortiz). Djent artists also benefitted from the internet and specifically the social media platforms that had begun to proliferate in the early 2000s, such as SoundClick, which provided a means of sharing musical ideas and songs. In a guest post for the *MetalSucks* website Acle Kahney summarised the circumstances of djent's emergence and the importance of the internet:

It was probably back in 2002/2003 when the online community of producer-musicians who spawned the bands of this new wave of progressive metal, or 'djent', began to come together. A key unique factor that set this community/scene/then-to-be-genre apart from others is that it had no geographical base; people from all over the world were (and still are) sharing ideas, recording parts for each other and even jamming via the internet. Like punk came from the bars, clubs and rehearsal rooms of New York, this scene started in chat rooms, forums and home studios. This made it easy for many like-minded people to find each other, something which would have been impossible without the internet.[8]

For Kahney, who was based in Milton Keynes (UK), the internet afforded the opportunity to form a fruitful collaborative relationship with Mansoor, based in the United States (Bethesda, Maryland), with whom he exchanged ideas on equipment and the use of DAW software for recording and the programming of drum parts. Mansoor has indicated that djent evolved organically through the free exchange of ideas and a willingness to share and re-use one another's material:

We had these ways of making songs on our own and appropriated them to our bands. I remember some of their riffs would be like TesseracT riffs and some would be Fellsilent riffs – whatever would fit. I don't think any of us had any huge plan. It just sort of evolved over time.[9]

Djent artists were thus early pioneers of online collaboration, a concept now increasingly accepted as the norm in contemporary record production practice.

The technological circumstances of the production of djent, including the use of the DAW for recording and programming musical parts and digital effects to process guitar sounds, played an important role in shaping the aesthetics of the subgenre. These technologies engendered a unique sonic fingerprint, summarised in the words of got-djent.com spokesman Sander Dieleman as a 'simulated', 'processed' aesthetic with 'no rough edges'.[10] A particular preoccupation of djent artists was with achieving an ideal 'djenty' guitar tone. This was the subject of continuous debate and discussion within the djent community on online forums such as got-djent.com, and amongst bloggers and YouTubers. As limited technological resources precluded the use of complex hardware set-ups, djent artists achieved their sound using a combination of characteristic guitar pickups (such as Bare Knuckle's Aftermath humbucker) and software and hardware-based digital amplifier modelling technologies, including Fractal Audio Systems' Axe FX and the Line 6 Pod Farm software and HD Pro hardware. They also experimented with freeware plugins, audio software made available at no charge on the internet by third-party developers, to simulate the required signal chains, another consequence of the budgetary constraints of the bedroom production scenario.[11]

With this equipment, djent guitarists were able to evolve a distorted guitar timbre that exhibited both a low-range heaviness appropriate to metal and a distinctively crisp, dry character. Here digital tools permitted precise control of the signal path via gating, compression and simulated amplifier configurations, together with the facility to build up a detailed inventory of easily retrievable presets. The cultivation of djent tone served more than a merely aesthetic purpose, being designed to allow for clear articulation of the relatively sophisticated pitch structures found within the power chords typically employed by these artists, as explained by Shelvock in reference to Animals as Leaders, Periphery and TesseracT:

The traditional guitar power chord, spelled Root-Fifth-Root on the guitar's lowest strings is modified–usually in a drop A (or lower) tuning – to be spelled Root-Fifth-Root-Fifth in this genre. This four-string chord necessitates a guitar tone which provides more clarity than metal of the past, where power chords would consist of two or three string power chords. In addition to using these expanded power chords, some progressive metal artists favour a harmonic palette which lies outside of the typical metal milieu. It is not uncommon to hear suspended chords, and some artists even choose to employ 7th and 9th voicings both with and without the application of distortion.[12]

Also fundamental to the post-digital character of the djent sound were the MIDI-programmed drum parts, which were drawn from software-based drum sample libraries. In the early period, these were often created using Toontrack's now-iconic *Drumkit from Hell*, a resource that had significance for djent artists, as it was one of the earliest sample libraries to be designed specifically for a metal performance context. Adding to the aura, this particular sample library had also been recorded by Meshuggah's drummer Tomas Haake at Dug-Out Studios in Uppsala, Sweden.[13] Djent artists programmed their drum parts using sequencing software such as Steinberg's Cubase and Propellerhead's Reason, the latter emulating a real-world rack-based studio set-up and including digital modelling of earlier sampler technologies.

Another popular software tool amongst djent artists was Native Instruments' dedicated drum sampler plugin, Battery (released in 2002), which enabled highly refined editing of sampled drum sounds.[14] Interestingly, the drum programming aesthetic remained central to djent bands' creative processes even when they had moved fully into live band performance. In some cases, this was a matter of practicality. Misha Mansoor, for example, who began his musical life as a drummer before moving to the guitar, has commented that, compared to the degree of control afforded by sampled drums, he found live drums to be far more troublesome to record, edit and mix.[15] Elsewhere, drum programming served a particular creative purpose, as in the case of Animals as Leaders, who retained this approach on their second album, *Weightless* (2011), despite having recruited an actual drummer – Navene Koperweis – in the meantime. Discussing the making of the album in an interview for *Modern Drummer*, Koperweis gave a succinct account of the MIDI-based process of creating the album's drum parts:

We used Cubase to write the MIDI, and I use a Yamaha electronic kit with the Toontrack *Drumkit From Hell* as the samples. You're able to play beyond your abilities [this way]. We're using MIDI. It's not audio; we manipulate it and run it through the Toontrack software. I can play a bunch of fills and put them where I want, then program or play beats. It's seamlessly arranged and then rammed through the *Drumkit From Hell* software. I did play a lot on the electronic kit, but sometimes I'd program a part, because then I'm not restricted to what I can play in the moment. And it's a lot faster to not [play the drum tracks] right off the bat. It's a weird, futuristic way of making music. It's 60/40 programmed/live drums. Every song has a mixture. And I never program anything I can't actually play.[16]

TesseracT drummer Jay Postones also developed his drumming in relation to software tools, typically evolving his drum performances from demos provided by guitarist Acle Kahney, containing parts programmed using

Superior Drummer, which he would attempt to replicate physically on the kit. Postones implied that this would entail trying to find a way to play a programmed part that at first sight might seem impossible: 'Sometimes I'll hear it and think, "Yup, that's something I can't play – I've got to learn how". I like trying to re-create the ideas he's had. I don't try to overstep the mark, because Acle has got a clear vision of what he wants it to sound like'.[17] Postones also remarks on the importance of using DAW software (Cubase in this instance) as a vehicle for clarifying a drum pattern idea before attempting to realise it using the kit:

Obviously I prefer to sit behind the kit and jam it out. But if I get an idea for a pattern, like putting fives and fours together, or sevens and nines and elevens, I might end up having to put it into a computer first to really hear it. . . . Occasionally . . . something will be quite tricky, and if I want to turn it into a triplet feel or whatever, I'll need to put it into a computer so that I can hear it played back perfectly first. That's the benefit of technology these days. You can slow it down to a tempo that makes sense, digest that, and then try to get it to a stage that you're not counting things – you're just kind of feeling things.[18]

The comments of Koperweis and Postones illustrate the extent to which digital tools informed the conception and realisation of djent, with the software here taking on an essentially collaborative role by assisting in the generation of rhythmic material that might not have been imagined when using the drumkit in a more traditional fashion. Even the very fact of engaging with the DAW from the perspective of more conventional performance activities, such as the tracking of guitar parts, left a mark on the character of djent as Mansoor observed regarding the evolution of his own very precise guitar performance style: 'When you're playing that way you start to focus on parts of your technique that make all the difference in the world. Things you'd never have noticed if you weren't sitting in front of a computer and hearing your playing back. It taught me how to play guitar'.[19]

Djent as a Style of Music

Djent began to crystallise as a recognisable genre of music around 2011, by which point the term was being used to describe the work of a wide range of artists. Joel McIver's *Metal Hammer* feature (April 2011),[20] for example, included the following in its 'league of djentlemen': Periphery, Vildhjarta, Animals as Leaders, Elitist, Of Legends, After the Burial, Born of Osiris, Skyharbor, Chimp Spanner and Mnemic, several of whom were now signed to high profile established, or up and coming, metal labels including Roadrunner, Century Media, Prosthetic, Sumerian, Nuclear Blast and Basick.[21] Having surveyed the output of these artists, McIver noted that 'the djent tag' was becoming applicable 'to a relatively wide range of sounds'.[22] Unsurprisingly, given the subgenre's progressive musical provenance, virtuosic rhythm and lead guitar performance skills are central to djent. The influences here are wide-ranging, including the progressive metal styles of guitarists such as Dream Theater's John Petrucci, but also (in the cases of Misha Mansoor and Tosin Abasi, for example) styles from outside metal, including contemporary jazz and jazz-rock fusion.[23] Hence the harmonic language of djent is often constituted of complex chords and dense textures derived from the polyrhythmic layering of guitar parts, sometimes involving up to three instruments simultaneously (see Periphery's work, for example).

At the same time, djent guitarists also showed leanings towards more traditional styles of top-line lead playing, such as Chimp Spanner, whose melodic approach is reminiscent of Steve Vai or Joe Satriani. While djent riffing is certainly a defining aspect of the style, as encapsulated by the characteristic djent 'breakdown', djent artists also favoured calmer, more ambient material in the form of reverb saturated and/or delay-effected clean arpeggiated guitar, employed as intro/outro material or to provide interludes between tracks. Instances can be found in much of the work of TesseracT, including the early *Concealing Fate* EP (2010) and subsequent debut album, *One* (2011), Periphery on *Periphery* (2010), Uneven Structure on *Februus* (2011), Chimp Spanner on *At the Dream's Edge* (2009), Skyharbor on *Blind White Noise: Illusion and Chaos* (2012), and Vildhjarta on *Måsstaden* (2011).

While a number of djent bands employ vocals prominently, the styles adopted can vary considerably, one key characteristic (seen in the work of TesseracT, for example) being the frequent alternation between clean sung and death metal style screaming, which is sometimes amusingly referred to as 'good cop, bad cop' technique. It should not be assumed that vocals are central to the work of all djent artists, however, as illustrated by Chimp Spanner and the trio Animals as Leaders, whose music is entirely instrumental in conception. Misha Mansoor's remark that Periphery's self-titled first album (2010) 'was written to be an instrumental album and vocals were thrown on top'[24] suggests that djent artists did not necessarily see themselves as beholden to song formats. Indeed, many djent compositions appear conceived in a manner consistent with instrumental music, adopting elaborate formal structures worked out over extended time frames, with many tracks lasting between 5 and 7 minutes, and in some cases even longer (see, for example, the 15-minute 'Racecar', which concludes Periphery's debut LP). Djent albums and EPs are likewise conceived as multi-movement compositional structures linked by conceptual themes, in some cases, such as TesseracT's *Altered State* (2013) and Periphery's double album *Juggernaut – Alpha/Juggernaut – Omega* (2015), on a grandiose scale befitting 1970s progressive rock.

Many djent recordings also show a marked influence of electronic music aesthetics, which manifest themselves in various ways. Often electronic styles are introduced for short periods at certain points in tracks to add colouristic interest, such as the chiptune-esque arpeggio introduction to Chimp Spanner's 'Bad Code' (2009), or the Aphex Twin-like beats heard briefly at the beginning of Periphery's 'Jetpacks Was Yes!' (2010) and outro to their track 'Totla Mad' (2010). Elsewhere, electronic music gestures are integrated more substantially into the proceedings, such as Animals as Leaders' track 'On Impulse' (2009), which includes 'glitch' style passages of mangled percussion and, in the acoustic guitar introduction, looped material, giving the impression of skipping audio.[25] Such examples can be regarded as a further by-product of the post-digital context of djent production, engendered by exposure to the possibilities of the DAW for the creative manipulation of sound. Looping, for example, is a DAW-induced compositional construct, which encourages the user to copy and paste short passages of recorded audio – bass lines, guitar riffs and drum parts – producing the effect of literal repetition more commonly associated with sample-based music.[26] Another interesting instance is Swedish band Vildhjarta's track 'Benblåst' (2011), which contains *musique concrète*-like passages of metallic clanking juxtaposed with a delay-effected noise loop, suggesting links to industrial music.

Working in the DAW also encouraged artists to utilise software-based sound design tools, including synthesisers and samplers. Chimp Spanner's sound on *At the Dream's Edge* (2009) and the *All Roads Lead Here* EP (2012), for example, is strongly defined by the synthesiser, which he uses to generate introductions, interludes and ambient backdrops to his riff and lead playing. Unsurprisingly, he has listed Brian Eno and Vangelis as particular influences on his musical thinking.[27] Elsewhere, French guitarist Rémi Gallego, known as The Algorithm, engaged directly with tropes of contemporary EDM, fusing characteristic djent-style riffing with elements of dubstep (see the track 'Trojans' on the 2012 album *Polymorphic Code*). Gallego's approach, which was aptly labelled 'djent-step', was consonant with developments that had been taking place in US metal, most notably in the work of Korn on their 2011 album *The Path of Totality*.

As djent began to proliferate during the early-2010s, it also showed itself to be amenable to fusion with a range of other popular music genres. One notable synthesis was 'rap-djent', pioneered by the British band Hacktivist, hailing from Milton Keynes (also the home of TesseracT). The band's eponymous debut EP, released in 2012, melds typical djent riffing with clean singing and a rapped element that has obvious roots in British grime.[28] Rap-djent was in one sense an iteration of the rap-metal fusion that had characterised 1990s US-American nu metal and its earlier proto-types, but now with a distinctly British tint.[29] One of the most contrived fusions of djent with the wider popular music sphere occurred on *Djent Goes Pop* (2011), an album released for free on Facebook by the Djent-Lemen's Club.[30] This multi-authored (and almost parodical) effort included mash-up style re-workings of (then) contemporary material, such as Lady Gaga's 'Poker Face' (2008) and Rihanna's 'Russian Roulette' (2009), utilising audio samples from the original recordings, as well as imaginative cover versions of earlier mainstream pop favourites such as George Michael's 'Careless Whisper' (1984) and A-ha's 'Take on Me' (1984). What this, and the work of Gallego and Hacktivist, tended to highlight was the extent to which djent's most recognisable elements – particularly its power chord riff – had quickly become self-contained clichés that could be readily re-inserted into other musical contexts, rather as a hip hop artist might treat an iconic drum-break. It also served as reminder of the general ambivalence of djent artists towards being pigeonholed in terms of any one specific musical genre – including metal.

The Reception of Djent

A survey of the critical literature (typically magazine articles, posts on blogs and forums, and YouTube videos) that appeared in response to djent from the time of its emergence in the late 2000s reveals that its effect was to polarise the metal community, in some quarters being welcomed for its freshness and innovation, while in others inviting vociferous ridicule and derision. The main sticking points for commentators negatively inclined towards djent can be succinctly summarised in the remarks made by The Mad Israeli, a regular blogger for the *No Clean Singing* website (writing in November 2011):

What do I think of djent? I honestly think it's pretty f**king stupid. Now, I didn't always think that, mind you, but for several reasons I've come around to that way of thinking: The word 'djent', the community centred around it, the scene kids, the desensitization of the style for commercial or widespread appeal, and the butchering of original-sounding production due to its foundation in totally digital recording technology.[31]

Elaborating each of these reasons, in turn, The Mad Israeli painted a picture of a subgenre that had become a cliché. This included criticism of the onomatopoeic use of the word 'djent' itself, which had become even more problematic since it had also taken on verb status ('to djent', 'djenting') as well as the presence of the 'scene kids', who had seized upon and over-exposed particular djent characteristics: 'All they have are 7- and 8-string guitars and a load of unnecessary clean and ambient overlays to boring, open-note grooves that are, dare I say, worse than the drivel Slipknot put out'. His criticisms of djent production were levelled at the homogeneity of the djent sound that had been engendered by the persistent use of digital tools in the music's creation:

I also dislike the growing trend of ultra-slick, ultra-clean production. Nowadays, mix is too often cast aside as an integral tool for conveying the songwriters' conception of the music, and in its place we have nothing more complicated than a simple desire to make the music shiny and pretty, because that sells better ... Many bands today sound the same because everything is done via Axe-FX recorded guitars and bass with Superior or EZ-drummer replacing a real person on the kit. It's very disheartening, and it's getting quite old.[32]

John Hill, another outspoken metal critic, wrote a particularly scathing commentary on djent for *Vice* in 2014, entitled, 'It's time for djent to djie [sic]'. Hill's article's overall position was that djent was little more than a fashionable offshoot of metalcore:

Djent is what happens after years of trolls tell metalcore kids in YouTube comment sections they should listen to 'real metal'. Instead of staying in their own lane and doing their own thing, metalcore bros have had their feelings hurt to the point that they feel they must prove to 'real metalheads' that they can also be edgy.[33]

Then, taking Periphery as the exemplar djent's shortcomings, Hill deconstructed the subgenre further:

If you remove the off-time guitar parts and the boring noodly bits, the track is reduced to your standard fare of Hot Topic-core scene metal. Breakdowns, lame-o scream-sing tradeoffs, and not much else make this band sound like Saosin covering Meshuggah at a high school talent show.

Elsewhere, the *MetalSucks* website, which acted as a placeholder for much of the online commentary on djent during the 2010s,[34] was less abrasive in its approach, tending to take a more tongue-in-cheek attitude to representing the scene, as illustrated by the titles of posts such as, 'The Debate Rages On: Is "Djent" a Genre' (2015) and 'Scientific Proof that Djent is a Genre' (2015). It also featured video content, which gently poked fun at the clichés of the music, such as YouTuber metal guitarist Jared Dines' annual parodies of djent guitar style, Andrew Baena's[35] 'Random Djent Breakdown Generator', a software algorithm, which triggered short pre-recorded segments of djent riffing over a drum loop, and Rob Scallon's 'The Discovery of Djent', which suggested that creating a djent track was simply a matter of copying and pasting a single power chord multiple times on a DAW arrange page. Much of the commentary was curated by *MetalSucks* blogger Vince Neilstein who, while generally sympathetic to the more high-profile djent bands, was outspoken in his criticism of djent hybrids such as djent-step and djent-rap.[36]

The more serious and balanced online commentary on djent tended to come from journalists representing commercial metal magazines, such as Europe's *Metal Hammer* and *Kerrang!*, which provided strong promotional support for the music as it emerged into the mainstream. *Metal Hammer* (UK), for example, published several articles devoted to djent artists from the early 2010s onwards, particularly TesseracT and Periphery, who were undoubtedly the most prevalent (and as time went on, least djent-like) of the bands associated with the scene.[37] Writing for *Metal Hammer* in April 2011, Dom Lawson remarked of djent that 'as daft as its name might be, this burgeoning scene sounds a lot more like the future of heavy music than anything else out there right now'.[38] Djent was also given significant coverage in guitar hobbyist publications such as *Total Guitar* and *Guitar Player*, which naturally foregrounded the music's guitar-centred virtuosity and the 'gear' culture surrounding it. There were also occasional articles in the British press, such as Jamie Thomson's 'Djent, the Metal Geek's Microgenre' (another somewhat tongue-in-cheek framing), which situated djent in relation to recent electronic music and the soloistic practitioner innovations associated with that field:

While such home recording techniques have been the preserve of digital recording artists producing techno, dubstep and electronica for some years now, it took the perseverance of one guitarist, Misha Mansoor, to bring this 21st-century philosophy to the metal realm.[39]

Thomson also suggested that djent's proliferation via the internet represented an important paradigm shift for metal music:

More than most genres, metal has a chequered history when it comes to the internet, not least Metallica's public spat with file-sharing website Napster. For the old guard, it has been something to fear; but for this new generation, it represents opportunity and a way to circumvent the established networks.[40]

Situating Djent within/without Metal

Having outlined the circumstances of djent's emergence, its characteristic features and given a sense of its reception by the metal community, it remains to offer some concluding thoughts on how djent may be situated in relation to the metal genre. It is interesting to note, given what has already been highlighted regarding the polarization of opinion on djent, that the position of the djent community has itself been one of ambivalence towards the 'djent' label. In an interview published by the Djentle-Music website in 2014, got-djent.com spokesman Sander Dieleman observed that 'the word djent just seems to cause a lot of polarized reactions . . . most of them [the djent bands] don't actually identify themselves as djent, like if someone says "hey you're djent" then they'll reluctantly acknowledge it'.[41] The main issue here is clearly the limited onomatopoeic signification of the word 'djent' itself, which most djent artists recognise is simply insufficient to encapsulate the scope of their individual musical remits. One of the most outspoken critics of the djent label has been Misha Mansoor, to whom (ironically) the origin of the word 'djent' is credited. Interviewed for the *Kerrang* podcast in 2011, Mansoor acknowledged that while the word djent was certainly applicable to aspects of Periphery's music, namely the djent style riffs employed, this was a relatively insignificant facet of a far less easily definable whole.[42] Instead, Mansoor preferred to see Periphery's music, and that of his djent contemporaries, as simply 'progressive'. This was also Dieleman's conclusion:

I think the term djent might probably disappear in the long term. It's going to be modern progressive metal again because that's a little more marketable maybe – and I think the distinction between the djent bands on the one side and then other progressive metal on the other side's kinda gonna fade away.[43]

Djent's affinities with the progressive metal subgenre, as has been observed, are not difficult to discern, being rooted in the musical styles of foundational bands such as Dream Theater and Tool and foregrounding 'specialist' approaches derived from technical and 'math' metal (Watchtower, Meshuggah, Dillinger Escape Plan) and less easily classifiable forms of postmodern metal (SikTh). Considered in relation to such predecessors, djent's sophisticated guitar-centric harmonic and melodic languages, its rhythmic and formal complexity and openness to musical perspectives outside metal, are hardly out of place. In these terms, djent may thus be considered to reside comfortably within the lineage of progressive metal as outlined by commentators such as Sam Dunn and Jeff Wagner.[44]

There is also an alternative approach to situating djent, however, which relates to the technological circumstances of the music's evolution. Specifically, djent can be regarded as a standalone post-digital form, whose musical identity, while founded upon key metal tropes (such as the distorted power chord riff), is at the same time uniquely the product of its practitioners' engagement with digital tools and the musical aesthetics these engender. In particular, this can be seen in the centrality of digital amp modelling software and programmed drums to djent's sonic identity, and more generally in the DAW-engendered electronic music traits that can be detected in many djent recordings. Robert Strachan, recognising this fact, has gone so far as to conclude that djent is an example of a 'cyber-genre', whose characteristics are 'simultaneously resultant from, and reflective of, the contexts of digitization', and to which the 'widespread availability of computer-based production technologies' is integral.[45] Where recent metal music is concerned, this description is not applicable only to djent, but also to the music of many contemporary metal-oriented artists, whose output in various ways reflects the consequences of the new digital tools for genre-situated musical practice. It is a relevant perspective, for example, on the work of Genghis Tron, whose use of Ableton Live facilitated their stark metal-EDM fusions in the mid-2000s, and Igorrr (Gautier Serre), an architect of 'cybergrind', whose accomplished death metal pedigree was radically re-contextualised through DAW-based micro-edited genre mash-ups.[46] It is also applicable to the work of veteran metal artists Korn, who on their album *The Path of Totality* (released in 2011, hence coincident with djent's emergence into the mainstream) purposefully re-aligned their metal outlook with the emerging North American dubstep scene, necessitating the radical re-thinking of their idiom through the paradigm of the DAW.[47] These, together with djent, illustrate the ways in which metal, like many other forms of late twentieth-century popular music, has inevitably become implicated in new forms of post-digital musical practice in which genre constructs appear to have become largely redundant.

Notes

1. See Robert G. H. Burns, *Experiencing Progressive Rock: A Listener's Companion* (Rowman & Littlefield, 2018); Allan F. Moore and Remy Martin, *Rock, the Primary Text: Developing a Musicology of Rock* (Routledge, 2018); Steven Gamble, *How Music Empowers: Listening to Modern Rap and Metal* (Routledge, 2021).

2. See Matt Shelvock, 'The Progressive Heavy Metal Guitarist's Signal Chain', in Russ Hepworth-Sawyer, Justin Paterson and Rob Toulson (eds.), *Innovation in Music* (Future Technology Press, 2013), pp. 126–38; Mark Marrington, 'From DJ to Djent-Step: Technology and the Re-coding of Metal Music since the 1980s', *Metal Music Studies* 3/2 (2017): 251–68; Robert Strachan, *Sonic Technologies: Popular Music, Digital Culture and the Creative Process* (Bloomsbury, 2017).

3. See Joel McIver, 'Periphery', *Metal Hammer* (Summer 2012), pp. 60–3. The definitive Meshuggah riffing sound can be heard on the 1995 album, *Destroy, Erase, Improve*, on tracks such as 'Future Breed Machine' and 'Soul Burn'.

4. For further discussion see Burns, *Experiencing Progressive Rock*.

5. Such elements can also be seen to reflect the influence of earlier progressive metal bands such as Rush and Dream Theater. For an involved discussion of Meshuggah's rhythmic approach, see Jonathan Pieslak, 'Re-casting Metal: Rhythm and Meter in the Music of Meshuggah', *Music Theory Spectrum* 29/2 (2007): 219–45.

6. As showcased by guitarists Dan Weller and Graham 'Pin' Pinney.

7. Burgess has used the expression 'artist' producer to describe this kind of autonomous DAW-based practitioner. See Richard J. Burgess, *The Art of Music Production: The Theory and Practice* (Oxford University Press, 2013).

8. See Acle Kahney, 'Tesseract's Acle on the Birth of Tesseract and the Djent Movement', *MetalSucks* (6 October 2010). www.metalsucks.net/2010/10/06/tesseracts-acle-on-the-birth-of-tesseract-and-the-djent-movement (accessed 29 June 2021).

9. Rob Laing, 'What Is Djent?', *Total Guitar* (May 2011), p. 51.

10. Djentle Music, 'Interview with Sander Dieleman from Got-Djent.Com', *SoundCloud* (2010). https://soundcloud.com/djentle-music/sets/interview-with-sander-dieleman (accessed 12 August 2021).

11. For further discussion see Shelvock, 'The Progressive Heavy Metal'.

12. *Ibid.*, pp. 129–30.

13. See Anon, 'Drum Software: High-Powered Sample Players for Today's Electronic Drummer', *Modern Drummer* (April 2009), pp. 30–1. This article also includes discussion of Toontracks' Superior Drummer and EZ Drummer, which were popular tools for djent drum programming.

14. See Laing, 'What Is Djent?'.

15. See Boyinaband, 'Interview: Misha Mansoor of Periphery [Part 1]' (2011). www.youtube.com/watch?v=qXNeoBaZH9w (accessed 23 August 2021).

16. Ken Micallef, 'Navene Koperweis', *Modern Drummer* (January 2012), p. 34.

17. Ben Meyer, 'Jay Postones', *Modern Drummer* (August 2015), p. 61.

18. *Ibid.*

19. Laing, 'What Is Djent?', p. 52.

20. Joel McIver, 'The League of Djentlemen', *Metal Hammer* (April 2011), pp. 66–7.

21. Basick has a particular association with djent, as can be heard on its 2012 Basick Records 'sampler' at https://basickrecords.bandcamp.com/album/basick-2012-free-sampler (accessed 12 August 2021).

22. McIver, 'The League of Djentlemen', p. 67.

23. For example, Animals as Leaders frontman Tosin Abasi has cited the influence of contemporary jazz players Kurt Rosenwinkel and Adam Rogers, while Periphery's Misha Mansoor references 'fusion' artists such as Allan Holdsworth and Guthrie Govan.

24. Kalin Pashaliev, 'Interview: Misha Mansoor of Periphery', *The New Age* (22 September 2016).

25. Looping is also a feature of the track 'Behaving Badly' on the same album. Tosin Abasi has referenced electronic artists Siriusmo, Reso, and Flying Lotus as influences.

26. This particular album, which was essentially a Tosin Abasi solo project, was also notable for its being wholly built on sampled drums, here programmed by Misha Mansoor who produced, mixed and mastered the recording.

27. See Chimp Spanner's SoundClick profile at www.soundclick.com/artist/default.cfm?bandID=77752 (accessed 12 August 2021).

28. See, for example, the track 'Blades' (2012). For further discussion of Hacktivist see Gamble, *How Music Empowers*.

29. Other notable rap-djent bands that emerged during this period were Devastator (later named DVSR), hailing from Australia, and Issues, originating from Atlanta, Georgia.

30. A follow-up album, *Djent Goes Christmas*, was released in December of the same year.

31. The Mad Israeli, 'Senseless Rambles – Djent', *No Clean Singing* (2011). www.nocleansinging.com/2011/11/06/senseless-rambles-djent (accessed 19 July 2021).

32. *Ibid.*

33. John Hill, 'It's Time for Djent to Djie', *Vice* (8 October 2014). www.vice.com/en/article/r3xdb6/its-time-for-djent-to-djie (accessed 9 July 2021).

34. *MetalSucks* on occasion provided djent artists with a forum to discuss their work, such as Kahney, 'Tesseract's Acle'.

35. Guitarist in the band Galactic Pegasus.

36. Among Neilstein's more amusingly titled articles were 'I hate myself enough to check out the djent-rap band Hacktivist's new song and video for you' and 'The latest metal micro genre bastardization: Dubstep+Djent=Djentstep'.

37. See, for example, Dom Lawson, 'TesseracT', *Metal Hammer* (April 2011), pp. 64–5; McIver, 'Periphery', pp. 60–3; Dom Lawson, 'Progs of War', *Metal Hammer* (March 2015), pp. 66–8.

38. Lawson, 'TesseracT', p. 65.

39. Jamie Thomson, 'Djent, the Metal Geek's Microgenre', *The* Guardian (3 March 2011). www.theguardian.com/music/2011/mar/03/djent-metal-geeks (accessed 3 February 2017).

40. *Ibid.*
41. Djentle Music, 'Interview with Sander Dieleman'.
42. See Kerrang!, 'Kerrang! Podcast: Periphery' (2011). www.youtube.com/watch?
v=IJFe8Vlw22I (accessed 2 August 2021). See also McIver, 'Periphery', p. 60.
43. Djentle Music, 'Interview with Sander Dieleman'.
44. See Sam Dunn, *Metal Evolution: Episode 11 – Progressive Metal* (Banger Films,
2012); Jeff Wagner, *Mean Deviation: Four Decades of Progressive Heavy Metal*
(Bazillion Points Books, 2010).
45. Strachan, *Sonic Technologies*, p. 135.
46. Two recordings of interest here are Genghis Tron, *Board up the House* (2008),
and Igorr, *Savage Sinusoid* (2017).
47. For a detailed discussion of Korn's strategy on this recording see
Mark Marrington, 'The DAW, Electronic Music Aesthetics, and Genre
Transgression in Music Production: The Case of Heavy Metal Music', in
Russ Hepworth-Sawyer, Jay Hodgson and Mark Marrington (eds.), *Producing
Music* (Routledge, 2019), pp. 52–74.

Contempt-of-Core

A Reception History of Metalcore Subgenres as Abject Genres

ERIC SMIALEK

Genre is complicated. Musical genres at once seem intuitive, yet any closer examination of them yields contradictions and uncertainties. Disagreements inevitably arise surrounding genre labels, boundaries, levels of generality, properties, connotations, chronologies, and any other tangible evidence that genres exist in a meaningful way. Despite these traps, genre categories continue to facilitate communication as much as confuse it and, as much as musicians may insist on not being funnelled into them, there remains a pervasive fascination with them among anyone who wishes to make sense of music. Rather than do away with genre, or strive to demarcate its details with increasingly Herculean taxonomies, I have found that the most meaningful discussions of musical categories tease out the sometimes counterintuitive ways that they behave in practice. How do genres come to exist? How do they compare with one another? Why are some relationships between genres and texts more complicated than others? This chapter aims to introduce readers to debates about musical genres through a historiographical study of metalcore, a particularly slippery genre term and thus an instructive one.

My understanding of metalcore (a genre portmanteau of '[heavy] metal' and 'hardcore [punk]') differs somewhat from other authors, whose historical narratives and timelines will be outlined further below. For one, I understand it to be an umbrella category that encompasses other genre terms such as the New Wave of American Heavy Metal (widely abbreviated NWOAHM), screamo and deathcore. As Lewis Kennedy has shown,[1] many metalcore enthusiasts separate these categories entirely or assign the term metalcore to different repertories covering different time periods than I do. I treat metalcore as an umbrella term that combines those subtypes because they overlap somewhat in style traits and audience demographics, and because they have comparable reception histories. With reception history in mind, I view metalcore as an especially challenging example of what I call an abject genre of metal music.[2]

To introduce readers to this concept, my chapter begins with an overview of commonalities that metalcore shares with other abject genres. It then outlines diverse historical accounts by other authors to argue for a more complex view of chronological and conceptual boundaries than an individual narrative might allow. Finally, an analysis of Currents' 'Silence' (2017) provides an example of metalcore as an amalgamation of stylistic qualities from multiple sources, following Kennedy.[3] This chapter demonstrates the utility of abject genres as a concept for understanding metalcore from multiple angles. Using metalcore as a particularly challenging case study in genre historiography, it argues that metalcore's complexity as a genre can teach broad lessons about genre in popular music.

Metalcore as an Abject Genre Category

Setting aside momentarily what abjection entails, abject genres may be thought of as categories of metal music that are frequently viewed with suspicion by metal fans as inauthentic imitations of 'real' metal, which gain popularity as fashionable trends. Moreover, in their derision of these genres, fans tend to invoke groups of people who face discrimination in the metal scene and broader society.[4] Thus, abject genres involve several key concepts that reveal aesthetic beliefs within the metal scene and socio-political relations between fans. These concepts and their associated traits are summarised in Table 20.1.

A time dimension subtends an abject genre's emergence and fall from popularity. While, in practice, this is more complicated than simply assigning a chronological start and end date to a genre, rough timeframes of decades do align with the three major instances that I argue characterise metal history since the 1980s: glam metal during the 1980s, nu metal during the 1990s, and metalcore during the 2000s. These may each be thought of as moments in time when certain styles of metal gained mass popularity with audiences that may not otherwise listen to metal. Such popularity draws a well-documented suspicion amongst metal fans towards the apparent inauthenticity of mass commerce.[10] While a full exploration of this value system lies outside the scope of this chapter, it is common among fans of more traditional forms of metal to perceive abject genres, like metalcore, as a diluted misinterpretation of metal's stylistic codes by non-fans.

Stylistically, abject genres are frequently dismissed as simplified metal with an exaggerated gimmick. All three instances involve verse-chorus forms that fit within a radio-friendly four-minute format. Nu metal

Table 20.1 Abject genres and their characteristics

Abject Genre	Glam metal	Nu metal	Metalcore[5]		
			NWOAHM	Screamo	Deathcore
Time Range	Mid-'80s to Late-'90s	Mid-'90s to Early-'00s	Early-'00s	Mid-'00s	Late-'00s
Examples	Poison, Mötley Crüe	Korn, Limp Bizkit	Lamb of God, Killswitch Engage	The Devil Wears Prada, Attack Attack!	Emmure, The Acacia Strain
Stylistic Traits	Verse-chorus form, radio-friendly length				
	Diatonic harmony, catchy tunes	Downtuned grooves, high-register dissonances, rap	Melodic death metal riffs, roared[6] verse with sung chorus	Stark contrast between screamed[7] verse and sung chorus	Downtuning, especially low roars, breakdowns
Lyrical Themes	Hedonism	Trauma and catharsis	Conflict, loyalty, empowerment	Romantic strife	Conflict, casual misogyny[8]
Sartorial Trends	Teased hair, tight clothes, makeup	Baggy clothes, tracksuits, jewellery, dreadlocks	Short hair, tight clothes	Asymmetrical hair, styled with clay, tight clothes	Short hair, gauged earlobes, sportswear
Aesthetic Goals	Rebellious appropriation of women's glamour	Aesthetic of affliction	Down-to-earth, blue-collar, toughness	Emotional intensity, sensitivity	Cathartic aggression, intensified NWOAHM
Social Connotations	Male appropriations of female 'to-be-looked-at-ness'[9] ('glam', 'lite', 'hair')	Teenage, white suburban appropriations of Black styles	Masculine, tough, violent	Teenage scenesters, Christian, feminine	Fraternity 'bros', intensified NWOAHM

eliminated guitar solos while exaggerating downtuned guitars for groove-driven riffs. That is, while bands like Pantera were routinely lowering their tunings by as much as one-and-a-half steps, nu metal bands like Korn added a seventh string to accommodate tunings as low as a perfect fifth below standard tuning. Metalcore, especially deathcore, became known for its 'breakdown' sections that conventionalised the slowed sections that thrash and death metal bands had explored in the late 1980s to early 1990s[11] and that Suffocation had especially developed in the early 1990s for death metal.[12] In contrast to the chromatically shifting power chords of

Suffocation's breakdowns, deathcore breakdowns nearly dispense with pitch changes altogether, emphasising rhythm, sometimes on a single, low open guitar string. In a particularly extreme example, 'Word of Intulo' (2011) by Emmure is a breakdown-like track that consists entirely of a single note for over a minute. Despite exhibiting multiple forms of rhythmic complexity – syncopations, hemiolas, cross rhythms, motivic extensions – it has been mocked over YouTube by fans who sarcastically cover it with apathetic expressions and provide 'guitar tablatures' consisting of strings of zeros. While such covers are done affectionately by fans of deathcore, the punchline about apparent simplicity draws from the same critiques made by its detractors.

A lyrical dimension can be observed that unifies each of the abject genres in opposition to other forms of metal. As I have shown in more detail elsewhere, this difference can be thought of as a split between heavy metal's traditional emphasis on supernatural themes and abject genres' emphasis on quotidian lyrics.[13] While Iron Maiden's 'The Number of the Beast' (1982) epitomises heavy metal's fantastical lyrical imagery, glam metal band Poison's 'Nothin' but a Good Time' (1988) focuses its fantasy escape around themes of everyday life. In contrast to the black metal lyrics of Emperor's 'I am the Black Wizards' (1993), Korn's 'Faget' (1994) presents its audiences with relatable nu metal lyrics about high-school bullying. The death metal lyrics of Hate Eternal's 'Two Demons' (2005), rife with archaisms ('reveal thyself') and references to 'beings' and 'souls', cultivates a decidedly supernatural feel compared to the NWOAHM band Lamb of God's 'Laid to Rest' (2004), which depicts the potentially supernatural theme of a murder victim's revenge with everyday slang. As Marcus Erbe notes in his analysis of male frustrations in deathcore lyrics, metalcore vocalists construct authenticity around their lyrics being expressions of personal experience[14] in contrast to what Michelle Phillipov sees as a lack of personal identification in 1990s death metal lyrics.[15] I have argued elsewhere that death metal vocalists do undergo a more figurative kind of identification in their physiological imitations of large beasts.[16] One might infer then that this figurative identification with beasts would also apply to deathcore vocalists whose growls are similar to those used in death metal. However, lyrical differences between death metal and deathcore parallel how the two genres construct authenticity differently. And it is that difference between quotidian, personal identification and supernatural, figurative identification that generally distinguishes abject genres from more traditional forms of metal.

A social dimension characterises each of the abject genres, reflective of socio-political tensions within the metal scene. Glam metal, as Robert

Walser's pioneering study of gender-play within the style demonstrates, dealt with male anxieties towards women by appropriating the spectacle of androgyny to express control over women and rebel against dominant men.[17] Nu metal incorporated musical and visual codes of Black cultures through its use of rap and DJ scratching from hip hop as well as its baggy clothes and visual celebration of commodities (i.e., jewellery, cars); dreadlocks became increasingly fashionable during the 1990s as worn by the members of Korn, Soulfly and Coal Chamber. Screamo, whose loose status as a '-core' genre can be seen in derisive nicknames like 'Christcore',[18] bears a connection to the demographic category of teenage youth, as did nu metal with the nickname 'mallcore' (which is sardonically gendered as well). In music journalism of the 2000s and retrospective writings more currently, one finds screamo (and its root term 'emo') associated with terms like 'scene kids' that accompany fashion stereotypes associated with dark, asymmetrical hairstyles, black eyeliner and Myspace selfies.[19] Thus, in their criticisms of why they find abject genres uncool, metal fans frequently invoke subtle antagonisms towards three categories of identity: women, racial Blackness and teenage youth. Tensions around these demographics reflect continuing forms of discrimination broadly found within the metal scene and are an important reason why I unify those genres with the descriptor 'abject'.

Abjection, a concept analysed in Julia Kristeva's *The Powers of Horror: An Essay on Abjection*, refers to something unknown and threatening that provokes disgust and terror.[20] While its literal manifestation might lie in various forms of human waste, the urge it provokes to destroy it can be transferred psychically to social entities such as threatening demographics of people, upsetting kinds of discourses, or troubling categories of music. Intense discomfort, essentially, is the experience of abjection, coupled with the need to obliterate it and rid oneself of the threat. Such an explanation may bring to mind some of the darkest examples, such as mass genocides and hate crimes. Indeed, as metal studies have shown during the past two decades,[21] serious forms of discrimination continue to affect the global metal scene, and the ways that abject genres are denigrated within fan discourses is one useful window into those often subtle prejudices.

Historiography of Metalcore

As one might expect with any genre of popular music, authors have presented conflicting accounts of what the term metalcore means. In some ways, acknowledging this diversity of accounts is almost a historiographical truism, not merely because different authors inevitably harbour different subjective viewpoints. More subtly, it also relates to the unstable ways in which genres emerge. As one finds with hard rock and heavy metal during the 1970s – terms that were used inconsistently and interchangeably at the time – authors writing about metalcore during its emergence write about it differently than those writing a decade or more later. But even speaking of an emergence of metalcore, as though such a time reference exists within a stable time frame, oversimplifies the history of the term. Any time frame, such as the one I provisionally gave above, will conflict with some accounts that give other dates. A bounded numerical range like 2004–2007 also simplifies chronological boundaries, not merely because one might debate whether a point of origin ought to be placed at 2003 or 2004, but also because genres, as a rule, do not emerge from the head of Medusa without precedent. Rather, they gradually coalesce in a process of discursive iteration and citation. That is, with every new iteration – such as a recording, concert review, rock interview and conversation among fans – the existence of a genre category becomes cited and re-cited, and thus more recognisable. This process occurs inconsistently over long or short spans of time, more in certain spaces (geographical, subcultural, discursive) than others, and variously among different agents (e.g., fans, critics and musicians) who engage with music in sometimes separate ways with differing levels of intensity. As a result of this rather chaotic soup of communication, any historical origin must be stipulated with some arbitrariness and any time span necessarily represents an approximation.[22]

While this is true of genre in general, metalcore is especially messy. To begin with, the term itself suggests hybridity and points to its roots in speed metal and hardcore punk, known in combination during the mid-1980s as 'crossover'.[23] Ian Christe, a music journalist writing in 2003, frames metalcore as being interchangeable with crossover: 'in 1987 most new names played a cross-pollinated S.O.D.-style hybrid called metalcore, or simply crossover'.[24] Each of the examples he lists comes from the 1980s, an early chronological focus that fits the relatively early date of his publication. More so than authors writing in the late 2000s and in contrast to those of the 2010s, Christe's perspective took place when metalcore was beginning to be recognised in the form that later authors know it. In other words, the emergence of the NWOAHM and its growing popularity as an abject subgenre (i.e., broadly popular, yet suspect in the metal scene for that popularity) would likely have seemed to be a curious but vague development at the time of writing. However, one does get a fascinating glimpse at Christe's view of these bands in his afterword, where he intriguingly positions a wide range of 2000s metalcore as an authentic antidote to inauthentic pop punk. For Christe, the 'new breed metalcore scene' – represented by the more melodic strand of Himsa, Freya, (early) Poison the Well; and the more aggressive strand of Hatebreed and Converge – functions as a response to pop punk in the same way that 1980s crossover bands rebelled against glam metal ('hair metal' for Christe) in the mid-1980s.[25] The inauthentic status of an abject genre, it is clear, is relative to the observer.

Jon Wiederhorn and Katherine Turman's *Definitive Oral History of Metal* gives a precise time range for metalcore (1992–2006) and mentions a start date for deathcore (2007).[26] Such an account indicates that they view the genre terms as separate categories, ones that have a historiographical relationship of chronological succession. In Wiederhorn and Turman's oral history, metalcore ends as deathcore takes its place. Like Christe above, Wiederhorn and Turman trace the history of these genres back to crossover in the 1980s, providing an end date for that music in 1992, the same year that they state metalcore begins.

Another notable aspect of their history is their framing of subgenre tributaries. Their chapter on metalcore begins by alerting readers to how metalcore cannot simply be a combination of metal and hardcore punk but rather should be viewed as a collection of influences, among them 'American post-punk and noise-rock', as well as 'avant-garde prog rock, straight-edge, and/or screamo'.[27] For Wiederhorn and Turman, then, these subgenres represent related influences but not metalcore proper. Rather than debate whether these subgenres belong inside or outside metalcore, a better point might be to acknowledge the porousness of genre boundaries in general and observe how Wiederhorn and Turman's account reveals the richness of different subgenres that make metalcore a complex concept. Certain subgenres may seem more centrally relevant to metalcore, depending on one's vantage point: straight-edge might seem most pertinent if one views metalcore in terms of lifestyle and attitude, American post-punk might seem more related than avant-garde prog rock if one thinks chronologically and geographically with the NWOAHM in mind (more on that below), and from a reception standpoint of abject genres, screamo appears most targeted for ridicule, which is why my earlier work on abject genres treats it as a subgenre of metalcore.[28]

Lewis Kennedy's research on metalcore represents the most theoretically sophisticated and complete account of the genre to date. An expert on its bands and recordings as a fan and musician, his dissertation[29] and publications related to it[30] synthesise research on hardcore punk and metal and offer compelling historical narratives that take current genre theory into account. One of his arguments is that metal and hardcore punk exist in a symbiotic relationship. Despite uneasy tensions existing for decades between fans and musicians devoted to one tradition or the other, Kennedy observes that metal and punk are 'very difficult to separate from one another' due to their reliance 'upon one another for continued influence and inspiration',[31] and that factions from within both traditions continuously fail to. Some genre purists within hardcore attempt to resist what they see as the stylistic dilution of hardcore within hybrid styles like crossover and metalcore. Thus, he cites the members of hardcore band Madball affirming their allegiance to hardcore in their lyrics and titles.[32] This gatekeeping by hardcore fans and musicians mirrors similar discourses among metal fans.[33] From both sides, metalcore is viewed with suspicion in a futile attempt to police the mixing of styles and ideologies. It is also against that suspicion that crossover and metalcore bands – metalcore positioned as potentially the 'spiritual successor of crossover' – construct a narrative of themselves as struggling in opposition to genre purists.[34]

The other important argument Kennedy makes is that metalcore became recognisable in its present form due to a stylistic process he calls codification, involving the so-called New Wave of American Heavy Metal. A loose nod to the more widely known NWOBHM (New Wave of British Heavy Metal), the NWOAHM is a subgenre of metal that emerged in popularity around 2004. It combined stylistic traits taken from melodic death metal, thrash metal and groove-oriented bands like Pantera with the tough, no-nonsense sensibilities (e.g., titles and band names, ideals of authenticity) and quotidian lyrics of hardcore punk. In a way suited to its awkward acronym, the NWOAHM was only loosely recognised as an emerging style, debated by fans and critics as to its significance. The codification taking place is the retrospectively recognisable process of moving from an initially loose observation that comparable bands like Lamb of God, Shadows Fall and Killswitch Engage were gaining popularity towards a 'reification of certain elements of style and the simultaneous diminution of others'.[35] Kennedy cites how writers around 2005 were including the odd time signatures and non-standard song forms of The Dillinger Escape Plan as representative of metalcore, while later authors such as Wiederhorn and Turman exclude those as precursor traits.[36] Gradually, the most recognisable musical features of metalcore became breakdowns, riffs influenced by melodic death metal, high-fidelity production and clean singing alternating with vocal roars (a distorted style communicative of quotidian anger more than the inhuman stylisations of death metal grunts). The codification of these traits, I would argue, stylistically unites subgenres like deathcore, screamo and the NWOAHM, which is another reason why I treat metalcore as an umbrella term.

The Sound of Metalcore

'Silence' (2017), a song by the metalcore band Currents, offers an example of metalcore understood in its post-codified sense, as an exemplar of narrowed stylistic traits,[37] as well as its abject sense, as a mixture of genre markers associated with different abject subgenres. Some of these markers are extra-musical and exemplify the lyrical divide between the supernatural themes of extreme metal and the quotidian themes of metalcore. According to an interview with vocalist Brian Wille, the lyrics of 'Silence' focus on the relatable, everyday theme of different pressures he and his fans might encounter in life:

It's basically about feeling that pressure to impress other people and having that pressure of expectation from all different parts of your life. You know you got your parents, they have an idea of where they want you to be or what they want you to do. You have your job, you know, and you have people that expect things of you. And then even with like the band and stuff like that, there's pressure to like, you know, do certain things and play a certain way and all of this. So it's kind of a song about me dealing with all of those pressures and trying to just bounce them off.[38]

In ways seldom encountered in death and black metal lyrics, 'Silence' is thus partly autobiographical and, if the nod to parents is significant, relatable to a youth audience. This aspect bears emphasis when speaking of metalcore as an abject genre. Much scholarship on metal treats the music as an emblem of youth cultures.[39] Rarely is youth discussed in metal scholarship as a target for discrimination.

Musically, the song contains all the elements of metalcore cited by Kennedy: 'the combination of clean and distorted vocals, high-fidelity, polished production, and a clear influence from melodic death metal'.[40] That clear influence is partially found in the verse-chorus song form shown in Table 20.2. Familiar verse-chorus song structures are, as I have shown,[41] one of the features of melodic death metal that contribute to its reputation for being 'melodic', or musically accessible. Another influence from melodic death metal can be heard in some of the song's diatonic guitar riffs that focus on higher-register melodic figurations (Figures 20.1a, 20.1b).

Table 20.2 Song form for Currents' 'Silence' (2017)

	Verse	Chorus	Verse	Chorus	Breakdown	Chorus	Verse	Chorus		Breakdown
Intro	1	A	2	B	1	A	2	B	Bridge	2
0:00	0:17	0:37	0:55	1:19	1:46	2:12	2:30	2:47	3:13	3:30

Figure 20.1a Melodic figuration during the first verse (0:20) (© Eric Smialek)
Figure 20.1b Melodic figuration during Breakdown 1 (2:03) (© Eric Smialek)

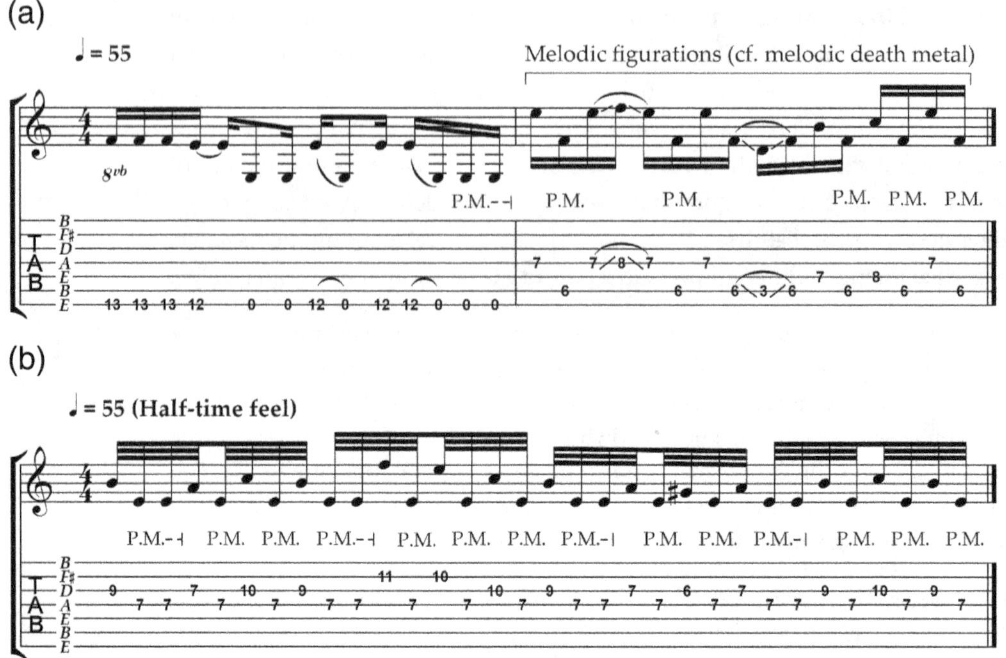

Looking at other features in Kennedy's quote above, the song's use of clean and distorted vocals demarcates the change from screamed verse to sung chorus, changing the mood from frustration to vulnerable, emotive reflection. Such introspection, and the characteristic shifts in song form that accommodate it, are strong markers of related abject subgenres like screamo and nu metal.[42] When combined with a second-person lyrical address, screamed and sung settings dramatise romantic conflict, emotional exasperation and intensity with a highly personal feel. Indeed, all of those things can be heard at the pivotal, stop-time moment that ends the song's bridge at 3:29 and acts as a pickup to the final breakdown section. At this moment, the accompaniment stops to emphasise the roared words, 'f**k you, I'm moving on!'. This is the kind of direct, quotidian catharsis that I argue is generally antithetical to extreme metal and more traditional forms of metal centred around supernatural or mythological themes. Even the obsession with murder found in death metal tends towards exaggerated, 'brutal' violence rather than personal, relatable disputes.

Lastly, the song does indeed boast a hi-fi, polished production with a careful mix of sounds, balanced throughout different registers and skilfully varied for rhetorical effect as the song moves through different sections.

Perhaps the most dramatic instance of this rhetorical effect comes in the song's two breakdown sections. In metalcore, the breakdown represents a song's sectional climax,[43] the peak of a song understood as a sectional plateau rather than a brief instance. Breakdowns represent moments of climactic contrast during a song that emphasise slower tempos and unison rhythmic playing between the guitars and kick drums while vocals perform independently of the rhythmic groove. In his article devoted to exploring the breakdown and its varied meanings in twenty-first-century metal, Steven Gamble explains that breakdowns serve a communal and cathartic function during live shows, when vocalists sometimes create anticipation for them during stage banter and prompt fans to mosh extra hard when they happen.[44] To demonstrate their primacy for fans, Gamble points to the significance of online curatorial collections of breakdowns extracted from their song contexts in 'best-of' compilations. As Gamble notes, 'no such curatorial practice exists around the best metalcore verses' or other metalcore song sections, demonstrating that 'it is clearly the breakdown which constitutes the climax and key section of [metalcore] tracks'.[45] He observes that fans in YouTube comment sections provide time stamps for breakdowns, singling out those sections for discussion.[46] In fact, according to YouTube's 'most replayed' feature, the most replayed moment of 'Silence' is the beginning of Breakdown 2 at 3:30, about which I will say more further below.[47]

While the breakdown normally functions similarly to the bridge section of a verse-chorus song, that is, as a contrasting section two-thirds of the way through the song, it is arguably even more prominent in 'Silence'. Here, two breakdowns occur in important places, midway through the song and at the end, each punctuating the end of a verse-chorus grouping. One significance of this double appearance is that the song breaks from its usual atmosphere twice to rhetorically intensify the song. In other words, what happens during these sections is marked for semiotic importance because fans recognise that breakdowns are meant to be extra heavy. The other aspect of significance is that the song's two separate breakdowns draw their semiotic codes from different subgenres – nu metal, melodic death metal, NWOAHM and djent – providing an opportunity to analyse how codes from different subgenres can operate within the same song and contribute to metalcore in similar ways.

The first breakdown is quite representative of the kinds of deathcore breakdowns that gained popularity in the mid-to-late 2000s. Like the

Emmure track 'Word of Intulo' mentioned above, the beginning of the breakdown distils the guitar to a single low pitch (or power chord) that stutters through a syncopated rhythm (Figure 20.2).[48] This is the characteristic, low open-string approach to breakdowns in deathcore in contrast to the shifting power chords of earlier precedents in the 1990s.[49] That reduction in pitch activity focuses attention on rhythm and creates a jarring, strobe-like effect through the guitar's syncopations. Even though there is plenty of musical activity throughout, the breakdown is arranged in such a way as to make time feel like it has slowed. If one measures tempo through snare pacing on beats two and four, the breakdown occurs in half-time relative to the previous chorus. That contrast between sections is further dramatised through the impact of the breakdown's initial downbeat. Heard best with headphones, it involves a diving low pitch, likely made by a drum trigger, which makes the power of the downbeat linger until the syncopations take over on beat two. That combination of half-time and an explosive downbeat that lingers through a pitch descent creates the extra slow, weighty feel of the breakdown conducive to moshing.

Some genre markers further colour the atmosphere of this breakdown as well. The middle-register melodic pull-offs heard near the end of the breakdown (2:03) suggest an influence from melodic death metal, typical of the NWOAHM. The minor-second dissonances that serve as a pickup to the initial downbeat and that recur as a momentary slide (1:50; see also the later instance marked 'loco' in Figure 20.3) and as a background effect (1:55) recall the aesthetic of affliction characteristic of nu metal bands like Slipknot and Korn before them. The voice as well carries signifiers of genre through the roared vocals heard in the verse. Its appearance in the breakdown continues the earlier alternation between intensity (verse roars) and introspection (chorus singing) typical of metalcore. In this particular breakdown, one can even hear a simultaneous contrast between the

Figure 20.2 Single-note, syncopated rhythm Breakdown 1 (1:46) (© Eric Smialek)

Figure 20.3 Markers of djent during the second breakdown (3:30) (© Eric Smialek)

more lyrically decipherable roars of metalcore and the less decipherable growls of death metal partway through (1:55), useful for comparing the two vocal styles.

The second breakdown, which ends the song, involves a similar punctuation of the downbeat and stuttering low guitar, much like the first breakdown. However, here one can hear markers of djent, arguably a newer abject subgenre that emerged following deathcore at the beginning of the 2010s.[50] Djent, a genre term that onomatopoetically imitates the sound of its guitars, focuses on rhythmic and metric complexity, influenced by the style traits of the progressive metal band Meshuggah, its progenitor. Like Meshuggah, djent bands eschew power chords in favour of single-note riffs around one octave below standard tuning. This extra-low pitch makes an appearance in the second breakdown of 'Silence' and is perhaps most noticeable in the slow, Meshuggah-like bend at 3:39 (see Figure 20.3). Djent sounds in the second breakdown not only contribute to the section's sense of heaviness but also continue earlier instances where the genre can be heard: the clean-tone introduction is reminiscent of djent/progressive-metal band Animals as Leaders' 'CAFO' (2009); the first verse (0:17) also involves the extra low E, which provides it with a djent feel; the muted rhythm guitar during Chorus A (0:37) also resembles Meshuggah.

Finally, the rap-like delivery of the roars in Verse 2 (0:59) and Chorus B (1:22) suggests the influence of nu metal; and the gang vocals – collective shouting (or singing in this case) to accent particular lyrics – that occur in Chorus B (1:18) recall conventions from hardcore punk.

All of these strong markers of different genres mix together to reveal how metalcore in 2017 had assimilated numerous earlier styles. Most notably, with the exception of the gang vocals from hardcore punk, each of these styles could be said to come from abject subgenres. Thus, stylistically, as well as lyrically – and sartorially as a glance at the band's short haircuts and skinny jeans will show – Currents break from the generic conventions of metal in ways that better suit metalcore, understood broadly as a combination of multiple abject subgenres.

Conclusion

This chapter has provided a condensed overview of metalcore in terms of genre theory, historiography and musical style. I began with some theoretical observations about genre in general, noting that metalcore represents an especially tangled instance of genre that can be instructive for learning about popular music genres more broadly. The notion of an 'abject genre' served as a conceptual lens throughout the chapter, necessitating an extended review of how metalcore fits within a decades-long, ongoing history of abject genres in metal. One of the reasons why that frame is pedagogically helpful is that it foregrounds the importance of nuance and uncertainty in historiography. Questions of what counts as an abject genre and what time frames apply to an example naturally arise when investigating trends in mass popularity, and their answers tend to be more elusive the closer one's example gets to the present. More than other abject genres, metalcore has proven to be slippery for assigning dates and delimiting what subgenres count within it as an umbrella category. While I have stipulated some provisional answers – namely NWOAHM, screamo and deathcore for subcategories and a *terminus post quem* of 2003 or 2004 – a closer examination of other authors' historiographies reveals those answers to be one among several narratives. Indeed, those authors have unique explanations for how the above subgenres relate to metalcore historically: Kennedy views the NWOAHM as codifying metalcore during the mid-2000s, and Wiederhorn and Turman view deathcore separately from metalcore, suggesting an upper limit around 2006, just prior to deathcore's early popularity. The advent of djent at the end of the 2000s may be another upper limit, depending on whether one sees a shift taking place at that time, from metalcore to djent, comparable to the shift that took place during the early 2000s from nu metal to metalcore. Arguably, in both instances, metal fans redirected their suspicions from one 'inauthentic' trend to similarly dismissing the newer one that replaced it in mass popularity.

My analysis of 'Silence' reveals a musical side to that possibility by exploring a track that involves both the stylistic features of metalcore and some djent traits within the same song. Within the span of a single track, one can hear multiple markers of abject genres: a verse-chorus format within a radio-friendly timespan, breakdown sections, lyrics involving introspection and vulnerability, rap-like vocal delivery reminiscent of nu metal, melodic guitar riffs that were central to the NWOAHM's codification of metalcore, and markers of djent in multiple sections. Taken together, these features demonstrate metalcore's assimilation of earlier metal styles, especially traits associated with other abject genres.

Throughout, I argued for reasons why I conceive of metalcore as an umbrella term and an example of what I call 'abject genres'. Those reasons involve key intersections with other abject metal subgenres, detailed throughout the chapter, and key differences between metalcore and more traditional forms of metal. Importantly, those observations are not limited to musical sound but extend to traits such as lyrical subject matter, sartorial fashions and sometimes implied audience demographics. While the scope of this chapter does not permit a thorough investigation of fan statements, reception studies reveal that their discussions of genre and value judgment are frequently framed with categories of identity.[51] It is this broad range of observations – musical, lyrical, sartorial, verbal/discursive – that reveals the social importance of abject genres as a concept. My application of the term is not meant to be a personal value judgment about metalcore but rather a recognition of metalcore's turbulent reception within the broader metal community.

Notes

1. Lewis F. Kennedy, *Functions of Genre in Metal and Hardcore Music*, doctoral dissertation (University of Hull, 2018), pp. 225–8.
2. Eric Smialek, *Genre and Expression in Extreme Metal Music (1990–2015)*, doctoral dissertation (McGill University, 2015), p. 66 and *passim*.
3. Kennedy, *Functions of Genre*, p. 247.
4. See Smialek, *Genre and Expression*, pp. 81, 94, 101–4.
5. Like their genre boundaries, metalcore timelines are complex and indeterminate. These dates are approximate and represent times of flourishing popularity rather than origins or endings.
6. My use of the term 'roar' follows Kennedy's distinction between three distinctive trends in vocal delivery that roughly correspond with different metal genres: roars (metalcore), growls (death metal), screams (black metal) (Kennedy, *Functions of Genre*, pp. 73–9).
7. While 'scream' does refer to a higher-register use of the voice, the technique is distinct from the screamed vocals of black metal referred to in Kennedy, *Functions of Genre*, pp. 73–9.
8. See the 'Suffer Bitch' t-shirt released by Heart of a Coward, referencing lyrics to their song, 'Shade' (2012). In personal correspondence, Lewis Kennedy observed a trend around this time of the word 'bitch' featuring prominently in deathcore lyrics.
9. Robert Walser, *Running with the Devil: Power, Gender, and Madness in Heavy Metal Music* (Wesleyan University Press, 1993), p. 124.
10. Keith Kahn-Harris, *Extreme Metal: Music and Culture on the Edge* (Berg, 2007); Nicola Allett, 'The Extreme Metal "Connoisseur"', *Popular Music History* 6/1–2 (2011): 164–79; Eric Smialek, 'The Unforgiven: A Reception Study of Metallica Fans and "Sell-Out" Accusations', in Andy R. Brown, Karl Spracklen, Keith Kahn-Harris and Niall Scott (eds.), *Global Metal Music and Culture: Current Directions in Metal Studies* (Routledge, 2016), pp. 106–24.
11. Steven Gamble, 'Breaking Down the Breakdown in Twenty-First Century Metal', *Metal Music Studies* 5/3 (2019): 342–433.
12. Smialek, *Genre and Expression*, pp. 92–4, 230.
13. *Ibid.*, pp. 77, 85, 88, 104.

14. Marcus Erbe, '"This Isn't Over 'til I Say It's Over!" Narratives of Male Frustration in Deathcore and Beyond', in Florian Heesch and Niall Scott (eds.), *Heavy Metal, Gender and Sexuality* (Routledge, 2016), pp. 182–92.

15. Michelle Phillipov, *Death Metal and Music Criticism: Analysis at the Limits* (Lexington Books, 2012), pp. 75, 79, 101–4.

16. Smialek, *Genre and Expression*, pp. 258–60.

17. Walser, *Running with the Devil*, pp. 128–9.

18. 'Christcore' is a nickname for Christian screamo music, given by the creator of an online set of cartoons that satirized different subcultural stereotypes. See Smialek, *Genre and Expression*, p. 82.

19. See *ibid.*, pp. 79, 82.

20. Julia Kristeva, *The Powers of Horror: An Essay on Abjection* (Columbia University Press, 1982). See also Julia Kristeva, 'Approaching Abjection', John Lechte (trans.), *Oxford Literary Review* 5/1–2 (1982): 125–49.

21. Karl Beckwith, '"Black Metal Is for White People": Constructs of Colour and Identity within the Extreme Metal Scene', *M/C Journal* 5/3 (2002). https://doi.org/10.5204/mcj.1962; Kahn-Harris, *Extreme Metal*, pp. 160–5; Caroline Lucas, 'White Power, Black Metal and Me: Reflections on Composing the Nation', in Rosemary Hill and Karl Spracklen (eds.), *Heavy Fundamentalisms: Music, Metal and Politics* (Inter-Disciplinary Press, 2010), pp. 43–53; Benjamin Hedge Olsen, 'Voice of Our Blood: National Socialist Discourses in Black Metal', *Popular Music History* 6/1–2 (2011): 135–49; Laura Wiebe-Taylor, 'Nordic Nationalisms: Black Metal Takes Norway's Everyday Racisms to the Extreme', in Niall Scott (ed.), *Reflections in the Metal Void* (Inter-Disciplinary Press, 2012), pp. 185–97; Karl Spracklen, 'To Holmgard . . . and Beyond: Folk Metal Fantasies and Hegemonic White Masculinities', *Metal Music Studies* 1/3 (2015): 359–77.

22. See Michel Foucault, *The Archeology of Knowledge*, A. M. Sheridan Smith (trans.) (Routledge, 2002 [1969]), pp. 21, 25.

23. Steve Waksman, *This Ain't the Summer of Love: Conflict and Crossover in Heavy Metal and Punk* (University of California Press, 2009), pp. 238–40.

24. Ian Christe, *Sound of the Beast: The Complete Headbanging History of Heavy Metal* (Harper Collins, 2003), p. 184.

25. *Ibid.*, p. 373.

26. Jon Wiederhorn and Katherine Turman, *Louder than Hell: The Definitive Oral History of Metal* (It Books, 2013).

27. *Ibid.*, pp. 979–80.

28. On the derision of screamo, see Smialek, *Genre and Expression*, pp. 79–85.

29. Kennedy, *Functions of Genre*.

30. Lewis F. Kennedy, 'The Symbiotic Relationship between Metal and Hardcore in the 21st Century', in Toni-Matti Karjalainen and Kimi Kärki (eds.), *Modern Heavy Metal: Markets, Practices and Culture* (Aalto University Press, 2015), pp. 424–33; Lewis F. Kennedy, 'Intersections of Genre, Heritage and Place in

the New Wave of American Heavy Metal', in Liam Maloney and John Schofield (eds.), *Music and Heritage: New Perspectives on Place-Making and Sonic Identity* (Routledge, 2021), pp. 126–35.

31. Kennedy, *Functions of Genre*, p. 428.
32. *Ibid.*, p. 431.
33. *Ibid.*, p. 432; Smialek, *Genre and Expression*, pp. 83, 98. One satirical commentary, on a cartoon caricature of a screamo-turned-deathcore fan, describes him as 'draining all originality from that genre before moving to the next' (*Ibid.*, p. 83).
34. Kennedy, *Functions of Genre*, p. 429.
35. *Ibid.*, p. 247.
36. *Ibid.*
37. *Ibid.*, p. 238.
38. Original Rock, 'Interview: Currents' Brian Wille at Exchange, Bristol' (14 February 2018). www.youtube.com/watch?v=Z61OMdoDSME (accessed 19 January 2022).
39. Harris Berger, *Metal, Rock, and Jazz: Perception and the Phenomenology of Musical Experience* (Wesleyan University Press, 1999), p. 284; Natalie Purcell, *Death Metal Music: The Passion and Politics of a Subculture* (McFarland, 2003), p. 99; Deena Weinstein, *Heavy Metal: The Music and Its Culture* (Da Capo Press, 2000 [1991]), pp. 106–11.
40. Kennedy, *Functions of Genre*, p. 238.
41. Smialek, *Genre and Expression*, pp. 195–234.
42. *Ibid.*, p. 77. See the examples in Jonathan Pieslak, 'Re-casting Metal: Rhythm and Meter in the Music of Meshuggah', *Music Theory Spectrum* 29/2 (2007): 219–45 and Scott Wilson, *Great Satan's Rage: American Negativity and Rap/Metal in the Age of Supercapitalism* (Manchester University Press, 2008), p. 113.
43. Brad Osborn, 'Subverting the Verse-Chorus Paradigm: Terminally Climactic Forms in Recent Rock Music', *Music Theory Spectrum* 35/1 (2013): 23–47.
44. Gamble, 'Breaking Down the Breakdown', pp. 347–50.
45. *Ibid.*, p. 345.
46. *Ibid.*, p. 346.
47. SharpTone Records [Currents' record label], 'Currents – Silence (Official Audio Stream)' (2018). www.youtube.com/watch?v=WlhlnVLfv-c (accessed 18 July 2022).
48. Transcriptions throughout are based on the anonymously authored tablature available at www.songsterr.com/a/wsa/currents-silence-tab-s458406 (accessed 17 July 2022).
49. Smialek, *Genre and Expression*, pp. 230–1.
50. Gamble, 'Breaking Down the Breakdown', pp. 343–4.
51. Smialek, *Genre and Expression*, pp. 65–114.

Global Metal

Personal Take IV – Malcolm Dome

Proud to Be Loud

Like any journalist, those of us who write about metal can sometimes face a moral dilemma: where is the line between public and private? Of course, usually you interview bands solely about their music. Occasionally, you can stray into more uncertain territory and discuss topics outside the domain of safe subjects. But at what point have you gone too far?

As an example, people in the metal media always knew Rob Halford was gay. But none of us ever brought this up with him during interviews. It was respected as a taboo subject. This was his private business and should be kept off-limits. The corollary to this was the situation when Hanoi Rocks drummer Razzle died in a car being driven by a less than sober Mötley Crüe vocalist Vince Neil. The consequences of this were played out in public, and nobody felt awkward about bringing this up with the Crüe.

More recently, there has been controversy surrounding Marilyn Manson. Not for the first time. Only on this occasion, it has not been of his own manufacture. Actress Evan Rachel Wood, a one-time girlfriend, revealed she had once been in an abusive relationship. People speculated that it could have involved Manson. Let's stress here, the speculation wasn't based on any facts. But one magazine decided to ask him how he felt about this accusation. The result? Manson abruptly terminated the interview. Yes, he could have handled it better. However, one also has to wonder if this was a fair line of questioning.

This is far removed from the early, and I would say glory, days of *Kerrang!*. The best compliment we were paid back in that era was when someone called the magazine a 'professional fanzine'. That's precisely what we set out to create. Despite the sybaritic activities of the time, it was something of an innocent period. There was no demand on us to put only major artists on the cover. So, we could take the risk with Bon Jovi, Guns N' Roses and Metallica. All of them graced the cover of *Kerrang!*, and this was before becoming huge selling acts.

There was a close relationship between the writers of the magazine and many of the musicians from the genre. We were committed to promoting talented bands and eschewed controversy for the most part. And it was always a delight to see any young name we had actively supported finally come good and make the leap to major status.

We strenuously guarded our independence. Naturally, record companies were keen to see their acts in the magazine. But, while it was usual policy in other countries to almost buy positive coverage by taking adverts in exchange for this, that was never the case in the UK. That's why it was believed a good album review from *Kerrang!* meant so much.

It has to be admitted that back in those days, record companies were awash with cash, and there were regular trips offered to exotic climes to interview bands. Now there was an expectation from the labels that if a journalist and photographer were taken overseas to cover any artist, then they'd receive considerable space. That was the trade-off, and you could make the point that, in effect, this was buying pages in *Kerrang!*. But at no time did we cover anyone just because there was the chance of a trip to, say, Bermuda. No, the band in question had to be worth covering in their own right.

Looking back, there was considered naivety in the way we worked. And we did work very hard. It was incredible to remember that *Kerrang!* was seen by the publishers' Spotlight as being nothing more than a nuisance, an irritant, to be hidden away from the supposedly more legitimate, weighty publications. Until that is, the company owners realised we were the biggest money earner they had in their portfolio of titles. And that was when the interference began. The magazine became a weekly instead of being a fortnightly, which led to a decline in quality. And eventually to a number of us leaving towards the end of 1987.

These days, there's more emphasis on playing it safe, looking for angles to cover bands that go beyond the music. That's why controversy is seen as a boost for magazine sales and a way of ramping up the clicks on social media. There's more pressure on those of us still lucky enough to write about metal. This is the new realism and reality.

Malcolm Dome, metal journalist (*Kerrang!, Total Rock*)

21 | Metal in the Middle East

PIERRE HECKER

Metal in the Middle East has been described as 'loud, liberating and on the rise', as a 'political statement' and as a musical genre that 'feeds on revolution and change'.[1] 'Counterculture' and 'resistance' in response to repression, war and religious extremism are perhaps the most commonly used terms to delineate the role of metal in the region. Metal has also been said to represent a 'cultural challenge to pious conservatism'[2] and an 'antidote to religious extremism'.[3] Against the backdrop of the wave of political upheavals that have shaken the region in recent years, metalheads have been furthermore portrayed as 'children of the revolution'[4] who took to the streets during the 'Arab Spring', the Iranian 'Green Movement' and the Turkish 'Gezi Park Protests'.

A casual perusal of the growing number of publications and documentaries on metal in the Middle East might give the impression that this musical genre represents a strictly *political* rather than a *subcultural* movement. In some instances, metal is cast as a powerful countercultural force, one capable of challenging both the authoritarian state and the rise of political Islam. The significance ascribed to metal on a political and cultural level is indeed remarkable. And yet, after (re)reading some of the meticulously researched books and articles published in recent years, I have become increasingly uncomfortable about the ways in which metal in the Middle East has been presented to a wider audience.

It is this feeling of discomfort and unease that leads me to the purpose of this chapter. Its goal is to critically assess *how* metal in the Middle East has been seen and represented in journalism and academia. The chapter also addresses the question of *who* controls or contributes to the discourse on metal in the Middle East, and *who* is being left out or excluded. In line with these goals, this chapter conceptualises metal as a discursive formation, which carries the risk of reproducing Orientalist notions of the Middle East.

The chapter begins with a necessarily brief and incomplete summary of previous research on metal in the region. It then reflects on the influence of Orientalist discourse over the study of metal music and culture. In my opinion, this discourse has led to the politicisation and exoticisation of a particular figure – the 'Middle Eastern' and/or 'Muslim metalhead'.

Finally, this chapter attempts to discern specific characteristics and challenges that need to be considered when studying metal music and culture in the Middle East.

Studying Moral Panics, Acknowledging Societal Change

The origins of scholarly debate on metal in the Middle East date back to Keith Kahn-Harris's early works on Israel's extreme metal scene of the late 1990s.[5] Based on extensive fieldwork in Israel, Kahn-Harris examined the dynamics and conspicuous ambivalences of identity construction among Israeli metalheads. Members of this demographic, he found, frequently considered themselves 'marginalized' and 'alienated from the Zionist project'.[6] Kahn-Harris described their situation as one of 'double marginality': marginal to the construction of Jewishness and national identity in Israel, and marginal to the production of metal music and culture in the world. Indeed, Kahn-Harris conducted extensive interviews with Israeli metal bands, including Azazel, Bishop of Hexen, Grimoire, Melechesh, Orphaned Land, Salem and others. Based on this empirical work, it became clear that metal was virtually invisible in both Israeli popular culture and global metal.[7]

Kahn-Harris also touched upon another issue that has frequently resurfaced in the works of other authors: moral panics over metal and Satanism. In his work, he briefly mentions that Israel's metal scene has been subjected to media allegations of Satanism.[8] Gabriel Cavaglion and Revital Sela-Shayovitz's detailed analysis of Israeli newspapers further indicated that heavy metal has been central to the Israeli narrative on Satanism.[9] They found that Israeli newspapers overwhelmingly tended to portray metal as a violent Satanic cult, as a menace to the central pillars of Judaism, and as a threat to the Zionist project. Israeli youngsters were allegedly being brainwashed into devil worship and, in the process, losing their religion.

The narrative conveyed by the Israeli media is strikingly redolent of similar moral panics over metal and Satanism in the Arab World, Turkey and Iran. Over the past three decades, the media of practically every country in this region has at some point generated a discourse around metal and Satanism. The triggers for these discourses invariably came in the form of public astonishment at the sudden spectacle of large crowds of long-haired metalheads dressed in black, or the supposedly inexplicable suicides of teenagers from wealthy families. The public visibility of metal music and culture was commonly limited to isolated events (festivals, concerts), which a broader mass audience was not accustomed to and, consequently, proved unable to decode. Metal thus assumed meaning in relation to concepts already collectively shared among a wider public, such as cultural imperialism (i.e., 'Westernisation') and apostasy. Satanism, by contrast, remained largely unknown, which obliged journalists, politicians and religious leaders to introduce and explain the term to their audiences. Ultimately, however, Satanism was neatly classified as yet another sign of moral dilapidation caused by Westernisation, and thus intimately associated with a wider postcolonial discourse.

Precisely such a moral panic was the focus of a paper presented by Ted Swedenburg at the American Anthropological Association Annual Meeting in San Francisco in November 2000.[10] Swedenburg gave a detailed account of how a series of sensationalist reports published in *Rouz Al-Yousef* in November and December 1996 had triggered an unprecedented set of events that, taken together, showed all the signs of a full-scale 'moral panic'. *Rouz Al-Yousef*, one of Egypt's oldest and most venerable political news magazines, depicted a lurid scenario of widespread Satanic rituals that involved young men and women from privileged Cairene families. All of those implicated listened to heavy metal music. The papers accused the metal fans of taking drugs, engaging in illicit sexual acts, slaughtering small animals and worshipping the devil. The alleged Satan worshippers were subsequently accused of apostasy and contempt of religion, both of which constitute a criminal offence under Article 98 of the Egyptian Penal Code. Things became really serious after Nasr Farid Wasil, Egypt's grand mufti, publicly condemned the spread of Satanism in the country. He also reportedly urged Hasan Al-Alfi, Egypt's minister of the interior, to take immediate action and arrest the Satanists. In January 1997, the Egyptian police arrested over ninety people, and Egypt's public prosecutor opened an official investigation. After less than two months, however, the accused Satanists were cleared and acquitted of all charges, and the panic abruptly dissipated.

Most studies on metal in the Middle East point to the outbreak of similar moral panics across the region. These studies have either analysed newspaper articles and media reports or interviewed local metalheads about the consequences of the events. It would go beyond the scope of this chapter to mention all of these studies in detail.[11] Moreover, I do not wish to suggest that the story of metal in the Middle East comprises nothing but an unceasing cycle of moral panics over alleged connections to

Satanism. Nonetheless, I would like to provide an idea of the scale and character of the aforementioned 'moral panics'.

For this purpose, I have chosen excerpts from two newspaper articles. The first article, published in the Turkish daily *Sabah* on 14 October 1990, was written by a well-known newspaper columnist named Engin Ardıç. It was responsible for the first moral panic over metal and Satanism in Turkey and provided a blueprint for countless other newspaper reports in the late 1990s and early 2000s.[12] Ardıç states the following:

Calling themselves 'children of Satan', their main characteristics are tattered clothes . . . Some of them are wearing swastikas and some are cutting themselves with razor blades here and there, ripping themselves left and right and making themselves bleed . . .

They have symbols. [They] stretch the index and the little finger of the right hand into the air and yell, bursting out 'metaaaaal' from deep inside your throat! . . . Every Saturday the 15th [sic!], they gather to celebrate a mass with wads of smoke, black cowls, crosses, sharp knives and a mystic number of magic murmurs. Stark-naked chicks. The abbot mixes the blood of the person attending the ritual with his own blood and signs a contract with Satan. After that, they copulate like dogs in front of the group! . . . They are the servants of Satan – everything is permitted; homosexual relationships are fostered. Among them, there are even villains who molest small children.

If our honourable Islamist brothers just gave up killing secular intellectuals with guns or mail bombs and 'tackled' this kind of true degeneration . . . We said 'tackling', but your hand should not immediately pull the trigger or the pin [out of the hand grenade]; there are a thousand ways of 'tackling'. You see, we are unaware of how 'Westernised' the country is, for heaven's sake.[13]

The second article is taken from the Lebanese news website *Al-Joumhouria*. It was published on 10 January 2012, mere months before Joe Malouf, a popular Lebanese journalist and TV host, presented a sensationalist report on metal and Satanism on MTV Lebanon. The report led to a public outcry and the arrest of several local metalheads by the Lebanese police.[14] The article seeks to maintain authority by lengthily quoting a Christian priest. The priest, whose name is revealed to the readers as Father Marwan Khoury, describes the evil deeds of the devil worshippers. *Al-Joumhouria* begins by quoting Father Marwan on how one of the devil worshippers convinced a young girl to have sex with him and bear his child:

After the girl voluntarily submits to the request of her partner, they take the foetus and prepare a ritualistic feast with the mother. They would cut it [the foetus], roast the pieces over the fire, then eat it with greed and joy. They believe the devil will provide them with eternal life . . . after eating this foetus.

The priest continues to unfurl his narrative by citing further unspeakable crimes:

Some years ago, I was asked to go to the Roumieh prison after the Intelligence Division had arrested a demon-worshipping squad, calling themselves 'Dragoons'. They had been arrested in the Mansouria cemetery while raping a deceased girl, who was only two days old. They were caught pulling her out of the grave and taking turns raping her. Satan worshipers usually wear black clothes, let their hair grow, and tattoo Swastikas or the Star of David on their chests and arms. They can be distinguished by their own signs and symbols, including their own gesture, which entails raising two fingers, the symbol of Satan.[15]

Satan, sex, seduction, Nazism, Zionism (!), violence and child abuse. Anything goes in Engin Ardıç and Father Marwan's fictional reports, as long as it signifies deviance, transgression and, ultimately, the representation of absolute evil. It would be tempting to dismiss all of this as laughable, were it not for the real-life consequences of such reports. The authors not only presented a list of heinous crimes, but they also listed numerous visual markers which purportedly signified Satanism in everyday life (long hair, black clothes, the sign of the horns, etc.). Those whose appearances corresponded with the aforementioned signifiers were left vulnerable to verbal and physical abuse. In the case of Ardıç's article, this was combined with concrete political demands and a call for Islamists to take violent action. Indeed, many of the moral panics over metal and Satanism have been accompanied by human rights violations. These have included extra-judicial arrests, police brutality and, in a few cases, torture.

Generally speaking, Middle Eastern states and societies have reacted harshly toward metal music and culture. Public vilification, police repression and arrests, or the confiscation and closure of fanzines have resulted from temporary media frenzies. Nonetheless, it should be emphasised that the kind of moral panics described above commonly comprise only temporary discursive events. Usually, those arrested were released and acquitted after a short period of time in police custody, while court cases were quietly dropped, and the public rapidly lost interest. An exception to this overall trend might be the situation in Iran, and specifically, the case of the black metal band Confess. The members of this band fled Iran to evade legal prosecution over blasphemy charges.[16]

Generally speaking, however, the depiction of metalheads in the Middle Eastern public sphere has not been entirely negative, despite media manipulation, police repression and public polemics. Mohammad Magout, for instance, points out that the Syrian TV series *Hajiz Al-Samt* (*The Wall of*

Silence) featured a gang of young men, who could easily be identified as metalheads by their long hair, metal shirts, tattoos and goatees. The TV series notably portrayed these somewhat suspicious-looking youngsters as loyal and honest friends who had simply been misjudged by society.[17] Similarly, the depiction of a laughing young metalhead on a poster for the Turkish Directorate of Religious Affairs' official Ramadan campaign in 2009 might be read as another example of pious conservatism's attempted incorporation of metal. With his long hair and black Iron Maiden t-shirt, the young metalhead could be perceived as 'transgressive', but also as pious and kind.

This leads us to a broader point about the current status of metal in the Middle East. In short, the recurrence of moral panics has been increasingly accompanied by a slow but gradual process of normalisation and accommodation towards metal music and culture. This may not hold true for the entire Middle East. To be sure, resentment from pious conservative sections of society toward metal remains marked. Nonetheless, certain events and reactions indicate an appreciable paradigm shift. For example, June 2013 saw the passing of Zeki Ateş, the founder of Kemancı, Istanbul's first rock and metal bar. Ateş was widely commemorated. Several major daily newspapers reported on his death, and even Kadir Topbaş, Istanbul's mayor and a leading figure of Turkey's pious conservative Justice and Development Party (Adalet ve Kalkınma Partisi, AKP), sent a large bouquet of flowers to his funeral. And yet, in the late 1990s and early 2000s, Kemancı had been pilloried as a hotbed of Satanism. Ateş's famous bar had provided an early stage for many of Turkey's best-known rock artists (Şebnem Ferah, Teoman, Özlem Tekin, Duman, Aylin Aslım, Mor ve Ötesi, Pentagram, etc.).

It seems that, today, an appreciation of Turkish metal is no longer confined to Turkey's metal community. A wider public seems readier to acknowledge the cultural (and political) value of this genre. Indeed, many 'ordinary citizens' now take pride in Turkey's rock tradition and the musicians representing it. Legendary figures of Anatolian rock music, such as Barış Manço (1943–1999) or Cem Karaca (1945–2004), have long become part of Turkey's collective memory, even among conservative sections of society. This does not mean that rock and metal music have been fully accepted by the mainstream. Rock and metal are still redolent of a secular way of life. They are thus loathed by Turkey's pious conservative elite for providing a putative alternative to its attempt at raising a new 'pious generation'. It is nonetheless important to point out that, today, the discursive construction of metal is very different from the discursive construction of metal twenty, thirty or even forty years ago. This is true not only of Turkey; it is certainly the case for other Middle Eastern societies.

Metal and Orientalism?

When I was first asked to write this chapter, I was hesitant to accept the offer, particularly because the very title – 'Metal in the Middle East' – carries serious semiotic baggage. At least since the publication of Edward W. Said's *Orientalism* in 1978,[18] it is no longer possible to use terms such as 'the Orient' or 'the Middle East' innocently. Said, a Professor of English and Comparative Literature at Columbia University, delineated an alliance between Western academic scholarship and modern imperialism. He exposed the concept of 'the Orient' as a European invention that had been used to legitimise European imperialist aspirations and establish 'Western' superiority over 'the East'. The tradition of representing 'the Orient' as ignorant, backward, violent and incapable of democracy has served to essentialise and patronise the 'Oriental other' and to mobilise fear, hatred and disgust. Orientalism can be seen as an ideological project that imagines the Orient as Europe's exotic but inferior adversary, one that must be tamed and dominated.

The effectiveness of Orientalism lies in the fact that the distinction between the Orient and the Occident – or, alternatively, Islam and the West – has become naturalised and part of common knowledge. Indeed, over the course of the nineteenth and twentieth centuries, the concept of the Orient became accepted by a sufficiently large number of authors as something self-evident, something that 'goes without saying'. In this way, Orientalist thought came to provide the basis for further research and reflection on any topic or issue relationally positioned in the context of the Orient or the Middle East.

The term 'Middle East' also traces its roots to European imperialism and denotes a Eurocentric perspective on the world. From the late nineteenth century onwards, the term was used to designate the British zone of influence in the Levant, Mesopotamia and the Arab Peninsula, and to distinguish these territories from the 'Far East' – that is, East and Southeast Asia. Attempts to detach the term from its imperial provenance, to define the region according to other criteria (climate, natural boundaries, religion, culture, language, etc.), are far from convincing. Therefore, the term 'Middle East' must be seen as a strictly geopolitical term. It evokes the memory of a long history of foreign domination and represents a reference point for a wider postcolonial discourse about cultural domination and power.

Metal in the Middle East must thus be carefully examined within this context. This includes recognising and addressing the myriad of implications that Orientalist discourse has for scholarly research on metal in the Middle East. Orientalist discourse might influence how authors see and represent metal in the Middle East. The 'Orientalist lens' they unconsciously wear may colour the questions they ask and the answers they generate. To date, it is mainly scholars from Europe and North America who hold authority over the discourse on metal in the Middle East. This obvious deficit in the research agenda requires us to direct a series of critical questions at ourselves. For example, if research were conducted by scholars from the region, would they produce a different picture of metal in the Middle East? Does the research deficit identified above comprise a continuation of Orientalism in academia, or does it result solely from a lack of academic interest in metal studies in the region? By studying and presenting the histories of local metal scenes to a broader, (non-)academic audience, do metal scholars reproduce cultural representations of the Orient? Are these scholars reflective enough of how Orientalist discourse might impinge on their ways of seeing and studying local metal cultures?

It is my contention that the discourse on metal in the Middle East has been directly influenced by Orientalist discourse. This becomes obvious if we examine certain procedures of exclusion which, in my opinion, should induce us to rethink the ways in which we see and represent metal music and culture to our audiences. Some discursive strands and events have been overemphasised, while others have been excluded, or at least neglected. Examples include a consistently intensive engagement with 'repression' and 'moral panic', as well as the absence of the lives of 'ordinary metalheads' from many studies.

Another procedure of exclusion relates to the case studies chosen by various authors to represent metal in the Middle East. The choice of protagonists often appears to be selective and repetitive and, therefore, reductive. What I mean by this is that some bands and musicians are repeatedly quoted and referred to in various studies, while others remain largely invisible. Researchers and journalists often tend to interview and thus over-represent those who speak English and can be easily contacted on social media or met face-to-face in the European or North American diaspora.[19] To date, the discourse is clearly dominated by researchers and journalists from Europe and North America. Authors from the Middle East itself play a strikingly limited role in reporting and representing local scenes and their histories. I would therefore argue that we need to reflect on how Orientalist discourse has contributed to exoticizing the 'Muslim metalhead', and how an examination of metal in the Middle East has helped to re-establish 'Western' moral superiority.

Rethinking the Exoticisation of the 'Muslim Metalhead'

> I'm gonna start with the most obvious question. How do you feel, JP [Haddad], when people express surprise that there is a metal scene in Lebanon? Is there really a metal scene in Lebanon?
>
> Actually, the Lebanese metal scene existed since the 1990s, and it's nothing new at all . . .[20]

This very brief dialogue has been taken from a round-table discussion on metal in Lebanon hosted by World Metal Congress co-founders Alexander Milas and Lina Khatib. The webcast, aired on 24 November 2020, also involved Anthony Kaoteon, Derek Roddy and Kimaera's Jean-Pierre Haddad. The latter is quoted above, responding to Milas's opening question. But why is this 'the most obvious question', and why would 'people express surprise' about the existence of a metal scene in Lebanon? Metal in Lebanon is indeed 'nothing new at all', and one might wonder why metalheads from the region still have to explain themselves and prove their existence to the outside world.

From where does this surprise originate, and when will journalists and academics stop asking these 'obvious' questions? In reflecting on this, I returned to a scene report written thirty years ago by Luk Haas for *Maximum Rocknroll*. Haas had apparently spent some time in Istanbul in 1989, from where he delivered the – by his reckoning – very first scene report from Turkey. His observations came with a concert photo that depicted thrash metal veterans Metafor, a potentially racist cartoon of a stereotyped Arab attacking a punk rocker with a sword, and the contact details of several punk and thrash metal bands in Turkey (Blessfamous, Headbangers, Kronik, Metafor, Noisy Mob):

Turkey has a fairly well-developed underground scene . . . consisting of metal, thrash, punk and hardcore bands, which are all friends and close together for they're all facing the same problems: they have to resist daily against the police oppression as well as Islamic fundamentalist aggressions. Turkey, as a Muslim country, is really a hard place for any kind of non-conformity. The police bother you if you wear earrings, have long hair or a mohawk. They can arrest you and question you in the police office. Deviant outlooks are considered as 'un-Turkish' . . . and they also accuse you of being homosexual.[21]

What, then, might the reader pick up from Haas's observations? That Turkey is a hard place for underground scenes to flourish because Turkey is a Muslim country. Certainly, I am sure that many punks and metalheads who lived in

Turkey at the time would agree with Haas. They would surely come forward with their own stories of how they were exposed to 'police oppression as well as Islamic fundamentalist aggressions'. However, I would also argue that Haas's report fulfils the expectations of a 'Western' audience and a worldview shaped by Orientalist discourse. The reader might well establish a meaningful connection between Islam and violence, repression, intolerance, human rights abuses and an absence of the rule of law. From this perspective, reports on metal in the Middle East contribute to and confirm existing stereotypical images of the Muslim world. But a central historical fact is apparently lost in translation in Haas's scene report: Turkey has been a secularist state since its foundation in 1923 and is home to millions of 'ordinary Muslim citizens' who, for decades, have been resisting the encroachments of political Islam. And even thirty years after Haas's report, similar lines of analysis are still being formulated. For instance, a recent article by Beth Winegarner concludes that 'in heavily Islamic nations like Lebanon, Morocco, and Egypt, the genre's popularity was followed by crackdowns, arrests, and government bans, leaving nascent heavy-metal communities in shreds'.[22]

It seems that, for researchers and journalists who grew up in Europe and North America (including myself), punk and metal in the Middle East was something unexpected and therefore somewhat exotic. In her early work, for instance, Deena Weinstein presumed that Islam would preclude metal from gaining a foothold among Muslim youths.[23] Similarly, Mark LeVine was honest enough to admit that 'the possibility of a Muslim heavy-metal scene came as a total surprise' – whereupon he immediately reminded himself that he 'shouldn't have been surprised at the notion of Muslim metalheads or punkers'.[24] Furthermore, I sometimes cannot escape the feeling that particular reports on metal in the Middle East read like the story of the discovery of an exotic new world, one in need of 'revelation' to a 'Western' audience.

Anecdotal Evidence?

Much of the existing literature on metal in the Middle East builds on anecdotal evidence. Metal scholars often compose their studies as a sequence of anecdotal encounters with local metalheads. The interviewees invariably retell the legends of particular discursive events (a 'legendary' concert, a police raid, etc.) that have shaped the collective memory of a local scene. This is usually reinforced by accumulating first- or second-hand observations and a certain degree of socio-political contextualisation. To be sure, anecdotal evidence combined with frequent eye-witness accounts provides a sense of authenticity and commonly resonates strongly with metalheads around the world. However, it often lacks analytical substance, not only regarding the empirical material laid out in a particular study but to the positionality of the metal scholar involved in its accumulation.

With that said, I will now lay out a few of my own anecdotal encounters. This is not a (potentially ridiculous) attempt to prove my 'street credibility' as a seasoned metal scholar in the Middle East. The goal here is to critically reflect on how I have approached the field. As the reader will quickly notice, these anecdotes tell us less about metal in the Middle East than about my own positionality.

In the summer of 1996, a friend and I decided to go backpacking through Egypt. It quickly turned out that our rather naïve concept of backpacking was not well-established in Egypt. After two-and-a-half weeks, we were sick, tired, confused and unable to decode much of the buzzing society around us. I neither understood the pervasive and mostly friendly interest of ordinary people, nor the hatred and overt racism we encountered on several occasions. Above all, I will never forget the shocked expression on the face of a local butcher who caught our eye when we were getting off a bus in the town of Rasheed (Rosetta). He literally froze, the cleaver he had been chopping meat with still raised over his head. Two white, long-haired guys wearing black clothes and Doc Martens probably presented our butcher with his own problems in decoding.

In 1996, it was relatively uncommon to see men with long hair and black clothes on the streets of a small Egyptian town. The only artefact that pointed to the existence of a local metal scene was a bootleg cassette of Pantera's *The Great Southern Trendkill* (1996), which I discovered while flipping through the display of a local street vendor in downtown Cairo. The street vendor, a young guy in his early twenties, was generous enough to play the tape on my request. To my regret, the sudden blast of sound that emerged from the cassette player made him frantically hit the stop button and terminate the 'noise' as quickly as possible.

I visited Istanbul for the first time in the spring of 2002 due to a stopover that allowed me to roam the city for a few days. My first walk led me directly along İstiklal Caddesi, Istanbul's famous pedestrian shopping road and the modern heart of the city. At this time, Slayer's *God Hates Us All* (2001) album was officially released and promoted in Turkey. The release of foreign rock albums was quite common at the time, but the release dates often came with a delay of several months. On that particular day in 2002, *God Hates Us All* was 'everywhere'. Posters advertised the album release, and a book and record store at the centre of İstiklal Caddesi blasted the title song out into the street. Several small music stores located around Tünel Square had electric guitars, amplifiers and, of course, a variety of the renowned Istanbul Agop and Istanbul Mehmet Cymbals on display. The impression of a vivid and well-established metal scene was provided by a plethora of small rock bars and the presence of numerous rockers and metalheads, with their long hair, boots and black shirts overtly signifying their 'metalness'.

My experience in Turkey was dramatically different from my experiences in Egypt, Syria or Morocco. Why, then, would I feel justified in drawing some kind of connection between these countries and their local scenes? Because they are referred to as 'Muslim' or 'Middle Eastern' in 'the West?' I am sure that most of my friends in Turkey would loathe the idea of being classified as Middle Eastern. Indeed, the history of Turkey could be written as a European history.

A few years later, I convinced some friends to join me on a trip to Istanbul's Ümraniye district. At this time, Ümraniye had the reputation of being a run-down, working-class neighbourhood dominated by pious conservatives – an unsafe place for long-haired metalheads. Only a few days earlier, I had interviewed a local black metalhead from Ümraniye, who told me about the daily fights and conflicts he encountered. And indeed, my friends, who had all grown up in middle-class families, had never visited Ümraniye. They initially ridiculed and rejected my idea ('They'll kill us!'). In the end, no one got killed, and we had a lovely encounter with a socialist family that invited us to their home. Most of the people on the streets simply ignored us. However, when we were on our way back to the minibus, we had to dodge out of the way of a middle-aged woman and her young daughter. The former briefly stared at us, especially at my friend Zehra, with her long, black dreadlocks and black leather jacket. Then she very audibly hissed the word 'Satanist'.

The woman's reaction indicates that popular media discourses had indeed influenced the public perception of rockers and metalheads in Turkey. Her reaction also made me aware of the fact that metal was an issue of social class. 'Ordinary people' commonly associated metal and Satanism with supposedly rich kids from secularist families. Certainly, to some extent, metal music was also popular among young men and women from working-class backgrounds. However, I generally found it difficult to get in touch with them. Social class set a boundary between metalheads, simply because not everyone had the money or leisure time to visit a rock bar or concert. Consequently, well-educated metalheads from middle-class families were over-represented in my research. This surely holds true for other studies on metal in the Middle East.

Language and cultural knowledge were also key issues here: Do I speak the language(s) well enough to understand and analyse texts, conversations and social encounters in daily life? And how reliable and potentially Orientalist does this make my own research?

Conclusion

In conclusion, I would like to point out five aspects that, in my opinion, pose a challenge to metal in the Middle East:

(1) Metal in the Middle East has always found itself at the peripheries of global metal. *Participation in global metal* has been limited due to a digital and economic divide. To be sure, the advent of the internet and the invention of new and cheaper recording and communication technologies (social media applications, audio recording software, etc.) have contributed to narrowing this gap. Even so, international travel restrictions or unfavourable currency exchange rates still pose a challenge to metalheads in the Middle East. Festivals in Europe or North America are mostly out of reach, and bands have difficulties organising gigs abroad.

(2) All local metal scenes in the Middle East have one thing in common: they are situated in religionormative societies. *Religionormativity* denotes a situation in which being religious and believing in a particular god or gods represents the commonly accepted norm. Religionormativity also comes with particular societal expectations. The individual is commonly expected to respect religious values and act accordingly. Non-religious persons are often discriminated against and marginalised, especially when the legal system happens to be aligned with religious principles. In the Middle East, metalheads have been branded as un-Islamic, un-Christian or un-Jewish. They have been accused of undermining the 'true' and 'authentic' spirit of the religiously imagined nation. Doing metal in religionormative environments thus often triggers negative reactions from 'ordinary believers', who consider their religious beliefs to be disrespected. Drinking alcohol in public, criticising religious teachings or dignitaries or incorporating (anti)religious symbols into lyrics and artwork constitute a contestation of religious norms.

(3) The collapse of pro-democracy movements throughout the Middle East (Egypt, Iran, Qatar, Turkey, etc.) has given rise to *authoritarian populist regimes* that threaten the freedom of artistic and individual expression, not only in metal but in all fields of popular culture.

(4) The ways of seeing and representing metal in the Middle East have been affected by *Orientalist discourse*. Consequently, it could be argued that studies on metal in the Middle East help to reproduce Orientalist representations of the past and re-establish 'Western' superiority over the 'Muslim world'.

(5) Within *postcolonial discourse*, metal music and culture are often considered to represent a form of cultural imperialism. This position has been common among representatives of political Islam, but it is also held by nationalist and socialist groups. A metalhead who was actively involved in Turkey's socialist movement once told me that he had temporarily stopped listening to metal because he and his comrades saw it as a representation of Western imperialism. Part of this postcolonial discourse is to imagine a nation's 'authentic self' in distinction from what is considered 'Western' and therefore intrusive. The appropriation of 'Western' popular culture is seen as an act of self-colonisation and surrender to Western values. In this context, doing metal appears alien, even hostile, an act that needs to be denied an active presence in the public sphere and eradicated from national memory. The attempt to reinvent the supposedly authentic culture of a nation corrupted by Western imperialism is arguably as essentialist and paternalistic as Western Orientalism. Indeed, Edward W. Said himself once described this phenomenon as 'Orientalism in reverse' or, using the medical suffix -osis to signify a sickness, 'Occidentosis'.[25] The whole debate on Westernisation fails to recognise that metal and other forms of popular culture are not just passively 'copied'; they are renegotiated, reshaped, 'authenticised', and thus integrated into local and individual identities.

Notes

1. Al Jazeera, *Playlist*, series 2, episode 6, hosted by Richard Gizbert (2009). www .youtube.com/watch?v=R5Bm4uOMbwE&t=32s (accessed 15 November 2021). Other documentaries on metal in the Middle East include Ufuk Önen, *Black, Not Grey. Ankara Rocks!* (2017); Ahmed Boulane, *Les Anges de Satan* (2007); Monzer Darwish, *Syrian Metal is War* (2018).

2. Pierre Hecker and Douglas Mattsson, 'The Enemy within: Conceptualizing Turkish Metalheads as the Ideological "Other"', in Bryan A. Bardine and Jeroem Steuart (eds.), *Living Metal: Metal Scenes Around the World* (Intellect, 2021), pp. 55–77.

3. Mark LeVine, *Heavy Metal Islam: Rock Resistance, and the Struggle for the Soul of Islam* (Three Rivers Press, 2008).

4. Orlando Crowcroft, *Rock in a Hard Place: Music and Mayhem in the Middle East* (Zed Books, 2017).

5. Keith Kahn-Harris, 'An Orphaned Land? Israel and the Global Extreme Metal Scene', in Keith Kahn-Harris (ed.), *New Voices in Jewish Thought*, Vol. 2 (Limmud, 1999), pp. 1–21; Keith Kahn-Harris, '"I Hate this Fucking Country": Dealing with the Global and the Local in the Israeli Extreme Metal Scene', in Richard A. Young (ed.), *Music, Popular Culture, Identities* (Brill, 2002), pp. 119–36.

6. Kahn-Harris, 'An Orphaned Land?', pp. 1–2.

7. Kahn-Harris, 'I Hate this Fucking Country'.

8. Kahn-Harris, 'An Orphaned Land?', p. 2.

9. Gabriel Cavaglion and Revital Shaytovitz, 'The Cultural Construction of Contemporary Satanic Legends in Israel', *Folklore* 116/3 (2005): 255–71.

10. Ted Swedenburg, 'Satanic Heavy Metal in Egypt', unpublished paper presented at the panel 'Counter/Culture: Worlding the Alternative', *American Anthropological Association Annual Meeting*, San Francisco, 16 November 2000.

11. See, for instance, LeVine, *Heavy Metal Islam*; Pierre Hecker, *Turkish Metal: Music, Meaning, and Morality in a Muslim Society* (Ashgate, 2012); Ralph Kronauer and Luca Tommasini, 'Metal in Egypt', *Norient* (1 February 2013). http://norient.com/stories/metal-in-egypt (accessed 19 November 2021); Benjamin J. Harbert, 'Noise and its Formless Shadows: Egypt's Extreme Metal as Avant-Garde *Nafas Dawsha*', in Thomas Burkhalter, Kay Dickinson and Benjamin J. Harbert (eds.), *The Arab Avant-Garde: Music, Politics, Modernity* (Wesleyan University Press, 2013), pp. 229–72; Crowcroft, *Rock in a Hard Place*; Beth Winegarner, *Tenacity: Heavy Metal in the Middle East and Africa* (2018).

12. Hecker, *Turkish Metal*, pp. 79–128.

13. Translated from Turkish to English.

14. Crowcroft, *Rock in a Hard Place*.

15. Translated from Arabic to English.

16. Pasqualina Eckerström, 'Extreme Heavy Metal and Blasphemy in Iran: The Case of Confess', *Contemporary Islam* 16 (2022): 115–33.

17. Mohammad Magout, *Heavy Metal in Syria*, MA thesis (Aga Khan University, 2010), p. 40.

18. Edward W. Said, *Orientalism* (Pantheon Books, 1978).

19. For instance, Cherine Amr and Nancy Mounir of the Egyptian band Massive Scar Era were interviewed for the works of LeVine, *Heavy Metal Islam*; Kronauer and Tommasini, 'Metal in Egypt'; Crowcroft, *Rock in a Hard Place*;

and Winegarner, *Tenacity*. This band also appeared in a number of European and North American rock and metal magazines and, today, resides in Canada. Another example could be Adel Saflou of a widely unknown Syrian band called Orchid. I interviewed Adel in June 2013, after he had relocated from Syria to Lebanon. A few years later, he also appeared in Orlando Crowcroft's *Rock in a Hard Place* and a documentary that covered his new life in the Netherlands as a refugee.

20. World Metal Congress, 'Heavy Metal in Lebanon', Webcast episode 5, hosted by Alexander Milas and Lina Khatib (24 November 2020). www.youtube.com /watch?v=Yzx09PXgsmM&t=1117s (accessed 19 November 2021).
21. Luk Haas, 'Scene Report Turkey', *Maximum Rocknroll* 84/5 (1990): 60.
22. Winegarner, *Tenacity*, p. 41.
23. Deena Weinstein, *Heavy Metal: The Music and its Culture* (Da Capo Press, 2000), p. 120.
24. LeVine, *Heavy Metal Islam*, p. 2.
25. Edward W. Said, *Power, Politics and Culture: Interviews with Edward W. Said* (Bloomsbury, 2005), p. 221.

22 | Asian Metal Rising

Metal Scene Formation in the World's Most Populous Region

JEREMY WALLACH

Of his band's Japanese admirers, Testament's Alex Skolnick writes:

> These fans seemed to really notice the emotion expressed in my guitar solos, as though they related my pain to their own lives. This was incredibly interesting to me – here was this culture that was largely based on keeping expression and emotions in private. Yet they were actually hearing what I'd been trying to express through all the double kick drums, crunchy riffing, and growling vocals.[1]

There are many possible reasons for metal's extraordinary popularity in Asia – and this chapter reviews some of them – but perhaps it is as simple as this ability to convey musical meaning across cultural boundaries.

Whatever the causes, metal's popularity in Asia is a social fact. While metal music is occasionally dismissed (even haughtily so) in the United States as nostalgic 'dad rock' or marginal esoterica for self-selecting elitists, in Asia the genre has remained vital, and its popularity appears to be growing. Composed of tens of millions of avid enthusiasts, the Asian metal music scene is an increasingly interconnected territory that has forged ties to other world regions through its most successful, distinctive-sounding groups, including Chthonic from Taiwan, Burgerkill, Seringai and Voice of Baceprot from Indonesia, Rudra from Singapore, The Hu Band from Mongolia, Bloodywood from India, and Babymetal from Japan. While it would not be inaccurate to state that online platforms enabled the global conquest of these bands, such an assertion would also be incomplete – even facile. The emergence of viable local music scenes and the culmination of a painstaking decades-long process of metal indigenisation were also necessary prerequisites for this success. In order to make an impact on the global scene, Asian metal acts also had to overcome Westerner listeners' resistance to Asian musics, a dismissal rooted in long-enduring colonial and racist stereotypes.[2] Among these stereotypes, as students of postcolonial theory are well aware, is the offensive notion that Asians are weak and emasculated compared to white Europeans. Thus the ability of Asian people, especially young Asian women, to master a music genre that extols strength and power is consequential within the larger history of cultural representations. The following survey of metal music in Asia assesses major developments since the genre's 1970s introduction to the region by focusing on three contemporary, internationally acclaimed artists. There are obviously many other important groups representing every imaginable metal subgenre, but our present purposes will be served by these few examples.

Historical Background and Overview

Foreign popular musics, from Christian hymns to tangoes, have influenced local musical life in Asia for centuries; this intensified following the global dispersion of American jazz recordings in the early twentieth century.[3] Following post-WWII decolonisation, fledgling Asian governments decried Western popular music as a corrosive cultural pollutant,[4] resulting in a climate in which metal music was not only oppositional in a broad sense (the genre's conventional trafficking in transgressive imagery, sounds and behaviours) but specifically in that enthusiasm for metal culture became unavoidably anti-government and anti-censorship. While metal music's foreignness and racial otherness were at first barriers to its wholesale adoption, Asian metallers were inspired by Sepultura from Brazil, proof that metal could thrive in the non-Anglophone Third World, and Death Angel, a thrash metal band from the San Francisco Bay Area composed of Filipino cousins, taken as proof that Asians could play this music too. Many also knew of the partial Asian ancestries of Metallica guitarist Kirk Hammett (Filipino) and Eddie and Alex Van Halen (Indonesian).

Along with punk, hardcore and underground hip hop, metal is a form of Extreme Youth Music that has transformed the global musical and political landscape over the last fifty years.[5] In the contemporary milieu, massive, long-established metal scenes in Japan, Indonesia, Malaysia, Singapore and Nepal exert influence on rapidly expanding ones in India, China, mainland Southeast Asia and other regions on the continent. Japan is home to Asia's oldest metal community, with Loudness and EZO its best-known 1980s exports, and metal labels are powerful enough to even sign bands from other countries.[6] Though men are still the majority, Japan is the world's most gender-balanced metal scene; this is likely due to the popularity of *visual kei*, a national hard rock genre with an ardent audience of mostly Japanese women.[7] The connected metal scenes in the adjoining Southeast Asian nations of Brunei, Indonesia, Malaysia, Philippines and Singapore[8] can trace their roots to the popularity of hard rock music in the region in the 1970s and 1980s[9] but accelerated in the 1990s as underground networks of bands, gigs and DIY cassettes sprang up with links to the global tape-trading underground.[10] This 'Nusantara' metal scene has produced bands representing every subgenre, from the atmospheric black metal of Jakarta's Vallendusk to the traditional thrash of Shah Alam's Cromok. Elsewhere in Asia, the megacity of Kathmandu became the epicentre of a massive Nepalese metal scene, with bands such as Cobweb and Ugra Karma,[11] while a smaller, tightly-knit metal scene arose in Bangladesh centred on the capital city of Dhaka.[12] Nascent scenes in Burma[13] and other mainland Southeast Asian nations, China[14] and the Indian subcontinent constitute fertile zones for future metal development. There has been little scholarly research on metal scenes in Central Asia, yet the region has produced some excellent groups, including Kazakhstan's Aldaspan and Azerbaijan's Violet Cold.

In recent years, awareness of other scenes within the region has increased, with more collaborative ventures undertaken. Founded in 2015 by Hong Kong musician Riz Farooqi, the website *Unite Asia* is a centralised source for information about Asian punk and metal bands. In October 2021, *Unite Asia* and other outlets announced that the early albums of the Singaporean 'Vedic metal' band Rudra, whose pathbreaking compositions combine Indian classical music and Hindu sacred texts with dissonant extreme metal,[15] were being re-released by the Chinese independent metal label Awakening Records.

Rudra is the first old-school Asian metal band, and the first with such a distinctive locally developed sound, to be picked by the Chinese label. 'I didn't know what Vedic metal was, and I liked Rudra because of their music', said Li Meng, Awakening Records' manager. 'In my mind, they are the true leaders of Asian extreme metal music'.[16]

As of this writing, such cross-regional collaborations are still uncommon, but their frequency is increasing as linguistic and logistical obstacles fall away.

The Metallification of Asian Music

I have written of four necessary steps in the integration of an Anglo-American popular music genre into a non-English-speaking country[17]: In the *first stage*, bands play English-language covers of songs by their favourite metal groups. Any original material in this stage is also performed in English to sound like the original source material. Bands who stay at this stage can develop reputations in the local concert circuit but do not record albums and usually do not have nationwide profiles.

The *second stage* is characterised by linguistic hybridity, in which metal bands devise ways to deploy the national language in metal contexts. Once this difficult hurdle has been cleared, bands become commercially viable to national recording industries, and their members can pursue music careers. The Chinese band Tang Dynasty, whose classic heavy metal debut was one of the most commercially successful albums in 1990s China, is a good example of this second stage. So are legendary Indonesian bands Burgerkill and Seringai, who combine virtuosic musicianship, intense drive and a range of twentieth-century heavy metal influences with a deep engagement with Indonesian society and politics.

The Taiwanese band Chthonic, formed in 1995 in Taipei and one of the most politically active metal groups in the world, represent the pinnacle of the *third stage*, that of musical hybridity. While Tang Dynasty used traditional Chinese music in song intros and interludes, Chthonic developed a unique form of folk metal[18] that combines the *erhu* (Chinese spike fiddle), called *hena* in Taiwan, with death, black and symphonic metal. Other East Asian stringed instruments such as the Japanese *koto* and the *yueqin* (Chinese moon lute) are added to song textures as well. Chthonic are well known for their outspoken support of Taiwan's independence from mainland China. After the pro-democracy, youth-driven Sunflower Movement dramatically reversed a long trend in Taiwanese politics toward assimilation into mainland China, lead singer Freddie Lim, previously chair of the local Amnesty International chapter, gained a parliamentary seat in 2016 as a member of the pro-independence New Power Party.

Chthonic are quite popular in their home country, despite the extremity of their sound. Due to the success of the nation of Taiwan in controlling the Coronavirus, Chthonic have been able to play large concerts on their home turf, attracting thousands of masked spectators. The band's CD recording of their massive 27 March 2021 concert in Takao, Taiwan, which is shipped in a box with customised face masks, a hand sanitiser bottle and a face mask chain, attests to their continuing appeal to young Taiwanese.

While Chthonic now also enjoy an enthusiastic global audience, this was built slowly over the twenty-five years of the band's existence. The remainder of this chapter will discuss two groups that exemplify even better the *fourth stage* of genre indigenisation: the phase of *internationalisation*, when a band's unique sound attracts a global audience. The two bands, Babymetal and Voice of Baceprot, were founded more recently, and while their composition is unusual, they both exemplify this phase.

Enter Babymetal

Babymetal, whose name rhymes with the Japanese pronunciation of 'heavy metal', were created in 2010 by a Japanese record producer (Kei Kobayashi, later known as 'Kobametal') out of a subgroup of a school-themed pop idol collective called Sakura Gakuin (Cherry Blossom Academy). The group, three teenaged singer-dancers backed by experienced session players and programmed accompaniment, performed an audacious amalgam of chirpy J-pop and thrash/death metal, a combination that took many by surprise and was widely thought at first to be nothing more than a bizarre novelty. Indeed, at one time, the success of Babymetal in the international metal arena would have seemed improbable, since by featuring Japanese teenagers in a clearly manufactured pop group, Babymetal appeared to violate so many of the sacrosanct genre rules of metal.[19] Yet Babymetal now play to packed stadiums around the world and are featured regularly in major metal magazines such as *Revolver* and *Metal Hammer*, the latter featuring the two remaining members of the group (Suzuka Nakamoto ['Su-metal'] and Moa Kikuchi ['Moa-metal']) on the cover of its July 2021 issue, marking the band's tenth anniversary. In the words of staff writer Stephen Hill, 'A decade on from their inception, Babymetal's mix of hyperactive J-pop, brutal riffs and heavy metal bombast has seen them sell out arenas, stun major festivals, conquer the mainstream, befriend legends of the genre and make some members of *Hammer*'s Facebook page throw proper toddler tantrums'.[20] One reason for their success, controversial though it may be, is that the energetic synthesis of pop music and death metal Babymetal wound up performing by their second album was really a form of power metal, a subgenre that *already existed* in the metal pantheon, a subgenre that combines uplifting, melodic songs of self-empowerment, often employing Mixolydian or Ionian modes, with churning extreme-metal riffs.

To the Babymetal story I have two additional observations. First, the basic pattern of singer flanked by two backup dancers has strong East Asian antecedents. The Korean superstar and popular music trailblazer Seo Taiji, who started his career as a heavy metal bass player, was the first artist to have two hype dancers and perform intricate pop-music choreography to speed metal[21] – Babymetal is really just following in their footsteps. Furthermore, since they combine metal with a national style of music (J-pop) and sing mostly but not exclusively in their national tongue, Babymetal could be viewed as the world's most commercially successful folk metal band.

Second, as Lorraine Plourde has observed, Babymetal can be said to epitomise the Japanese ideal of *kawaii*, loosely translated as 'cute'.[22] Yet this is a version of cuteness that includes the concealed menace of that which is coded as harmless and feminine (such as a kitten's sharp claws and teeth). As stated above, much of Asian heavy metal's aesthetic potency in the West derives from its capacity to overcome Orientalist expectations. The sight and sound of young Asian women mastering a powerful style of music confounds underestimations born of anti-Asian, ageist and sexist bias, rendering such performances compelling and memorable. And thus there is now a whole metal subgenre pioneered by Babymetal: kawaii metal.

Even before Babymetal's massive global popularity (for example, as the first Asian act to top the Billboard Rock Chart in 2019, it is the most popular Japanese band in the history of the United States), there was no shortage of Japanese women metal artists who play their own instruments, including in bands on the most extreme end of the spectrum. Contemporary groups include Aldious, Bridear, Gallhammer, Hagane and the veteran grindcore group Flagitious Idiosyncrasy in the Dilapidation. Yet the group of young woman metal musicians who eventually captured the Western media's imagination came not from Japan but from Asia's other massive metal scene, Indonesia, which has its own proud history of female participation.

Voice of Baceprot: The Future of Metal Is Now

'Move Over, Babymetal' announces the title of an article in online fansite *The Mary Sue*, 'Indonesian All-Girl Metal Band Voice of Baceprot Is Here to Rock'.[23] Originally from a rural village approximately 20 kilometres outside the town of Garut, West Java, the members of Voice of Baceprot (roughly, 'chatterbox'), singer/guitarist Firdda Kurnia (Marsya), bassist Nidi Rahmawati (Widi) and drummer Euis Siti Aisyah (Sitti), have been celebrated for their instrumental virtuosity and their willingness to challenge entrenched expectations regarding gender, religiosity and metal performance. The trio, who all wear the Muslim headscarf that is typical modest attire of village women in West Java, was first introduced to metal by their music teacher, who eventually became the band's manager, Cep Ersa Eka Susila (known as Abah). Significantly, Abah is, unlike Kobametal, less of a Svengali figure and more of a facilitator/collaborator; when the group toured Europe for the first time in the fall of 2021, he stayed behind.

Voice of Baceprot play an aggressive amalgam of thrash and nu metal; the bands the three musicians mention most often in interviews as influences are Gojira, Metallica, Rage Against the Machine, Red Hot Chili Peppers, Sepultura, Slipknot and System of a Down. They are quite adept at their instruments, and their skill level individually and collectively is far above most ensembles twice their age. Voice of Baceprot have received a great deal of attention from Western media outlets, but in fact headscarf-wearing Muslim women playing heavy metal are not that unusual in Indonesia. Vocalist Asri Yuniar (Achie) of Gugat, virtuoso guitarist Meliana Siti Sumartini and drummer Siti Nurjanah of Soul of Slamming are some of the best-known figures currently in the scene. Moreover, the vast Indonesia metal scene is a place where countless women of varying degrees of adherence to Islamic practice (and female members of non-Muslim minorities) have long found avenues of self-expression.

Generally, the stages of music genre adoption slowly build on each other over decades, but because they are such a new band, Voice of Baceprot encapsulate all four at once: they still perform English-language covers, they play original songs in a combination of Indonesian and English, and recently they even debuted an instrumental based on the Sundanese pentatonic scale. Finally, of course, they have definitely impacted the international scene. The group have yet to record a whole album of original material but have already been covered by National Public Radio (US), *The Guardian* (UK), *The South China Morning Post* (Hong Kong), the *New York Times* and the international metal music press. While this chapter was being completed, the trio finished their first European tour (Covid-19 notwithstanding, though they had to cancel a few dates) and seems poised to win increasing numbers of fans overseas.

While touring Europe, the members of Voice of Baceprot were surprised and somewhat dismayed to encounter so many interviewers' questions about their headscarves rather than their music. Since Europeans are more familiar with Middle Eastern Islam and the perennial conflicts between fundamentalist religion and heavy metal,[24] it is not surprising that they would not grasp the nuances of the Indonesian situation. Though Voice of Baceprot have certainly encountered staunch opposition from conservative religious forces in their own country, Islam itself is not regarded as problematic by most Indonesian metalheads, as opposed to certain strict, intolerant interpretations of it. In fact, numerous commentators, including Islamic scholars, have held up the members of Voice of Baceprot as religious and feminist role models for fellow Indonesians.[25] The trio have also received a great deal of support from members of Indonesia's longstanding metal scene, including Stevie Item from death metal supergroup DeadSquad[26] and Stephen Santoso from the traditional metal band Musikimia.

Conclusion

Heavy metal has a long history in Asia. After first entering the region surreptitiously, in the form of rare and frequently unauthorised recordings, the music is now performed regularly by local groups and, while still not a mainstay of popular entertainment, is easily accessible through the internet.

As the social disruptions of neoliberal capitalist development and proletarianization of nonaffluent classes progresses in Asian nations, metal music only increases in appeal for those marginalised by modernity's depredations, with the music's ability to express the strong emotions that attend social upheaval, ethical unmoorings, and the psychic wounds of increasing and conspicuous economic inequality. At the same time, the emergence of unique Asian metal 'alloys' has caught the attention of the international metal scene. Asian metal studies is not yet a recognised subfield, but it is only a matter of time.

As Asian bands have attracted the enthusiastic attention of international audiences, they have compelled a shift in dominant representations of Asian musics, which in the West have either been dismissed as boringly derivative, inauthentic pop or abstruse traditional styles inaccessible to non-Asian ears. Asian metal is decidedly neither, and its hold upon the imagination of the global music scene has arguably just begun. This chapter has argued that in order to understand Asia's best-known metal exports, it is crucial to learn about the vibrant scenes from which they came.

Notes

1. Alex Skolnick, *From Geek to Guitar Hero* (Louder Education, 2013), p. 254.
2. See Robyn Perry, *'Ersatz as the Day Is Long': Japanese Popular Music, the Struggle for Authenticity, and Cold War Orientalism*, MA dissertation (Bowling Green State University, 2021).
3. E. Taylor Atkins, *Blue Nippon: Authenticating Jazz in Japan* (Duke University Press, 2001).
4. Steven Farram, 'Wage War against Beatle Music! Censorship and Music in Soekarno's Indonesia', *RIMA: Review of Indonesian and Malaysian Affairs* 41/2 (2007): 247–77.

5. Pierre Hecker, Mark LeVine, Nahid Siamdoust and Jeremy Wallach, 'Epilogue: The Joys of Resistance', in Mark LeVine (ed.), *We'll Play Till We Die: Journeys across a Decade of Revolutionary Music in the Muslim World* (University of California Press, 2022), pp. 251–86.

6. Kei Kawano and Shuhei Hosokawa, 'Thunder in the Far East: The Heavy Metal Industry in 1990s Japan', in Jeremy Wallach, Harris M. Berger and Paul D. Greene (eds.), *Metal Rules the Globe: Heavy Metal Music Around the World* (Duke University Press, 2011), pp. 247–69.

7. Oliver Seibt, 'Asagi's Voice: Learning How to Desire with Japanese *Visual-kei*', in Christian Utz and Frederick Lau (eds.), *Vocal Music and Contemporary Identities: Unlimited Voices in East Asia and the West* (Routledge, 2013), pp. 248–66. Gender and the role and status of women in the scene have been central preoccupations of studies of heavy metal from the beginning. There has been relatively limited attention paid to heavy metal and gender in Asia, however, though see Hinhin Agung Daryana, Aquarini Priyatna and Raden Muhammad Mulyadi, 'The New Metal Men: Exploring Model of Flexible Masculinity in the Bandung Metal Scene', *Masculinities and Social Change* 9/2 (2020): 148–73; Marissa Saraswati and Annisa R. Beta, 'Knowing Responsibly: Decolonizing Knowledge Production of Indonesian Girlhood', *Feminist Media Studies* 21/5 (2021): 758–74; and Seibt, 'Asagi's Voice'.

8. This multinational, multicultural ecumene, often called the Nusantara region, has a long and robust history of musical cross-pollination and exchange. See Adil Johan and Mayco Santaella (eds.), *Made in Nusantara* (Routledge, 2021).

9. See Marco Ferrarase, 'Southeast Asian Glamour: The Strange Case of Rock Kapak in Malaysia', in Ian Chapman and Henry Johnson (eds.), *Global Glam and Popular Music: Style and Spectacle from the 1970s to the 2000s* (Routledge, 2016), pp. 232–44; Steve Ferzacca, *Sonic City: Making Rock Music and Urban Life in Singapore* (National University of Singapore Press, 2020).

10. Emma Baulch, *Making Scenes: Reggae, Punk and Death Metal in 1990s Bali* (Duke University Press, 2007); Amalina Timbang and Zawawi Ibrahim, 'Malay Metalheads: Situating Metal Music Culture in Brunei', *Situations* 10/2 (2017): 7–26; Jeremy Wallach, *Modern Noise, Fluid Genres: Popular Music in Indonesia, 1997–2001* (University of Wisconsin Press, 2008).

11. Paul D. Greene, 'Electronic and Affective Overdrive: Tropes of Transgression in Nepal's Heavy Metal Scene', in Jeremy Wallach, Harris M. Berger and Paul D. Greene (eds.), *Metal Rules the Globe: Heavy Metal Music Around the World* (Duke University Press, 2011), pp. 109–34.

12. Shams Bin Quader and Guy Redden, 'Approaching the Underground: The Production of Alternatives in the Bangladeshi Metal Scene', *Cultural Studies* 29/3 (2014): 1–24.

13. Heather MacLachlan, '(Mis)representation of Burmese Metal Music in the Western Media', *Metal Music Studies* 2/3 (2016): 395–404.

14. Cynthia P. Wong, '"A Dream Return to Tang Dynasty": Masculinity, Male Camaraderie, and Chinese Heavy Metal in the 1990s', in Jeremy Wallach, Harris M. Berger and Paul D. Greene (eds.), *Metal Rules the Globe: Heavy Metal Music Around the World* (Duke University Press, 2011), pp. 63–85. In 2016, Yu Zheng located active metal bands in every Chinese province consulting a combination of English- and Chinese-language social media. See Yu Zheng, *'The Screaming Successor': Exploring the Chinese Metal Scene in Contemporary Chinese Society (1996–2015)*, MA dissertation (Bowling Green State University, 2016).

15. Eugene I. Dairianathan, 'Vedic Metal and the South Indian Community in Singapore: Problems and Prospects of Identity', *Inter-Asia Cultural Studies* 10/4 (2009): 585–608.

16. Marco Ferrarase, 'Southeast Asian Vedic Heavy Metal Rocks China's Extreme Music Scene', *Nikkei Asia* (16 July 2021).

17. Jeremy Wallach, 'Global Rock as Postcolonial Soundtrack', in Allan Moore and Paul Carr (eds.), *The Bloomsbury Handbook of Rock Music Research* (Bloomsbury, 2020), pp. 469–85.

18. Folk metal, which strategically combines local instruments with metal music, originated in twentieth century Europe and has flourished in diverse locales, from Latin America to East Africa. Numerous Asian bands specialise in this subgenre, such as Eternal Madness (Bali, Indonesia), Nine Treasures (Inner Mongolia, China), Black Kirin (Jilin, China) and the aptly named Japanese Folk Metal (Kanagawa, Japan). While they are more hard rock than metal, Mongolia's celebrated Hu Band also fit the folk metal template.

19. Lewis Kennedy, 'Is Kawaii Metal? Exploring Aidoru/Metal Fusion through the Lyrics of Babymetal', in Riitta-Liisa Valijärvi, Charlotte Doesburg and Amanda Digioia (eds.), *Multilingual Metal Music: Sociocultural, Linguistic and Literary Perspectives on Heavy Metal Lyrics* (Emerald, 2020), pp. 201–19.

20. Various Authors, '10 Years of Babymetal: The Story of a Modern Metal Phenomenon', *Metal Hammer* (July 2021), p. 37.

21. Sarah Morelli, '"Who Is a Dancing Hero?" Rap, Hip Hop, and Dance in Korean Popular Culture', in Tony Mitchell (ed.), *Global Noise: Rap and Hip-Hop Outside the USA* (Wesleyan University Press, 2001), pp. 248–58.

22. Lorraine Plourde, 'Babymetal and the Ambivalence of Cuteness', *International Journal of Cultural Studies* 21/3 (2018): 293–307.

23. Teresa Jusino, 'Move Over, Babymetal: Indonesian All-Girl Metal Band Voice of Baceprot Is Here to Rock', *The Mary Sue* (15 August 2017).

24. See Mark LeVine, *Headbanging against Repressive Regimes: Censorship of Heavy Metal in the Middle East, North Africa, Southeast Asia and China* (Freemuse, 2009).

25. Endrizal Ridwan and Bardi Rahmawan, 'The Heavy Metal Genre in an Islamic City of Padang: Struggle and Promotion', *Attarbiyah: Journal of Islamic Culture and Education* 6/1 (2021): 1–14; Saraswati and Beta, 'Knowing Responsibly'.

26. For more on the Indonesian death metal scene, which is likely the largest in the world, see Kieran James and Rex Walsh, 'Bandung Rocks, Cibinong Shakes: Economics and Applied Ethics within the Indonesian Death-Metal Community', *Musicology Australia* 37/1 (2015): 28–46; Dennis W. Lee, '"Negeri Seribu Bangsa": Musical Hybridization in Contemporary Indonesian Death Metal', *Metal Music Studies* 4/3 (2018): 531–48.

23

Distortions in the Last Frontier

Metal Music in Africa

EDWARD BANCHS

Once referred to as metal music's 'last frontier',[1] Africa's entry into the heavy metal dialogue is reflective of this genre's universal appeal. Its arrival in the African continent has come as no surprise to headbangers, who have grown aware of the genre's reach in recent decades through internet chat rooms and social media platforms that have allowed for an international dialogue between fans. But how has metal music been able to successfully establish itself in the African continent?

This chapter will discuss sub-Saharan Africa's entrance into the rock and metal world. Because heavy metal's presence on the nations of North Africa has been detailed elsewhere,[2] I have chosen to focus my work primarily on sub-Saharan Africa. Whether in Madagascar, South Africa, Kenya or the budding scenes in West Africa, African metal stories reflect economic and political challenges that Westerners have likely never encountered. Metal's expansion into Africa has not only been validated by fervent fanbases in at least a dozen countries, but it has also been solidified by the establishment of national scenes producing bands, original recordings, record labels and media that cater to this specific industry, as well as the ever-increasing presence of metal festivals.

Overview of Metal in Africa

The countries where metal has found itself situated are those with strong colonial experiences and where connections to the former colonial country remain by way of imports of goods and culture. Though I would not argue that the colonial presence introduced rock music into Africa, what connects the threads more apparently is the direct link that colonialism has established to Europe for Africans in the form of stronger expatriate communities within and outside of Africa and the linguistic links that stem from this era.

Before metal scenes were born, a culture of rock music established itself quite well in the African continent. Different regions, in fact, had budding scenes that began to form after the Second World War in the lead-up to the continent's independence movements. Notable scenes sprouted in Kenya, South Africa, Somalia, Nigeria, Ghana, Mali, Niger, Zimbabwe and Zambia. Guitar-driven music, whether infusing the revered tones of American blues or the 'fuzzy' psychedelic sounds that enamoured Western audiences in the 1960s and 1970s, was nothing out of place in a continent that has long celebrated chordophones. As Michael E. Veal notes, 'sub-Saharan Africa has in fact been one of the world's richest spheres of guitar playing since World War II',[3] adding the instrument's history in the continent[4] 'has been a prismatic, syncretic dialogue between Western popular music and indigenous musical traditions'.[5]

Whether it was through the exposure to the music that Africans who served in the war brought home, or by way of imports and radio play, American artists such as Bill Haley, Buddy Holly and Elvis Presley were introduced to the continent to the same fanfare they enjoyed at home and in Europe. Perhaps the continent's most recognisable rock and metal scene today belongs to South Africa, whose introduction to rock music came by way of media exposure – with one exception: Black artists were not granted the same exposure as white artists as a result of the nation's policy of segregation known as apartheid. Thus, some of rock's notable artists that preceded the names mentioned above, such as Chuck Berry and Little Richard, did not enjoy the same success in South Africa as their white peers.[6]

Elsewhere in Southern Africa, the nation of Zambia enjoyed a successful psychedelic-inspired rock scene that emerged in the years following the nation's independence and was known as Zamrock. This style of 'fuzzy-rock', also known as *kalindula*, is a 'distinct musical style, (that) typically features a lead funky/fuzzy electric guitar and a rock/rumba beat mixing English and local languages'.[7] Following an economic crisis that hit Zambia during the late 1970s, Zamrock left the collective conscious until a rejuvenated interest sparked by the re-releasing of the seminal albums of the era and a feature documentary in the 2010s reignited this music's memory.[8]

In Kenya, too, during the decades that followed the Second World War, the country was enjoying a rich array of guitar-led music.[9] Further, musicians in the country enjoyed the opportunity to perform and release original music through a budding recording industry that included famed labels His Majesty's Voice and Equator Records. Noted musicians from this era included guitarists Daudi Kabaka and Fundi Konde – often cited as the first electric guitar players in East Africa – and later the fuzzy, psychedelic sounds of Black Savage, one of the country's earliest rock bands.[10] However, the government's grip on political subversions, along with economic difficulties that plagued the country throughout the 1980s and 1990s, greatly affected the aspirations of musicians.

North of Kenya, the nation of Somalia also enjoyed a vibrant music scene between the 1960s and 1980s, highlighted by the vibrant nightlife and venues that featured an array of funk, jazz and rock artists in what was known as the country's 'golden age'.[11] Sadly, the nation's perilous fall into a failed state has provided deleterious and nearly dangerous conditions for a rock or metal scene to exist in the country today. However, with regional shifts toward democratisation, only time will tell if the conditions for a new cultural revolution are in place.

On the opposite side of the continent, the region of West Africa has also seen once vibrant scenes disappear as a result of political and economic matters. Nigeria once housed a rich rock scene that saw acts such as Semi Colon, The Funkees, The Hykkers and Grotto[12] garner national fame. With rock's introduction to Nigeria in the 1960s by way of the film *Rock Around the Clock*,[13] the scene continued through the nation's civil war before fading from collective memory in the late 1970s.[14] Psychedelic rock also influenced acts in Ghana in the years following independence, notably the band Magic Aliens,[15] who drew influence from acts such as Jimi Hendrix and Cream.

Metal's entrance into sub-Saharan Africa in many ways follows the genre's trajectory in the West and was itself a natural evolution out of national rock scenes that were well-cemented in the 1970s. The music spread through an array of international magazines or cassette trading that circulated throughout Africa by way of expatriate and 'pen pal' exchanges, which was a common practice in the 1980s and early 1990s, allowing fans the opportunity to hear the music of Western bands. In the following decades, the internet and file sharing replaced this practice, greatly accelerating the spread of metal into new countries.

With the establishment of scenes throughout various periods of development and political uncertainty in Africa, a diverse swath of acts has been able to navigate through an assortment of troubled waters and have survived dictatorships in Zimbabwe, authoritarian rule in South Africa and Kenya, overwhelming poverty in Madagascar, and a brutal civil war in Angola. Other nations with well-established metal scenes also include those with varied political circumstances, such as the single-party-led Togo, war-torn Mozambique and the African success stories of Botswana and Mauritius.

Within sub-Saharan Africa, metal has placed itself prominently within four regions: Southern Africa, East Africa, West Africa and the Indian Ocean islands. Though the continent's Sahel regions boast of a proud history of guitar-driven music within Tuareg communities, the existing scene in the region sees only a handful of acts. Further, the region of Central Africa, which includes the nations of the Democratic Republic of Congo, Chad, Central African Republic and the Republic of Congo (Brazzaville), have little rock or metal to report as of this writing, likely because of ongoing conflicts in the region, infectious poverty, derelict living conditions and ever-present low levels of health and education. Rock and metal scenes are likelier to be found within a 'metacultural context of modernity'[16] in nations that enjoy better political and economic stability,[17] and support an infrastructure that maintains an exchange of goods between Western countries, as well as steady electricity and internet connection.

But, as I note in the following sections, rock and metal's arrival into the African continent is not uniform throughout as the genres unfolded during different periods in different countries under different circumstances. And many scenes have come to life in spite of the various difficulties that citizens in African nations face, both political and economic. Metal's reach has shown that this music can speak to anyone, regardless of identity, because of its own brutal honesty and the unquestionable fervour that it invokes among its fans.

Southern Africa

The nation of South Africa has established a powerhouse scene that includes international touring acts and is also steadily receiving professional touring acts from the West. As a result of this country's success with rock and metal, regional nations, including Botswana, Mozambique, Namibia and Zimbabwe, were able to benefit from South Africa's musical infrastructure, as acts from the country were able to influence others in regional states through various transmissions, notably radio signals and expatriate communities that tethered to South Africa's economy for employment and educational opportunities. South Africa's metal scene, however, ascended through one of the more tumultuous periods in modern history: apartheid.

A policy of racial segregation that was implemented in 1948, apartheid saw the nation's white minority population control the nation's economy and land ownership. South Africa's non-white majority were not granted the same rights of citizenry as their white counterparts, nor did they benefit from the economy equally, which is still felt today, as the country remains one of the more unequal societies in the world.[18] Authoritarianism affected musicians and artists through an aggressive police state and a censorship board that monitored what music was being consumed and imported into the country through the Publications Act of 1974.[19] Apartheid further ostracised the country politically and economically through the various sanctions by the world's economic powers.

Provided the difficulties of forming a metal scene under an authoritarian rule that monitored the activities of musicians no longer a part of the nation's identity, post-apartheid South Africa has now become home to the largest and most successful metal scene in the African continent, which boasts of acts that have not only released albums internationally but also performed outside of the continent, including Groinchurn, Voice of Destruction and Vulvodynia. South Africa has also benefitted from an international touring economy, allowing local bands the opportunity to engage in the transfer of musical and industry acumen between Western acts.

One nation that has become synonymous with metal music in Africa is Botswana. This sparsely populated, landlocked nation that borders South Africa has benefitted from the access provided by that nation's radio stations and accessible border crossings. It has become home to a metal scene that is the most documented of all of Africa, receiving coverage from media outlets such as *CNN*,[20] *The BBC*,[21] *The Guardian*,[22] *Metal Hammer*,[23] *The Wall Street Journal*,[24] and has been the subject of various documentaries.[25] Much of the attention focused on this scene, though, is on the local fan culture, which is marked by the presence of leather and outrageous – at times gaudy – props that include swinging chains, wooden guns, animal skulls and head-to-toe studded leather dresses. Fans in Botswana are also known to display hyperbolic behaviour, whether through their full-body handshakes or exaggerated sauntering that has been the focal point of the international press.

Much like their southern neighbours, the scene in Botswana traces its origins to the 1970s with the formation of the country's first rock band Nosey Road. By way of this influence, Botswana's first metal act, Metal Orizon, formed in the early 1990s, followed the path set by Nosey Road and performed original music marked by their heavier European influences. In the years since, acts such as STANE, Remuda, Dust N' Fire, Raven In Flesh, Overthrust, Wrust, and Skinflint have helped put Botswana's metal scene on the international map – with the latter three having performed outside of the continent, in both Europe and the United States.

With the international imprint being made by these two nations, nearby nations have also seen metal scenes come into existence to varying degrees, regardless of their political and economic circumstances. Known for its stability, Namibia's scene has kept a low profile in relation to its neighbours. Highlighted by two seminal acts, subMission and Arcana XXII, as well as rockers Penilane, the country has hosted various touring acts from within and outside of the continent, even staging its own metal festival in the national capital, the Windhoek Metal Festival, which attracted bands from neighbouring countries and the United States.

The nations of Zimbabwe, Angola and Mozambique highlight metal music's tenacity as the preferred music for those reaching for an art form that best articulates their lived experiences through tumultuous circumstances, notably the latter two, whose scenes have come into being on the heels of devastating civil wars. Though the two lusophone nations are on opposite sides of the continent, both experienced similarities between their conflicts, leaving an emotionally scarred generation to navigate a new identity. Angola's civil war ended after 27 years in 2002, leaving over half a million dead, according to the United Nations.[26] It was from these ashes of devastation that a generation searching for their own hope gravitated toward heavy metal as part of their efforts to confront their new post-war surroundings, including the pummelling metalcore of Before Crush and the thrash-tainted sounds of Dor Fantasma. The country's first-ever metal festival was documented in the film *Death Metal Angola*.[27]

Mozambique's nascent metal generation also grew up sheltering from the sounds of gunfire and bombs and has adopted the thunderous sounds of metal to best reflect the process of healing. The civil war that ravaged the country for fifteen years officially ended in 1992, having taken nearly one million lives,[28] yet sporadic conflict did not see the warring factions reaching peace until 2019.[29] Under these circumstances, which are documented in the film *Terra Pesada: An Unexpected Documentary*,[30] bands such as the extreme Morghelarisy, groove-influenced Mikaya and the metalcore act Damning Cloudiness have performed and recorded original music, with some acts garnering exposure in neighbouring South Africa.

Formed in 2012, the Afro-groove of Zimbabwe's Dividing The Element has ignited this country's small metal scene. What sets them apart from other regional acts is their alacrity in performing in the dominant local language Shona,[31] an indication to metal fans that they are a band riding their Western influences while paying respect to their nation's musical history. Dividing The Element's existence in a country that has suffered through one of the more nefarious leaderships in the twentieth century, marked by record-setting inflation, disastrous poverty, nefarious land grabs and a well-documented intolerance for political dissent, has proven a remarkable resilience for a band existing in a country whose musicians are better known for their lives in exile than in their home.

Metal's place in Southern Africa shows that through resilience and determination, metal can reach fans longing for a voice that pushes down restrictive barriers because 'heavy metal can promote values in opposition to dominant power structures and damaging hegemonies such as oppression, restricting freedoms of expression, racism and sexism and thus also addresses political issues',[32] that would need to be addressed for the sake of building not only a scene but also a nation.

East Africa

Much like their counterparts in South Africa, Kenyan metal fans have similarly seen their scene develop while confronting authoritarianism and state-sanctioned censorship. For Kenyans, the 2002 election, the first to be held without Daniel arap Moi, the strong-armed president who had led Kenya since 1978, set the country free of its authoritarian leadership. The scene, primarily centred in the capital city, Nairobi, had previously stumbled forward with a small number of acts, including Rock of Ages and the punk acts Class Suicide, Impish and Bloodshed, who were able to access rock and metal through motion picture soundtracks, expatriate connections and local black-market record shops. Though these acts, mainly formed at universities, were performing do-it-yourself (DIY) styled shows, the overreaching police and military were not far behind threatening scene participants and their families. Once Moi's party (KANU) was voted out, economic and democratic liberalisation brought forward more fans, as acts were now able to perform openly without fear.

Since multi-party elections have taken hold, Kenya's metal scene has been able to make a global imprint with acts such as Last Year's Tragedy and Duma garnering international press[33] and even an annual metal festival, the Nairobi Metal Festival.[34] However, performers in the scene today are not without their difficulties. Subsequent elections have seen the country spiral into ethnically motivated violence following contested results, having personally affected the identity of local metal fans who have embraced this identity as one without the onus of the ethnic cleavages that remain a vestige of the country's colonial legacy.

The Kenyan scene's imprint and continued success is necessary for regional nations to step up, including neighbouring Uganda, whose rock scene came to light during the late 2000s and early 2010s, and includes the

'African doom' duo of Vale of Amonition and alternative-metal rockers Phyv5. Elsewhere, atmospheric black metal act Nishaiar and 'Ethio rock' act Jano have stepped forward as the only two acts performing electric guitar-driven music in Ethiopia. Though this represents only a handful of acts in the region outside of Kenya, it is clear that the presence of acts, albeit in modicum in the region, signals a shift in the right direction for electric guitar music to once again return to prominence.

Indian Ocean Islands and West Africa

Another country in Africa that attributes the formation of its rock and metal scene to a political transition is Madagascar. The island nation that is home to over 25 million – primarily descendants of Austronesians and Black Africans – has since the early 1990s embraced aspects of Western life, including the public enjoyment of rock and metal, which had already found a small audience in the country by way of migrant workers and expatriates.

This reach westward came via the government's termination of a national policy of seclusion that was necessary for Madagascar to be able to 'obtain credit from the World Bank and the International Monetary Fund' after the country found itself bankrupt during its Second Republic.[35] These expansions allowed for rock and metal to reach an even larger audience and for the prospective musicians to access instruments and other Western goods previously unavailable to them. Early bands in the country include Apost, Green and Kazar. The sound of these acts was in line with their Western influences yet is distinguished by the use of the Malagasy language in place of English and French, the former being rock and metal's primary language, and the latter being the nation's colonial language.

Since its inception, the rock and metal scene in Madagascar has grown to be one of the largest in any African country in terms of the number of acts, based on my personal observations, with a very diverse metal scene that features a wide array of styles and sees the nation's most popular acts enjoying wide levels of success nationally. This is the only scene in the entirety of Africa where hard rock acts are not only performing on national television but also in front of stadium-sized crowds. Further, what is remarkable about this particular scene is that musicians in Madagascar have carved out this scene in one of the poorest nations in the entire world. The World Bank estimates that 75 per cent of the population lives below the poverty line, and only 13 per cent of the population has access to steady electricity.[36] Internet service remains feeble, the equipment necessary to perform metal is financially out of reach for many, as evidenced by the fact that musicians here routinely share equipment, and political strife has continued to plague the country in the early decades of the twenty-first century.[37] Unlike their counterparts on the African mainland, the Malagasy metal scene lacks an international presence; bands are not receiving international press like others in Africa, and acts from the country are seldom afforded the opportunity to embark on performances outside of their island, nor are they presented with the fortunes of being able to release music by way of international labels.

What has likely contributed to the lack of international attention toward the scene is the use of the Malagasy language, which is prominent among acts in the country. Madagascar's metal scene is the only example of an African nation where metal bands perform primarily in their national language. Yet this metal scene's embrace of their cultural roots has also separated metal bands here from their African contemporaries. Utilising a pre-Francophone style of speech known as the *hainteny,* an ornamented form of speech ladened with metaphors gifted from their ancestors[38] alongside traditional time signatures, acts here have distinguished themselves in ways that place their culture and history at the forefront of what they do.

Elsewhere in the Indian Ocean islands, near Madagascar, sit Reunion Island and Mauritius. Both islands have benefitted from a strong economic and modern infrastructure and have continually maintained a close relationship with the European continent, notably Reunion Island, whose status as a French overseas territory benefits its populations with the privileges of French citizenship. Both islands' scenes exist with similar access to goods and Western musical resources and have been closely linked since their inception in the late 1950s.[39]

The region of West Africa is among the continent's quietest with regard to rock and metal. As alluded to earlier, the nations of Nigeria and Ghana at one time enjoyed vibrant rock scenes and are both slowly seeing a resurgence, with Ghana's Dark Suburb and Nigeria's The Isomers stepping forward. Regionally, nearby Niger and Mali are known for their 'African rock' scenes that are dominated by internationally known artists such as Mali-based Tinariwen, Nigerian bands Group Bombino and Group Inerane, and the Western Saharan band Group Doueh. While these particular acts owe more to the 'rawness of garage rock'[40] than their predecessors of the 1950s and 1960s, they have also welcomed traditional infusions into their music.

The lone heavy metal band in the nation of Togo, Arka'n Asrafokor, also converges local musical proclivities of the members' native Ewe sounds by including a traditionally-trained musician in their band, blending this aspect effortlessly alongside their Western influences into a hybrid sound best described by the band's vocalist as 'metal in our own language'.[41] Though rarely performed, a few other bands throughout the continent have begun to incorporate local sounds into their brand of rock and metal, including the previously mentioned act Dividing The Element from Zimbabwe, who lean on Shona influences for their sound, and Botswana's Wrust, who have incorporated a few aspects of Setswana clapping, call and response and 6/8 time signature with their brutally aggressive sound. What these infusions have allowed is for Africans to share their locales, their origin stories and their lived experiences through an already familiar style while paying homage to the sounds that are seeped into their consciousness. This approach serves to enhance the listenership of local fans who may otherwise be put off by the genre's abrasiveness.

Conclusion

Although various African metal scenes have been recognised through a variety of press outlets and publications in recent years, metal in Africa has become a curiosity because it is the last place on the planet that metal fans, musicians and academics alike would have expected the genre to blossom. Yet, African metal's existence should not be treated differently.

African metal stories speak of a genre that is empowering performers and fans alike. Metal has been able to elevate this platform because of the honesty this music provides, one that Western acts have also embraced by highlighting social and political issues in challenging the status quo through metal music. As Niall Scott states, '[h]eavy metal, both its music and culture, are in a position to resist the popular where the popular in music is an infantilized submission to sameness'.[42] It is precisely for this reason that metal's arrival in the continent has been embraced by a generation eager to perform a soundtrack that reflects their lives.

However, for African metal acts, an overwhelming challenge remains: validation from their Western peers. How could their efforts be compromised by way of their geographic origins? And how would 'othering' affect the manner in which their work and contributions could be valued with the same dignity and respect that Western contributions are held? Only time will tell. It is not up to Africans to change their image, their sound or their location in order to succeed. It is up to the Global North to open their ears to an already familiar sound from an otherwise unfamiliar continent for the sake of truly embracing the ultimate panacea of a collective global metal scene that many fans have long proclaimed exists, yet with little inclination to invite members of the Global South to the table. Heavy metal's presence in Africa serves to embolden fans and empower performers in a manner that could ultimately provide the necessary validation from Westerners and send a signal that Africa is now this genre's ultimate frontier.

Notes

1. Eroll Barnett, 'Meeting up with Botswana's "Metal Heads"', *CNN* (2 July 2012). www.cnn.com/videos/international/2012/07/02/inside-africa-botswana-metal-music-a.cnn (accessed 27 August 2020).
2. Orlando Crowcroft, *Rock in a Hard Place: Music and Mayhem in the Middle East* (Zed Books, 2017). See also Mark LeVine, *Heavy Metal Islam: Rock, Resistance, and the Struggle for the Soul of Islam* (Three Rivers Press, 2008).
3. Michael E. Veal, 'Dry Spell Blues: Sublime Frequencies across the West African Sahel', in Michael E. Veal and E. Tammy Kim (eds.), *Punk Ethnographies: Artists & Scholars Listen to Sublime Frequencies* (Wesleyan University Press, 2016), pp. 210–34.
4. Veal states, 'It is generally accepted that the guitar was introduced to Africa by the Portuguese in the fourteenth century', *Ibid.*, p. 214.
5. *Ibid.*
6. Charles Hamm, 'Rock "n" Roll in a Very Strange Society', *Popular Music* 5 (1985): 159–74.
7. Henning Goranson Sandgerg, 'Why Zamrock is Back in Play', *The Guardian* (22 July 2013). www.theguardian.com/world/2013/jul/22/zamrock-zambia-music-rerelease (accessed 3 March 2021).
8. See Gio Arlotta, *We Intend to Cause Havoc* (Pantheon Pictures, 2019).
9. John Low, 'A History of Kenyan Guitar Music: 1945–1980', *African Music* 6/2 (1982): 17–36.
10. Thomas Gesthuizen, 'Here's Some 1970s Psychedelic Rock from Kenya', *OkayAfrica* (23 May 2018). www.okayafrica.com/kenya-music-psychedelic-rock-black-savage (accessed 1 March 2021).
11. BBC Africa, 'Somalia's Lost Tapes Revive Musical Memories' (26 August 2017). www.bbc.com/news/world-africa-40966656 (accessed 2 March 2021).
12. The Guardian, 'Lighting Up Lagos: The Stars of 1970s Nigerian Rock Music – In Pictures' (6 June 2016). www.theguardian.com/artanddesign/gallery/2016/jun/06/1970s-nigerian-rock-music-stars-wake-up-you (accessed 2 March 2021).

13. Fred Sears, *Rock Around the Clock* (Columbia Pictures, 1956).

14. Michel Martin, '"Wake Up You!" Explores the Transitional, Post-war Rock "n" Roll of Nigeria', *NPR: All Things Considered* (24 April 2016). www.npr.org /2016/04/24/475138787/wake-up-you-explores-the-transitional-post-war-rock-n-roll-of-nigeria (accessed 3 March 2021).

15. John Collins, 'Afro-Rock', in David Horn and John Shepherd (eds.), *Bloomsbury Encyclopedia of Popular Music of the World*, Vol. 12, Genres: Sub-Saharan Africa (Bloomsbury, 2019), pp. 30–4.

16. Jeremy Wallach and Alexandra Levine, 'I Want You to Support Local Metal: A Theory of Metal Scene Formulation', *Popular Music History* 6/1–2 (2011): 116–34.

17. Donald Maguire, 'Determinants of the Number of Heavy Metal Musicians per Capita', *Metal Music Studies* 7 (Supplement, 2021): 1–41; Cameron DeHart, 'Metal by Numbers: Revisiting the Uneven Distribution of Heavy Metal Music', *Metal Music Studies* 4/3 (2018): 559–71; Richard Florida, 'How Metal Tracks the Wealth of Nations', *CityLab* (26 May 2014). www.bloomberg.com /news/articles/2014-05-26/how-heavy-metal-tracks-the-wealth-of-nations (accessed 15 March 2021).

18. Aryn Baker, 'What South Africa Can Teach Us as Worldwide Inequality Grows', *Time* (2 May 2019). https://time.com/longform/south-africa-unequal-country (accessed 15 March 2021).

19. Michael Drewett, 'Music in the Struggle to End Apartheid: South Africa', in Martin Cloonan and Reebee Garafolo (eds.), *Policing Pop* (Temple University Press, 2003), pp. 153–65; Ole Reitov, 'Encounters with a South African Censor: Confrontation and Reconciliation', in Maria Korpe (ed.), *Shoot the Singer! Music Censorship Today* (Zed Books, 2004), pp. 82–93.

20. Benazir Wehelie, 'Heavy Metal Finds a Home in Botswana', *CNN* (20 August 2016). www.cnn.com/style/article/cnnphotos-heavy-metal-botswana/index .html (accessed 7 December 2020).

21. BBC, 'In Pictures: Renegades – The Heavy Metal Sub-Culture of Botswana' (20 February 2013). www.bbc.com/news/in-pictures-21509571 (accessed 27 August 2020); Ade Adepitan, 'Where Traditional African Culture and Heavy Metal Collide', *BBC* (5 February 2016). www.bbc.com/travel/story/ 20151218-where-traditional-african-culture-and-heavy-metal-collide (accessed 27 August 2020).

22. Edward Banchs, 'Desert Sounds – Kalahari Metalheads Pursue a Dream', *The Guardian* (10 February 2013). www.theguardian.com/world/2013/feb/10/ kalahari-metalheads (accessed 27 August 2020); Paul Shiakallis, 'The Leather-Clad Rock Queens of Botswana – In Pictures', *The Guardian* (25 December 2015). www.theguardian.com/world/gallery/2015/dec/25/the-leather-clad-rock-queens-of-botswana-in-pictures (accessed 27 August 2020).

23. Kim Kelly, 'The Queens of Botswana', *Metal Hammer* 306 (2018): 70–2.

24. Patrick McGroarty, 'Shout of Africa: Heavy Metal Maniacs Swarm the Kalahari – Botswana is Home to a Raucous Festival, Starring Overthrust and a Lot of Leather', *Wall Street Journal* (8 June 2016): A-1.

25. Raffael Mosca, *March of the Gods: Botswana Metalheads* (Self-Released, 2014); Samuli Pyykkönen, *Freedom in the Dark: A Roadtrip to Trans-Kalahari Rock 'n' Roll* (Self-Released, 2018); Sarah Vianney, *Queens of Botswana* (1091 Media, 2019).

26. UNHRC, 'Angola: Current Political and Human Rights Conditions in Angola', *Refworld* (4 December 2020). www.refworld.org/docid/3dedf3204.html (accessed 27 January 2021).

27. Jeremy Xido, *Death Metal Angola* (Vladar, 2012).

28. Milton Leitenberg, 'Deaths in Wars and Conflicts in the 20th Century', Occasional Paper #29, 3rd ed. (Cornell University Peace Studies Program, 2006), pp. 1–83.

29. VOA, 'Mozambique President, Opposition Leader Sign Peace Agreement', *VOA Africa* (1 August 2019). www.voanews.com/africa/mozambique-president-opposition-leader-sign-peace-agreement (accessed 28 January 2021).

30. Leslie Bornstein, *Terra Pesada: An Unexpected Documentary* (Last Grasp Productions, 2020).

31. Edward Banchs, 'Mbira Goes Metal: Zimbabwe's Nascent Rock Scene', *Afropop* (21 June 2018). https://afropop.org/articles/mbira-goes-metal-zimbabwes-nascent-rock-scene (accessed 27 January 2021).

32. Niall Scott, 'Heavy Metal as Resistance', in Brenda Gardenour Walters, Gabby Riches, Dave Snell and Bryan Bardine (eds.), *Heavy Metal Studies and Popular Culture* (Palgrave Macmillan, 2016), pp. 19–35.

33. Thomas O'Boyles, 'Kenyan Noise Kings Duma Make Industrial Grindcore Like You've Never Heard Before', *Metal Hammer* (23 October 2020). www.loudersound.com/features/kenyan-noise-kings-duma-make-industrial-grindcore-like-youve-never-heard-it-before (accessed 5 March 2021).

34. Edward Banchs, 'Nairobi Metal Fest: Inside Kenya's Flourishing Metal Scene', *Metal Hammer* (30 October 2019). www.loudersound.com/features/nairobi-metal-festival-inside-kenyas-flourishing-metal-scene (accessed 5 March 2021).

35. Markus Verne, 'Heavy Metal in Madagascar (Metaly Gasy)', in David Horn and John Sheperd (eds.), *Bloomsbury Encyclopedia of Popular Music of the World*, Vol. 12, Genres: Sub-Saharan Africa (Bloomsbury, 2019), pp. 190–4.

36. World Bank, 'The World Bank in Madagascar' (31 July 2020). www.worldbank.org/en/country/madagascar/overview (accessed 1 February 2021).

37. Barry Bearak, 'Mayor Declares a Coup in Madagascar', *The New York Times* (31 January 2009). www.nytimes.com/2009/02/01/world/africa/01madagascar.html (accessed 1 February 2021).

38. Elinor O. Keenan, 'A Sliding Sense of Obligatoriness: The Poly-Structure of Malagasy Oratory', *Language in Society* 2/2 (1973): 225–43.
39. Thomas Arcens and Vincent Pion, *Bourbon Rock: Une Autre Histoire de la Musique a La Réunion* (le corridor bleu, 2013).
40. Veal, 'Dry Spell Blues', pp. 222–3.
41. Nils Bourdin, 'Arka'n: "Metal is African"', *Pan-African Music* (5 February 2020). https://pan-african-music.com/en/arkan-metal-is-african (accessed 6 February 2021).
42. Scott, 'Heavy Metal', p. 33.

24

What Has Latin American Metal Music Ever Done for Us?

A Call for an Ethics of Affront in Metal Music

NELSON VARAS-DÍAZ AND DANIEL NEVÁREZ ARAÚJO

Maybe we should begin our contribution to this book with a disclaimer. A statement on what this brief chapter aims to be, and more importantly, what it is not. It is not our intent to portray an all-encompassing picture of Latin American metal for the reader. That endeavour is too extensive to be contemplated here and merits a more extensive and comprehensive reflection that does justice to the music created in the region. For most readers, Latin America will seem, from the outside, like a monolithic region. Far from this conceptualisation, the countries, peoples and communities that make up Latin America are greatly varied and diverse, as manifested in their languages, traditions, histories and geographies. Latin America is an incarnation of plurality, albeit sometimes a systematically silenced one. We will not foster this silence with the plethora of metal scenes in the region, which are diverse and marked by varied socio-political experiences. Consequently, this chapter does not aspire to offer a summary of metal in Latin America, and we invite readers to look to the emerging research on the region for such a purpose. Instead, what we aim to do in this chapter is examine one of the endeavours Latin American music has predominantly engaged in, namely decoloniality, and use this as a bedrock to examine what we consider to be a pertinent question: What has Latin American metal ever done for the international metal scene? We believe that the answer to this question lies at the juncture of and brings forth a call for ethics in metal music, as we aim to succinctly explain throughout this chapter.

As most metal music researchers will attest, sometimes the answer to our research questions manifests unexpectedly. In a casual conversation with a fan or a musician, one comment can open up an unanticipated area of reflection. We would like to use one example to highlight this argument. While interviewing Pablo Trangone, singer for the Argentinian metal band Arraigo, our conversation on metal music veered drastically towards the topic of Latin America proper. Pablo was less interested in talking about the sounds of metal music in his country and more concerned with what metal music was doing, or should be doing, to address the plights of local people in the wider Latin American region. He posed poignant questions: 'what is metal if not that scream that makes visible all the people that will be struck down in Latin America during the coming years? What is metal, if it's not that? If it's not that … then it's nothing'. Pablo's reflection during our conversation made two things clearly palpable. First, that he saw the plight faced by local communities from a regional perspective. He was not concerned solely with Argentinian agony but rather with Latin American suffering. This suffering was currently manifested as exploitative neo-liberalism, but this just happened to be the most recent expression of a deeper experience defined by a history of colonialism. Second, that Pablo interpreted metal music as an artistic endeavour with an underlying responsibility towards its context; in this case, that meant an oppressive context. In his opinion, music demanded an agenda marked by visibility. If it did not assume this agenda, then it would be relegated to futility. This sentiment has been echoed by metal musicians in every Latin American country we have engaged with in our ethnographic work. Pablo was not alone in his call for a socially committed metal music that understood the historical plights of individuals and communities under colonialism and its ongoing effects throughout Latin America. He was, even if inadvertently, pointing to the decolonial role of metal music in Latin America.

Decolonial Metal Music

In light of many encounters like the one with Pablo, we have argued that metal music in Latin America has engaged in critical reflections pertaining to the colonial history of the region.[1] It explicitly recognises that the colonial process is not over, and that its consequences remain an ongoing concern, representing a process that Peruvian sociologist Aníbal Quijano has termed *coloniality*.[2] We have posited that metal confronts coloniality through *extreme decolonial dialogues*.[3] We define these as 'invitations, ones particularly interested in promoting transformation, made through metal music to engage in critical reflections about oppressive practices faced by Latin American communities in light of coloniality'. We label these experiences *dialogues* in order to highlight the interaction between those who are informed about coloniality and those who have yet to, or sometimes refuse to, comprehend it. These dialogues are an exchange of information between equals, as proposed by Paulo Freire,[4] posited in opposition to a didactic top-down approach where only one part of the dyad possesses correct information. They are decidedly *decolonial* precisely because 'metal bands engage in dialogues that are concerned with the historical process of oppression faced by the region, stemming from 15th-century colonialism and its lingering effects into the present day'. Finally, these dialogues are *extreme* primarily because they are perceived as threatening to 'those unfamiliar to metal aesthetics and sounds' and because they address issues related to 'death, violence, and oppression', which tend to 'worry unfamiliar listeners in the region; this includes politicians and the media'. They address issues of extremity (for example, violence, murder, political repression) that some people in the region would rather soon forget. These decolonial reflections in metal music have also found their relevance in metal studies throughout the Global South.[5]

As we continue to unpack the utility of *extreme decolonial dialogues* to better understand what metal does throughout Latin America, we wish to take this opportunity to reflect on the ethical dimensions of these dialogues. To delve into these dimensions, we will focus here on a certain quality or aura of defiance and confrontation, which we have found manifested in the ethics performed by many practitioners embedded in the region; as such, we have come to call these a *metal ethics of affront*.

A Metal Ethics of Affront

The debate over the ethical and unethical use of music, its sounds, lyrical messages and accompanying imagery has always cast a long shadow over metal music. We would be repetitive in discussing the censorship of the music espoused by the Parents Music Resource Center (PMRC) in the United States during the 1980s. Still, it is important to note that these perceptions are very much still present in some places of the world as we write this chapter. The legal battle between Behemoth's singer, Nergal, and the Polish government over accusations of blasphemy would be just one example of current concerns over the unethical dimensions of metal music.[6] Still, as scholars, we are aware that the call for an examination of the unethical uses of music has not always been based on moral panics, but rather on very fair concerns over the ways music can be utilised to oppress people and trample on their well-being. The work of Steve Goodman highlights, for example, the use of music during warfare.[7] The same could be said of Bruce Johnson and Martin Cloonan's reflection on the use of music as part of State violence.[8] These contributions serve today as important invitations to continuously reflect on the ethical dimensions of music. But how useful are ethical conceptualisations of music in our understanding of metal in Latin America and its decolonial endeavour?

This question has received little attention in metal scholarship, and we understand the field is prime to finally engage it.

An examination of two important publications on music and ethics is useful to understand how an ethical approach stemming from metal music in Latin America would benefit from a new set of conceptual tools. The first is Kathleen Marie Higgin's book on music and ethics, entitled *The Music of Our Lives*.[9] In it, she offers an important and comprehensive analysis of the ways music can impact our lives in an ethical manner. Still, throughout her work, there is an almost homeostatic view of ethics and music. By this, we mean that music is seen as an alleviator of conflict. For example, she proposes that listening to music 'gives us a very immediate sense of enjoyably sharing our world with others'.[10] This idea is driven home by an idealised view of the world when she posits that music 'involves a sense of sharing life with others'.[11] These positions reflect not only a particular view of the relation between music and ethics but of the world itself, one where the world and life itself are enjoyably shared with others. This conceptualisation might stem from her overall view of ethics as a way of 'living at ease with one's environment' and how music 'develops our ability to approach others in a nondefensive, noncompetitive manner'.[12] Although these views on ethics, music and the sharing of life with others might seem useful for some readers, we posit that they are particularly idealistic. They seem to present a homeostatic view of the world where balanced and just interactions amongst people are achieved. They leave little room to understand how music, used in an ethical manner, has little to do with homeostasis, and is more closely linked to challenging historical patterns of oppression through confrontation. In a homeostatic social scenario, the need for social change seems like a chimaera.

Subsequent reflections on music and ethics have pushed back, to an extent, on these homeostatic views. For example, in their book entitled *Music and Ethics*, Marcel Cobussen and Nannette Nielsen explore music as an artform to encounter the other; those who are different from oneself and therefore experience the world in a dissimilar manner.[13] Although they cement their reflection on multiple views on ethics, it seems particularly significant to us that they reference Zygmunt Bauman's conceptualisation of ethics as 'being *for* the other' in light of the oppressions presented by the European modern project on particular populations.[14] Although this is an important step away from the more homeostatic view on music and ethics outlined earlier, we still feel it is too ambiguous to understand the ethical dimensions of metal music in Latin America. The other is presented as an indistinct figure, devoid of a specific context, political geography, particular history and precise oppressive experiences. For example, in their reflection on the ethical role of music, the colonial experience is not mentioned outright. It remains a moot point.

We would like to posit that metal music in Latin America, particularly that which has a decolonial tone, dominant or inflexion, provides its listeners with a radically different ethical experience; one that is less concerned with fostering homeostatic relations and prefers to explore the tensions generated by social oppression. In essence, metal in Latin America posits an ethics that is strengthened by its specificity regarding the oppressive experiences people live through and the tensions generated in the encounters between the oppressors and the oppressed. The reflections generated by this ethical approach have little to do with enjoyably sharing life with those who oppress us or living at ease with the effects of coloniality. Instead, what we see is an ethics of affront. An ethics that recognises everyday life as a constant struggle for liberation from oppression and uses the arts, in this case metal music, to practically and symbolically confront this positionality via sounds, images and practices that disrupt the illusions of social homeostasis by generating emotional discomfort. We wish to identify three of its guiding principles while simultaneously recognising that there could be, and should be, many more.

Principle 1: Acknowledging the humanity of those oppressed by coloniality: One of the main drivers of coloniality has been the devaluation of indigenous people, their experiences and knowledge-producing practices through systematic racism, violence and epistemicide. Indigenous people in the Americas have suffered a great burden in this process, which has aimed to deprive them of the very basic notion of humanity. The colonial experience of the fifteenth century, with its practices and laws, deprived the members of these communities of their right to be considered human, or of even being seen as having a soul. Nelson Maldonado-Torres has worked extensively on this form of colonial oppression and has labelled this mechanism as 'the coloniality of being'.[15] Metal music in Latin America has challenged this type of colonisation by placing the indigenous peoples of the region, and more importantly, their plights, at the forefront of their musical endeavour.[16]

Some important examples include Peruvian band Kranium's song 'El Obraje' (1999), which describes the exploitation of indigenous people through forced servitude. More importantly, metal songs have been able to advocate for the humanity of indigenous people by describing them as powerful, knowledgeable and, equally important, visible. Other examples include Puya's (Puerto Rico) depiction of *taíno* ceremonial practices in the song 'Areyto' on *Areyto* (2019) Werken's (Argentina) conceptualisation of Indian blood as a source of power (Sangre India) on *Plegaria Al Sur* (2010),

Yanacona's (Argentina) celebration of indigenous warriors and leaders (Tupac Amaru) on *Por La Sangre Derramada* (1999), and Ch'aska's (Peru) telling of indigenous war victories. Equally important is metal music's celebration of indigenous worldviews and ideas, as exemplified by the band Egregor (Chile) in their album *Pachakuti* (2020); it represents a term used to depict Inca legends and conceptualisations of time. These are but some examples of the way decolonial metal music recognises the humanity in others impacted by coloniality.

This ethical positioning through metal music could be best understood by relying on the conceptualisation of ethics that stems from the region itself and recognising the ongoing implications of its colonial experience. The work by Argentinian philosopher Enrique Dussel on ethics and the philosophy of liberation seems to us like the perfect example.[17] After specifically examining the oppressive practices embedded in the colonial process in the Americas, Dussel calls for a philosophy of liberation that fosters an 'ethical conscience' as a strategy to challenge coloniality. This is the 'capacity one has to listen to the other's voice' in order to understand the injustices they face. Notice how this call is not universalist in nature but rather specific to the region's experiences. Decolonial metal music in Latin America echoes this call via its *extreme decolonial dialogues* by listening to the voices of those most affected by coloniality, placing them front and centre, and amplifying not just their experiences of oppression but, perhaps more importantly, their stories of emancipation.

Principle 2: Acknowledging the reality of the socio-political context: When Latin America is viewed by people from a Global North perspective – that is, from the geographies and worldviews that initiated fifteenth-century colonialism and foster coloniality today – some of the events that have taken place in our socio-political contexts might seem too extraordinary to be true. Dictatorships, the systematic disappearance of political activists, the extermination of indigenous populations, and government-sponsored murder of local communities are just some of the oppressive practices that have plagued the region. Some of them are so extraordinary, so distant from the comforts of the Global North, that they might seem like exaggerations, as mere artefacts of our imagination. But they are very real and, most concerning, many are ongoing.

Decolonial metal music in Latin America has aimed to make those events, and the socio-political contexts that foster them, visible to the rest of the world. An examination of the lyrical content of some metal bands will evidence discussions on colonisation and its social implications: Aggressive's (Colombia) 'Predator's Mind'; A.N.I.M.A.L.'s (Argentina)

'Gritemos Para No Olvidar'; Dremis Derinfet's (Colombia) 'Cruz, Corona y Guerra'; Huinca's (Chile) 'América Letrina'; Hermética's (Argentina) 'La Revancha de América'; Ratos de Porão's (Brazil) 'Amazônia Nunca Mais'. Other bands have focused on very specific local events, including nineteenth- and twentieth-century regional wars and conflicts: Custom71's (Argentina) 'Alas de Gloria'; Tren Loco's (Argentina) 'Acorazado Belgrano'; Abäk's (Costa Rica) 'Santa Rosa'; Gillman's (Venezuela) 'La Batalla de Carabobo'. Perhaps the crudest and most lyrically compelling songs are those that address local massacres: Azeroth's (Argentina) 'Campaña del Desierto'; Demolición's (Ecuador) 'Noviembre Negro'. Taken together, these are all efforts from metal bands to validate their local histories, even when they might seem all too incredible to be believed by outsiders.[18]

We understand that decolonial metal music echoes practices found in regional literature that aim to validate these histories as real. For example, Cuban writer Alejo Carpentier developed the notion of *lo real maravilloso* (the awe-inspiring real) as a way to describe the West's inability to comprehend the elusive quality of life as lived in Latin America.[19] He aimed to reflect the idea that, to the outside world, certain events associated with the region might seem unbelievable. We believe his term, when juxtaposed with what metal music in the region does, helps us understand the relationship between Latin America and the rest of the world. It serves to stress that, for Latin Americans, the above-mentioned events are part of our history and reality. We are witnesses to them today. Therefore, we understand that metal music engages in an ethics of affront when echoing *lo real maravilloso* to account for its context against those who would deny them. What is being described in these songs is all too real, regardless of how unbelievable it may seem to others.

We would be remiss if we limited this ethical acknowledgement of the Latin American context to an examination of song lyrics. It is also intimately related to the local sounds integrated into the metal music created in the region. Thus, the incorporation of instruments like the *quena, zampoñas, batá* and the *charango* are frequently described by musicians as ways of transmitting socio-political messages to listeners in the Global North. For example, the *batá* as a rhythmic instrument has been used in Cuban metal as a way to clearly link the genre to Afro-Caribbean roots.[20] The *quenas* and *zampoñas* are local wind instruments integrated into metal to transmit emotions, specifically melancholy, over the oppressions experienced in the Andean region.[21] These sounds, alien to metal music in the Global North, serve this ethical principle by telling its listeners something about the socio-political context in which they were generated. This is vitally important since, as Cobussen and Nielsen have argued, the ethical dimension of music goes beyond the words being sung, and includes the 'sounds penetrating the body, cutting across the duality of physical and emotional processes'.[22]

<u>Principle 3: Fostering activist action as a task for metal music</u>: A third principle that we wish to stress in describing the ethics of affront posed by decolonial metal music in Latin America is activist action. That is, the use of metal music and culture to call for engagement in social activism against the varied manifestations of coloniality in the region. This call echoes invitations from scholars and artists to engage in varied forms of 'artivism', or the use of the arts as social protest, which has been called for in the Latin American context.[23] This has happened through various local bands' lyrical content, support for other activist communities and via direct participation in protests.

The lyrical content of metal music in Latin America has demonstrated support for social justice movements throughout its history. Two significant examples can be seen in Mexican and Venezuelan metal music. In Mexico, the band Leprosy dedicated their 1998 album *Llora Chiapas* to the Zapatista movement in open support of the indigenous people of the region. The Venezuelan band Gillman addressed the 1989 protest, known as *El Caracazo*, against the neoliberal practices of the Carlos Andrés Pérez government on *El Regreso Del Guerrero* (1990). These are examples of the most prominent ways in which metal music engages in social protest through critical reflections about the manifestations of coloniality in their settings.

Other bands have gone from singing about activist groups or events to accompanying local communities in their plights. Such is the case of the Ecuadorian band Curare, who have worked alongside communities affected by mining in the Imbabura region. They are known for being in constant collaboration with these communities and supporting them by playing music in their educational events as a way to foster the building of knowledge related to environmental exploitation. This role of support to the ongoing battles faced by communities echoes the call made by Boaventura de Sousa Santos to use the arts as a way to make visible the plights of groups impacted by coloniality and how they generate knowledge through these experiences.[24] In this manner, bands like Curare become part of what he has termed a sociology of emergences that aims to make visible the abyssal line dividing the world between the oppressors and the oppressed, stress the value of the knowledge produced by those affected, and highlight how they resist. Bands like Curare make that line visible, albeit sonically.

Finally, it must be stressed that Latin American metal music's call for engagement in social activism has not been limited to lyrical content or signs of support; it has called for the taking of the streets. As we write this chapter, Colombia has erupted in protests against tributary reforms that echo the most sinister agenda of neoliberalism. The government has deployed the police and armed forces to face the protestors, and as so many times in the region, violence and death have been the outcome. There have been a plethora of Colombian metal bands posting messages of support on social media and, more significantly for our reflection on ethics, taken to the streets. One important example is the band Corpus Calvary from Bogotá, who have joined protesters in marches and public demonstrations. They posted a video on their Facebook wall sending out a message in support of the national strike. It showed masked members of the band on the streets while tires burned behind them and black smoke filled the street. 'Long live the resistance', one of the members stated in the short video.

Discussion and Conclusion

Metal fans in the Global North, particularly those who saw themselves as part of the international metal scene during the 1980s, will probably recognise, even if unconsciously, some of our conceptual positionings in this short chapter. They will surely remember that moment when they held in their hands their first Sepultura tape. There was a sense of foreignness to it. This was a band from Brazil, a place where they probably had never set foot in; therefore, it did not occur to them to think of the ways in which life played out for the youth there. They read the magazine articles describing how the band's young musicians came from poverty, used the *favelas* as backdrop images for their music, and had recently survived a military dictatorship.[25] One thing was clear: these people were different from metal musicians in the Global North. The band's linkages with indigenous populations later in their career would drive this point home even more. Latin America was something else, and metal music there reflected it. Of course, many would limit their gaze to this singular Brazilian band and neglect to understand that this difference was embodied and musicalized by many others in the region. Now, several decades later, we can see how these explicit differences, embodied by bands like Sepultura and many others, were initial indicators of the emerging ethics of affront we have described here.

Let us revisit the question that serves as the title for our chapter. What has Latin American metal music ever done for us? We posit that it has fostered in metal music a reflection on oppression that distances itself from the more general critiques of modernity we see in a lot of metal in the

Global North. It is a specific reflection that reminds listeners that for people in the Global South, modernity cannot be understood outside coloniality.[26] Therefore, metal music's examination of the social conditions lived through in the region constantly references the colonial past and its present-day consequences. In presenting these patterns of oppression, and critiquing them vehemently, metal music in Latin America called for an ethical positioning of the music genre and its practitioners. The observations posed by metal in the Global North, general in nature and seemingly devoid of any reference to our conditions, were not enough for us. The European universalist perspective, manifested in their knowledge-building practices, and therefore also in the music emanating from the North, did not account for our experience. We needed to tell our colonial history through sounds, images and words. We needed to use them, simultaneously, to challenge that colonial history. We needed them, and still do today, to believe there is a way to move beyond the colonial experience and the modern project, what Dussel has called *transmodernity*.[27] Latin American metal infused the international scene with a call to ethics, a specific ethics of affront that sees little room for social homeostasis in a world still dominated by coloniality.

The ethics of affront posed by metal music in Latin America also has implications for metal-related scholarship. They are a call to examine metal as more than a musical genre, more than a sequence of musical notes to be dissected, and more than a passing fad of youth. Rather, metal music should be studied as a way of understanding how people in Latin America, and the Global South in general, use extreme forms of music to learn about their context and gather a deeper understanding of the social and political forces that sustain oppressive practices. This will be key to the expansion of, and critical engagement with, some of the ideas posed by metal scholars in the Global North. For example, the sometimes tense relation between metal and politics that has been stressed by some scholars clearly comes to mind.[28] Something different has happened in Latin American metal, and there seems to be little room, or at least a rapidly diminishing space, for those who support metal music's 'reflexive anti-reflexivity', described by Keith Kahn-Harris.[29] The ethics of affront seems to be gaining ground. Its three principles (acknowledging the humanity of those oppressed by coloniality, recognising the reality of the region's socio-political context, and fostering activist action as a realm for metal music) now permeate the work of a growing number of metal bands in Latin America.

'What is metal if not that scream that makes visible all the people that will be struck down in Latin America during the coming years? What is metal, if it's not that? If it's not that . . . then it's nothing', stated Pablo while sitting in his living room in Argentina. His question served as a call to the ethics of affront. As if his interrogation had been heard by others in the region, the answers seemed to spawn everywhere at once: Chilean metal musicians running for political office and working to change the Pinochet era constitution; Colombian metal singers being recognised by their local governments for fostering historical memory against violence; Cuban metal bands battling for State support of the arts; Venezuelan musicians denouncing the US imperialist blockade of their country; Ecuadorian metal musicians engaging in environmentalist activism. They are all participants of an ethics of affront in Latin American metal. They stand as examples of what metal in the Global North could do now. What has Latin American metal music done for us? A lot. It has shown the way. More work needs to be done. But if we are to hear the echoes of that scream, this is a pattern setting up further opportunities for sonic, physical and sociocultural and political forms of affront. Metal was always rebellious and in your face, and that remains the case. It is just that the stakes of that rebelliousness in certain sociocultural theatres are undeniably higher. In a theatre like Latin America, we are witnessing a masterclass of the type of work and transformation that is possible.

Notes

1. Nelson Varas-Díaz, *Decolonial Metal Music in Latin America* (Intellect, 2021); Nelson Varas-Díaz, 'Decolonial Hope: From the "Nueva Canción" to Heavy Metal Music in Latin America', paper presented at the *4th International Society for Metal Music Studies Biennial Research Conference* (ISMMS, 2019).
2. Aníbal Quijano, 'Coloniality and Modernity/Rationality', in Walter D. Mignolo and Arturo Escobar (eds.), *Globalization and the Decolonial Option* (Routledge, 2010), pp. 22–32.
3. Varas-Díaz, *Decolonial Metal Music*, p. 9.
4. Paulo Freire, *Pedagogy of the Oppressed* (Bloomsbury Academics, 2000).
5. Melina Aparecida dos Santos Silva and Beatriz Medeiros, '"This Gave Me a Mastodong": A Decolonial Analysis of the Black Twerking Dancers in Mastodon's The Motherload Music Video', *European Journal of Cultural Studies* 2 (2021): 1–17; Mark LeVine, *Heavy Metal Islam: Rock, Resistance, and the Struggle for the Soul of Islam* (Three Rivers Press, 2008); Anthony J. Thibodeau, *Anti-Colonial Resistance and Indigenous Identity in North American Heavy Metal*, MA dissertation (Bowling Green State University, 2014); Jeremy Wallach, 'Global Rock as Postcolonial Soundtrack', in Allan

F. Moore and Paul Carr (eds.), *Bloomsbury Handbook for Rock Music Research* (Bloomsbury, 2020), pp. 469–85.

6. Michael Hann, 'Nergal: The Extreme Metal Musician Fighting Poland's Blasphemy Laws', *The Guardian* (2021). www.theguardian.com/music/2021/mar/18/nergal-the-extreme-metal-musician-fighting-poland-blasphemy-laws (accessed 18 March 2021).

7. Steve Goodman, *Sonic Warfare: Sound, Affect, and the Ecology of Fear* (MIT Press, 2012).

8. Bruce Johnson and Martin Cloonan, *Dark Side of the Tune: Popular Music and Violence* (Ashgate, 2009).

9. Kathleen Marie Higgins, *The Music of Our Lives* (Temple University Press, 1991), pp. 155–69.

10. *Ibid.*

11. *Ibid.*

12. *Ibid.*

13. Marcel Cobussen and Nannette Nielsen, *Music and Ethics* (Routledge, 2016).

14. Zygmunt Bauman, *Postmodern Ethics* (Blackwell, 1993), p. 7.

15. Nelson Maldonado-Torres, 'On the Coloniality of Being: Contributions to the Development of a Concept', *Cultural Studies* 21/2–3 (2007): 240–70.

16. Manuela Belén Calvo, 'Indigenista Perspectives in Argentine Metal Music', *Metal Music Studies* 4/1 (2018): 155–63.

17. Enrique Dussel, *Philosophy of Liberation* (Wipf and Stock, 1985), p. 59.

18. Nelson Varas-Díaz, Daniel Nevárez Araújo and Eliut Rivera-Segarra, 'Conceptualizing the Distorted South: How to Understand Metal Music and its Scholarship in Latin America', in Nelson Varas-Díaz, Daniel Nevárez Araújo and Eliut Rivera-Segarra (eds.), *Heavy Metal Music in Latin America: Perspectives from the Distorted South* (Lexington Books, 2020), pp. 7–36.

19. Alejo Carpentier, *De Lo Real Maravilloso Americano, Tientos y Diferencias* (Universidad Autónoma de México, 1967).

20. Nelson Varas-Díaz and Sigrid Mendoza, 'Ethnicity, Politics and Otherness in Caribbean Heavy Metal Music: Experiences from Puerto Rico, Dominican Republic and Cuba', in Toni-Matti Karjalainen and Kimi Kärki (eds.), *Modern Heavy Metal: Market, Practices and Culture* (Aalto University Press, 2015), pp. 291–9.

21. Nelson Varas-Díaz, *Songs of Injustice: Heavy Metal Music in Latin America* (Puerto Rico Heavy Metal Studies, 2018). https://filmfreeway.com/projects/1489724 (accessed 22 June 2021).

22. Marcel Cobussen and Nannette Nielsen, *Music and Ethics* (Routledge, 2012), p. 102.

23. Eva Aladro-Vico, Dimitrina Jivkova-Semova and Olga Bailey, 'Artivismo: Un Nuevo Lenguaje Educativo Para La Acción Social Transformadora', *Comunicar* 57 (2018): 9–18; Suzanne Nossel, 'Introduction: On "Artivism," or Art's Utility in Activism', *Social Research* 83/1 (2016): 103–5; Alberto

López Cuenca and Renato David Bermúdez Dini, '¿Pero Esto Qué Es? Del Arte Activista Al Activismo Artístico En América Latina, 1968–2018', *Revista de Artes Visuales* 8 (2018): 17–28.

24. Boaventura de Sousa Santos, 'Toward and Aesthetics of the Epistemologies of the South: Manifesto in Twenty-Two Theses', in Boaventura de Sousa Santos and Maria Paula Meneses (eds.), *Epistemologies of the South: Knowledges Born in the Struggle – Constructing the Epistemologies of the Global South* (Routledge, 2020), pp. 117–25; Boaventura de Sousa Santos, *The End of the Cognitive Empire: The Coming of Age of Epistemologies of the South* (Duke University Press, 2018).

25. Idelber Avelar, 'Heavy Metal Music in Postdictatorial Brazil: Sepultura and the Coding of Nationality in Sound', *International Journal of Phytoremediation* 21/1 (2003): 329–46.

26. Ramón Grosfogel and Ana Cervantez-Rodríguez, 'Unthinking Twentieth-Century Eurocentric Mythologies: Universal Knowledges, Decolonization and Developmentalism', in Ramón Grosfogel and Ana Cervantez-Rodríguez (eds.), *The Modern/Colonial/Capitalist World-System in the Twentieth Century: Global Processes, Antisystemic Movements and the Geopolitics of Knowledge* (Praeger Press, 2002), pp. xi–xxix; Walter D. Mignolo, *The Darker Side of Western Modernity: Global Futures, Decolonial Options* (Duke University Press, 2011).

27. Dussel, *Philosophy of Liberation*, p. 59.

28. Niall Scott, 'Heavy Metal and the Deafening Threat of the Apolitical', *Popular Music History* 6/1 (2012): 224–39; Vivek Venkatesh, Jeffrey S. Podoshen, Kathryn Urbaniak and Jason J. Wallin, 'Eschewing Community: Black Metal †', *Journal of Community & Applied Social Psychology* 25/1 (2014): 66–81.

29. Keith Kahn-Harris, *Extreme Metal: Music and Culture on the Edge* (Berg, 2007).

25

Pioneers and Provocateurs

Australian Metal Music, Distance and Disregard

SAMUEL VALLEN

Despite the country's remoteness, Australian metal music has remained largely in line with developments in metal music globally. Practically every major chapter in metal bears a timely parallel Down Under, and the Australian adoption of these global movements, from metal's late sixties advent to the commercial success of contemporary metalcore, is rarely relayed without some distinctive variation. Exactly what common qualities one could ascribe to these myriad and diverse musics is at the heart of a growing scholarly literature on Australian metal, often contained within the broader question of the music's Australian identity. This literature comes at this question from various angles. Most scholars, oftentimes echoing the larger precursory literature on Australian popular music more broadly, examine the cultural tropes which underpin the music's development and character. They identify irreverent humour,[1] working-class masculine identities and a predominance of white performers as common traits.[2] Some look at how these characterisations are implied or explicated in paramusical[3] texts, from incendiary political or ideological materials,[4] to provocative record titles and deliberately offensive lyrics, and the juxtaposition of the brutal and the mundane.[5] Some scholars, albeit a limited subset, consider the musical texts themselves, expounding on themes of stylistic hybridisation and pushing at the limits of convention, both in style and intensity.[6] Although offering a multifaceted sense of this music, this literature is young, and there is abundant space and scope with which to develop understandings of Australian metal moving forward.

Australia, as a country, is notable for being dominantly Western in its culture but geographically isolated from its Western counterparts. Further, it is a country where major population centres are spread farther apart than many European countries, and where scenic hubs are likewise scattered and isolated. It has historically been unavoidable for Australian metal artists to negotiate with distance on both international and national scales.

A manifestation of this relationship is artists who, because of their isolation, are removed from the pronounced scenic pressures in metal music hubs worldwide, and whose music is accordingly singular and challenging of norms.

This chapter explores how this circumstance, alongside aspects of Australia's culture, has instigated unique artistic statements in many of its most prominent metal artists. There are instances of such artists spanning the history of Australian metal in myriad substyles and scenes, and while not wholly unique to Australia, this quality's presence across time and style establishes it as a useful concept through which to frame Australian metal. This chapter will cursorily explore the history of Australian metal, focusing on three diverse bands who demonstrate varying negotiations with this quality in different periods. These bands are Buffalo, a rough and provocative Sydney-based proto-heavy metal band from the early seventies; Sadistik Exekution, an extraordinarily heavy and influential Sydney-based death metal band formed in the mid-eighties; and Ne Obliviscaris, a sophisticated and innovative Melbourne-based progressive extreme metal band with a career spanning the 2000s to the present.

The Emergence of Australian Heavy Metal

Australia is a vast and sparsely populated island distanced from its Western cultural counterparts, and indeed most places, by days on a plane. Its population, around 25 million at the time of writing, are spread out across a landmass a little under 80 per cent of the size of the continental United States. Its sparse population and geographical diffusion have had a profound impact on the development of its music industry, often portrayed as hinderingly careful and conservative.[7] While each of Australia's eight states and territories has a capital city, two amongst them – Sydney (New South Wales) and Melbourne (Victoria) – currently bear approximately 50 per cent of the Australian music industry,[8] although the former has had significantly less governmental support than the latter in recent years.[9] These two have historically been represented as rivals.[10] In a musical example, Rosemary Overell describes Melbourne's grindcore scene as being constructed in part by their distance from Sydney's counterpart scene, the latter being portrayed tendentiously by Melbourne scene members as weak, inauthentic and feminine.[11] Next to Sydney and Melbourne in population size are Brisbane (Queensland) and Perth (Western Australia), the latter being particularly isolated with almost 2,700 km (by car) of desert distancing it from its nearest major city-neighbour, Adelaide, the capital of South Australia. Smaller still are Canberra, Australia's capital city situated in the small Australian Capital Territory, Darwin in the sparsely populated Northern Territory, and Hobart in the small southern island of Tasmania. All these cities and their respective states have produced metal bands and scenes of varying influence and success.

Australian music artists negotiate with a host of challenges due to their location: it is expensive for them to tour internationally or nationally beyond the largest cities, the country has had a historical dearth of quality recording studios,[12] and it has been traditionally challenging to disseminate Australian music worldwide, especially outside of the ambit of major labels. Moreover, compared to its UK and European cultural counterparts, Australia has had relatively little national or state governmental support for developing its musical exports, especially compared to other forms of media like cinema, where there has been a more tangible project of developing a 'national film culture'.[13] Australia's policy support for its music industry has remained, since the late sixties, cautious, exclusive and occasionally corrupt.[14] It has taken the rise of a handful of globally successful musical exports over the span of decades – the Bee Gees, INXS, etc. – for Australian popular music to be treated as a 'site for national cultural assertion'.[15]

Considering the span of this industry and its capitalist stakes, it is little surprise that promoting an Australian identity – whatever that might mean – has been a low priority for record companies. Resultantly, many of Australia's biggest musical exports, especially prior to the advent of the internet, have been arguably stylistically alike to their counterparts in the United States and UK.[16] Of course, this industry prudence and emphasis on reinforcing a global, saleable standard over stimulating more original directions in this music filters down in even more concentrated manners to less commercially viable musics like metal. Nevertheless, while relatively few Australian metal acts have reached the upper tiers of commercial success, the country has always had a persistent and reasonably influential metal music underground.

Paul Oldham dates the earliest characteristics of a proto-heavy metal musical style in Australia to around 1965.[17] In this period, Australia's remoteness precluded it from the touring schedules of American and European artists, and so a handful of acts rose to occupy this space. The earliest Australian proto-heavy metal acts, for the most part constituting Australia's celebrated Oz Rock or pub rock lineage, were Lobby Loyde, Billy Thorpe & The Aztecs, and Buffalo. Loyde, who first led Melbourne-based hard rock bands the Purple Hearts and the Wild Cherries in the mid to late sixties before forming the highly influential Coloured Balls in the early seventies, is lauded as Australia's first rock guitar hero.[18] Coloured Balls' music is muscular, tongue-in-cheek and experimental. Although founded in blues, it shows prototypical strains of punk and progressive rock and acts as something of a bellwether for the forming pub rock movement's heavier contingent. Heavily influenced by Loyde, with whom he collaborated and from whom he received guitar lessons, Billy Thorpe & The Aztecs would perform blues-derived hard rock music remembered for its ear-splitting volume due to Thorpe's amassing and combining of PA equipment. Thorpe, nicknamed 'King Yobbo' at the time – a term inferring a boisterous and brash character – would become the infamous star of pub rock, often arrested for profanity and raucous behaviour on stage.

The latter, Sydney's Buffalo (formed in 1971 in Sydney out of the ashes of Brisbane-formed band Head), have the strongest claim at being Australia's first heavy metal band,[19] personifying a style reasonably alike Black Sabbath, who had formed three years prior. Buffalo released their debut album, *Dead Forever* (1972), through Vertigo, an imprint of Philips/Phonogram, the home of proto-heavy metal bands like Black Sabbath and Status Quo; prog rock bands like Gentle Giant and Van Der Graaf Generator; and later, Metallica. Buffalo were the first non-European or British band to be signed to this label, arguably a failed attempt by A&R Dermot Hoy to establish an Australian identity in the label's Sydney base. It saw little promotion in Britain, although it was distributed to several Western European countries, and the band remained mostly unknown on the isles.[20] Despite these circumstances, the band's debut managed to sell 25,000 copies[21] and achieve a limited following in Europe. Interestingly, this route, including signing to a European record label, would be repeated similarly in the eighties by thrash/death metal bands like Hobbs' Angel of Death and Mortal Sin. This period is discussed in the next section.

Buffalo's music is reminiscent of British blues-derived proto-heavy metal, although bearing some notable musical properties. Guitarist John Baxter, called 'the heart and soul of [Buffalo]', purportedly had no instinct for, nor interest in, the blues, which founded the band's earliest stylistic practice.[22] This imprinted on the largely harmonically static and rhyth-mically pummelling character of Buffalo's mid-seventies work. Their music, even within its more psychedelic and exploratory elements, retains a harder, more overtly masculine edge than much European or North American psychedelic music in the period, practically bereft of the folk leanings, spacey extemporisations, or studio effects manipulations respectively common to many of the most prominent bands in this style.

The more notable element of Buffalo's work, though, is the character of their paramusical material: album covers, lyrics and song titles. The band were ignored by radio and so needed to capture attention in different manners. Their answer was provocative imagery, like the album art of *Volcanic Rock* (1973), where a fully nude androgynous figure holds a statue of what appears to be a penis over their head while standing on an erupting volcano, itself reminiscent of a menstruating female figure; or the cover to its 1974 follow-up, *Only Want You for Your Body*, which shows a woman strapped to a torture rack with her dress hiked up to her neck. Buffalo's lyrics are celebratory of conservative concepts of hetero-normative masculinity and misogyny: sexual conquest, machismo, ideation of domination and power, and light homophobia. Most of these qualities are represented to varying degrees in concurrent global hard rock and heavy metal music, but Buffalo's demonstration of these themes and their provocativeness seems especially deliberate. Indeed, the act of being confrontational and incendiary was a proclaimed goal of the band; its effect justified as necessary to garner attention in an otherwise conservative cultural milieu. But it was avowedly light-hearted. This quality, using the jocular intention of something to soften or justify its provocativeness, proves reasonably common in discussions of Australian metal music and will be problematised further in the next section.

Buffalo's negotiation with distance is multifaceted. In their hometown of Sydney, they were effectively a local band, relegated, due to both relatively low demand and draconian liquor licensing laws, to gigs in schools and municipal halls.[23] The sites of performance would move to pubs through the early seventies alongside a broad liberal cultural shift, but the band's (ample) national touring remained limited to the scope of this underground scene, despite their record deal and overseas sales.[24] Buffalo's isolation is an important factor in their global uptake, but the more interesting scope, at least in terms of the band's sound and character, is their engagement with local music institutions. Their assiduously provocative paramusical materials were ostensibly a direct result of being ignored or cast aside by Australia's own music media and radio. Their contrarian-charged attitude of avoiding the trappings of pop stardom, too, seems custom-made for the idiosyncratic space they occupied in the Australian music industry. Perhaps this embodies an engagement with the mounting modernist discourse in rock music in the late sixties and early seventies: the pervasive sense of being individualistic, artistic and uncorrupted by capitalist machinations.[25] In Buffalo's case, though, the theme bears a more comedically rebellious tone invocative of the Australian larrikin, an archetype explored in the next section.

The late seventies saw Australia's answer to the New Wave of British Heavy Metal steadily emerge, reaching a high in terms of both the number of acts and their respective prominence in the early to mid-eighties. This was something of a watershed period in Australian metal's development, offering a host of stylistically diverse bands in varied metal substyles spanning the country's capital cities, from the progressive metal of Melbourne's Taramis to Canberra-founded proto-death metal act Armoured Angel, to Melbourne speed metal pioneers Nothing Sacred, and dozens of others. The profusion of new bands and growing underground interest was supported by several important individuals and institutions, which provided limited platforms for their distribution. These included radio shows and deejays like Allan Thomas from 3RRR in Melbourne; record stores like Sydney's Utopia Records and Melbourne's Central Station Records, which acted as scenic hubs as well as distributors; and eventually concerts like the famed yearly event, Metal for Melbourne, which started in 1981 and which – for five non-consecutive instalments ending in 1986 – acted as the premier Australian heavy music festival.[26] These identities and circumstances laid the groundwork for several more idiosyncratic and unique stylistic trajectories to develop throughout the eighties with an increasing presence in, and influence on, the global metal scene. The following section will explore the case of Australian extreme metal in the mid to late eighties and specifically the challenges faced, and the imprint left, by Sydney's Sadistik Exekution.

Australian Extreme Metal

The advent of extreme metal in the early to mid-eighties embodied a significant shift in the character of metal music up to that point. Key extreme metal scenes and bands included British grindcore led by Napalm Death (formed 1981); the Bay Area death metal scene led by Possessed (formed 1983), Floridan death metal (the Tampa Scene) including Morbid Angel and Death in the mid-eighties; contemporaneous Swedish death metal including Morbid and Entombed; and the formative embodiment of Norwegian black metal, Mayhem (formed 1984). All these substyles were underground musics entrenched in paramusically transgressive and widely sonically unpalatable genre markers. Both Australia's first extreme metal act, Slaughter Lord, and their most successful extreme metal export at this time, Mortal Sin, formed throughout 1985, essentially concurrent to these global developments in extreme metal music.

Early Australian extreme metal artists and fans were able to remain abreast of developments thousands of kilometres away due primarily to two technologies: tape trading and zines. The former describes private mail distribution of demo tapes and bootlegs, often between 'pen pals' and sometimes through small-scale mail-order operations. The latter describes self-published, printed and distributed magazines. While facilitating the spanning of global distance, these avenues also influenced the emerging music, encompassing simultaneously curation and consumption. It was due to these technologies that many of Australia's earliest extreme metal exponents were known outside of the country before they had any significant name nationally. Melbourne's Hobbs' Angel of Death, an early Australian death metal band, exemplify this situation. The band's grisly output, styled as 'virgin metal' to allude to its purity and uncompromising nature, earned the band a record deal with German label Steamhammer and relatively strong sales abroad while remaining relatively unknown at home.

Sydney's Sadistik Exekution (formed in late 1985) provide an especially compelling example of how isolation and obstinate ideals facilitated a singular and influential musical statement. The band formed alongside the burgeoning Norwegian black metal scene and were known to key players like Øystein 'Euronymous' Aarseth of Mayhem and Jon 'Metalion' Kristiansen, the editor of perhaps the most pivotal zine on the development of black metal in Northern Europe, *Slayer*. Kristiansen, a member of the infamous 'inner circle' of Norwegian black metal, claims that Sadistik Exekution was 'the most important band in *Slayer* mag history'.[27]

Sadistik Exekution's output is as fierce and intense as that of any of their contemporaries in the late eighties and early nineties. Their music blends a hellish Norwegian black metal-styled tremolo-heavy guitar approach with a primal and ceaseless drum battery, largely constituted of blast beats. Their music, which they considered death metal, is sometimes taken to be prototypical of the 'war metal' substyle, merging black and death metal.[28] In addition to this hybrid foundation, the band have two notable elements which differentiate them from most contemporaneous extreme metal. First, their bassist, Dave Slave, often featured in a prominent melodic role in the band, is far more virtuosic and foregrounded than is normal of the time and style (an interesting parallel to draw with the next case study, Ne Obliviscaris). Secondly, their singer, Rok, covers a wide range of atypical vocal and lyrical approaches. Rok's vocals veer from black metal shrieks and guttural barks to comedic yells, theatrical moans, and barrages of decisively Australian profanity and insults delivered in a thick Australian drawl. This vocabulary includes slang and expressions such as 'drongos', 'how ya's going?', 'bloody crook', and myriad other instances of Australian vernacular and idiom. Viewed within the context of early extreme metal, such affectations are unusually self-aware, highlighting an intrinsic absurdity. This activity relates to Kahn-Harris' 'reflexive anti-reflexivity': a concept in metal studies used to explain how metal practitioners and fans can simultaneously champion the thematic integrity of something while actually comprehending it as the opposite.[29] The difference in Sadistik Exekution's work, as compared to most of their contemporaries, is the temerity with which they rejected metal coding, specifically its pursuit of thematic pretence and po-faced seriousness. Further, they considered this very seriousness and pretence as weak and inauthentic; to quote Rok: 'we were Australian, not Norwegian, we were rough and aggressive, not thin and feminine sounding'.[30] In this late eighties and early nineties extreme metal milieu, no bands were as brazen as they were in highlighting and revelling in absurdity and madness (and its inherent comedy). This awareness of the ludicrousness of one's approach alongside an effectively intense and thematically transgressive artistic output would later become a mainstay of much Australian extreme metal, from Ballarat's Damaged to Melbourne's Blood Duster and Frankenbox, and, more recently, to King Parrot, also from Melbourne.

Sadistik Exekution's isolation explains much of this character. The band developed in a space largely bereft of stylistic contemporaries, thereby sidestepping the strict inter-scenic proliferation of codes like those seen in, for example, Norwegian black metal. Their tether to global scenes – zines and tape trading – provided a broad stylistic pallet embodying many global developments in metal music. But due to the band's isolation, they experienced little pressure to follow any of these movements precisely, and so their output became distinctively hybridised, bearing the qualities of many substyles. The fact that they did this while maintaining scenic authenticity and respect from their overseas contemporaries is notable. One potential justification for this could be the sense of unpredictability and untethered chaos in their public personas, as though to insinuate that their breaks from metal coding are simply symptoms of being completely socially and culturally unhinged, a quality which is clearly celebrated in much of their media coverage.[31]

The character founding Sadistik Exekution's persona, and echoed throughout the history of Australian metal and rock more generally, is that of the Australian larrikin.[32] Although a constant figure in Australian folk culture, 'larrikin' has meant different things in different eras, from savage urban criminality in the early nineteenth century through to a pervasive and treasured vestige of contemporary Australian culture celebrating brashness, irreverence and roguishness.[33] Larrikinism is expressed in the idiom 'taking the piss' – a Commonwealth expression, which describes making fun of someone or something with a friendly redress, often to bring that thing or person down to earth. In this ostensibly light-hearted manner, larrikins push incessantly at convention and good taste. The implication is that the joke may be pushed far, but it will remain essentially harmless. Perhaps unsurprisingly, such a jocular attitude (observed, too, in the work of Buffalo) deflects from a host of potentially dysfunctional behaviours, rendering them as little more than idiosyncratic quirks of the Australian national identity despite sometimes concealing and even justifying more problematic activities, such as violence, racism and misogyny. While this persona is exemplified by myriad bands in all styles of Australian music, its situation in Sadistik Exekution's brand is particularly obvious, justifying both the band's raucous, hysterical and uncouth public persona as well as its wanton aversion to following the codes of extreme metal authenticity. The band's distance from the origins of its style, the methods of the music's arrival (and consequent dissemination), and the culture surrounding and suffusing the band members' lives all play a part in this distinctively unhinged and chaotic musical statement and its, perhaps surprising, legitimation.

Contemporary Australian Metal and Ne Obliviscaris

The eighties saw the stylistic ambit of Australian metal broaden, but it proliferated far further throughout subsequent decades to the present. Indeed, there is a theme in international metal media that Australia's current metal offerings are notably artistically and sonically varied. While the overall output of the country matches its population, a sizable portion of these bands occupy unique and oftentimes influential positions in global metal. Bands like Northlane, Voyager, Karnivool, Psycroptic, Twelve Foot Ninja, Dispossessed, Portal and Caligula's Horse illustrate this diversity. Some of these bands, such as Karnivool and Northlane, acted as fountainheads for burgeoning metal substyles. All occupy singular positions in Australian metal, demonstrating little creative tether to contemporaneous scenes, local or global. Some employ distinctive musical practices while some explore paramusical theming which is novel and unusual in the context of global metal. While the distance-related pressures have been different for each of these bands, many of whom experienced at least a portion of their career with the presence of the internet, their location and output reveal parallels to their forebearers, namely them being stylistically idiosyncratic and dismissive of metal codes and authenticity.

Melbourne's Ne Obliviscaris, formed in 2003, are an interesting case study in this regard. They embody a high degree of stylistic hybridity, melding styles which would regularly be taken as incompatible in discourses of (extreme) metal authenticity (for example, black metal and progressive rock), as well as perpetuating a confident and fully formed voice from early in their career without scenic contemporaries in similar styles to emulate. Ne Obliviscaris's music is founded in extreme metal, and numerous extreme metal substyles find place in different aspects of their music. Drummer Dan Presland foregrounds ferocious and relentless death metal-derived double kick and blast beat patterns; vocalist Xenoyr utilises both death metal-styled guttural vocals and high-pitched shrieked vocals, more redolent of black metal; guitarists Benjamin Baret and Matt Klavins employ machine gun rhythmic riffing with a lineage to thrash metal by way of death metal, as well as more colourful and chord-based black metal patterns played either harmonically or as tremolo-picked arpeggios. These approaches are manifestly wide-ranging but still situated under the umbrella of extreme metal style markers.

Of more interest, though, are the ways the band actively undermine these recognisable hybrid extreme metal qualities. Ne Obliviscaris employ a violinist, Tim Charles, who also acts as their melodic vocalist. Charles's virtuosic violin, rather than behaving like a (reasonably normalised in metal) symphonic layer, occupies a role more akin to a lead guitar, establishing key melodies and countermelodies and acting, continuously, as an Apollonian foil to the brutality of the underlying metal music.[34] This is especially evident in the fiddle-like performative timbre often utilised, as well as a whole range of expressive nuances and articulations like harmonics, portamento (sliding between notes) and pizzicato (plucking with fingers rather than bowing). The fragile, human qualities of these techniques and others provide a distinctive contrast to the machine-like metal foundations of the band's music. In a similarly creative approach, Martino Garattoni's bass relatively rarely performs in unison with the guitars nor occupies the lower fundamental qualities of the song's harmony. It often acts, instead, as another smooth melodic voice, foiling the music's harshness and density. Moreover, Ne Obliviscaris generally convey the influence of non-metal musics like flamenco, Gypsy jazz and classic psychedelic and progressive rock, all compositionally situated to provoke the greatest drama by contrast to the band's metal underpinnings.

Ne Obliviscaris sound like no other band in the metal landscape, and this uniqueness has attracted a significant underground following the world over. Regardless, the band often describe the same pressures experienced by essentially all Australian underground artists: cost of touring, less support from industry and policy in the country, and so forth.[35] Their answer to these oft-repeated issues was an unconventional one: crowdfunding. While the band are signed to an independent label, Season of Mist, they have, since 2016, been funded primarily by their fans through the American membership platform Patreon.[36] Over 700 fans, at the time of writing, contribute almost $9,000 AUD (the equivalent of around $6,500 USD) to Ne Obliviscaris each month. Although reasonably accepted now, Ne Obliviscaris were early adopters – as a metal band – of this avenue and were criticised by many for the approach at the time. The band continue to emphasise how necessary this approach has been to their longevity.[37]

While the outrageous larrikinish character shared by Sadistik Exekution and many other Australian bands is not necessarily evident in Ne Obliviscaris's identity, their defiance for convention is no less charged. On the one hand, their particular sonic hybrid, crystallising without scenic contemporaries or clear overseas antecedents, is brazen and original. On the other, their answer to problems catalysed by their geographical distance and underground scenic positioning is clearly built from a stubborn ingenuity, one echoed – albeit in parallel and sometimes contrasting manners – across Australian metal.

Ne Obliviscaris arguably do not embody an 'Australian' aspect to their sound, at least not in the same way bands like King Parrot, Twelve Foot Ninja or Dead Kelly might be said to through their direct (paramusical) employment of Australian accent and argot. This observation could be extended to many acknowledged Australian metal bands, perhaps more than the inverse, and so this marker has limited use in characterising Australian metal. Rather, what Ne Obliviscaris, Sadistik Exekution, Buffalo and many other Australian metal bands share is a negotiation with their mutual circumstances: isolation, distance from scenic hubs, and the absence of large or well-established local scenes. They also share in stubbornly surmounting these problems, often resulting in mutually inventive and novel sonic and aesthetic outcomes. In any case, these common variables have some effect on the bands' identity and practice. Buffalo are largely characterised through their offensive and inflammatory paramusical materials, created as a response to a disinterested and conservative media and public. Sadistik Exekution are known for their tremendously heavy and out-of-control music made as a response to their estimation that pretence and authority, a pervasive target of the larrikin character, diminishes metal purity. Ne Obliviscaris forged a genuinely novel sonic hybrid and, after battling with geographical handicaps for over a decade, disseminated it through an equally novel funding platform, one which cyclically allowed and allows the band supreme freedom over their stylistic vision.

Conclusion

The history of Australian metal is dotted with novelty, with necessity driving invention and defiance plotting courses against convention. Considering just how varied, how hybrid and how singular many leading Australian metal bands are, defining common qualities is a difficult undertaking. This chapter considered, instead, some of the distance-related negotiations faced by Australian metal acts as a means of grouping and conceptualising their practice and situated this quality in the work of three key bands from across the music's historical trajectory. While the particularities of this quality are respectively unique, negotiation with distance remains a pervasive aspect of Australian metal, one with broad and tangible ramifications across the style's musical and paramusical developments. One cannot write the history of Australian metal without considering this ongoing negotiation.

Notes

1. Rosemary Overell, 'Brutal Belonging in Melbourne's Grindcore Scene', *Studies in Symbolic Interaction* 35/1 (2010): 79–99.
2. Catherine Hoad, 'We are the Sons of the Southern Cross', *Journal of World Popular Music* 3/1 (2016): 90–107.
3. Tagg defines paramusical as 'literally alongside the music, i.e. semiotically related to a particular musical discourse without being structurally intrinsic to that discourse'. See Phillip Tagg, 'Glossary of Terms, Neologisms, etc. Used in Writings by Philip Tagg', *Tagg.org* (n.d). https://tagg.org/articles/ptgloss.html (accessed 12 September 2021).
4. Benjamin Hillier and Ash Barnes, 'Wolf in Sheep's Clothing', *IASPM Journal* 10/2 (2020): 38–57.
5. Sam Vallen, 'A Blaze in the Northern Suburbs', in Catherine Hoad (ed.), *Australian Metal Music* (Emerald, 2019), pp. 37–54.

6. Benjamin Hillier, 'Investigating the Australian Sound in Australian Extreme Metal', *12th Annual Graduate Research Conference* (University of Tasmania, 2018).

7. Ian McFarlane, *The Encyclopedia of Australian Rock and Pop* (Allen & Unwin, 1999).

8. Andy Bennett, David Cashman and Natalie Lewandowski, 'Twice the Size of Texas', *Popular Music and Society* 42/5 (2019): 561–75.

9. Andrew Taylor, 'Melbourne v Sydney', *The Sydney Morning Herald* (2018). www .smh.com.au/entertainment/music/melbourne-v-sydney-which-city-has-the-better-live-music-scene-20181005-p5082h.html (accessed 12 September 2021).

10. Mel Campbell, 'Sydney v Melbourne: A History', *Crikey* (2019). www .crikey.com.au/2019/07/25/melbourne-sydney-rivalry-history (accessed 12 September 2021).

11. Rosemary Overell, 'I Think Sydney's Pretty Shit', in Catherine Hoad (ed.), *Australian Metal Music* (Emerald, 2019), pp. 71–90.

12. Shane Homan, 'An "Orwellian Vision"', *Continuum* 22/5 (2008): 601–11.

13. Phillip Hayward, 'Introduction Charting Australia', in Phillip Hayward (ed.), *From Pop to Punk to Postmodernism: Popular Music and Australian Culture from the 1960s to the 1990s* (Allen & Unwin, 1992), pp. 1–10.

14. Shane Homan, 'From Coombs to Crean: Popular Music and Cultural Policy in Australia', *International Journal of Cultural Policy* 19/3 (2013): 382–98.

15. Hayward, 'Introduction Charting Australia', p. 3.

16. *Ibid.*

17. Paul Oldham, 'Heavy Metal Kids: A Historiographical Exploration of Australian Proto-Heavy Metal in the 1960s–1970s', in Catherine Hoad (ed.), *Australian Metal Music* (Emerald, 2019), pp. 19–36.

18. Paul Oldham, 'Lobby Loyde: The G.O.D. Father of Australian Rock', *Thesis Eleven* 109/1 (2012): 44–63.

19. Geoff Barton, 'Were Buffalo the Original Aussie Heavy Metal Band?', *Classic Rock* (31 December 2015). www.loudersound.com/features/were-buffalo-the-original-aussie-heavy-metal-band (accessed 12 September 2021).

20. Ian McFarlane, 'Buffalo: 1972 & Dead Forever', *Third Stone Press* (2006). www .thirdstonepress.com.au/archive-blog/2018/4/30/buffalo-dead-forever (accessed 12 September 2021).

21. Brian Giffin, *The Australian Metal Guide* (Moonlight, 2002).

22. McFarlane, 'Buffalo'.

23. It should be noted that, while largely relegated to the conditions described, Buffalo played two shows with Black Sabbath on the band's first Australian tour in 1974 and featured on a line-up with Slade and Status Quo later that year.

24. Klemen Breznikar, 'Buffalo Interview with Dave Tice', *Psychedelic Baby Magazine* (2011). www.psychedelicbabymag.com/2011/08/buffalo-interview-with-dave-tice.html (accessed 12 September 2021).

25. Sam Vallen, *Rock Vanguards: Exploring Artistic Progressiveness in Popular Music and Progressive Rock*, doctoral dissertation (Queensland Conservatorium, 2020).

26. Nick Calpakdjian, *Metal Down Under* (MGM, 2014).

27. Jon Kristiansen, *Metalion: The Slayer Mag Diaries* (Bazillion Points, 2015), p. 117.

28. Usually defined as a black and death metal hybrid performed by Australian bands like Deströyer 666 and Bestial Warlust. See Hoad, 'We are the Sons of the Southern Cross'.

29. Keith Kahn-Harris, *Extreme Metal: Music and Culture on the Edge* (Berg, 2007).

30. Sparky, 'Rok: No Words Needed', *The Coroner's Report* (2020). www.thecoronersreportmag.com/post/rok-no-words-needed-1 (accessed 12 September 2021).

31. Niklas Göransson, 'Rok (Sadistik Exekution)', *Bardo Methodology* (2019). www.bardomethodology.com/articles/2019/06/06/rok-sadistik-exekution-interview (accessed 12 September 2021).

32. See Vallen, *Rock Vanguards*.

33. Melissa Bellanta, *Larrikins: A History* (University of Queensland Press, 2012).

34. Weinstein has detailed the Dionysian qualities of metal against which such an Apollonian contrast is set. See Deena Weinstein, *Heavy Metal: The Music and its Culture* (Da Capo Press, 2000).

35. Andrew Massie, 'Interview: Tim Charles Ne Obliviscaris', *The Rockpit* (2016). www.therockpit.net/2016/interview-tim-charles-ne-obliviscaris (accessed 12 September 2021).

36. www.patreon.com/neobliviscaris (accessed 12 September 2021).

37. Staff Writer, 'Ne Obliviscaris Violinist Responds to Patreon Criticism', *Killyourstereo.com* (2016). www.killyourstereo.com/news/1082303/ne-obliviscaris-violinist-responds-to-patreon-criticism (accessed 12 September 2021).

Select Academic Bibliography

Adorno, Theodor W., *The Culture Industry* (Routledge, 1991).

Alapatt, Eothen and Uchenna Ikonne, *Wake Up You! The Rise and Fall of Nigerian Rock 1972–1977*, Vols. 1 and 2 (Now-Again, 2016).

Alapatt, Eothen and Leonard Koloko, *Welcome to Zamrock! 1972–1977: How Zambia's Liberation Led to a Rock Revolution* (Now-Again, 2017).

Arthur, W. Brian, *The Nature of Technology: What It Is and How It Evolves* (Penguin, 2009).

Ashcroft, Bill, Gareth Griffiths and Helen Tiffin (eds.), *Postcolonial Studies: The Key Concepts* (Routledge, 2013).

Attali, Jacques, *Noise: The Political Economy of Music*, trans. Brian Massumi (University of Minnesota Press, 1985).

Banchs, Edward, *Heavy Metal Africa: Life, Passion, and Heavy Metal in the Forgotten Continent* (Word Association, 2016).

Banchs, Edward, *Scream for Me Africa! Heavy Metal Identities in Post-Colonial Africa* (Intellect, 2022).

Bardine, Bryan and Jerome Stueart, *Living Metal: Metal Scenes Around the World* (Intellect, 2021).

Barone, Stefano, *Metal, Rap, and Electro in Post-Revolutionary Tunisia: A Fragile Underground* (Routledge, 2019).

Barratt-Peacock, Ruth and Ross Hagen (eds.), *Medievalism and Metal Music Studies: Throwing Down the Gauntlet* (Emerald, 2019).

Baulch, Emma, *Making Scenes: Reggae, Punk and Death Metal in 1990s Bali* (Duke University Press, 2007).

Bauman, Zygmunt, *Identity* (Polity Press, 2004).

Bayer, Gerd (ed.), *Heavy Metal Music in Britain* (Routledge, 2016).

Bellanta, Melissa, *Larrikins: A History* (University of Queensland Press, 2012).

Berkers, Pauwke and Julian Schaap, *Gender Inequality in Metal Music Production* (Emerald, 2018).

Biasutti, Michele, 'Group Music Composing Strategies: A Case Study within a Rock Band', *British Journal of Music Education* 29/3 (2012): 343–57.

Birnie-Smith, Jess and Wesley C. Robertson, 'Superdiversity and Translocal Brutality in Asian Extreme Metal Lyrics', *Language and Communication* 81 (2021): 48–63.

Bourdieu, Pierre, 'The Field of Cultural Production, or: The Economic World Reversed', in Richard Nice (trans.), *The Field of Cultural Production* (Columbia University Press, 1993 [1983]), pp. 29–73.

Boynik, Sezgin and Tolga Güldallı (eds.), *An Interrupted History of Punk and Underground Resources in Turkey 1978–1999* (Bas Yayınları, 2007).

Brackett, David, '(In Search of) Musical Meaning: Genres, Categories and Crossover', in David Hesmondhalgh and Keith Negus (eds.), *Popular Music Studies* (Arnold, 2002), pp. 65–83.

Brown, Andy R., 'The Importance of Being Metal', in Niall Scott and Imke von Helden (eds.), *The Metal Void: First Gatherings* (Inter-Disciplinary Press, 2010), pp. 105–34.

Brown, Andy R., 'Everything Louder than Everyone Else: The Origins and Persistence of Heavy Metal Music and Its Global Cultural Impact', in Andy Bennett and Steve Waksman (eds.), *The SAGE Handbook of Popular Music* (Sage, 2015), pp. 261–77.

Burke, Peter, *What Is Cultural History?* (Polity Press, 2004).

Burkitt, Ian, 'Emotional Reflexivity: Feeling, Emotion and Imagination in Reflexive Dialogues', *Sociology* 46/3 (2012): 458–72.

Burns, Robert G. H., *Experiencing Progressive Rock: A Listener's Companion* (Rowman & Littlefield, 2018).

Cardwell, Tom, 'Battle Jackets, Authenticity and "Material Individuality"', *Metal Music Studies* 3/3 (2017): 437–58.

Cardwell, Tom, *Heavy Metal Armour: A Visual Study of Battle Jackets* (Intellect, 2022).

Christe, Ian, *Sound of the Beast: The Complete Headbanging History of Heavy Metal* (Alison and Busby, 2004).

Clifford-Napoleone, Amber, *Queerness in Heavy Metal Music: Metal Bent* (Routledge, 2015).

Coggins, Owen, *Mysticism, Ritual and Religion in Drone Metal* (Bloomsbury Academic, 2018).

Coggins, Owen, 'Ecology, Estrangement and Enchantment in Black Metal's Dark Haven', *Green Letters* 24/4 (2021): 1–13.

Cope, Andrew L., *Black Sabbath and the Rise of Heavy Metal Music* (Ashgate, 2010).

Côté, James and Charles Levine, *Identity Formation, Agency, and Culture: A Social Psychological Synthesis* (Lawrence Erlbaum Associates, 2002).

Crowcroft, Orlando, *Rock in a Hard Place: Music and Mayhem in the Middle East* (Zed Books, 2017).

Dawes, Laina, *'What Are You Doing Here?' A Black Woman's Life and Liberation in Heavy Metal* (Bazillion Points, 2012).

Dodds, Sherril, *Dancing on the Canon: Embodiments of Value in Popular Dance* (Palgrave Macmillan, 2011).

Elovaara, Mika and Bryan Bardine, *Connecting Metal to Culture: Unity in Disparity* (Intellect, 2017).

Endean, Gareth, *Half a Ton of Metal: 50 Years of the Loudest Music on Earth* (Blurb, 2020).

Erbe, Marcus. '"This Isn't Over 'til I Say It's Over!" Narratives of Male Frustration in Deathcore and Beyond', in Florian Heesch and Niall Scott (eds.), *Heavy Metal, Gender and Sexuality* (Routledge, 2016), pp. 182–92.

Fellezs, Kevin, 'Black Metal Soul Music: Stone Vengeance and the Aesthetics of Race in Heavy Metal', in Eric James Abbey and Colin Helb (eds.), *Hardcore, Punk, and Other Junk: Aggressive Sounds in Contemporary Music* (Lexington Books, 2014), pp. 121–38.

Fletcher, K. F. B., 'Classical Antiquity, Heavy Metal Music, and European Identity', in Fernando Lozano Gómez, Alfonso Álvarez-Ossorio Rivas and Carmen Alarcon Hernandez (eds.), *The Present of Antiquity: Reception, Recovery, Reinvention of the Ancient World in Current Popular Culture* (Presses universitaires de Franche-Comté, 2019), pp. 223–46.

Fletcher, K. F. B. and Umurhan Osman (eds.), *Classical Antiquity in Heavy Metal Music* (Bloomsbury, 2019).

Frith, Simon and Simon Zagorski-Thomas (eds.), *The Art of Record Production: An Introductory Reader for a New Academic Field* (Ashgate, 2012).

Gaines, Donna, *Teenage Wasteland: Suburbia's Dead End Kids* (University of Chicago Press, 1998).

Gamble, Steven, 'Breaking Down the Breakdown in Twenty-First Century Metal', *Metal Music Studies* 5/3 (2019): 337–54.

Gamble, Steven, *How Music Empowers: Listening to Modern Rap and Metal* (Routledge, 2021).

Gibson, Chris and John Connell, *Music Festivals and Regional Development in Australia* (Ashgate, 2012).

Greene, Paul D., 'Electronic and Affective Overdrive: Tropes of Transgression in Nepal's Heavy Metal Scene', in Jeremy Wallach, Harris M. Berger and Paul D. Greene (eds.), *Metal Rules the Globe: Heavy Metal Music Around the World* (Duke University Press, 2011), pp. 109–34.

Hagen, Ross, 'Black Metal', in Jeremy Wallach, Harris B. Berger and Paul D. Greene (eds.), *Metal Rules the Globe: Heavy Metal Music Around the World* (Duke University Press, 2011), pp. 180–99.

Hagen, Ross, *Darkthrone's A Blaze in the Northern Sky* (Bloomsbury, 2020).

Halnon, Karen Bettez, 'Inside Shock Music Carnival: Spectacle as Contested Terrain', *Critical Sociology* 30/3 (2004): 743–79.

Halnon, Karen Bettez, 'Heavy Metal Carnival and Dis-Alienation: The Politics of Grotesque Realism', *Symbolic Interaction* 29/1 (2006): 33–48.

Hecker, Pierre, 'Taking a Trip to the Middle Eastern Metal Scene: Transnational Social Spaces and Identity Formations on a Non-National Level', *Nord-Süd aktuell* 19/1 (2005): 57–66.

Hecker, Pierre, *Turkish Metal: Music, Meaning, and Morality in a Muslim Society* (Ashgate, 2012).

Hecker, Pierre and Douglas Mattsson, 'The Enemy within: Conceptualizing Turkish Metalheads as the Ideological "Other"', in Bryan A. Bardine and Jerome Steuart (eds.), *Living Metal: Metal Scenes Around the World* (Intellect, 2021), pp. 55–77.

Heesch, Florian, 'Metal for Nordic Men: Amon Amarth's Representations of Vikings', in Niall Scott (ed.), *The Metal Void* (Inter-Disciplinarity Press, 2010), pp. 71–80.

Heesch, Florian and Niall Scott (eds.), *Heavy Metal, Gender and Sexuality* (Routledge, 2016).

Herbst, Jan-Peter, 'Heaviness and the Electric Guitar: Considering the Interaction between Distortion and Harmonic Structures', *Metal Music Studies* 4/1 (2018): 95–113.

Herbst, Jan-Peter, 'Teutonic Metal: Effects of Place- and Mythology-Based Labels on Record Production', *International Journal of the Sociology of Leisure* 4 (2021): 291–313.

Herbst, Jan-Peter and Mark Mynett, 'Nail the Mix: Standardisation in Mixing Metal Music', *Popular Music & Society* 44/5 (2021): 628–49.

Herbst, Jan-Peter and Mark Mynett, '(No?) Adventures in Recording Land: Engineering Conventions in Metal Music', *Rock Music Studies* 9/2 (2021): 137–56.

Herbst, Jan-Peter and Mark Mynett, 'What Is "Heavy" in Metal? A Netnographic Analysis of Online Forums for Metal Musicians and Producers', *Popular Music & Society* 45/5 (2022): 633–53.

Herbst, Jan-Peter and Mark Mynett, 'Toward a Systematic Understanding of Heaviness in Metal Music Production', *Rock Music Studies* 10/1 (2022): 16–37.

Herron-Wheeler, Addison, *Wicked Women: Women in Metal from the 1960s to Now* (Self-published, 2014).

Hill, Rosemary Lucy, *Gender, Metal and the Media: Women Fans and the Gendered Experience of Music* (Palgrave Macmillan, 2016).

Hillier, Benjamin, 'Investigating the Australian Sound in Australian Extreme Metal', *12th Annual Graduate Research Conference* (University of Tasmania, 2018).

Hillier, Benjamin, 'Considering Genre in Metal Music', *Metal Music Studies* 6/1 (2020): 5–26.

Hillier, Benjamin and Ash Barnes, 'Wolf in Sheep's Clothing: Extreme Right-Wing Ideologies in Australian Black Metal', *IASPM Journal* 10/2 (2020): 38–57.

Hoad, Catherine, 'Hold the Heathen Hammer High: Viking Metal from the Local to the Global', in Oli Wilson and Sarah Attfield (eds.), *Shifting Sounds: Musical Flow – A Collection of Papers from the 2012 IASPM Australia/New Zealand Conference* (IASPM, 2013), pp. 62–70.

Hoad, Catherine, 'We Are the Sons of the Southern Cross', *Journal of World Popular Music* 3/1 (2016): 90–107.

Hoad, Catherine (ed.), *Australian Metal Music* (Emerald, 2019).

Holt, Fabian, *Genre in Popular Music* (University of Chicago Press, 2007).

Homan, Shane , '"I Tote and I Vote": Australian Live Music and Cultural Policy', *Arts Marketing* 1/2 (2011): 96–107.

Hudson, Stephen, *Feeling Beats and Experiencing Motion: A Construction-Based Theory of Meter*, doctoral dissertation (Northwestern University, 2019).

James, Kieran and Rex Walsh, 'Bandung Rocks, Cibinong Shakes: Economics and Applied Ethics within the Indonesian Death-Metal Community', *Musicology Australia* 37/1 (2015): 28–46.

Jenks, Chris, *Transgression* (Psychology Press, 2003).

Jocson-Singh, Joan, 'Vigilante Feminism as a Form of Musical Protest in Extreme Metal Music', *Metal Music Studies* 5/2 (2019): 263–73.

Kahn-Harris, Keith, *Extreme Metal: Music and Culture on the Edge* (Berg, 2007).

Karjalainen, Toni-Matti (ed.), *Sounds of Origin in Heavy Metal Music* (Cambridge Scholars Publishing, 2018).

Karpe, Matthew, *Nu Metal Resurgence* (FastPrint, 2018).

Kawano, Kei and Shuhei Hosokawa, 'Thunder in the Far East: The Heavy Metal Industry in 1990s Japan', in Jeremy Wallach, Harris M. Berger and Paul D. Greene (eds.), *Metal Rules the Globe: Heavy Metal Music Around the World* (Duke University Press, 2011), pp. 247–69.

Kearney, Mary Celeste, *Gender and Rock* (Oxford University Press, 2017).

Kennedy, Lewis F., 'The Symbiotic Relationship between Metal and Hardcore in the 21st Century', in Toni-Matti Karjalainen and Kimi Kärki (eds.), *Modern Heavy Metal: Markets, Practices and Cultures* (Aalto University Press, 2015), pp. 424–33.

Kennedy, Lewis F., *Functions of Genre in Metal and Hardcore Music*, doctoral dissertation (University of Hull, 2018). https://hydra.hull.ac.uk/resources/hull:16545.

Kennedy, Lewis F., 'Intersections of Genre, Heritage and Place in the New Wave of American Heavy Metal', in Liam Maloney and John Schofield (eds.), *Music and Heritage: New Perspectives on Place-Making and Sonic Identity* (Routledge, 2021), pp. 126–35.

Kristeva, Julia, *The Powers of Horror: An Essay on Abjection* (Columbia University Press, 1982).

Kruse, Holly, 'Abandoning the Absolute: Transcendence and Gender in Popular Music Discourse', in Steve Jones (ed.), *Pop Music and the Press* (Temple University Press, 2002), pp. 134–55.

Laing, Rob, 'What Is Djent?', *Total Guitar* (May 2011): 49–54.

Lake, Daniel, *USBM: A Revolution of Identity in American Black Metal* (Decibel Books, 2020).

Lawler, Steph, *Identity: Sociological Perspectives* (Polity Press, 2008).

Leonard, Marion, *Gender in the Music Industry: Rock, Discourse and Girl Power* (Ashgate, 2007).

LeVine, Mark, *Heavy Metal Islam: Rock, Resistance, and the Struggle for the Soul of Islam* (Three Rivers Press, 2008).

LeVine, Mark, *We'll Play Until We Die: Journeys Across a Decade of Revolutionary Music in the Muslim World* (University of California Press, 2022).

Liew, Kai Khiun and Kelly Fu, 'Conjuring the Tropical Spectres: Heavy Metal, Cultural Politics in Singapore and Malaysia', *Inter-Asia Cultural Studies* 7/1 (2006): 99–112.

Lucas, Olivia, '"Shrieking Soldiers … Wiping Clean the Earth": Hearing Apocalyptic Environmentalism in the Music of Botanist', *Popular Music* 38/3 (2019): 481–97.

Marrington, Mark, 'From DJ to Djent-Step: Technology and the Re-coding of Metal Music since the 1980s', *Metal Music Studies* 3/2 (2017): 251–68.

Marrington, Mark, 'The DAW, Electronic Music Aesthetics, and Genre Transgression in Music Production: The Case of Heavy Metal Music', in Hepworth-Sawyer Russ, Jay Hodgson and Mark Marrington (eds.), *Producing Music* (Routledge, 2019), pp. 52–74.

Mattsson, Douglas, '"Spreading VX Gas Over Kaaba": Islamic Semiotics in Turkish Black Metal', in Pierre Hecker, Ivo Furman and Kaya Akyıldız (eds.), *The Politics of Culture in Contemporary Turkey* (Edinburgh University Press, 2021), pp. 49–67.

McFarlane, Ian, *The Encyclopedia of Australian Rock and Pop* (Allen & Unwin, 1999).

McIver, Joel, *Extreme Metal* (Omnibus Press, 2000).

McIver, Joel, 'Periphery', *Metal Hammer* (Summer 2012): 60–3.

Mudrian, Albert, *Choosing Death: The Improbable History of Death Metal & Grindcore* (Feral House, 2004).

Muggleton, David, *Inside Subculture: The Postmodern Meaning of Style* (Berg, 2000).

Mynett, Mark, *Metal Music Manual: Producing, Engineering, Mixing, and Mastering Contemporary Heavy Music* (Routledge, 2017).

Mynett, Mark, 'Defining Contemporary Metal Music: Performance, Sounds and Practices', *Metal Music Studies* 5/3 (2019): 297–313.

Negus, Keith, *Music Genres and Corporate Cultures* (Routledge, 1999).

Newsom, Daniel, 'Rock's Quarrel with Tradition: Popular Music's Carnival Comes to the Classroom', *Popular Music and Society* 22/3 (1998): 1–20.

O'Donoghue, Heather, *From Asgard to Valhalla: The Remarkable History of the Norse Myths* (I. B. Tauris, 2008).

O'Hagan, Lauren, '"My Musical Armor": Exploring Metalhead Identity through the Battle Jacket', *Rock Music Studies* 9/1 (2022): 34–53.

Overell, Rosemary, 'Brutal Belonging in Melbourne's Grindcore Scene', *Studies in Symbolic Interaction* 35/1 (2010): 79–99.

Overell, Rosemary, *Affective Intensities in Extreme Music Scenes: Cases from Australia and Japan* (Palgrave MacMillan, 2014).

Patterson, Dayal, *Black Metal: Evolution of the Cult* (Feral House, 2013).

Pichler, Peter, 'The Power of the Imagination of Historical Distance: Melechesh' "Mesopotamian Metal" as a Musical Attempt of Solving Cultural Conflicts in the Twenty-First Century', *Metal Music Studies* 3/1 (2017): 97–112.

Pichler, Peter, *Metal Music, Sonic Knowledge, and the Cultural Ear in Europe since 1970: A Historiographic Exploration* (Franz Steiner, 2020).

Quader, Shams Bin and Guy Redden, 'Approaching the Underground: The Production of Alternatives in the Bangladeshi Metal Scene', *Cultural Studies* 29/3 (2014): 1–24.

Reyes, Ian, *Sound, Technology, and the Interpretation in Subcultures of Heavy Music Production*, doctoral dissertation (Pittsburgh University, 2008). http://d-scholarship.pitt.edu/7194/1/Reyes_ETD.pdf.

Reyes, Ian, 'Blacker than Death: Recollecting the "Black Turn" in Metal Aesthetics', *Journal of Popular Music Studies* 25 (2013): 240–57.

Reynolds, Simon, *Blissed Out: The Raptures of Rock* (Serpent's Tail, 1990).

Riches, Gabrielle, 'Brothers of Metal! Heavy Metal Masculinities, Moshpit Practices and Homo-sociality', in Steven Roberts (ed.), *Debating Modern Masculinities: Change, Continuity, Crisis?* (Palgrave Macmillan, 2014), pp. 88–105.

Riches, Gabrielle, Brett Lashua and Karl Spracklen, 'Female, Mosher, Transgressor: A "Mo-shography" of Transgressive Practices within the Leeds Extreme Metal Scene', *IASPM Journal* 4 (2014): 87–100.

Rivera-Segarra, Eliut, Jeffrey W. Ramos and Nelson Varas-Díaz, '"A Scream That Makes Us Visible": Latin American Heavy Metal Music and Liberation Psychology', in Nelson Varas-Diaz, Daniel Nevárez Araújo and Eliut Rivera-Segarra (eds.), *Heavy Metal Music in Latin America: Perspectives from the Distorted South* (Lexington Books, 2020), pp. 287–304.

Rowe, Paula, 'Global Metal in Local Contexts: Questions of Class among Heavy Metal Youth and the Structuring of Early Metal Identity Formations', *Metal Music Studies* 3/1 (2017): 113–31.

Rowe, Paula, *Heavy Metal Youth Identities: Researching the Musical Empowerment of Youth Transitions and Psychosocial Wellbeing* (Emerald, 2018).

Rowe, Paula and Bernard Guerin, 'Contextualizing the Mental Health of Metal Youth: A Community for Social Protection, Identity and Musical Empowerment', *Journal of Community Psychology* 46/4 (2018): 429–41.

Scott, Niall, 'Heavy Metal and the Deafening Threat of the Apolitical', *Popular Music History* 6/1 (2012): 224–39.

Shadrack, Jasmine, *Black Metal, Trauma, Subjectivity and Sound: Screaming the Abyss* (Emerald, 2020).

Sharpe-Young, Gary, *Metal: The Definitive Guide* (Jawbone, 2007).

Shelvock, Matt, 'The Progressive Heavy Metal Guitarist's Signal Chain', in Russ Hepworth-Sawyer, Justin Paterson, Jay Hodgson and Rob Toulson (eds.), *Innovation in Music* (Future Technology Press, 2013), pp. 126–38.

Smialek, Eric, *Genre and Expression in Extreme Metal Music, ca. 1990–2015*, doctoral dissertation (McGill University, 2015). https://escholarship.mcgill.ca/concern/theses/qv33s018k.

Smialek, Eric and Méi-Ra St-Laurent, 'Unending Eruptions: White-Collar Metal Appropriations of Classical Complexity, Experimentation, Elitism, and Cultural Legitimization', in Ciro Scotto, Kenneth Smith and John Brackett (eds.), *The Routledge Companion to Popular Music Analysis: Expanding Approaches* (Routledge, 2019), pp. 378–99.

Spracklen, Karl, *The Meaning and Purpose of Leisure: Habermas and Leisure at the End of Modernity* (Palgrave Macmillan, 2009).

Spracklen, Karl, *Constructing Leisure: Historical and Philosophical Debates* (Palgrave Macmillan, 2011).

Spracklen, Karl, *Digital Leisure, the Internet and Popular Culture: Communities and Identities in a Digital Age* (Palgrave, 2015).

Spracklen, Karl, *Metal Music and the Re-imagining of Masculinity, Place, Race and Nation* (Emerald, 2020).

Stolz, Nolan, *Experiencing Black Sabbath: A Listener's Companion* (Rowman & Littlefield, 2017).

Strachan, Robert, *Sonic Technologies: Popular Music, Digital Culture and the Creative Process* (Bloomsbury, 2017).

Stratton, Jon (ed.), *Australian Rock: Essays on Popular Music* (Network Books, 2007).

Thibodeau, Anthony J., *Anti-Colonial Resistance and Indigenous Identity in North American Heavy Metal*, MA dissertation (Bowling Green State University, 2014).

Thomas, Niall, 'Innovation and Tradition in Metal Music Production', *Metal Music Studies* 7/3 (2021): 423–43.

Thomas, Niall and Andrew King, 'Production Perspectives of Heavy Metal Record Producers', *Popular Music* 38/3 (2019): 498–517.

Trafford, Simon, 'Viking Metal', in Stephen C. Meyer and Kirsten Yri (eds.), *The Oxford Handbook of Music and Medievalism* (Oxford University Press, 2020), pp. 563–85.

Trafford, Simon and Aleks Pluskowski, 'Antichrist Superstars: The Vikings in Hard Rock and Heavy Metal', in David W. Marshall (ed.), *Mass Market Medieval* (McFarland, 2007), pp. 57–73.

Turman, Katherine and Jon Wiederhorn, *Louder than Hell: The Definitive Oral History of Metal* (It Books, 2013).

Turner, Daniel, 'Outlining the Fundamental Production Aesthetics of Commercial Heavy Metal Music Utilising Systematic Empirical Analysis', *Art of Record Production Conference* (2009). www.artofrecordproduction.com/aorpjoom/ symposiums/21-arp-2009/117-turner-2009 (accessed 14 April 2021).

Umurhan, Osman, 'Heavy Metal Music and the Appropriation of Greece and Rome', *Syllecta Classica* 23 (2012): 127–52.

Varas-Díaz, Nelson, *Decolonial Metal Music in Latin America* (Intellect, 2021).

Varas-Díaz, Nelson, Daniel Nevárez Araújo and Eliut Rivera-Segarra, *Heavy Metal Music in Latin America: Perspectives from the Distorted South* (Lexington Books, 2021).

Varas-Díaz, Nelson and Niall Scott (eds.), *Heavy Metal and the Communal Experience* (Lexington Books, 2016).

Vasan, Sonia, 'The Price of Rebellion: Gender Boundaries in the Death Metal Scene', *Journal for Cultural Research* 15/3 (2011): 333–49.

Vasan, Sonia, 'Gender and Power in the Death Metal Scene: A Social Exchange Perspective', in Andy R. Brown, Karl Spracklen, Keith Kahn-Harris and Niall Scott (eds.), *Global Metal Music and Culture: Current Directions in Metal Studies* (Abingdon, 2016), pp. 261–76.

Von Helden, Imke, *Norwegian Native Art: Cultural Identity in Norwegian Metal Music* (LIT, 2017).

Wagner, Jeff, *Mean Deviation: Four Decades of Progressive Heavy Metal* (Bazillion Points Books, 2010).

Wallach, Jeremy, 'Unleashed in the East: Metal Music, Masculinity, and "Malayness," in Indonesia, Malaysia and Singapore', in Jeremy Wallach, Harris M. Berger and Paul D. Greene (eds.), *Metal Rules the Globe: Heavy Metal Music Around the World* (Duke University Press, 2011), pp. 86–105.

Wallach, Jeremy, 'Distortion-Drenched Dystopias: Metal in Island Southeast Asia', in Niall Scott (ed.), *Reflections in the Metal Void* (Inter-Disciplinary Press, 2012), pp. 101–19.

Wallach, Jeremy, 'Global Rock as Postcolonial Soundtrack', in Allan F. Moore and Paul Carr (eds.), *Bloomsbury Handbook for Rock Music Research* (Bloomsbury, 2020), pp. 469–85.

Wallach, Jeremy, Harris M. Berger and Paul D. Greene (eds.), *Metal Rules the Globe: Heavy Metal Music Around the World* (Duke University Press, 2011).

Wallach, Jeremy and Esther Clinton, 'Theories of the Post-Colonial and Globalization: Ethnomusicologists Grapple with Power, History, Media, and Mobility', in Harris M. Berger and Ruth Stone (eds.), *Theory for Ethnomusicology: Histories, Conversations, Insights* (Prentice Hall, 2019), pp. 1114–39.

Walser, Robert, *Running with the Devil: Power, Gender and Madness in Heavy Metal Music* (Wesleyan University Press, 1993).

Weinstein, Deena, *Heavy Metal: The Music and its Culture* (Da Capo Press, 2000 [1991]).

Wiederhorn, Jon and Katherine Turman, *Louder than Hell: The Definitive Oral History of Metal* (It Books, 2013).

Williams, Duncan, 'Tracking Timbral Changes in Metal Production from 1990 to 2013', *Metal Music Studies* 1/1 (2015): 39–68.

Wilson, Scott (ed.), *Melancology: Black Metal Theory and Ecology* (Zero Books, 2014).

Wong, Cynthia P., '"A Dream Return to Tang Dynasty": Masculinity, Male Camaraderie, and Chinese Heavy Metal in the 1990s', in Jeremy Wallach, Harris M. Berger and Paul D. Greene (eds.), *Metal Rules the Globe: Heavy Metal Music Around the World* (Duke University Press, 2011), pp. 63–85.

Zinn, Howard, *The Politics of History* (University of Illinois Press, 1990).

Select Journalistic Bibliography

Anselmi, J. J., *Doomed to Fail: The Incredibly Loud History of Doom, Sludge, and Post-Metal* (Rare Bird Books, 2020).

Arnopp, Jason, *Slipknot: Inside the Sickness, Behind the Masks* (Ebury Press, 2001).

Arvizu, Reggie, *Got the Life: My Journey of Addiction, Faith, Recovery, and Korn* (It Books, 2010).

Beaujour, Tom and Richard Bienstock, *Nothin' but a Good Time: The Uncensored History of the '80s Hard Rock Explosion* (St Martins Press, 2021).

Blush, Steven, *American Hair Metal* (Feral House, 2006).

Brown, Jake, *Motörhead in the Studio* (John Blake, 2010).

Brown, Jake, *Iron Maiden in the Studio: The Stories Behind Every Album* (John Blake, 2011).

Brown, Jake, *Rick Rubin: In the Studio* (ECW Press, 2013).

Brown, Rex, *Official Truth, 101 Proof: The Inside Story of Pantera* (Da Capo Press, 2014).

Buhszpan, Daniel, *The Encyclöpedia öf Heavy Metal* (Sterling, 2012).

Byford, Biff, *Saxon – Never Surrender (or Nearly Good Looking): An Autobiography* (IP Verlag, 2002).

Cavalera, Max and Joel McIver, *My Bloody Roots: From Sepultura to Soulfly and Beyond: The Autobiography* (Jawbone, 2022).

Christe, Ian, *Sound of the Beast: The Complete Headbanging History of Heavy Metal* (It Books, 2003).

Curl, James, *Dokken: Into the Fire and Other Embers of 80s Metal History* (JC Publications, 2020).

Daniels, Neil, *Killers: The Origins of Iron Maiden, 1975–1983* (Soundcheck Books, 2014).

Darnielle, John, *Black Sabbath's Master of Reality* (Continuum, 2004).

Darski, Adam, *Confessions of a Heretic: The Sacred and the Profane: Behemoth and Beyond* (Jawbone, 2015).

Dickinson, Bruce, *Bruce Dickinson: An Autobiography* (Harper Collins, 2018).

Downing, Kenneth Keith, *Heavy Duty: Days and Nights in Judas Priest* (Constable, 2020).

Eglinton, Mark, *Of Metal and Man: The Definitive Biography of James Hetfield* (Music Press Books, 2017).

Ekeroth, Daniel, *Swedish Death Metal* (Bazillion Points Book, 2019).

Endean, Gareth, *Half a Ton of Heavy Metal: 50 Years of the Loudest Music on Earth* (blurb, 2020).

Evdokimov, Aleksey, *Doom Metal Lexicanum*, Vols. 1 and 2 (Cult Never Dies, 2021).

Ferris, D. X., *Slayer's Reign in Blood* (Bloomsbury, 2014).

Fischer, Tom Gabriel, *Are You Morbid? Into the Pandemonium of Celtic Frost* (Sanctuary, 2000).

Fischer, Tom Gabriel, *Only Death is Real: An Illustrated History of Hellhammer and Early Celtic Frost* (Bazillion Points Books, 2010).

Franklin, Dan, *Heavy Metal: How Metal Changes the Way We See the World* (Constable, 2020).

Gehlke, David E., *Damn the Machine: The Story of Noise Records* (Deliberation Press, 2017).

Gehlke, David E., *Turned Inside Out: The Official Story of Obituary* (Decibel Books, 2022).

Glasper, Ian, *Contract in Blood: A History of UK Thrash Metal* (Cherry Red Books, 2018).

Hagen, Ross, *Darkthrone's A Blaze in the Northern Sky* (Bloomsbury, 2020).

Halford, Rob, *Rob Halford Confess: The Autobiography* (Headline, 2021).

Halmshaw, Paul, *Peaceville Life* (Crypt, 2019).

Hann, Michael, *Denim and Leather: The Rise and Fall of the New Wave of British Heavy Metal* (Constable, 2022).

Herron-Wheeler, Addison, *Wicked Women: Women in Metal from the 1960s to Now* (Create Space, 2014).

Hilton, Christopher P., *The Rise, Fall and Rebirth of Hair Metal* (Independent, 2020).

Iommi, Tony, *Tony Iommi: Iron Man: My Journey through Heaven and Hell with Black Sabbath* (Simon & Schuster, 2012).

Johannesson, Ika and Jon Jefferson Klingberg, *Blood Fire Death: The Swedish Metal Story* (Feral House, 2018).

Jourgensen, Al, *Ministry: The Lost Gospels According to Al Jourgensen* (Da Capo Press, 2015).

Karpe, Matt, *Nu Metal: Resurgence* (Fastprint, 2018).

Karpe, Matt, *Korn on Track: Every Album, Every Song* (Sonicbond, 2021).

Karpe, Matt, *Nu Metal: A Definitive Guide* (Sonicbond, 2021).

Korolenko, Jason, *Relentless: Thirty Years of Sepultura* (Rocket 88, 2014).

Kristiansen, Jon, *Metalion: The Slayer Mag Diaries* (Bazillion Points Books, 2011).

Kudlow, Steve and Robb Reiner, *Anvil! The Story of Anvil* (Bantam Press, 2009).

Lake, Daniel, *USBM: A Revolution of Identity in American Black Metal* (Cult Never Dies, 2020).

Makkonen, Markus and Kim Strömsholm, *Rotting Ways to Misery: The History of Finnish Death Metal* (Cult Never Dies, 2020).

Malmsteen, Yngwie J., *Relentless: The Memoir* (Wiley, 2013).

Masciotra, David, *Metallica's Metallica* (Bloomsbury, 2015).

McIver, Joel, *Nu-Metal: The Next Generation* (Omnibus Press, 2002).

McIver, Joel, *Slipknot: Unmasked* (Omnibus Press, 2003).

McIver, Joel, *Extreme Metal II* (Omnibus Press, 2005).

McIver, Joe, *Justice for All: The Truth about Metallica* (Omnibus Press, 2009).

McIver, Joel, *The Bloody Reign of Slayer* (Omnibus Press, 2010).

McIver, Joel, *Crazy Train: The High Life and Tragic Death of Randy Rhoads* (Jawbone, 2011).

McIver, Joel, *Overkill: The Untold Story of Motörhead* (Omnibus Press, 2011).

McIver, Joel, *Machine Head: Inside the Machine* (Omnibus Press, 2012).

McIver, Joel, *Unleashed: The Story of Tool* (Omnibus Press, 2012).

McIver, Joel, *Sabbath Bloody Sabbath* (Omnibus Press, 2014).

McIver, Joel, *Slipknot Bam: All Hope Is Gone* (Omnibus Press, 2016).

Meller, Lauro, *Iron Maiden: A Journey through History* (Editora Appris, 2018).

Moores, J. R., *Electric Wizards: A Tapestry of Heavy Music, 1968 to the Present* (Reaktion Books, 2021).

Moynihan, Michael and Didrik Soderlind, *Lords of Chaos: The Bloody Rise of the Satanic Metal Underground* (Feral House, 2003).

Mudrian, Albert, *Choosing Death: The Improbable History of Death Metal & Grindcore* (Bazillion Points Books, 2016).

Mustaine, Dave, *Rust in Peace: The Inside Story of the Megadeth Masterpiece* (Hachette Books, 2020).

O'Shea, Mick, *Cemetery Gates: Saints & Survivors of the Heavy Metal Scene* (Plexus, 2011).

Ollila, Mape, *Once upon a Nightwish: The Official Biography* (Bazillion Points Books, 2008).

Osbourne, Ozzy, *I Am Ozzy* (Sphere, 2010).

Patterson, Dayal, *Black Metal: Evolution of the Cult* (Feral House, 2013).

Popoff, Martin, *Black Sabbath FAQ: All That's Left to Know on the First Name in Metal* (Backbeat Books, 2011).

Popoff, Martin, *2 Minutes to Midnight: An Iron Maiden Day-by-Day* (Backbeat Books, 2013).

Popoff, Martin, *So Far, So Good . . . So Megadeth!* (Wymer, 2017).

Popoff, Martin, *Iron Maiden: Album by Album* (Voyageur, 2018).

Popoff, Martin, *Swords & Tequila: Riot's Classic First Decade* (Wymer, 2019).

Popoff, Martin, *This Means War: The Sunset Years of NWOBHM* (Wymer, 2019).

Popoff, Martin, *Who Invented Heavy Metal?* (Wymer, 2019).

Popoff, Martin, *Born Again! Black Sabbath in the Eighties & Nineties* (Wymer, 2020).

Popoff, Martin, *Sabotage! Black Sabbath in the Seventies* (Wymer, 2020).

Popoff, Martin, *Denim and Leather: Saxon's First Ten Years* (Wymer, 2021).

Popoff, Martin, *Judas Priest: Decade of Domination* (Wymer, 2021).

Popoff, Martin, *Judas Priest: Turbo 'til Now* (Wymer, 2021).

Popoff, Martin, *Wheels of Steel: The Explosive Early Years of NWOBHM* (Wymer, 2021).

Purcell, Natalie J., *Death Metal Music: The Passion and Politics of a Subculture* (McFarland, 2003).

Quirk, Justin, *Nothin' but a Good Time: The Spectacular Rise and Fall of Glam Metal* (Unbound Digital, 2020).

Rosen, Steven, *The Story of Black Sabbath: Wheels of Confusion* (Castle Communications, 1996).

Sharpe-Young, Gary, *A-Z of Power Metal* (Cherry Red Books, 2003).

Sharpe-Young, Gary, *Thrash Metal* (Zonda Books, 2007).

Slagel, Brian and Mark Eglinton, *For the Sake of Heaviness: Metal Blade Records* (BMG, 2017).

Smith, Adrian, *Monsters of River and Rock: My Life as Iron Maiden's Compulsive Angler* (Virgin Books, 2021).

Stolz, Nolan, *Experiencing Black Sabbath: A Listener's Companion* (Rowman & Littlefield, 2017).

Stubberud, Jørn, *The Death Archives: Mayhem 1984–94* (Ecstatic Peace Library, 2018).

Suction, Chris, *Black Sabbath in the 1970s: Decades* (Sonicbond, 2022).

Tucker, Jon, *Neat & Tidy: The Story of Neat Records* (Iron Pages Books, 2015).

Wall, Mick, *Run to the Hills: The Authorised Biography* (Sanctuary, 1998).

Wall, Mick, *Metallica: Enter Night: The Biography* (Orion, 2012).

Wall, Mick, *Black Sabbath: Symptom of the Universe* (Orion, 2014).

Wall, Mick, *Ronnie James Dio: Rainbow in the Dark: The Autobiography* (Constable, 2021).

Welch, Brian, *Save Me from Myself: How I Found God, Quit Korn, Kicked Drugs, and Lived to Tell My Story* (HarperOne, 2008).

Welch, Brian, *With My Eyes Wide Open: Miracles and Mistakes on My Way Back to KoRn* (TN Nelson Books, 2017).

Wiederhorn, Jon, *Raising Hell: Backstage Tales from the Lives of Metal Legends* (Divison Books, 2020).

Wiederhorn, Jon and Katherine Turman, *Louder than Hell: The Definitive Oral History of Metal* (It Books, 2013).

Winwood, Ian and Paul Brannigan, *Into the Black: The Inside Story of Metallica, 1991–2014* (Faber & Faber, 2016).

Zazula, Jon, *Heavy Tales: The Metal. The Music. The Madness* (Zazula, 2019).

Index